AP

The Story Of News

AP

THE STORY OF NEWS

BY

OLIVER GRAMLING

Illustrated by
HENRY C. BARROW

FARRAR AND RINEHART, INC.

NEW YORK   TORONTO

To

Frank B. Noyes

446332

A NOTE BY THE AUTHOR

The idea of putting this story into words goes back a dozen years. It was then that the author began to learn that honest news reporting didn't just happen—that even though the "freedom of the press" ideal had been incorporated in the Bill of Rights more than a hundred years before, systematic news gathering had to earn its place as a self-respecting public service through slow but dramatic evolution.

The actual writing and refining of *AP—The Story of News* required two years, but other years of research and study preceded that final effort. Even two years may seem a long time to devote to such a work, yet the fact is that the author alone could not have produced the story as it now appears in that length of time. Indeed, the chances are he never could have produced it without the assistance of William A. Kinney, now of the Washington staff of The Associated Press, whose brilliant research abilities and keen perception as to detail contributed so much.

Many sources were drawn upon in tracing the story to its end. Bits turned up in odd places: from yellowed, time-worn records; from various books and publications of one sort or another, many of them long since out of print; from hundreds of newspaper files going back as far as 1800, and from all AP organizational reports and news files over a period of many years. No attempt is made here to list all such references and authorities, which fill a score of closely typed pages, but it can be said that more than three thousand books and publications were examined and that the search of AP records alone entailed the reading of more than twenty million words.

And while it is not practical to list all the individuals who contributed in one way or another to the story, the author wishes to express thanks for their interest and help. To all of them, and the total runs to hundreds, he expresses the especial hope that in the following pages they will find some reward for their wholehearted co-operation in helping to make possible this story of news.

O. G.

New York, N. Y.
June 25, 1940.

CONTENTS

Contents

1925

PRELUDE

PRELUDE

A CHILL November rain blew in from Boston harbor. It swept across Long Wharf, up State Street and past the seven floors of the Exchange Coffee House, in 1811 the tallest building in the country.

Below, on the drenched cobblestones, merchants and citizens hurried by twilight to the recently established Reading Room on the second floor. They asked questions of one another and of travelers who had just arrived by schooner and stagecoach. They studied the dog-eared European newspapers. But they found no fresh news.

Down the seaboard, past New York and the southern shore line, lights flickered in farmhouses and in fishing shacks, and in the busy towns of this New World of five million people. Out on the Atlantic there were other and more ominous lights. They dipped and rolled with the dark hulls of British men-of-war. American commerce was being blockaded and Yankee seamen were seized for the service of the crown on the grounds that they were British subjects. Every incoming merchantman brought tales of warlike acts, and at the end of the day people gathered to wonder and to speculate.

In England George III brooded over the loss of his American colonies, and on the continent Napoleon traced new campaigns on his crinkling maps.

In Washington a young, ill-knit Congress was convened in the half-finished Capitol demanding war to avenge repeated indignities at the hands of Great Britain and France. Precise President Madison rocked in the newly invented swivel chair and pondered. Henry Clay and his "War Hawk" followers had served their ultimatum—Madison must see to it that war was declared or he would not be renominated.

Official Washington could feel the state of affairs, but even there citizens could only speculate on what the next day held. These were crucial times. Events moved in some puzzling world pattern, yet the people had no news.

2

There was no news because there were no real newspapers. True, newspapers and newsletters, of a sort, had existed for years. But the news they printed was old and almost always inaccurate. They took what little information came to them and made no effort to gather it for themselves. They found much else to print—flowery verses, erudite essays, political bombast, or solemn dissertations on religion.

Front pages, most of them, were given over to advertisements urging the purchase of slaves and livestock, of secondhand furniture, and of curious medicines. The size of the pages was often large and the number of pages few. These large pages were called "blanket" sheets because, when opened, they were almost as large as a blanket. The reason for their size was partly a holdover from pre-Revolutionary days when papers were taxed on the number of pages they contained, and partly because the crude printing presses were operated by hand and it was easier and quicker to run off a few large sheets than many small ones. A strong pressman, without interruption, could produce as many as two hundred copies an hour. The large journals did not hesitate to make capital of their size. One of them proclaimed itself: "The Largest Paper In All Creation." But in the matter of circulation not even the most prosperous papers had more than a few hundred.

The problem of hand presses and large pages was not the only one confronting printers. There was no telegraph, typewriter, or telephone. Copy was written out by pen, or set directly in type by hand. The only method of communication was by schooner or stagecoach. Public intelligence, more likely than not, traveled by word of mouth. The tavern or the coffeehouse, rather than the newspaper, was the best place to find out what was going on and Boston was the trading center of the New World.

This was the condition of newspapers, with few exceptions, until that November night in 1811 when the rain whistled in from the harbor and Boston citizens hurried along to the Exchange Coffee House Reading Room in quest of whatever intelligence they might find.

3

The popular Reading Room had been established a year before by Samuel Gilbert, one of the proprietors of the Exchange Coffee House, in an attempt to attract merchants and shipmasters to the trading center on the second floor. After the practice of European establishments of a similar kind, Gilbert stocked it with whatever old journals he could obtain. But he also was an innovator. He kept on hand two large books, in one of which he recorded marine intelligence and in the other incidental information.

The idea of recording news was immediately popular. Patrons thought so well of it that they donated a rowboat which Gilbert had used on occasions to meet incoming craft and learn details of their cargoes and voyages.

Things went along satisfactorily enough until Gilbert found the Reading Room was taking too much of his time. He decided he needed a helper. The merchants and patrons learned of his selection with pleasure. Boston's foremost newspaper, the semiweekly *Columbia Centinel*, printed an obscure announcement on November 20:

EXCHANGE COFFEE HOUSE BOOKS. These news-books &c commenced and so satisfactorily conducted by Mr. Gilbert are now transferred to the care of Mr. Samuel Topliff, Junr., a young gentleman of respectability, industry and information; and who will, we doubt not, continue the Marine and General News Books with great satisfaction to the patrons and friends of the Reading Room.

The son of a sea captain, this young Samuel Topliff, Jr., was born in a wooden house in Orange Street in 1789. His childhood was prosaic. He did the things other boys of his time did—sang in the choir at Hollis Street Church, marched in a memorial procession for George Washington in 1800, and went to school. He dreamed of a life at sea, but then in 1811 his father was murdered by a mutinous crew. When this news finally reached Boston Topliff knew that his earlier plans must be abandoned. He must support his mother and brothers and so he lost little time in undertaking his unusual assignment.

Topliff soon observed that the stories of travelers and seafarers became magnified with each retelling. He decided that the best way to make sure the information was reasonably accurate was to obtain it promptly and record it in the News Books before constant repetition destroyed its value.

He was completing his News Book entries for the day when the Reading Room door was thrown open by a runner who panted out that an unidentified boat was trying to negotiate the harbor. The runner, as was customary, had been stationed on the observation roof near the big dome of the coffeehouse. It was his duty to study the harbor by glass and report all arrivals and departures. Because of the descending darkness, he had been unable to distinguish the colors of the incoming craft, but unquestionably something unusual must be afoot, otherwise it was doubtful if any craft would attempt the harbor in such a squall.

This information caused an uproar among the readers in the room. For all they knew, the British might be planning an attack or the ship might be bringing word of more warlike acts against Yankee shipping and commerce.

Topliff listened to the hum of curious voices and made up his mind. The harbor was dark and treacherous, but he had handled a rowboat in bad weather before. While the Reading Room crowd continued its excited speculation, he left the coffeehouse and headed for Long Wharf, where the Reading Room rowboat was moored. He unshipped the oars and pulled out.

He was gone what seemed an interminable time. The cold rain continued to blow. Dim lights flickered in the storm and slipped deeper into the night. Then the blur of the small boat reappeared, zigzagging its way to Long Wharf with the bedraggled young man still at the oars.

Soon he was back at his desk in the Reading Room and while those nearest crowded around to read over his shoulder, he entered in the News Book the story of what he had learned.

The arriving boat was the brig *Latona*. She had had a stormy 68-day voyage from Archangel. Her master was Captain Blanchard, and he brought disturbing tidings. A few days before, in longitude 65, the *Latona* was running before moderate winds when she was overhauled by an English sloop-of-war which immediately broke out a signal for the brig to heave to. The sloop ran out her starboard guns to emphasize the order and when she came alongside a longboat of British marines boarded the *Latona*.

A cocky, talkative second officer ordered Blanchard to muster his crew while the brig was searched for "deserters from His Majesty's Navy." The officer spoke in belligerent tones. He told Blanchard that six British line-of-battle ships and twenty frigates already had arrived off Halifax, and that twenty more were expected. England was bringing her naval forces in North America up to wartime strength.

"To be prepared," the officer had explained condescendingly, "in case of a rupture with America. . . ."

Before Topliff had finished writing there were shouts and commotion. These Boston citizens could understand the inevitable. Britain

TOPLIFF UNSHIPPED THE OARS AND PULLED OUT.

was ready to risk another war with her former colonies, New England's rich commerce at sea faced destruction, and eventually America might even lose the independence it had won thirty years before.

The patrons of the Reading Room knew that Topliff had risked danger in order to bring back news at a time when everyone was eager for news. They toasted him for his courage and he knew that he had made a good beginning. But it is doubtful if any one of them realized the full significance of his act.

Topliff in his rowboat had started systematic news gathering.

4

The young man continued to meet incoming craft in the harbor. He also employed correspondents to send him regular newsletters from abroad. He kept his information as accurate as he could make it, and before long he was persuading a few newspapers to subscribe to regular reports which he wrote out in longhand and delivered by messenger or stagecoach. Newspapers themselves also slowly began to gather and print news.

The War of 1812 came and the rowboat method was adopted by others. A rowboater for the Charleston (S. C.) *Courier* obtained word of the war's end seven weeks after the treaty was signed at Ghent, Belgium, the Christmas Eve of 1814. That seemed an amazing feat, receiving word in such a comparatively short time, yet there was irony in it. In the last battle of the war Andrew Jackson won an overwhelming victory over the British at New Orleans, but it was a battle that would never have been fought had there been an adequate news system; peace had been declared two weeks previously.

By 1828 Boston had yielded to New York in news gathering as well as commerce. The vigorous, rough-and-tumble young metropolis sprawled along the lower tip of Manhattan and laughed at its growing pains. Plagues of yellow fever ravaged the populace, pigs roamed the thoroughfares, and brothels flourished along the water front. The shore line was a forest of spars, masts, and riggings, wagons rattled through Wall Street, and the graves of Potter's Field covered the meadow that is now Washington Square.

Rowboats were still being used, but owing to the jealousy and intrigue of rival publishers the harbor was a perilous place to venture, even in broad daylight.

The hurrying population of 180,000 had halfheartedly supported nine daily newspapers until a year before, when a tenth—unwelcome to the others—made its appearance. Among the nine were the *Commercial Advertiser*, the *Post*, the *Standard*, and the *Morning Courier*, the last published by violent, overbearing Colonel James Watson Webb. The tenth was the *Journal of Commerce*. It was owned by merchant-philanthropist Arthur Tappan and was managed by 37-year-old David Hale.

The nine papers originally had fought among themselves to be the first with the news. Constant threats that additional newspapers might enter the growing field, however, finally had drawn them together in a harbor combine served by the toughest collection of rowboaters who ever pulled an oar, more concerned with crushing outside opposition than with collecting and speeding the highly important intelligence from abroad.

It was against the cutthroat activities of this combine that David Hale and the new *Journal of Commerce* had to struggle.

Hale, a New Englander, was religious and would not gather news on Sunday. He had worked on an uncle's paper in Boston about the time Topliff was starting. He had taught school. He had started an importing business. He had tried auctioneering. He had invested in a powder mill only to have it blow up. During one brief period of prosperity he had lent a few hundred dollars to a friend, Gerard Hallock, who shortly after became the editor of the weekly New York *Observer*. That loan to Hallock was a fortunate one, for it was Hallock who recommended Hale to owner Tappan as a likely manager of the *Journal of Commerce*.

Hale was accustomed to failure and after several months with the unpopular *Journal of Commerce* he faced it again. He could not get past the harbor combine to gather news from Europe. His boatmen regularly came back from the water front with their heads laid open by belaying pins. As soon as they set foot on a ship's ladder they were knocked back into their rowboats. If the paper could not obtain news it could not survive. Owner Tappan was tired of his venture and wanted to sell out.

Early one morning in October, 1828, a small sloop sailed down the East River. It slipped past the spot where Brooklyn Bridge now stands and headed toward the entrance of the lower harbor and Sandy Hook. It was Hale's boat and on her side was painted the legend: JOURNAL OF COMMERCE, 1828.

The *Journal of Commerce* manager had fitted up the craft in a desperate effort to beat the harbor combine. He had tried to keep his intentions a secret, but word leaked out. The other papers accepted the challenge by rigging out a fast sloop they called the *Thomas H. Smith*. The *Journal of Commerce* then announced its plan in a notice which said:

An opportunity now will be offered for an honorable competition. The public will be benefited by such extra exertions to procure marine news, and we trust the only contention between the two boat establishments will be which can outdo the other in vigilance, perseverance and success. . . .

The two boats raced the eighteen miles to Sandy Hook and when the *Journal of Commerce* hove to in the rolling swells the combine craft was far behind. News gatherers never had ventured that far before, but Hale saw that it was an excellent spot. Arriving merchantmen started to trim their sails there and his sailboat could obtain whatever budgets of intelligence they brought and scuttle back to port.

The success of the *Journal of Commerce* jolted rival editors out of their lethargy and set the whole town talking. The bankers and merchants who foregathered at Holt's Hotel on Water Street discussed the commercial advantages that might come from this unprecedented enterprise in news. But there was more to it than the excitement it created in New York. Hale and his *Journal of Commerce* had introduced the vital stimulant of competition into the sluggish world of news gathering.

5

The *Journal of Commerce* went down the harbor many times. Larger, more seaworthy boats soon were cruising for news as far as a hundred miles off Sandy Hook.

The harbor combine, fighting back with all its resources, began to make use of a new marine telegraph which was constructed between the harbor entrance and the Battery at the lower end of Manhattan. This was a semaphore device of flagstaff stations. A man at Sandy Hook identified the incoming boats and signaled word to the next station, where it was picked up and resignaled to stations along the route all the way to the city.

But the difficulty with this system was that it could relay little more than the bare identity of the approaching ship. The news those ships carried was the thing, and Hale meant to have it first. Thereafter his boat put in at the outer tip of Staten Island, which sprawled between New York and Sandy Hook, and a waiting horseman took the news and galloped to the Manhattan ferry.

The contest still waged unabated with every man for himself after the old harbor combine finally disintegrated under the pressure of Hale's efforts. The *Journal of Commerce*, however, was prepared to cope with this multiplication of opponents. Hale and his friend Gerard Hallock purchased the paper.

The era of evening newspapers had not arrived, but Hale and Hallock gave New York its first "extra" by running off important news on their old hand presses for distribution during the afternoon hours. They broke precedent by putting their biggest news on page one, and they introduced credit lines proclaiming "25 DAYS LATER FROM EUROPE" to stress the speed with which they were obtaining the latest foreign reports.

The nation was growing. Domestic news was becoming more important. The *Journal of Commerce* met this situation by inaugurating a pony express.

Andrew Jackson's attack on the Bank of the United States was the exciting topic of 1830 when the two publishers announced they would run a special express from Washington to New York in order to obtain the presidential message to the opening of Congress. James Watson Webb, who had not hesitated to attack the methods of his rivals, hastily organized an express for his *Courier*, bewailing the fact that it cost him $300. The remaining papers pooled their interests in a third. New Yorkers marveled to read that Jackson's message reached the city in less than two days in spite of badly mired roads.

Yet the pony express remained only an occasional service until Hale and Hallock once more jogged the pace of progress. In 1833 they started a regular express from Washington with twenty-four horses racing day and night over a distance of 227 miles. It was a notable feat, for the paper's black ponies covered the distance in twenty hours, regularly beating the government's own express by one to two days.

6

While these exploits were increasing the importance of the owners of the *Journal of Commerce*, another newspaper personality moved boldly on the scene. He was a squinting Scotsman and his name was James Gordon Bennett. He did not hesitate to tread on the touchy toes of all the New York publishers, and before he was through he became the first to gather and print all kinds of news—fit or otherwise.

Bennett had emigrated to America as a youth in 1819 and found a shilling in the streets of Boston, which fed him for a day. After working in Boston and New York he became Washington correspondent for Webb's *Courier*. Years later people spoke of him as the first Washington columnist, but at the time he was more concerned with the problem of eating. He roamed the Capitol corridors gobbling information. Sometimes there was small importance in the facts he gathered—that the wife of a certain Cabinet officer was addicted to port laced with brandy, that Andrew Jackson was a good trencherman, or that people were calling the Executive Mansion the White House since it had been painted to cover the scars left by the War of 1812. Often enough, however, the information he obtained was important, and when it was he made the most of it.

Vigorous, inquisitive almost to the point of being obnoxious, Bennett appeared just the man choleric Webb was seeking as editor when he consolidated his *Courier* with the *Enquirer* in a determination to outdo Hale and Hallock. The Scotsman went to New York as a $12-a-week editor of the *Courier and Enquirer*. From the beginning the two personalities clashed. Webb's shifty policies grated on the Scotsman and the two parted in 1832.

Bennett tried other newspaper enterprises, but none of them succeeded. By 1835 his writing of cheap newspaper fiction had netted $500. He attempted to persuade a young printer to join him in the publication of a penny paper. The printer was Horace Greeley and he curtly declined. Bennett trudged down to the printing plant of Anderson and Smith at 34 Ann Street. His $500 talked and the partners agreed to print his paper as long as he could pay cash in advance.

The morning of May 6, 1835, saw the birth of the *Herald*. It was a one-penny paper—a fact calculated to appeal to the masses who could not afford the six-penny price of the established journals. The penny press had made its first positive appearance in New York two years earlier with the birth of the *Sun* and Bennett was shrewd enough to observe that such a popular-priced publication had a definite appeal. The city now had a population of 270,000, yet the combined circulation of all New York dailies was only 42,000. There was room for another paper.

Bennett resolved to become a real news gatherer. He actually did become the first reporter in the modern sense of the word. He promised to report the shady transactions in Wall Street, where the six-penny papers got their biggest support. He promised to print political news only for what it was worth. He said he would mirror the world in all its freaks and vagaries, that he would record facts on every public and proper subject. They were promises he kept for the remainder of his life.

This vigorous start of the *Herald* served notice on Hale and Hallock that they must look to their news-gathering laurels. To meet so boisterous a menace, the six-penny papers put forth redoubled efforts. Still faster newsboats were built, more pony expresses were run. It was a formidable competition because Webb's *Courier and Enquirer*, with a circulation of 3,300 and an advertising revenue of $65 daily, was accounted the most powerful paper in the country.

But Bennett was not to be annihilated. His news touch was like magic. He was thrashed in the streets, denounced from pulpits, and still the *Herald's* circulation climbed until it reached 20,000 by 1836. No matter what the six-penny papers did, Bennett outdid them. His newsboats were faster, his expresses quicker, his genius sharper. He used the few rattletrap railroads, canal barges, runners, any and all conceivable methods of getting news.

Brazen cock of the journalistic walk, the ill-looking Scotsman crowed long and loud over his triumphs. He mixed fact, fiction and fancy with an indiscriminate hand and served up the spicy mélange under the name of news.

And that was the salient weakness of the cause he did so much to help. He might get the news anywhere—in Wall Street and on the Exchange, in the police station and at church, at the theater and in court, at home and abroad—but when he gave it to the public in his rowdy, shocking way the news became a subordinate vehicle to express the incorrigible flamboyance of the man who presented it.

7

Back in Boston the urgency of a swifter method of delivery had impressed Daniel Craig, an ambitious printer's apprentice from New Hampshire. He had planned to start a penny paper in Boston, but instead he made himself one of the great news gatherers of his time.

"Carrier pigeons have been used for years in Europe to transmit messages," the heavy-set, square-jawed young man reflected. "They are fast; they can fly forty to seventy-five miles an hour. Why can't they be used to transmit news?"

He ordered a consignment of pigeons from Europe, and once the birds had been trained, he inaugurated his pigeon post. It was not long before newspapers were subscribing to the service. Craig met ships miles out at sea off Boston, summarized the news from abroad, and sent copies winging shoreward.

The pigeon service spread from Boston to New York and Baltimore. Moses Beach of the New York *Sun* was the first to appreciate the advantages that Craig could offer a metropolitan newspaper. In Maryland the New Englander found an enthusiastic supporter in Arunah S. Abell, who had just launched the Baltimore *Sun*.

James Gordon Bennett, unwilling to mark time while any opposition editor enjoyed a faster delivery of news, bought himself dozens of pigeons and before long he was shipping his birds to Craig, who loaded them with news and sent them winging back. At one stage Bennett was offering Craig $500 an hour for each hour that a pigeon could deliver news to the *Herald* ahead of its rivals. The *Herald* publisher also augmented his pony express routes with pigeon posts from Washington, Baltimore, Philadelphia, and the state capitol at Albany.

8

Only the highly successful journals could afford the heavy expense necessary to maintain the trinity of pigeons, ponies, and boats. The problem was a scientific one and Samuel Finley Breese Morse, a painter of international reputation with several minor inventions to his credit, had the solution. By 1847 his revolutionary new communications system, the electro-magnetic telegraph, was clattering away in a dozen or more cities.

There were real newspapers now—real enough for the times. The hand press had been replaced by faster but still crude mechanical presses.

Although the future of the telegraph was a foregone conclusion, it was expensive and its facilities still were too inadequate to handle all press dispatches with any degree of speed, even for papers in the few cities it connected. Until it could expand on a nation-wide scale—and the first pony express had not even reached the Pacific Coast—newspapers found it necessary to operate longer express routes, bigger newsboat systems, and more elaborate pigeon posts.

The War with Mexico did not simplify matters. Bennett, still the most daring news gatherer, was running a special pony express all the way from the border. With the collaboration of the Baltimore *Sun*, the Philadelphia *Public Ledger* and the New Orleans *Picayune*, his efforts to obtain news of the Mexican struggle were leaving other publishers far behind.

David Hale watched the *Herald's* expensive activities and realized the time had come to end the blind, cutthroat competition in which the New York papers had so long indulged. He didn't like Bennett any better than did the others among the so-called "Wall Street Press." Nevertheless, he had to admit that Bennett's contribution to news-gathering enterprise had been considerable. He saw that the progress of systematic news gathering had made newspapers indispensable in the lives of the people as the world grew slowly larger, extending difficult news frontiers. He was convinced that no one paper could continue indefinitely to meet the multiplying problems of individual news collection.

Others among the aloof New York press might continue to belittle Bennett in print and thrash him in the streets, as old James Watson Webb had done on more occasions than one. They might continue a "moral war" in which they had labeled him with such epithets as "obscene vagabond," "leperous slanderer," "rogue," "polluted wretch," and the like. But Hale did not propose to continue to do so. He felt that there was disaster ahead if the New York papers continued their headstrong course, and that there was no point in waiting longer to propose to Bennett what he had in mind.

He put on his tall hat, left the *Journal of Commerce* office and presently was at the corner of Nassau and Fulton, where the *Herald* building stood.

A few minutes later there was a knock on the door of Bennett's office.

"Come in," called the publisher.

He looked up from his desk, squinted his type-tired eyes, and finally recognized Hale. He got to his feet and stood waiting. Hale lost no time getting to the point.

"Mr. Bennett," he said, "I have called to talk about news with you. Do you have any objection?"

The publisher nodded his visitor to a chair.

"I am always pleased to talk on that subject," he said.

At last one of the publishers of the holier-than-thou Wall Street press had come to the offices of the despised penny paper.

Hale proposed that he and Bennett pool resources to cover the

Mexican War and the other big news of the day and Bennett, the Scotsman, accepted. That was the first positive step toward co-operative news gathering after years of fumbling, groping, and bitter competition. The next step came a year later.

1848

I. MILESTONES

TEN men, representing the six most important New York newspapers, sat around a table in the office of the *Sun* one day early in May, 1848. They had been in session for more than an hour and all that time they had been in stubborn argument. Some of them were belligerent, some were conciliatory, some were unconcerned, and some were worried. They were the autocrats of the city's newspaper world and one room never before had been big enough to hold them.

Bennett was there with his assistant, Frederic Hudson, for the *Herald*. Webb attended with his managing editor, Henry Raymond, of the *Courier and Enquirer*. Gerard Hallock and Hale represented the *Journal of Commerce*. Greeley of the *Tribune*, Moses Beach, publisher of the *Sun*, and Eustace and James Brooks of the *Express* completed the ten.

The meeting was the outcome of Hale's efforts over a period of months to bring the competing publishers together. He and Bennett had been pleased with the success of the co-operative effort which grew out of their meeting the year before, and Hale gradually had come to see a possible union of the foremost New York newspapers, each contributing its share to a general fund which could be used in a concerted effort to provide readers with wider coverage of all important world events. Now at the critical moment of his campaign he was tired and ill. He knew how difficult it would be to persuade the news titans to forget their antagonisms in the interests of the common good. But he faced the meeting and talked of news, its problems, and his proposal.

There was plenty of news to talk about. In Europe there were revolutions in progress and others brewing. At home the Mexican War was over, but the drums of another presidential campaign were beating for the war's two heroes, Zachary Taylor and Winfield Scott. The antislavery movement was growing daily; out in the wilderness of Utah the Mormons were establishing themselves on the shores of

Salt Lake, and from Chicago, a rough, frontier city of 24,000, the railroad was pushing slowly into the green prairies of the West.

But, aside from Hale and Bennett, the overlords of the New York press were suspicious and reluctant. Hale outlined his plan and saw marked signs of resentment. The rival publishers had not been pleased at the strides of the *Herald* and *Journal of Commerce* through their co-operative efforts. There were gruff questions and vigorous dissent.

James Watson Webb heard the plan through impatiently and reared to his feet. He had never forgiven Hale for breaking the harbor news monopoly with his sailboat years before, and he never would forgive Bennett for violating established newspaper practice by publishing a penny paper which gave the reader more than he was paying for. His *Courier and Enquirer,* he said, never would join any organization which contained Bennett and his *Herald.* He accused Hale and Bennett of concocting a scheme which had been so costly that they were now trying to bamboozle others into paying the bill. Puffing and angry, he turned to Henry Raymond for approval only to find Raymond's attention fixed on Hale, who had picked up the interrupted discussion.

Hale turned patiently to another phase of the problem. The situation on telegraph news was highly complicated. Each paper arranged for this news independently and paid the full rate to the company; there was only one wire available to serve all the New York papers; it had its terminus across the Hudson River on the New Jersey shore; the papers had to take fifteen-minute turns on the facilities, and all but the first in line were out of luck. News was read aloud from the crude Morse ticker to a representative of the receiving paper and there was deliberate eavesdropping and pilfering. The telegraph companies were in a precarious position because of their own competitive struggles and consequently they charged every penny the traffic would bear.

Although telegraph news already was expensive, Hale warned it might well become even more costly. It was common knowledge that the telegraph companies were selling news from their various offices to anyone with the price in spite of the fact that it had been gathered by representatives of the papers themselves. Hale also had been reliably informed that certain wire enterprises were secretly toying with the idea of setting up regular subsidiary organizations to gather and transmit news for sale. The dangers were obvious; with no governmental supervision, the telegraph companies could make it virtually impossible for any news but their own to move on limited wire facilities; papers would be forced to surrender the vital function of news gather-

HALE OUTLINED HIS PLAN AND SAW MARKED SIGNS OF RESENTMENT.

ing, and news itself would be reduced to a purely commercial and un-reliable commodity dished up for a price by outsiders on a take-it-or-leave-it basis.

As Hale concluded, Webb was drawn aside from the group by his able assistant. Raymond, who founded the New York *Times* three years afterward, was convinced of the wisdom of the proposal Hale had just made. A few minutes later the old stalwart of the *Courier and En-quirer* returned to the table and one glance told Hale and the others that the battle was over.

So in the *Sun* office in May, 1848, the first real co-operative news-gathering organization was formed. Its concept was limited and largely selfish. There was no immediate thought of benefiting any but these six papers and there was no disposition to look upon the collection of news as a great public service. The organization was by no means all that it might have been, but it was a beginning.

They called it The Associated Press.

2

The first step taken by the new organization was to perfect operat-ing procedure. Hallock was named president and the office of "general agent" was created. The man to fill this job would be responsible for actively collecting and distributing the news, so important a position that time was necessary to fill it. Therefore a committee was imme-diately named to supervise the first news-gathering efforts. Frederic Hudson, Bennett's editorial right-hand man, and Raymond, the bril-liant managing editor of Webb's *Courier and Enquirer*, were the two men selected.

The committee quickly began functioning. First it arranged for the charter of the steamer *Buena Vista* at Halifax to intercept all European boats, obtain what news they brought and rush it on to Boston, the northernmost terminus of the telegraph. Then it began negotiations with the wire company to secure precedence for the transmission of this news to New York at attractive rates. Raymond outlined what was needed in a letter on May 13, 1848, to F. O. J. Smith, a tight-fisted promoter then in charge of the Boston-New York telegraph line. He wrote:

The Journal of Commerce, Express, Courier and Enquirer, Herald, Sun, and Tribune, of this city have agreed to procure foreign news by tele-graph from Boston in common and have appointed a committee to make arrangements with you for its transmission.

Acting on behalf of that committee of the Association, I beg to propose that you give us, from the moment our dispatch shall be received at the telegraph office in Boston, the use of all the wires that may be in working order for the uninterrupted transmission of all the news we may wish to receive.

Upon its receipt here, we will make copies for each paper entitled to it and shall desire authority to prevent any part of the news leaving the office until we choose to send it out.

The arrangement is also intended to apply to steamer's news that may reach Boston for us by express from Halifax.

Upon what terms will you secure for us, for one year from the present date, the use of the telegraph as specified above? An immediate reply will greatly oblige Your obedient servant.

Smith realized the increased business such an arrangement would bring and two days later he outlined a plan, quoting tolls. Raymond confirmed the contract on May 18. His communication to Smith said:

I have received your letter of the 15th and have submitted it to Mr. Hudson, of the Herald, who with myself form the committee to act in behalf of The Associated Press. The object in making the arrangement proposed is to prevent the competition and the frequent changes of which you complain. We intend to forward the news so received, at once, to Philadelphia and Baltimore, so that the press of those cities will also be interested in the arrangement.

We understand your offer to be this: that our news shall come through without interruption; that for the first 3,000 words we pay a gross sum, $100, without reference to the parties using it; and that for the excess, we pay the regular rates, one full price and as many half prices as there are copies used, less one.

We therefore accept the offer and assent to the conditions you have named.

As the spring days moved on into another summer, it became obvious that Raymond had had definite plans in mind when he mentioned to Smith the possibility of forwarding news to other papers. The Philadelphia *Public Ledger* and the Baltimore *Sun* began receiving dispatches. They were not members of The Associated Press—the New York organization restricted that privilege—but they were its first paying clients, and as the association grew the profitable practice of selling news to outside papers was greatly expanded.

Once the channel was clear for foreign intelligence, the committee turned its attention to news at home. Already there were independent "telegraph reporters" scattered through the country who wrote and transmitted copy to any newspaper that would buy. The system under which they operated was unsatisfactory, but some of the men were good. There was serious need now for a man who was familiar not only with these free-lance sources, but also with the general operation of the telegraph. The association found the man for its general agent in Dr. Alexander Jones, a graduate in medicine whose early interest in communications had lured him into journalism. He had been a news gatherer on both sides of the Atlantic and he had devised the first cipher code to effect savings in telegraph tolls.

Jones opened a simple office at the top of a long, dim flight of seventy-eight stairs at the northwest corner of Broadway and Liberty Street. This served as the headquarters of The Associated Press for more than two decades. The annual rental was less than $500 and the weekly administrative expense less than $50. The general agent's salary was $20 a week and the entire cost of operations the first year was between $10,000 and $20,000. Payment for foreign news was the largest single item.

At first the entire New York staff consisted of Jones and one assistant, but later there was a second. Trained, capable men were few and those available needed months of instruction. Besides his work in New York, Jones was kept busy engaging correspondents, or "agents" as they were called, to obtain and telegraph news to New York. The major duties of the general agent were to receive and distribute the intelligence received from these men, to pay telegraph tolls and other expenses necessary to conduct the business, and to see to collections from the six member newspapers and the hinterland clients. Sufficient copies of each incoming dispatch were made on manifold tissue paper to cover the list of subscribers.

These were the first days of the sticky postage stamp—an innovation which seemed a curiosity—and the mails carried such obscure family tidings as the wedding of young Lieutenant Ulysses S. Grant and word that fifteen-year-old James A. Garfield had found a job as a mule driver.

The great rush was on to California and fantastic tales of fortunes in gold trickled overland to the East. But the exciting announcement of this discovery did not reach readers along the Atlantic until late in 1848 because pieces of ore, sent to the New York *Herald* by its Pacific Coast correspondent, lay for months before anyone thought to have them assayed.

But gold was only one story. The Associated Press covered its first presidential campaign; a Woman's Rights Convention at Rochester demanded suffrage; President Polk offered to buy Cuba for $100,000,000;

Garibaldi's red shirts battled the French; the King of Prussia became the hereditary emperor of the Germans; the latest census showed Parkersburg, West Virginia, the center of the nation's 25,000,000 population.

The 1848 presidential election was the first major assignment undertaken. It had a spectacular, if premature beginning. Public interest centered on the Whig National Convention at Philadelphia where four men were in the running for the party's nomination: General Zachary Taylor, Henry Clay, General Winfield Scott, and Judge McLean.

The New York terminus of the telegraph line still was in Jersey City—the problem of bridging wide rivers baffled the wire companies— and General Agent Jones intended to get the convention news across the Hudson as fast as possible. Flag signals, he decided, would do it. He went to Jersey City himself to make sure there would be no slip-up. At a pier near the Cortlandt Street Ferry on the New York side he stationed a boy from the *Courier and Enquirer*. The youngster had careful instructions. A white flag said Taylor; a red, Clay. Two white flags on the same staff meant Scott, and two reds, McLean.

Forty minutes after Jones crossed the river, the boy saw a white flag being waved vigorously from the New Jersey side. He raced off to notify the New York papers that General Taylor had been nominated. The news fled north along the telegraph to New England, arousing great excitement, and in Portland a salute of a hundred guns was fired. Meanwhile, Jones was waiting patiently in Jersey City. The signal the boy had seen was the white flag of a broker's representative in New Jersey wigwagging the latest Philadelphia stock quotations to a lookout on the Merchants' Exchange building in New York. Fortunately, General Taylor was nominated the next day.

Coverage of the election was an epochal thing. It cost more than $1,000—an awesome amount for 1848—to report General Taylor's defeat and the re-election of James K. Polk. For the first time telegraph offices remained open all night. Dr. Jones went seventy-two hours without sleep before the story was cleaned up.

Everything considered, the organization was off to a good start but the man who began it did not live to see The Associated Press through its first crucial years. Hardly a month after the meeting in the *Sun* office, David Hale had a stroke. He regained strength for a time but in January, 1849, death came to the pioneer of co-operative news gathering.

There were many difficulties those first years. Now that the association had been launched with a general agent to handle its affairs, the publishers wanted to believe their news troubles were over. Almost every successful newspaper was aligned with one political party or another, and without partisan support they would have had trouble making ends meet. But the political picture was changing and the real beginning of an independent press imminent. The old party of Whigs, long so powerful, was on the decline.

Jones did his best with his modest organization. He was handicapped by a lack of experienced help, the slow expansion of the telegraph, and the shortage of finances. The publishers saw the association as a money-saving creation and the $50 weekly allowed for office expense was not enough. Jones was kept busy day and night, Sundays and holidays. Years later he complained:

Our services were severe, and help with the proper tact and necessary prior instruction could not be had. Often on stormy nights in winter, when our errand boys were ill or absent in Jersey City [which still was the New York terminus of the telegraph] have we gone around at twelve and one o'clock and delivered messages with a snow or sleet storm beating in our face; and having, at many of the offices, to climb three or four pairs of stairs to find the composing room. For months at a time, we seldom retired before one o'clock and then had to be on duty through the next day.

He gave The Associated Press all his energy and ability, but without Hale's support and encouragement the strain soon began to tell. In May, 1851, he submitted his resignation.

II. HESITANT YEARS

I

DANIEL CRAIG, the hard-bitten Yankee who had started the first pigeon post, stood on the steps of the telegraph office in Halifax, Nova Scotia, one day in 1851. He could hear the industrious stutter of a Morse key and he could see in front of him the blue of the tumbling Atlantic. At any minute now his outgeneraled rivals would come racing up uneven Hollis Street to find they had been beaten once more.

He was a hard man to beat, this Craig. For the first several months of existence, The Associated Press had exerted every resource to outdo him, but had failed. The sensible thing, then, was to use him, so two years earlier he had become the association's first regular correspondent on foreign soil. He operated out of Halifax because that had become the first port of call of the new Cunard steamers, which were slowly replacing the sail. By boarding the craft there he could obtain any incoming news and rush it on to Boston and New York, first by pigeon post and pony express, and then by telegraph as the lines expanded north.

Fifteen years of news gathering had taught Craig to ignore the angry outbursts of his worsted opponents. But those rivals and their confederates were not above cutting telegraph wires, and Craig found it wise to be watchful until his budget of intelligence had cleared. He turned for a reassuring look at the lines which stretched from the office. Just then a clerk stepped up to him with a message. Craig read it. The Executive Committee of The Associated Press wanted him to come to New York immediately.

In the two years since Raymond and Hudson had prevailed upon him to act as foreign news agent, Craig had done well. He established the first Associated Press office on foreign soil at Halifax early in 1849. He arranged for the first Associated Press pony express that June to rush the exclusive news of an attempt to assassinate Queen Victoria in London. He sent The Associated Press's first all-wire message of European news from Halifax in November. He successfully advocated the first Associated Press controlled wire from New York to Boston to St. John to Halifax. And he brought The Associated Press its first large bloc of outside clients when he induced the papers in Boston to subscribe to the Halifax-European pony express before the telegraph reached Nova Scotia.

At the time Craig's assignment began, the telegraph lines extended only as far north as Portland, Maine, and getting the news to the wires was a headlong race. Once Craig's budget reached shore, an express rider was off with it at a breakneck gallop on the first lap of the 144-mile trip across the Nova Scotian peninsula from Halifax to Digby on the Bay of Fundy. Every eight miles a fresh mount waited. It took the express eight hours to cover the distance—a mile every three and a half minutes. The riders aroused terrific excitement as they pounded across the country, and villagers lined the roadsides to cheer them when they passed. Several miles outside of Digby a cannon was fired to notify the boat captain at Digby that the express had been sighted. The captain got up steam and sent a yawl ashore to meet the rider. Then the fast Digby boat dashed down the Maine coast to Portland and the telegraph.

Several months later the telegraph wires reached St. John, New Brunswick, and Craig sent his Digby packet to that port. The ship made the trip in three hours, enabling Craig to get his news to Boston on an average of thirty-five hours ahead of the ten-knot Cunarders on the Halifax-Boston run. Late in 1849 the telegraph bridged the gap between St. John and Halifax and direct wire communication was established with New York.

The hostility of the telegraph people interfered greatly with Craig's use of pigeons overland, even before the Halifax line was completed. They considered the birds unfair competition, and went to great lengths to harass anyone using them. At sea, however, it was different and the pigeons flew the most important news ashore. In calm weather Craig could board the incoming Cunarders, obtain his package of European papers, then return to his own boat and prepare the dispatches as he made for shore. When the seas were stormy, the steamers threw the packages overboard in water-tight half-gallon cans for Craig to pick up. During the daytime, the cans carried a small flag on a stick, and at night a flare to guide the news gatherer.

Innumerable hard knocks in the unending struggle to be first with foreign news had toughened Craig. One of his fiercest battles had been with a telegraph promoter who had schemed to create and control a foreign news monopoly. Somehow the promoter always seemed to have first call on the wire out of Halifax whenever Craig reached the office with news from the latest incoming boat. Craig's material accordingly was sidetracked. But Craig was equal to the emergency. As soon as a steamer was sighted off Halifax, he had an undercover employe send a cryptic message to another agent at Amherst, the next telegraph office along the line. The agent at Halifax understood what was then expected of him. He immediately passed a copy of the Bible over to the Amherst telegraph operator with word that he was to start sending "Associated Press Steamer News."

With a sigh the operator began sending: "Associated Press, New York, N. Y.: In the beginning God created the heaven and the earth. And the earth was without form and void." While this sending was being made, Craig was meeting the steamer at Halifax and dispatching his news by pony express to Amherst. It took five hours for the express to reach Amherst and, during that whole time, the Amherst operator continued his sending of Scripture to The Associated Press in New York. Sometimes he got through Genesis and well into Exodus before the express arrived and the local Halifax agent took back his Bible and substituted the newly arrived news.

Craig's job was to obtain the news and send it in the most expeditious way possible, and that was what he did.

"The advance receipt of European news by steamer at Halifax was so important," he said bluntly, "that no consideration of money or effort would have excused me for a single failure."

As his train rattled southward over the rough roadbed which set its smoky oil lamps swaying, Craig may have wondered why he was being called to New York. Before his interview with Hudson and Raymond was ended, however, the first foreign correspondent of The Associated Press had become its second general agent.

2

Craig had barely cleared a desk and established himself in the Broadway headquarters when another force entered the growing field of news. Raymond, who had resigned as editor of Webb's *Courier*, founded the New York *Times*, and he was so well liked that The Associated Press immediately welcomed his paper into membership.

The *Times* proved a beneficial influence. A definite division was slowly splitting the ranks of the membership. The *Herald*, the *Tribune*, and the *Sun* believed that the activities of the association should be increased. The *Express,* the *Courier and Enquirer,* and the *Journal of Commerce* were satisfied with things as they were. Raymond's *Times,* with its policy of initiative, broke the deadlock.

Another important factor appeared. In the earlier days of the Morse, the swelling volume of news had been a nightmare for editors who found their antiquated printing equipment incapable of handling it. Machinery had failed to keep pace with the abruptly increased speed and volume of news. Just as the trouble was becoming acute, Robert M. Hoe discovered that the secret of rapid printing was to take the type from the flat bed on which it had reposed so many centuries and put it on a cylinder. His first rotary press appeared two years before The Associated Press was founded, but only now was the improved equipment replacing outmoded machinery in the plants of the larger papers.

The revolving cylinder brought an era of faster editions, larger papers, and a greater use of news.

Activities of news pirates and bids of short-lived opposition agencies failed to check The Associated Press and the number of subscriber papers increased as urban centers enlarged. Payments from these "outside" sources supplied funds for expansion and at the same time made it possible for the seven New York members to receive a steadily larger report at a fraction of the expense that would have been necessary had the news organization been restricted to New York alone.

Gradually the subscriber papers began to gravitate into loosely defined geographical groups. Two major reasons prompted the rise of these groups. Their news was distributed to them on a regional basis, and a regional grouping facilitated their dealings with New York. In time these local associations were referring to themselves by such names as the Philadelphia Associated Press, New York State Associated Press, Southern Associated Press, Western Associated Press, and the like. Sometimes the word "Associated" was omitted and the papers were spoken of merely as the Baltimore Press, or the Southern Press.

To distinguish the parent organization from these loosely formed groups, the newspaper world began to speak of it as the New York Associated Press. It remained the only association which endeavored to obtain all important domestic and foreign news and the others looked to it for coverage on everything outside their various geographical divisions.

The telegraph slowly expanded, but Craig never completely abandoned a belief that his organization should take over communications facilities as subsidiary. He saw the telegraph as a logical "tail to The Associated Press kite." He feared the attempts of the telegraph companies to gather and sell news. Under the pretext of necessity—and he had a free hand most of the time—he went as far as he dared in efforts to convert the association's members to his point of view. Once, to assure delivery of his news without interference, he took a half interest in a line for a small amount and disposed of it in a few years at a profit of $100,000. He subsequently helped build other lines and controlled them temporarily in his capacity as general agent.

Dealing with the staff, he had considerably more success in enforcing his views. He was a stickler for correctness and insisted his men be likewise. He knew that it was a general practice for a reporter in one city to telegraph a few lines on the main facts of an event, leaving it to an imaginative editor on the receiving end to "blow up" the story into several hundred words with whatever "details" came to mind. Craig issued orders that if a story was important enough to warrant details the details were worth the wire costs. The rule shocked an experienced "telegraph reporter," who protested that editors did not know the difference between real and imaginary news. But the reporter did not raise the point a second time. He did things Craig's way.

Another reform was the end to the practice of sending news reports in bewildering codes or highly skeletonized jumbles. Codes and ciphers had been the first reaction to the high cost of telegraphy. With words costing so much each, an attempt was made to compress phrases and even parts of sentences into one polysyllabic combination. This produced such amazing "words" as caserovingedsable, hoveesness, rehoeingedableness, and retackmentativeness. Craig put a stop to that. He ordered all the association's dispatches sent in full, and woe betide telegraph men who took liberties with them. The change was a nine-day wonder in the newspaper world.

3

In 1856 Craig pointed out to the seven New York member papers that it was dangerous for the association to continue operations without more definitely defined rules of procedure. A meeting was held on October 21 and out of it came a formal reorganization which set the association on a more businesslike basis, promulgated a code of regulations and redefined methods. The reorganization emphasized the essentially selfish purpose of the association. It was a union of seven morning papers—there were still few afternoon editions—and the news collected was designed solely to meet their needs, without any consideration for the wants of subscriber papers. The subscribers, in effect, were journalistic vassals who dutifully paid tribute for such news as their New York overlords saw fit to provide.

One of the outstanding results of the reorganization was an order to the general agent to establish the first two formal Associated Press bureaus in the United States—at Washington and Albany. The association already had correspondents in most major centers and now it was logical to establish them in offices and to provide, in some cases, for assistants.

The Washington bureau, or "agency" as it was called, was put in charge of Lawrence Augustus Gobright, a veteran who had been reporting the capital's news for The Associated Press since 1848. He had been a familiar newspaper figure since the dim, half-forgotten days of Clay, Webster, and Calhoun. His service had been so long that they called him "Father" Gobright, though he was not yet forty.

With authority better defined, Craig did not hesitate to crack down vigorously. Even James Gordon Bennett had no immunity and twice when he was disciplined by the general agent he threatened to withdraw the *Herald* from membership. There was little attempt to disguise the fact that the object of the association was to create and perpetuate a news monopoly, and Craig bluntly stated: "We succeeded and compelled the editors to abandon their arrangements and come into ours."

However much he might be occupied with the details of administration, the general agent never forgot that his prime concern was news —lifeblood of the association. He had been compelled to devote most of his time to the development of domestic news, but he retained a keen interest in the European budget. When he left Halifax he had commissioned William Hunter, a resourceful, pugnacious man like himself, to represent The Associated Press. Craig could find no fault with the way the foreign news was sent to New York once it reached Canadian soil. But all of Hunter's efforts and all the swiftness of the telegraph could not change the fact that European news was weeks late. The telegraph had conquered the land but not the seas. Any news report was a mixture of fresh domestic intelligence and stale date lines from abroad.

III. "WE WILL GO ON"

IT WAS the evening of August 17, 1858. President Buchanan, in shirt sleeves, examined a remarkable message before him and drummed his fingers on the arm of his chair. He was sixty-eight and on this occasion he looked it because of the sultry heat of summer. Members of the Cabinet lounged about the White House study. The secretary of the treasury, Howell Cobb, relaxed on a sofa, shook his head in disbelief for the dozenth time. It was a hoax, he declared, and in these days of growing agitation there was sufficient deceit in the land without swallowing another fraud.

The brief, unexplained message purported to be a greeting composed abroad only that day by Queen Victoria and already delivered in Washington to the President of the United States!

Everyone, however, did not agree that the message was a hoax. The messenger said he had come from Agent Gobright of The Associated Press. Moreover, there had been word from Cyrus Field a fortnight before that he had brought the North American end of his Atlantic cable ashore at Trinity Bay, linking Newfoundland and Valentia, Ireland. Buchanan read the message again:

```
THE QUEEN DESIRES TO CONGRATULATE THE
PRESIDENT UPON THE SUCCESSFUL COMPLETION OF
THE GREAT INTERNATIONAL WORK, IN WHICH THE
QUEEN HAS TAKEN THE GREATEST INTEREST.
```

That was what the message said and Secretary of the Interior Thompson, most active of the indolent group, had been dispatched to the Associated Press office to find out the truth of the matter. The Cabinet idled on until he returned with Gobright, who soon cleared up the puzzle.

The greeting had, in truth, come by Field's new cable under the ocean from Valentia to Trinity Bay, and thence by land telegraph from Newfoundland. It had been received from Field along with other messages to The Associated Press. Although it was unknown at the time, the one-sentence message did not contain all that the queen had said. The following addition came through the next day:

... THE QUEEN IS CONVINCED THAT THE
PRESIDENT WILL JOIN WITH HER IN FERVENTLY
HOPING THAT THE ELECTRIC CABLE, WHICH NOW AL-
READY CONNECTS GREAT BRITAIN WITH THE UNITED
STATES, WILL PROVE AN ADDITIONAL LINK BETWEEN
THE TWO NATIONS, WHOSE FRIENDSHIP IS FOUNDED
UPON THEIR COMMON INTERESTS AND RECIPROCAL
ESTEEM. THE QUEEN HAS MUCH PLEASURE IN THUS
DIRECTLY COMMUNICATING WITH THE PRESIDENT, AND
IN RENEWING TO HIM HER BEST WISHES FOR THE
PROSPERITY OF THE UNITED STATES.

The President and his perspiring Cabinet finally were persuaded as to the authenticity of the Queen's brief greeting and the chief executive drafted a reply which he asked Gobright to send.

"I'll make a copy," the agent told the President, "and keep the original."

Secretary Cobb, still at ease on the sofa, felt that the original should be deposited in the public archives. But Gobright wanted it for himself and the President made the decision.

"It's yours, sir," he said.

The correspondent glanced at the first official message ever to be cabled from this country and hurried along to follow Buchanan's request. The message, which Gobright later donated to a historical collection, read:

THE PRESIDENT CORDIALLY RECIPROCATES THE
CONGRATULATIONS OF HER MAJESTY THE QUEEN ON THE
SUCCESS OF THE GREAT INTERNATIONAL ENTERPRISE
ACCOMPLISHED BY THE SKILL, SCIENCE AND INDOM-
ITABLE ENERGY OF THE TWO COUNTRIES. IT IS A
TRIUMPH MORE GLORIOUS BECAUSE FAR MORE USEFUL
TO MANKIND THAN WAS EVER WON BY A CONQUEROR ON
THE FIELD OF BATTLE. MAY THE ATLANTIC TELE-
GRAPH UNDER THE BLESSING OF HEAVEN PROVE TO BE
A BOND OF PERPETUAL PEACE AND FRIENDSHIP BE-
TWEEN THE KINDRED NATIONS AND AN INSTRUMENT
DESTINED BY DIVINE PROVIDENCE TO PURSUE ITS
RELIGION, CIVILIZATION, LIBERTY AND LAW THROUGH-
OUT THE WORLD. IN THIS VIEW WILL NOT ALL THE
NATIONS OF CHRISTENDOM SPONTANEOUSLY UNITE IN
THE DECLARATION THAT IT SHALL BE FOREVER NEUTRAL
AND THAT ITS COMMUNICATIONS SHALL BE HELD
SACRED IN PASSING TO THE PLACE OF THEIR DESTI-
NATION EVEN IN THE MIDST OF HOSTILITIES?

This had been a casual incident in the White House, but there was nothing matter-of-fact in the exuberant reception the nation gave the news that Field had succeeded after two costly failures. Papers clarioned the triumph by which Europe and America were linked by one slender wire snaking across the bottom of the Atlantic. In New York Bennett's *Herald* shouted its loudest, and city after city joined in the plans for a nation-wide celebration on September 1. Field was toasted, given medals and lionized. Cannon boomed, bells rang, and whistles shrieked. There were parades, dinners, and fireworks. Poets wrote flowery odes and red-faced orators declaimed on the new union of the two continents. General Agent Craig was personally very happy. He felt that the cable would immediately solve the problem of slow receipt of foreign news.

In the midst of this great rejoicing the first European cable news in the history of the world spanned the Atlantic. It was addressed to The Associated Press. The essence of condensation, it read:

```
    EMPEROR OF FRANCE RETURNED TO PARIS SATUR-
DAY.  KING OF PRUSSIA TOO ILL TO VISIT QUEEN
VICTORIA.  HER MAJESTY RETURNS TO ENGLAND 31ST
AUGUST.  SETTLEMENT OF CHINESE QUESTION: CHINESE
EMPIRE OPENS TO TRADE; CHRISTIAN RELIGION AL-
LOWED.  MUTINY BEING QUELLED, ALL INDIA BECOM-
ING TRANQUIL.
```

The next day, August 28, the station on the North American mainland was answering with a budget of American news which included yellow fever statistics from the South and brief details of the plans for formal celebration of the successful cable.

But cable signals were growing fainter and the operators were finding it difficult to understand them. The message was long in transit. There were uneasy periods during which the two stations could not hear each other and then, just as the September celebration was at its height, the last faint signals came over the lines.

The cable was dead.

The disappointment was tremendous. Those who had most loudly acclaimed Cyrus Field and his assistants damned the cable as a gigantic hoax. They claimed that no messages ever had been received or transmitted. There even was talk that the cable was a subterfuge for a stock-selling swindle. But the line was dead and The Associated Press was forced to lay aside its hurriedly formulated plans for use of the new link in international communications. The old reliable newsboats continued their assignments off Halifax and Cape Race.

Field met dejectedly with the directors of his company soon after the blow had fallen. Large sums of money had been lost and the

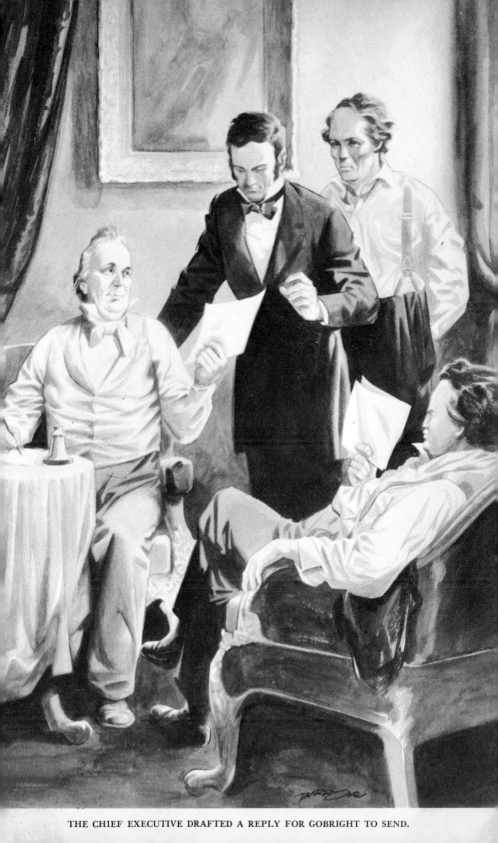

THE CHIEF EXECUTIVE DRAFTED A REPLY FOR GOBRIGHT TO SEND.

failure would make it difficult to find public backing for another attempt. Peter Cooper, the noted inventor, threw a consoling arm over Field's shoulder. As a director of the cable company, he had invested heavily in the venture.

"Do not give up hope," he said, "we will go on."

But black thunderheads were filling the horizon. The storm was inevitable and when its fury broke the nation and its news gatherers had little attention for Field or his persevering efforts. The storm had been brewing a long while. Its first cloud had appeared over Jamestown, Virginia, one August day two hundred and forty-nine years before. John Rolfe, husband of the Indian princess Pocahontas, had recorded the fact:

About the last of August, came in a Dutch man of Warre that sold us twenty negars.

446332

IV. BUGLES BLOW

I

WHAT would Lincoln do?

General Agent Craig stood at the news pulse of the anxious nation in the large, dingy, carpetless headquarters of The Associated Press in New York. He weighed the question. The mass of dispatches in his hand was far from reassuring that gloomy November day of 1860. They told of southern students quitting classes at Harvard to return home, of the Richmond *Enquirer* screaming "An Act of War" at Lincoln's election as President, and of General Scott's warning on the dangers of secession. National tension was mounting hourly and Craig debated his problem.

Some persons felt that the whole tide of sectional differences arose because a humanitarian North wished to free the slaves of a feudal South, but hardheaded Craig could see there was more to it than that. There were fundamental differences in the two sections and long years of ignorance had not helped to bring about an understanding. The differences between the two suspicious, badly informed sections were too many to be overcome. A truthful, alert press would have helped, but much of the press had been anything but that. The warped, fanatical opinions and the twisted reports in news columns, North and South, were almost as much to blame as any other single factor. In this atmosphere of sectional recrimination, Craig knew it was too late to do anything about the shortcomings of the past. The day had not yet arrived when newspapers drew a distinct line between the news columns and the editorial page, but he intended to use his influence to prevent distortion of Associated Press reports.

Craig could not recall when a president-elect had assumed such sudden importance in the destinies of the country. Overnight the home of the furrow-faced lawyer in Springfield, Illinois, had become the focal point for a troubled people's attention. In 1852 and again in 1856 the general agent had found that successful candidates produced news only occasionally in the preinaugural months and consequently required only casual attention. But with Lincoln it was different. Craig decided the time had come when the association must keep a correspondent constantly with the President-elect.

The unprecedented assignment went to a 25-year-old Mid-westerner, Henry Villard, who was excited by his novel and important mission. He received a warm welcome at Springfield. Lincoln held many conferences those fateful weeks and Villard reported them all. It became known that the President-elect would accept almost any compromise with the disaffected southern states except one sanctioning extension of slavery to the territories not yet ready for admission to the Union. That stirred up a furor; then the announcement of some members of his Cabinet brought another blast of condemnation.

Villard reported the facts, but no facts during those preinaugural days could stay the relentless march of events. On December 20, 1860, South Carolina adopted the first ordinance of secession and the Charleston *Mercury* shouted: "The Union Is Dissolved." Before 1861 was a week old other states followed and the office at Broadway and Liberty was flooded with dispatches which told of the seizure of federal arsenals and forts, of regiments being raised, of bellicose speeches.

Lincoln stood on the train platform at Springfield and looked down into the faces of the group of friends gathered to bid him good-bye as he left for Washington. He was somber with worry and the demonstration touched him. In a few brief sentences he said farewell. The speech caught Villard unprepared and as soon as the train pulled out the Associated Press man came to him and explained his predicament. Lincoln reached out, took the correspondent's pad and pencil, and while the train jolted eastward he carefully set down the words he had spoken. At the first telegraph station Villard filed the dispatch, which concluded with the eloquent words of Lincoln's parting:

MY FRIENDS, NO ONE NOT IN MY POSITION CAN
APPRECIATE THE SADNESS I FEEL AT THIS PARTING.
TO THIS PEOPLE I OWE ALL THAT I AM. HERE I
HAVE LIVED MORE THAN A QUARTER OF A CENTURY;
HERE MY CHILDREN WERE BORN AND ONE OF THEM LIES
BURIED. I KNOW NOT HOW SOON I SHALL SEE YOU
AGAIN. A DUTY DEVOLVES ON ME WHICH IS, PER-
HAPS, GREATER THAN THAT WHICH HAS DEVOLVED
UPON ANY OTHER MAN SINCE THE DAYS OF WASHING-
TON. HE NEVER WOULD HAVE SUCCEEDED EXCEPT FOR
THE AID OF DIVINE PROVIDENCE, UPON WHICH HE AT
ALL TIMES RELIED. I FEEL THAT I CANNOT SUC-
CEED WITHOUT THE SAME DIVINE AID WHICH SUS-
TAINED HIM, AND IN THE SAME ALMIGHTY BEING I
PLACE MY RELIANCE FOR SUPPORT; AND I HOPE YOU,

MY FRIENDS, WILL ALL PRAY THAT I MAY RECEIVE
THAT DIVINE ASSISTANCE, WITHOUT WHICH I CANNOT
SUCCEED, BUT WITH WHICH SUCCESS IS CERTAIN.
AGAIN I BID YOU ALL AN AFFECTIONATE FAREWELL.

It was easy for many newspapers to overlook that little speech in
the thickening sheaf of dispatches that passed over Craig's desk that raw
February. Jefferson Davis was inaugurated the first President of the
Confederate States of America. In Charleston harbor guns under the
brave new palmetto flag pointed menacingly across the water toward
Fort Sumter. "The Southern Excitement" or "The Southern Troubles"
became standing headlines in the North, and the secession spirit spread
even to New York where the council was asked to declare Manhattan
a free city, independent of the wrangling states.

On a melancholy March day the telegraph clicked and the story
went chattering into scores of newspaper offices that the one-time rail
splitter had taken his oath of office. Then came the text of the inaugural
address with its somber admonition: "In your hands, my dissatisfied
fellow countrymen, and not in mine, is the momentous issue of civil
war." Word for word the document went to Associated Press members
and clients. Lincoln had furnished his own printed copy with its numerous corrections and extensive interlineations so that it might be
telegraphed in full.

March swept on into April and there was nothing to report except
that the tense nation hovered on the brink. The animosities did not
appear to have touched all the people everywhere, and in the Associated Press office at Louisville, headquarters for the South, a representative of the client papers below Maxon and Dixon's line still worked
amicably enough with old Tyler, the Yankee agent there. The duty
of the southern representative was to select from the incoming telegraph report of the New York Associated Press a daily budget of news
for his own subscribers.

Then, at Washington, Gobright obtained the first authentic story
of the administration's complete policy toward the seceded states—and
two days later the four long, red years began.

They began, not in Washington, but miles southward. It was four-
thirty in the morning of April 12, 1861. The agent at Charleston
watched a signal rocket arch out over the harbor toward the Union
garrison of Fort Sumter and a second later saw the first Confederate
shell go screaming across the water. He sent his dispatch. Thirty-four

LINCOLN . . . CAREFULLY SET DOWN THE WORDS HE HAD SPOKEN.

hours later he reported the fort's surrender and in New York Bennett wrote an editorial in a single line: "Civil War has begun."

Resourceful as Craig might be, he had no precedent on which to model the activities of the association. The technique for reporting military action had to be learned by trial and error. Even by the loose standards of the day the number of experienced reporters in the service was few, for most of the agents who manned Craig's scattered outposts had been chosen primarily because of their ability to use the telegraph. Battles were not fought conveniently in the backyard of telegraph offices and wire facilities were rambling and insufficient.

Thus far, however, the agents were acquitting themselves well. Through the worried weeks since the 1860 election, while the crisis mounted and prejudices ran wild, their dispatches, even as read now, show factual directness and great restraint. These were the days of flowery, declamatory journalism, and frequently the correspondents for individual papers wrote with undisguised bias. In the news columns, side by side with such excitable accounts, the association's dispatches seemed strangely calm, direct, and terse. As the long bloody miles to Appomattox unrolled, many a successful skirmish was hailed by writers representing one journal or another as "a glorious, overwhelming victory," and many a sorry rout excused as "a strategic withdrawal before a vastly superior enemy." But somehow Craig's agents managed to cling close to a factual sanity and keep their dispatches reasonably free of gaudy, artificial heroics.

Gobright summed up the creed effectively:

My business is to communicate facts; my instructions do not allow me to make any comment upon the facts which I communicate. My dispatches are sent to papers of all manner of politics, and the editors say they are able to make their own comments upon the facts which are sent them. I therefore confine myself to what I consider legitimate news. I do not act as a politician belonging to any school, but try to be truthful and impartial. My dispatches are merely dry matters of fact and detail. Some special correspondents may write to suit the temper of their organs. Although I try to write without regard to men or politics, I do not always escape censure.

On April 15, 1861, Lincoln called for 75,000 militia "to suppress obstructions to Federal laws in the seceded states," and in Boston the bells rang all day. Jefferson Davis retorted with an appeal for 42,000 men to serve in the ranks of the Confederacy, and the South dreamed of a short, glorious fight to victory. In New York a mob marched on the *Journal of Commerce* demanding that Gerard Hallock, its pacifist editor and president of The Associated Press, display the union emblem. He quickly did so. Earlier the crowd had marched down to Fulton Street, where Bennett was not quite so well prepared. While they stormed the *Herald's* door and shouted threats, the agitated office staff sought frantically for a flag and the nervous publisher paced the floor. The frenzied search failed to produce a banner and an office boy was sent out the back door to the nearest Broadway department store. The crowd's temper had reached the boiling point by the time the youngster returned. The hastily purchased Stars and Stripes was broken out from a flagpole and then Bennett himself appeared smiling at the window.

War fever spread, and North or South it was: Follow the Flag or Wear Petticoats.

Then two awkward, amateur armies met near Bull Run in the blazing heat of July 21. The sloppy blue lines rolled forward in a fumbling attack which nevertheless seemed assured of victory and an officer in gray was shouting: "Look! There stands Jackson like a stone wall!" To Washington by courier and telegram went the exultant prediction of triumph and a raw agent with the Union Army, after seeing the Confederate forces so badly hammered, set off for the capital at a mad gallop with the details of the unfinished battle. It was his first experience under fire and he was so unstrung when he reached Washington that he was unable to write his account. Gobright took charge, pieced the story together, and dispatched the first eyewitness account to New York. He started writing at nine o'clock that night and it was after eleven before he finished.

The distraught correspondent would have preferred some whisky for his nerves, but Gobright ordered the telegraph line kept open and dragged his tired companion off to seek later arrivals from the field who might have additional news. It was just then that the first panic-stricken fugitives began to straggle into the city and from them Gobright learned the incredible news that the tide of battle had turned, transforming an apparent Union victory into decisive Union defeat. The details were sketchy but enough to send Gobright racing for the telegraph office to dispatch a description of the reversal of federal fortunes.

Gobright counted himself lucky in having held his night wire open long enough to obtain and send such important information, but the next day he discovered that not a single paper had printed his momentous story of the Union defeat. Instead, they had printed only the earlier material brought in by the field correspondent.

The North was hailing this incomplete report as the first "glorious victory" for the Union and the exuberant populace was celebrating with clanging bells and wild hurrahs. Gobright learned what had happened. As soon as Winfield Scott, general in chief of the northern forces, had heard of the disastrous turn in the battle's tide he dispatched a rider to the telegraph office with orders to prevent the transmission of any word of the defeat. Gobright's story never had left the wire company's office. It was the first instance of official censorship, but it was an unmistakable warning of what was to come.

2

The war was on in grim earnest and the federal government, lacking an adequate telegraph service of its own, commandeered the facilities of The Associated Press to handle military communications. This imposed a heavy handicap on the association. Henceforth military messages took precedence and the flow of news was increasingly restricted as the volume of these messages grew. Craig saw one advantage to be gained. His agents would be brought into close daily contact with the army and since many of them were telegraphers, they frequently would be privy to the contents of the messages they handled. Craig felt confident that in this way his men in the various cities would be able to keep well informed of facts throughout a war which already was spawning endless rumors and alarms.

But the campaigns were not fought in the cities, and Craig methodically set out to organize his corps of war correspondents to accompany the Union armies into the field. He began recruiting new men and dispatching them to the ill-defined fronts which were slowly taking shape—to Missouri, to Kentucky, to the strategic points along the Ohio, to West Virginia where the cocky star of McClellan had started its rise, and into Virginia where the Bonnie Blue Flag whipped defiantly over the Confederate outposts. His preparations went ahead independent of the pretentious individual efforts of the New York publishers.

For the first time in many years the hurried plans of the journalistic powers were minus the loud and bullying influence of one famous old personality. James Watson Webb no longer was on the scene. He had disposed of his paper and it was consolidated with the newly founded *World*, which acquired the *Courier's* Associated Press membership. The indefatigable Bennett was mapping a coverage campaign which cost him $525,000 and put sixty *Herald* correspondents in the field. Greeley's *Tribune*, Raymond's *Times*, and the others likewise were assembling their forces. The private news armies they marshaled were large, but Craig's forces were even more numerous. One of the *Herald's* staff, surveying the war zones, wrote: "The special correspondents of the several New York papers are nearly if not quite as numerous as the agents of The Associated Press."

They were a picturesque lot, these correspondents, some smoothshaven youths, some with long Quakerlike beards, some mustached in the approved style of the day. Kossuth hats and fancy vests were universal favorites and all wore stiff collars. Campaign kits were not elaborate—revolver, field glasses, notebook, blanket, haversack—although a good mount was indispensable. For the risks and arduous living demanded, the monetary return was not great. Salaries ranged from $10 to $25 a week for the men in the field, out of which they had to pay their own expenses, to a maximum of $35 for key men in such centers as Washington and Louisville. General Agent Craig received $3,000 annually.

From the flatlands of Virginia to the muddy Mississippi unseasoned armies maneuvered and feinted for advantage. But before another major battle followed the rout of Bull Run there was trouble on the home front which ended the career of Gerard Hallock, president of The Associated Press since its foundation.

Under Hallock's personal direction, the *Journal of Commerce* had been outspoken in its opposition to the Lincoln administration and the prosecution of "the present unholy war" with the South. He himself wrote most of the editorials which so offended fiery Union supporters. With the war fever at fanatical heat, a federal grand jury stepped in with a presentment denouncing the *Journal of Commerce* as disloyal and recommending that the paper be prosecuted along with several others. Later it was said that the foreman of the jury had reason to nurse a grudge against Hallock because of the editor's refusal to accept a bribe for publishing a "puff." A patriotic boycott was unloosed against the *Journal of Commerce*. Its circulation suffered, but Hallock stuck to his course, unmindful of threats against his life. Then came the second blow. The postmaster general barred the paper from the mails. Hallock fought the order as in violation of the Bill of Rights, but it was not revoked and the *Journal of Commerce* faced the certain loss of its profitable out-of-town circulation. Its evening edition was suspended and the morning edition was distributed only to those who did not receive their paper through the mail.

It was obvious that the *Journal of Commerce* could not continue to publish under such a handicap and so on August 31, 1861—the day the publication completed its thirty-fourth year—the editor stepped down to save the life of his paper. He disposed of his interest to David M. Stone, head of the *Journal's* commercial news department, and to William Cowper Prime, author and traveler, who immediately succeeded him as president of The Associated Press. Beyond Hallock's embarrassment at the stigma of "disloyalty" to the Union, his retirement had no consequences. The beliefs expressed in his columns represented his own personal feelings and were not reflected by the press association.

But Hallock never lost his absorbing interest either in the *Journal of Commerce* or in The Associated Press. For the next several years, even after he retired with his family to Connecticut, he watched news gathering pursue its uneven course. He wrote letters to the editor and from time to time he offered advice to his former colleagues.

He sat one winter afternoon beside the smoldering fire in the living room of his home overlooking the Connecticut River. A blanket rested across his legs and he was intent on the current edition of his favorite paper. Presently he called the members of his family to join him. He talked with them of the past and of the future and then asked if he might be alone.

When they returned ten minutes later the first president of The Associated Press was dead.

V. THE LONG CAMPAIGN

NORTH, south, east and west men marched and countermarched through 1861. Generally overlooked in those hectic days was the part the special correspondents of many northern newspapers were playing by disclosing Union strategy to the Confederacy. Not content with attempts to get news first, they tried to anticipate it and unwittingly served the Confederate cause. For a long time their stories kept the South remarkably well informed on federal plans. Southern spies in the North watched the newspapers closely, forwarding any important information they contained, sometimes even maps of projects, campaigns, or fortifications. In the South this problem did not develop so acutely. An official agency supplied the papers there with war news and the authorities were better able to control the information published.

It was not only this aiding of the enemy that was turning Union generals against the war correspondents as a group. Too many reporters were writing fantastic, erroneous stories. They embroidered "atrocity" reports. They set themselves up as experts in military strategy and they railed at any officer whose ideas on a campaign differed from their own. And woe to the general who did not acknowledge their dignity.

The Department of the Cumberland, the military designation for the area with Union headquarters at Louisville, had more than its share of these so-called correspondents in the autumn of 1861. William Tecumseh Sherman, the general commanding, made no attempt to conceal his contempt for them. The only two men he trusted were quiet old Tyler, the Associated Press agent, and Henry Villard, who had joined the *Herald* since his preinaugural press association work with Lincoln. Because the government had commandeered the association's telegraph facilities, the Associated Press agency in Louisville virtually became a part-time headquarters for Sherman. He was there night after night, tall, sharp-eyed, brusquely abstracted. When he talked at all, it was to Tyler or Villard.

Sherman was worried. He saw that the war would be a long and bloody one and he was afraid the Confederates would seize the strategic vantage points in Kentucky and along the Ohio before he had sufficient men to hold them. The special correspondents continued to ridicule him. One of them wrote that Sherman had the manners of a Pawnee Indian and when the general upbraided him the correspondent apologized in print—not to Sherman, but to the Indians!

Then many reporters for the private press seized upon his moodiness and whispers began to circulate that the general was suffering from mental depressions, spells, and aberrations. The whispers grew until they reached Washington. Sherman was relieved of his command and sent to an inconsequential "safe" post in Missouri. Then on December 11, 1861, the most abusive of all libels was splashed across certain front pages. "General William T. Sherman Insane!" was the headline in the Cincinnati *Commercial*, over a story which began:

> The painful intelligence reaches us in such form that we are not at liberty to disclose it, that General William T. Sherman, late commander of the Department of the Cumberland, is insane. It appears that he was at the time while commanding in Kentucky stark mad.

After months under a cloud, Sherman fought his way back as one of the greatest military figures of the war, but he never forgave that "slanderous insanity story." Two years later, at Vicksburg, three special correspondents were erroneously reported lost. The general received the news with caustic sarcasm. "That's good," he exclaimed. "We'll have dispatches now from hell before breakfast."

Although Associated Press men themselves had nothing to do with the libel, the entire press without distinction suffered the consequences for the remainder of the war. It multiplied the difficulties of obtaining official news and it made army officers openly hostile. Associated Press agents and other correspondents who tried to be accurate labored under as much disrepute as their careless, vindictive colleagues.

The first war Christmas passed and the New Year came—1862. In New York the association's headquarters had grown to five rooms and the office staff was enlarged to meet the demands which had come with the conflict. The general agent had two assistants and a corps of six copyists, or manifolders, who transcribed dispatches by hand on the flimsy, carbon-smeared tissue sheets which were distributed by four messengers to members and clients in the city.

Before the costly spring campaigns got under way the truculent new secretary of war, Edwin M. Stanton, clamped down on news gathering. "All newspapers publishing military news, however obtained, not authorized by official authority, will be excluded thereafter from receiving information by telegraph and from transmitting their publications by railroad." That was his order, aimed primarily at the papers which had been disclosing military secrets to the enemy. It aroused so much editorial opposition that he modified the regulations the next day to permit the publication of "past facts, leaving out details of military forces, and all statements from which the number, position and strength of the military forces of the United States can be inferred." Editors continued to storm, but Stanton was not to be trifled with. Already he had thrown one special correspondent into prison and, moreover, he was the wartime czar of both the telegraph and the railroad.

From Craig's agents in Virginia came accounts of defeat after defeat—the fierce Peninsular campaign, another rout at Bull Run, the awful slaughter at Antietam, and Burnside's butchery of an army before the heights of Fredericksburg. Only from the West came tidings to relieve the Union's gloom. A new leader, Ulysses S. Grant, was shouldering his way in a slam-bang fashion through the back door of the South. And that superannuated sea dog, Admiral Farragut, captured New Orleans. The London *Times* put mourning borders around the news when it reached Europe many days later.

Special writers signed their accounts with fancy pseudonyms, but there were no "by-lines" for the Associated Press agents on the many fronts. Occasionally a copyist might absently include the name of the agent at the end of a dispatch—McGregor with the Army of the Potomac, Weir with the Army of Tennessee, Tyler in Kentucky—but those were exceptions. For every exception there were hundreds of accounts which submerged the identities of the men on the battle lines with the impersonal description: "From the Associated Press Agent."

The dispatches which came to the general agent ordinarily were brief. The curtailment of wire facilities limited his correspondents to terse bulletins on important engagements. These were followed a day or more later by more extended eyewitness accounts. In the East the agents often found it quickest to jump a train immediately after a battle and write their stories en route to New York or some intermediate city where telegraphic transmission could be arranged. Sometimes they used messengers, sometimes they galloped the long miles themselves, and sometimes they relied on the mails. It was even more difficult for the men in the West where train service was erratic and infrequent.

They had to trust to the mails or the good graces of a military courier to carry the dispatches which supplemented the meager intelligence the army allowed on the telegraph. But, East or West, the anonymous agents somehow contrived to get their news through with a promptness that was creditable.

2

Like the troops in the winding blue columns they accompanied, Associated Press agents were mystified that year by the peculiar-looking two-horse wagon which followed the army. The soldiers called it the "What-is-it-wagon"—a name that stuck—and jested about the short-bearded man who rode after it in a battered buggy. He was Matthew B. Brady, the "What-is-it-wagon" was his traveling darkroom, and together they were the quiet heralds of the beginnings of news photography. In those days a camera still was an oddity and pictures had to be developed within five minutes after exposure or else they would spoil. Brady used the primitive equipment expertly to produce a pictorial history of the war. The newspapers were not equipped for engraving and reproduction, so Brady's photographs did not appear to illustrate dispatches from the field of battle.

The year dragged on to its end, and when the general agent totaled his expenditures for 1862 the amount reached the unheard peak of $123,408. The assessments against the seven papers had risen to $214 a week, and the afternoon papers in the city—three in number—were paying $119 each. Out-of-town subscribers were charged from $7 a week upward for the little they received. Craig accompanied his financial accounting with a report setting forth that he had been able to save $20,000 by various news arrangements. "Indeed," he told the members, "holding practically a monopoly of the telegraphic news of the country, you are saving the expenditure of many thousands of dollars which would be required in case you had determined opposition." He also reminded them that more than half the association's entire expense was met by subscribers who had no say about the report they received.

News-gatherings difficulties in New York were taking an unforeseen turn. There had been a steady drain of city reporters to the various fronts and the seven member papers soon found themselves hard put to arrange for adequate coverage of local news. Because of this shortage of man power, the newspapers filled some positions with women, but the problem still remained acute. The situation finally prompted an organizer named Thomas Stout to establish a private service which years later was considered a forerunner of the present New York City News Association, which gathers the news of the metropolis. He called it Stout's Agency and recruited a staff of ten men to cover local assignments ordered by short-handed city editors or the general agent.

The war went on and it was 1863. The price of newsprint soared. Small change had virtually disappeared and people paid streetcar fares with postage stamps. There was talk about an unknown "scribbler" named Walt Whitman who had burst upon the literary horizon, and there were advertisements for artificial limbs. Out in the West the dogged Grant was stubbornly hammering away at Vicksburg, and in Virginia the genius of Robert E. Lee seemed never surer.

June came and the whole anxious North was asking: "Where is Lee?" No one seemed to know. Gobright scurried about Washington, trying one official source after another. Then among the straggling crowds on Pennsylvania Avenue he met a friend who was with the army as a staff officer. After a hard ride from western Maryland the official had just arrived with a message for the secretary of war. Lee had invaded the Free State and was moving north on Pennsylvania at the head of an army of 80,000 men! The officer had few particulars, but what he had sent Gobright hurrying off to the room high up in the National Hotel where Stanton's censors operated. Gobright wrote his alarming dispatch that Lee was invading the North—it was not more than twenty lines—and pressed it upon the censor.

"It can't go," said the War Department official.

"But why?" asked Gobright.

"Because it gives information to the enemy."

Gobright was exasperated.

"Colonel," he asked, "do you suppose the enemy does not know what he himself is doing? And besides, is it not important that the people of Pennsylvania and New York should know of their danger?"

In the face of this logic, the censor finally agreed to pass the dispatch if Gobright qualified it with the cautious prefix: "It is said." So the dispatch sped to New York with the first staggering news that Lee and his gray legions were sweeping north.

Just one week from the day Gobright sent the news, the North was wildly rejoicing at the first meager tidings of the victory at Gettysburg. Church bells tolled and then a telegraph key tapped out a terse Associated Press message from the West: "Grant has captured Vicksburg." No single day in three years had brought such news, and the day happened to be the Fourth of July.

Battles were obvious things, and it took no great reportorial discernment to recognize an advance or a retreat, a victory or a rout. But too often news judgment was wanting and correspondents and editors alike stood unseeing in the presence of important history. It had been that way in January, 1861, when Confederate batteries drove off the relief ship bringing supplies and reinforcements to Fort Sumter; editors did not realize that those were the opening shots of civil war. It had been that way in March, 1862, when the *Monitor*, that "cheese box on a raft," fought the *Merrimac* in Hampton Roads; editors did not see that the long history of wooden navies was over. And it was that way, too, in November, 1863, when Lincoln delivered his Gettysburg address.

It was almost an afterthought that Lincoln had been asked to attend the dedication of a national cemetery on the battlefield. The President was given to understand that his part would be quite secondary. "It is desired," he was told, "that after the oration you, as chief executive of the nation, finally set apart these grounds to their sacred use by a few appropriate remarks."

So Lincoln sat on the platform and listened to the Honorable Edward Everett's elegant periods. Pencils of journalists raced. For more than an hour the famous orator spoke and when he reached his peroration there was a storm of applause. So intent were many on congratulating Everett that they missed the solemn opening words of the President. "Four score and seven years ago," he was saying, "our fathers brought forth upon this continent a new nation . . ."

The next day newspapers published long, laudatory columns on Everett's address, and most accounts ended with the brief sentence: "The President also spoke." Here and there an editor gave some obscure position to the text of what the President had said because The Associated Press had delivered it to his newspaper. Indeed, years afterward a story persisted that an unsung agent for The Associated Press was the only one to telegraph Lincoln's words just as he delivered them.

3

After three years of civil war it was 1864 and Lee was still master of the snowy Virginia flatlands. Across the Potomac political veterans of three years' hard campaigning at the Willard bar gulped their neat

whiskies on cold January nights and conceded Lincoln little chance of
re-election. Perennially hopeful, Cyrus Field haunted London, seeking
funds and waiting for the war to end so he might make still another
attempt to lay an Atlantic cable. And young Henry Villard, one-time
Associated Press agent with Lincoln, was back in Washington after his
siege as a war correspondent.

The general agent in New York presently heard of Villard's
return and of what he was doing. The ambitious Midwesterner had
conceived the idea for a news service to rival The Associated Press in
Washington news. It was not long before he had five papers subscribing
to his report and The Associated Press was in arms at the temerity of
this upstart. Competition might be the life of trade, but at this stage
neither Craig nor the seven members he served liked the idea. Villard
was an interloper and they attacked him.

While Villard and Craig fought, the secretary of war was still
cudgeling his brains for a foolproof method of combating the misin-
formation which appeared with increasing frequency in some publications. Censorship had not proved enough and there was no use in
suppressing papers when Lincoln permitted them to resume. Stanton
hit upon a solution. He would write a "war diary." Perhaps Lincoln
himself had something to do with the inauguration of the official
communiqués, for he believed the people should have the news and
on more than one occasion he made sure that important intelligence
was given to The Associated Press.

Stanton acted on his idea immediately. Each night he wrote a
dispatch summarizing the day's military events. The "war diary"
dispatches were addressed ostensibly to General John A. Dix, the chief
military authority in New York, but actually were prepared for The
Associated Press. Dated variously between eight o'clock in the evening
and two in the morning, the bulletins set forth with brevity and
restraint the daily progress of each command.

The entire Union perhaps never was so anxious for news as during
the first week of May, 1864, after Grant disappeared into the tangled
underbrush of the Wilderness to start his campaign against Lee and
Richmond. All communications were cut and for two days there was no
word. Then Henry J. Wing of the New York *Tribune*, after a
dangerous all-day journey, reached Washington with the first account
of the opening of a bloody battle. Lincoln was so overjoyed at the
information and at a private message Wing gave him from General
Grant ("Tell him for me that whatever happens, there will be no

turning back") that he impulsively kissed the youthful correspondent. Then apologetically the President told Wing he had robbed the *Tribune* of the beat. "He told me," the correspondent related, "that to relieve the anxiety of the whole country regarding Grant's first contest with Lee, he had arranged with my managing editor to give a summary to The Associated Press to appear in all the papers."

The fierce campaign in the Wilderness remained the biggest news one night two weeks later when a nervous messenger made the rounds of the newspaper offices in New York. He carried several copies of the same story. All bore the heading, "To The Associated Press," and told under a Washington date line that President Lincoln had issued a surprise call for 400,000 more troops and had appointed a national day of fasting and prayer for victory.

The boy stopped at the *Times*, at the *World*, at the *Sun*, at the *Herald*, and then at the *Express*. When he reached the *Tribune* building the door he tried was locked and he scuttled away. In a few minutes he was at the office of the *Daily News*, which only recently had begun to buy the news report. The boy passed the pages across the counter and was starting for the door when the editor hailed him. Why wasn't this dispatch in the usual Associated Press envelope? The messenger stuttered, then blurted out that the supply of envelopes had run out and the dispatch was too important to be delayed.

A presidential proclamation was important news. Although deadlines were near, grumbling editors began to rip out front pages to make room for it. But deadline or no deadline, the editor at the *Daily News* was dubious. The *Times* office was the nearest, so he sent a copy boy there to see if that paper had the same dispatch. The *Times* had the proclamation, but the inquiry aroused suspicion and an editor went hurrying to the *Tribune*. The mysterious messenger had tried the wrong door and consequently the *Tribune* men knew nothing about the story. There was a hurried dash to the Associated Press offices and there the dispatch was immediately branded a forgery.

The presses already were printing at the *Herald*, the *Express*, the *Journal of Commerce*, and the *World*, but the *Herald* discovered the truth in time to destroy its edition. The *Express*, too, learned in time, but word reached the *Journal of Commerce* and the *World* too late. The papers already were on the street, in the mails, and on steamers for delivery abroad. Rewards were posted for the perpetrator of the hoax and the general agent hurriedly sent off telegrams warning all subscribers not to pick up the counterfeit.

But the damage had been done and War Secretary Stanton's orders crackled over the telegraph to General Dix in New York. Blue-coated troops went tramping into the *World* and *Journal of Commerce* offices and publication was suspended. Manton Marble, editor of the *World*, and William C. Prime, *Journal of Commerce* editor and president of The Associated Press, were clapped into the military prison at Fort Lafayette.

For four days the bogus proclamation was a major mystery. Then the culprit was discovered. He was Joseph Howard, publisher of the struggling New York *Daily Star*. Acting at the behest of Wall Street promoters, his aim was to create a disturbance in the stock market and he had deliberately withheld delivery of his false intelligence until the early morning hours when it was unlikely that the copy would be carefully examined before use.

The *Journal of Commerce* and the *World* were not the only papers to suffer. In New Orleans, then in Union hands, the *Picayune* picked up the proclamation from a mail edition and fared even worse. General Banks suppressed the paper from May 23 until July 9, while Prime and Marble were exonerated at Lincoln's order and their publications resumed in a week. But there was a certain curious irony about the whole affair. Before two months were over Lincoln not only called for additional troops, but also set aside a national day of prayer for victory.

As soon as Howard had been thrown into prison, The Associated Press took steps to protect members and subscribers against a recurrence of such fraud. A special iron stamp was made and henceforth all dispatches bore its imprint.

The civil conflict was almost over now and the news reports added, day by day, the final details. Sherman reached the sea in December, 1864. Then bugles sang in the April dawn and Richmond fell. A week later—April 9, 1865—it was Palm Sunday and at half past one in the afternoon Grant and Lee met in the home of Wilmer McLean on a dusty road near Appomattox. At four o'clock they shook hands. McGregor, the Associated Press agent with the Army of the Potomac, watched them as they came out. Lee had surrendered.

Only a few newspapermen were awake, keeping the watch, when the news reached Washington. Telegraph keys began to click, and at dawn a tremendous thunder broke all the windows in Lafayette Square. Five hundred cannon were roaring out a salute. Even Stanton was affable.

The city was in a gala mood and when John Francis Coyle, editor of the *National Intelligencer*, encountered John Wilkes Booth shortly before noon on Good Friday he did not think it strange that the handsome actor should invite him to share a bottle of wine. Over their glasses Booth expressed anything but satisfaction with the outcome of the Union efforts and fumed against the President, the government, and the North.

"What would happen," he said, "if Lincoln were removed?"

The editor answered that and many other questions on the same subject. But Booth obviously had been drinking and Coyle did not bother to wonder what prompted such sudden technical interest.

They talked on into the afternoon until the actor tossed off his last glass of wine and then made his departure. He seemed in great spirits.

4

"Father" Gobright puffed on the big cigar that had been given him by a tipsy captain at the Willard bar and leaned back in his chair to scan the out-of-town editions. The Washington agent had written his last dispatch for the night and already it was on its way to the New York office. It stated that General Ulysses Grant had changed his mind and, instead of attending the play, *Our American Cousin*, at Ford's Theatre, as advertised, had departed with Mrs. Grant for New Jersey.

In the few days since Appomattox the ill-kempt city had taken on a crude and garish atmosphere of rejoicing. The dreary years of conflict and uncertainty had given way to a surging relief and even Lincoln was joining in the celebration. Along with other dignitaries, he and Mrs. Lincoln were at Ford's Theatre. Although General Grant had been able to persuade Mrs. Grant to go north instead, the President had not been successful with his suggestion to Mrs. Lincoln that an old newspaper friend, Noah Brooks, accompany her in his place.

Gobright sat in his office until the hands of the clock dragged to nine-thirty and on toward the hour. Just as he was turning another page, the office door burst open and a friend rushed in shouting. The story came in snatches. The man had raced from Ford's Theatre by hack. He was upset, but Gobright began to ask questions.

A few seconds later the agent was hurrying off the dispatch:

                              WASHINGTON, APRIL 14, 1865
TO THE ASSOCIATED PRESS:
    THE PRESIDENT WAS SHOT IN A THEATRE
TONIGHT AND PERHAPS MORTALLY WOUNDED.

Minutes after the assassin leaped from Lincoln's box Gobright was standing beside the chair in which the President had been shot. The military was in command and a cordon of bayonets and blue uniforms circled the theater. All doorways and passages were barred. A crowd materialized in the streets outside, but the assassin was gone.

Gobright had just entered the presidential box when William Kent, a theater employee, stooped beneath one of the seats, picked up a pistol, and placed the stubby firearm in the agent's hand. The audience was still horrified below. A young naval officer demanded that the gun be surrendered, but Gobright would give it to no one but the police.

He quickly got the picture of the attack as it had occurred. He examined the torn flag in which the assassin's spur caught as he jumped from the box to the stage to scream, "Sic semper tyrannis!" Then he followed the path of escape out a back door. Gobright was leaving the theater to get back to the telegraph office when he heard that Secretary of State Seward also had been attacked as he lay sick at home. In his commandeered hack Gobright hurried to the Seward residence. There he obtained all the information available and was off to the boarding-house to which the President had been carried. Then he returned to his office to send additional details.

Months afterward when there was time for reminiscing the agent recalled:

Returning to the office, I commenced writing a full account of that night's dread occurrences. While thus engaged, several gentlemen who had been at the theater came in, and, by questioning them, I obtained additional particulars. Among my visitors was Speaker Colfax, and as he was going to see Mr. Lincoln, I asked him to give me a paragraph on that interesting branch of the subject. At a subsequent hour, he did so. Meanwhile I carefully wrote my despatch, though with trembling and nervous fingers, and, under all the exciting circumstances, I was afterward surprised that I had succeeded in approximating so closely to all the facts in those dark transactions.

Long before Gobright began to prepare his full story of the attacks, his first dispatch had galvanized the New York office. Copyists on duty wrote furiously. Sleepy messengers were rushed out to deliver the news to the offices of member papers in other parts of the city, and there was driving haste to prepare the information for telegraphing to client papers. All this took time, yet the speed was considered exceptional.

Greeley's *Tribune* was ready to go to press as the messenger dashed in with the wrinkled sheet of copy. It was the first bulletin from Washington and page one was hurriedly dismantled. Typesetters went to work, headline writers scribbled, and the story was thrown together in the extreme left column—then the preferred front-page space. So sensational was the news that the *Tribune* crammed into its columns, in the order of arrival, every scrap of information that it received. Shortly after the first Associated Press dispatch, the *Tribune's* own correspondent in Washington was heard from, first in a message to "stop" the press association bulletin and later in dispatches that were not always accurate, particularly in the premature report of the President's death. And so details of the story appeared as received, the erroneous bulletins intermingled with the accounts from Gobright.

Next morning the *Tribune's* left column read:

HIGHLY IMPORTANT!
The President Shot!
Secretary Seward Attacked

First Dispatch

Washington, April 14, 1865

To The Associated Press:

The President was shot in a theatre tonight and perhaps mortally wounded.

Second Dispatch

To Editors: Our Washington agent orders the dispatch about the President sent "stopped." Nothing is said about the truth or falsity of the report.

Third Dispatch

Special to the New York Tribune:

The President was just shot at Ford's Theatre. The ball entered his neck. It is not known whether the wound is mortal. Intense excitement.

Fourth Dispatch

Special to the New York Tribune:

The President expired at a quarter to twelve.

Fifth Dispatch

Washington, April 15, 12:30 A.M.

To The Associated Press:

The President was shot in a theatre tonight and perhaps mortally wounded.

The President is not expected to live through the night. He was shot at a theatre.

Secretary Seward was also assassinated.

No arteries were cut.

Particulars soon.

Then came Gobright's long story under the heading "Particulars." Through the night, as additional reports were available, the details moved from Gobright's office to the office of the general agent and thence to subscribers. Secretary of War Stanton also sent an official announcement to Major General Dix in New York. It reached General Agent Craig in the early morning.

Gobright's longest telegram, the "Particulars," was unusually detailed and stood for many years as a model of the reportorial style of the day. It read:

Washington, April 14.

President Lincoln and wife, with other friends, this evening visited Ford's Theatre, for the purpose of witnessing the performance of the "American Cousin."

It was announced in the papers that General Grant would be present. But that gentleman took the late train of cars for New Jersey.

The theatre was densely crowded, and everybody seemed delighted with the scene before them. During the third act, and while there was a temporary pause for the actors to enter, a sharp report of a pistol was heard, which merely attracted attention, but suggesting nothing serious, until a man rushed to the front of the President's box, waving a long dagger in his right hand, and exclaiming, "Sic semper tyrannis" and immediately leaped from the box, which was in the second tier, to the stage beneath, and ran across to the opposite side, making his escape, amid the bewilderment of the audience, from the rear of the theatre, and mounting a horse, fled.

The screams of Mrs. Lincoln first disclosed the fact to the audience that the President had been shot; when all present rose to their feet, rushed toward the stage, many exclaiming, "Hang him! Hang him!"

The excitement was of the wildest possible description, and of course there was an abrupt termination of the theatrical performance.

There was a rush toward the President's box, when cries were heard, "Stand back and give him air!" "Has any one stimulants?" On a hasty examination, it was found that the President had been shot through the head, above and back of the temporal bone, and that some of the brain was oozing out. He was removed to a private house opposite to the theatre, and the Surgeon-General of the Army, and other surgeons, were sent for to attend to his condition.

On an examination of the private box, blood was discovered on the back of the cushioned chair in which the President had been sitting; also on the partition, and on the floor. A common single-barrelled pocket-pistol was found on the carpet.

A military guard was placed in front of the private residence to which the President had been conveyed. An immense crowd was in front of it, all deeply anxious to learn the condition of the President. It had been previously announced that the wound was mortal, but all hoped otherwise. The shock to the community was terrible.

At midnight the Cabinet went thither. Messrs. Sumner Colfax, and Farnsworth; Judge Curtis, Governor Oglesby, General Meigs, Colonel Hay, and a few personal friends, with Surgeon-General Barnes and his immediate assistants were around his bedside. The President was in a state of syncope, totally insensible, and breathing slowly. The blood oozed from the wound at the back of his head.

The surgeons exhausted every possible effort of medical skill, but all hope was gone!

The parting of his family with the dying President is too sad for description. The President and Mrs. Lincoln did not start for the theatre until fifteen minutes after eight o'clock. Speaker Colfax was at the White House at the time, and the President stated to him that he was going, although Mrs. Lincoln had not been well, because the papers had announced that General Grant and they were to be present, and, as General Grant had gone north, he did not wish the audience to be disappointed.

He went to the theatre with apparent reluctance, and urged Mr. Colfax to accompany him; but that gentleman had made other engagements, and with Mr. Ashmun, of Massachusetts, bade him good-bye.

When the excitement at the theatre was at its wildest height, reports were circulated that Secretary Seward had also been assassinated.

Reported Assassination of Mr. Seward

On reaching this gentleman's residence, a crowd and military guard were found at the door, and on entering, it was ascertained that the reports were true.

Everybody there was so excited, that scarcely an intelligible word could be gathered; but the facts are substantially as follows:

About ten o'clock, a man rang the bell, and the call having been answered by a colored servant, he said he had come from Doctor Verdi, Secretary Seward's family physician, with a prescription, at the same time holding in his hand a small piece of folded paper, and saying in answer to a refusal, that he must see the Secretary, as he was instructed with particular directions concerning the medicine. He still insisted on going up, although repeatedly informed that no one could enter the chamber. The man pushed the servant aside, and walked heavily toward the Secretary's room, and was then met by Mr. Frederick W. Seward, of whom he demanded to see the Secretary, making the same representation which he did to the servant. What further passed in the way of colloquy is not known, but the man struck him on the head with a billy, severely injuring the skull, and felling him to the floor almost senseless. The assassin then rushed into the chamber and attacked Major Seward, Paymaster United States Army, and Mr. Hansell, a messenger of the State Department, and two male nurses, disabling them all. He then rushed upon the Secretary, who was lying in bed in the same room, and inflicted three stabs in the neck, but severing, it is thought and hoped, no arteries, though he bled profusely. The assassin then rushed downstairs, mounted his horse at the door, and rode off before an alarm could be sounded, and in the same manner as the assassin of the President.

It is believed that the injuries of the Secretary are not fatal, nor those of either of the others, although both the Secretary and the Assistant Secretary are very seriously injured.

Secretaries Stanton and Welles, and other prominent officers of the government, called at Secretary Seward's house, to inquire into his condition, and there, for the first time, heard of the assassination of the President. They then proceeded to the house where he was lying, exhibiting, of course, intense anxiety and solicitude. An immense crowd was gathered in front of the President's house, and a strong guard was also stationed there, many persons supposing that he would be brought to his home.

The entire city to-night presents a scene of wild excitement accompanied by violent expressions of indignation and the profoundest sorrow. Many shed tears. The military authorities have dispatched mounted patrols in every direction, in order, if possible, to arrest the assassins. The whole metropolitan police are likewise vigilant for the same purpose.

The attacks, both at the theatre and at Secretary Seward's house, took place at about the same hour, ten o'clock, thus showing a preconcerted plan to assassinate those gentlemen. Some evidences of the guilt of the party who attacked the President are in possession of the police. Vice-President Johnson is in this city, and his headquarters are guarded by troops.

The story written, Gobright took up his vigil outside the house in which the dying President lay. More than once he had swapped stories with the chief executive and during the long early morning hours many pictures of the man came to mind. There was the Lincoln who could enjoy a joke even when it was on himself—the Lincoln who could fill with emotion at the sight of suffering—the Lincoln whose ready wit could be devastating in driving home an argument. Gobright had been a veteran in Washington even before Lincoln appeared on the scene as an Illinois congressman and at one time or another he had had occasion to write about every one of those Lincolns he now remembered.

Nevertheless, he did not write the final lines of the assassination. With other correspondents, he was excluded from the house. War Secretary Stanton took everything into his own hands.

Day dawned and it was raining. More hours of waiting. Another of the secretary's military couriers emerged from the shuttered house, swung into a saddle, and clattered off. No one knew at the time, but he was riding to the telegraph office and he carried one of the last of Stanton's hastily scribbled "war diary" messages. The message was for the New York Associated Press and it read:

```
        ABRAHAM LINCOLN DIED THIS MORNING AT
  TWENTY-TWO MINUTES AFTER SEVEN O'CLOCK.
```

VI. THUNDER IN THE WEST

I

THE long siege between the Union and the Confederacy had obscured events which ultimately exerted a decisive influence on the course of news gathering. During the war years hinterland publishers first began to chafe at the journalistic servitude in which they were held by the New York Associated Press. The most important stirrings of discontent were in the West.

As a geographical designation, "West" was a vague expression. Because the nation had been born along the Atlantic seaboard, anything beyond the Alleghenies was the West, and even before Chicago existed there were such thriving centers as Pittsburgh, Cleveland, Louisville, Cincinnati, Detroit, and St. Louis. Just as in other areas, the journals of the West had risen with the growth of populations and the increase of literacy. Like all the other "outside" papers, they paid their money as clients to the New York Associated Press and took whatever was doled out to them.

The inequity of this condition became greater as the West grew stronger. By the second year of the Civil War the publishers of western papers had started to prepare for journalism's own internal conflict. The call to arms—necessarily a discreet one—was sounded by Joseph Medill, the erect, sharp-featured publisher of the Chicago Tribune.

The lot of Medill's Tribune was neither better nor worse than that of its major western contemporaries. In spite of the feverish public interest in Civil War news, the service supplied by the New York Associated Press was far from adequate. Dispatches came by telegraph only four hours nightly—between six and ten o'clock—and Medill knew they represented only a minor portion of the daily file collected primarily for the New York papers. The arbitrary price exacted for that sketchy budget was out of all proportion.

A lawyer before he became a publisher, Medill realized the futility of protest. He was at the mercy of a firmly entrenched news oligarch and it would be absurd to attack it singlehanded. As matters stood, he was helpless. He must have news, however inadequate, and if he refused to meet New York's demands, he would be cut off in the midst of the biggest news period of the nation's history. General Agent Craig, spokesman for the owners in the East, tolerated no opposition.

Together with other papers beyond the Alleghenies, the Chicago *Tribune* belonged to the loosely grouped affiliation of journals known as the Western Associated Press. This was primarily a regional association which had not thought of mutual protection and advancement.

Medill took the initiative late in the war year of 1862. A letter went out from the Chicago *Tribune* to fellow publishers. It was time, it hinted, for Westerners to unite in a real alliance, but they must do it warily so as not to arouse the suspicions of New York or to provoke reprisals. Medill suggested a meeting. To all appearances it would be a casual, regional gathering to discuss limited, routine problems.

That meeting was held in Indianapolis late the same year. Medill and his colleagues took special care to let New York hear of it and they welcomed the representative sent by Craig. A model of circumspection, the meeting appointed an Executive Committee with Medill as chairman, to represent the group in all negotiations with the East. So discreet were requests that the New York representative was able to report that it had been a very friendly meeting in which entirely "satisfactory agreements" were reached for continuation of the existing relationship.

New York dismissed the meeting with little thought, but it marked the formal start of a real Western Associated Press.

The first tentative steps of organization begun, a meeting in 1863 at Dayton produced more tangible results. The Western Associated Press felt strong enough to experiment and voted to send a committee to New York to seek a larger and better prepared report. Medill described what was accomplished:

We succeeded in being allowed to put a news agent in the office of the New York Associated Press with authority to make up and send a three hundred word extra dispatch to afternoon papers and a one thousand word message to be put on the wire after ten P.M. for the morning papers. It was called the midnight dispatch and was published in an extra addition. We secured it at low tolls. The extra day dispatch was comparatively expensive as the wires were occupied at that time on commercial business.

Medill continued his interest and when the 1864 meeting convened in Cincinnati he urged that the Western Associated Press be put on a legal basis. After some discussion, the decision was made to seek a charter of incorporation. H. N. Walker of the Detroit *Free Press* was chosen to apply to the Michigan legislature for a special act making the charter possible.

Once the uncertainties of the Civil War had been banished, the West entered upon a truly epic period of expansion. Pioneers and their covered wagons were rumbling westward from the Mississippi, onward to the Rockies and the Sierras. Chicago was the hub from which the spokes of expansion radiated west. It was the capital of a broad new empire in which there were now 103 daily journals. On the plains sledge rang on spike as sweating labor gangs pushed forward the road of steel and ties.

Side by side with the advancing rails marched the telegraph, but in many places it struck out boldly for itself across prairie and mountain. The lines strung on into the purple distance and suspicious Indians inspected the strange strands. They listened to the hum of the wires and in time they learned how the magic of the telegraph could summon the "Long Swords" of the palefaces. This "talking wire" was evil medicine, and war parties went whooping forth to cut the wires, fell the poles and massacre the men in the isolated stations where the talking wire spoke. And in the Southwest, cowboys were finding the telegraph a source of sport. The insulators on the poles proved irresistible targets and blazing six-shooters kept linesmen busy repairing damaged lines. But the poles and wires kept moving onward.

The West was on the march. Yet when the publishers filed into Masonic Temple at Louisville on November 22, 1865, to perfect their recently chartered organization, there was a strange lack of belligerency and outspoken criticism on the subject of New York. The growing discontent in the Western Associated Press was well underground—a calm before the storm that broke within a year.

The meeting adopted resolutions designed to leave General Agent Craig under the impression that everyone was well content. In the light of later events, two of them stood out as shrewdly conceived. One was a friendly gesture to the publishers of the prostrate South, expressing disappointment that they had been unable to meet with the Westerners and suggesting that either they attend future sessions or "that they organize a Southern Associated Press." The other resolution outlined for the West's special agent in New York the factors he should take into consideration in selecting the limited reports he was permitted to send. It contained four rules for news handling which stood for many years to come:

Telegraph reports should above all else be reliable; they should be as brief as possible; information should be selected for its interest to the subscribing papers, not for its importance in New York, and in most cases editorial comment of New York papers should be disregarded; also news items should be compiled without giving credit to papers except where the authority is an essential part of the news.

Small papers as well as large were represented in the Western Associated Press and it was necessary that action be taken to dispel any fears of the little publishers that the wealthier newspapers would dominate. This feeling had manifested itself the year before. The small papers then were receiving the same budget as more affluent contemporaries, although at lower assessments, and in most cases the wordage was ample for their needs. They were afraid that a larger report would saddle them with increased expense for news which only the big papers could handle.

To reassure them, a resolution was adopted specifying that newspapers having the need and the large resources could obtain more news without obligating proprietors of the small papers. This regulation was made part of the working constitution in 1865. In order to allay any other fears, Medill stepped aside and J. D. Osborne, of the Louisville *Journal*, was chosen president to succeed him.

2

The first big event of 1866 was Cyrus Field's final triumph over the Atlantic. He had bounded back from his failure of years before with new backers and many more hundreds of miles of cable.

Dissatisfaction in the Western Associated Press was reaching intolerable proportions just about the time of Field's success. The papers felt confidence in the strength of their organization and they knew they could rely on the financial support of the bulk of their membership. The end of the Civil War had removed their fears of being arbitrarily cut off from vital news and they were free to assert themselves. With the new cable opening up broader news horizons, there was an added incentive to seek a voice in the management of news gathering and an end to the inequities which galled them.

The discontent was not confined to the West. Trouble was brewing among the seven members of the New York Associated Press. The balance of power was now in the hands of the ultra conservatives. The four members who held the reins underestimated the force which was rising elsewhere in the country. They were blind to the necessity for initiative in news gathering and failed to comprehend the ferment agitating the "outside" clients.

Back of the New York dissension was the old rule of the association forbidding any one of its members to publish telegraph news from any part of the world without first making it available to all six others. This was a discouraging burden for the minority because the less ambitious papers could sit back and feel perfectly assured that they would receive all the news the others compiled at great individual expense.

The cleavage thrust General Agent Craig into the most anomalous position of his regime. He agreed with the minority, yet he was forced to act counter to his beliefs. The strong-minded Yankee grew increasingly restive. Little by little rumors began to seep west that Craig was at loggerheads with the men who were dictating the policies at New York.

The Western Associated Press had waited a long time, but now the psychological moment had arrived and it was in an atmosphere of resentment that the membership convened in Detroit on August 7, 1866. Some members were for a quick and open action, but the knowledge that there was disagreement in New York—it was probable that the information had come from Craig himself—counseled more subtle tactics.

On the vital issue before the organization—independence of New York or equality with it—the entire course of action was placed in the hands of the Board of Directors. The breach in New York was becoming daily wider and the Western directors bided their time.

The bombshell exploded on November 5. To every client of the New York Associated Press went a telegraphic note declaring that Daniel Craig, for fifteen years the monarch of news gathering, "is discharged by unanimous vote of the members," and that "Mr. James W. Simonton has been appointed General Agent" in his place. It was signed by W. C. Prime, as president of the New York association, and Joseph P. Beach, as secretary.

The wires sizzled with a heated rejoinder by Craig denouncing the Prime-Beach statement as "utterly and infamously false." He denied he had been dismissed and volunteered the startling information that he was planning a new and better news service.

"My resignation," he declared, "has been in the hands of the Executive Committee for several weeks, and whether accepted or not,

I should have retired at the end of this time, at which time, as I have good reason to believe, every agent or reporter of the association will earnestly co-operate in the new movement, which I assure you is started with the most ample backers, and its results will largely promote the interests of all the papers outside of this city, and I shall confidently hope for your earnest approval."

The secret was out. Craig confidently expected to take with him all the employees of the New York Associated Press both at home and abroad. The seven squabbling New York members did not know every detail of his quietly devised plans, but the dominant faction had acted with lightning swiftness to oust him as soon as it learned that he proposed to start another news-gathering organization. Craig's summary dismissal ruined his plan to keep his project under cover until everything was ready and he could leave the stunned New York members in the lurch. He was forced to leave his old job at once and he turned all his energy to his audacious new undertaking.

Simonton, the new general agent and a close friend of Raymond of the *Times*, was catapulted overnight into a trying position. He was suddenly expected to do all things. He must direct the operation of the news report without interruption. He must meet the menace of Craig's bold promise to raid the profitable ranks of his news customers. And he must maintain control of the restless "outsiders" who already were eager to do business with Craig.

The New York Associated Press had been maneuvered into a perilous spot and the Westerners did not see how they could lose. Either New York must grant them the full concessions they were prepared to demand or else they could sever all relations and join Craig. Each passing day made the old association more vulnerable, and the strategists of the West watched for New York and its new general agent to make some overture. But New York was too busy fending off Craig's forays among its near-by clients.

3

On the day Craig's new service began the Executive Committee of the Western organization was on its way to New York. Murat Halstead of the Cincinnati *Commercial*, and Horace White of the Chicago *Tribune* carried with them complete authority to obtain the concessions desired or to "make such other arrangements as they should deem advisable" for another news service.

The envoys from the West were both young men. Halstead, a stubborn, fiery individual with the mustache and goatee of the traditional southern colonel, was thirty-eight and his companion several years younger. Both were experienced journalists and White had the added advantage of five years' experience as agent for the New York Associated Press in Chicago. He took the post in 1855 and covered the famous Lincoln-Douglas debates for the organization he was now ready to fight.

Halstead and White found New York an industrious city with a population close to the million mark. The wires from telegraph poles laced through the branches of shade trees along Broadway. Office forces worked ten hours a day, six days a week, and there were no female employes. The basement of the modest J. P. Morgan building in Wall Street was stacked with the wares of a retail wood and coal dealer, and inflated rubber bosom pads were the latest boon to the feminine figure.

The two Westerners went straight to the New York Associated Press offices on lower Broadway where boxlike containers rattled back and forth above the street on three miniature aerial railways, shuttling dispatches from the association's headquarters to the wires of the near-by telegraph company. The aging, one-time schoolmaster who presided over the messenger boys greeted them and led the way to the committee room.

There the powers waited—President Prime; Joseph P. Beach, manager of the *Sun;* George Jones, business manager of the *Times;* Samuel Sinclair, publisher of the *Tribune;* Manton Marble, of the *World,* and Simonton, the new general agent. The *Express* was not represented, but Halstead and White already knew that Erastus Brooks was on a hurried trip upstate in an effort to hold the wavering New York State Associated Press in line. Nor was there anyone from the *Herald.* Young James Gordon Bennett, who had succeeded his father, was busy getting his sleek yacht *Henrietta* ready for a transatlantic race.

Halstead, as spokesman for the West, told the New Yorkers that his association wanted an equal voice in all news-gathering affairs. Such a proposal shocked the monopolistic group.

"Any such proposal is out of the question," Prime declared. "Such an idea cannot even be considered."

"Why not?"

Baldish and slightly hunched, the president of the New York Associated Press wrinkled his brow and attempted to explain.

"The New York Associated Press," he said, "was founded by six publishers who have sponsored organized news gathering since 1848. We have facilities for carrying on the work and we do not propose to delegate any of our authority. It is unthinkable that an outside group should presume to feel it can have any voice in our affairs. News gathering is our business enterprise and we do not propose to share it with others. Consideration of your plan would imply that the Western Associated Press is entitled to be treated as an equal, and that would be an intolerable humiliation."

Halstead and White objected to such a narrow concept of news gathering, but, making no impression, suggested another meeting the next day. Prime and his colleagues consented—it would give these Westerners time to realize New York could not be frightened into agreement with their plan. The second meeting was inconclusive and a third was arranged.

But Halstead and White were not bluffing. They had proceeded cautiously pending an opportunity to appraise the preliminary success of Craig's new independent agency—the United States and Europe Telegraph News Association, which was backed by the Western Union.

The new service had begun auspiciously on November 24 and the reports for the first four days were workmanlike and promising. One of Craig's initial policies had been to provide, by way of the new cable, a good budget of foreign news, a large portion of it from sources formerly controlled by the New York Associated Press. This assured the West of some improvement in cable coverage and Craig had further promised to make up a special daily western report designed solely for the particular needs and requirements of that section.

The two Westerners spent no time on formalities at the third meeting. They put a prepared statement on the table in front of President Prime. It served notice that the West planed to assume control of its own news report and that it would obtain news on its own behalf from any outside organization which could provide what they wanted. It said:

To The New York Associated Press:

The Executive Committee of the Western Associated Press propose to get news from all parties who have news to sell, and to provide for its transmission to their respective journals. They propose to take the regular report of the New York (Associated) Press at Buffalo, and provide for its transmission to the various Western cities. For this news they will pay their own equitable proportion of the cost of collection. They propose also to appoint their own agent in New York to collect and buy additional news from all sources accessible to him and to provide for the transmission of the same to the various cities.

A hubbub broke loose. There were sharp words, loud threats, and a noisy storm of voices. Halstead and White sat through the turmoil, calm and unmoved, making no attempt to reply. The New York group quickly adopted a resolution prohibiting any subscriber from taking dispatches from a rival organization under the penalty of being cut off instantly from its news report. But this time the threat did not work. The two young men from the West rose.

"Gentlemen," Halstead said, "my colleague and I have made a most thorough examination of the entire situation. As matters now stand the press of the West is subservient to and dependent upon the New York Associated Press for all its news. We are not getting the kind of news we want and we have no voice in the direction of your organization. Our decision is that it would best serve the interests of the West if we aid in the establishment of another news service. Then we can get the kind of news we want. Accordingly we have made plans to supply ourselves with news without any further assistance from you. Gentlemen, we bid you good day."

The two men quit the room. They could hear another wrathful outbreak as they descended the stairs. The angry voices died, but Halstead and White would have been interested to hear the carefully studied observation of one of the men they left behind. General Agent Simonton had watched these Westerners in action. He saw they were progressive and might be impressed by some startlingly new development. The struggle was on, but he believed he could produce a news report that might play some part in bringing it to an end.

"Mr. President," he began, "I have a plan . . ."

VII. THEY CALLED IT PEACE

I

GENERAL AGENT SIMONTON'S plan was to take advantage of the new cable and improve New York's foreign news report. He would do this by sending an American-trained reporter to Europe—something the association had never done before. He looked around for a likely man and called in the son of a New Jersey senator.

When Alexander Wilson left Simonton and climbed down the long flight of stairs all had been decided. There was a raw, wintry bite in the early December air of 1866 as he stepped out onto Broadway and looked down Liberty Street toward the East River. He could see the graceful masts of clipper ships and California packets towering above the low water-front buildings, and the sooty columns of smoke from the less glamorous steamships. Wilson now felt a new, personal interest in these trim vessels. Somewhere along the docks of South Street was his transport to a great adventure.

This new foreign assignment at first had seemed a very ambitious experiment in news gathering, but as Simonton carefully explained its purpose Wilson realized how logical and inevitable it was. The foreign report of the past had been contributed by Europeans with no firsthand knowledge of what American papers needed. In consequence much copy of comparatively little interest was received at considerable expense. The completion of the cable brought the long-awaited opportunity to obtain foreign intelligence while it still was news and Simonton saw that, by sending his own man abroad, he would have a strong point in bargaining with the West.

Once his plan was approved by the New York majority, Simonton offered Wilson the assignment. The new correspondent had had experience on the New York *Times* and before that had been associated with both Simonton and Henry J. Raymond on the *Courier and Enquirer*. Now he was in his late forties and once he had recovered from his surprise at such an unexpected change he was impatient to begin his duties abroad.

A few days later he stood on the deck of an outbound vessel and watched the ragged Manhattan sky line fade into the morning mist. It would be his task henceforth to write Europe's daily history—the wary duels of the great Disraeli and Gladstone, the negotiations with Russia for the purchase of Alaska, Garibaldi's invasion of the Papal States, the rise of a strong German nation under Bismarck, and the troubled destiny of France.

He set up the first Associated Press office in London, and he did it in time to cable news of a contest which had all the East talking—the first transatlantic yacht race from Sandy Hook to Cowes. Young James Gordon Bennett brought his *Henrietta* in victorious on Christmas Day, 1866, with a record of 13 days, 21 hours, and 55 minutes for a tempestuous winter crossing of 3,106 miles. Bennett's two rivals, Pierre Lorillard, Jr., and George Frank Osgood, scudded in a day later to pay off the $30,000 stake each had posted.

As European agent for The Associated Press, Wilson inherited what Craig had left of a loosely-knit staff of foreign-born representatives. These were his lieutenants and to supplement them he had the reports of the foreign agencies, originally largely commercial in character, which were developing as news gatherers. There was the agency which Charles Havas established in Paris in 1836 to obtain financial intelligence, the German organization founded in Berlin by Dr. Bernhard Wolff in 1849, Guglielmo Stefani's Italian enterprise which had its beginnings in Turin in 1854, and most important, the service Julius de Reuter launched in London in 1858.

But Wilson's job was to do as much actual reporting as possible, and Simonton also wanted him to Americanize the foreign news for American consumption. Wilson had to do the job alone and the news conflict raging back home made his task an exacting one.

2

That conflict had been on in grim earnest for weeks. Immediately upon quitting the New York meeting of November 28, 1866, Halstead and White dispatched to their fellow members a full announcement of the break with New York. They reported that arrangements had been consummated with Craig to provide the service of his United States and Europe Telegraph News Association, and they instructed the publishers to refuse henceforth the budgets transmitted by the old organization.

Craig made his debut as the paladin of the "outside" papers he

. . . ALONG THE DOCKS WAS WILSON'S TRANSPORT TO A GREAT ADVENTURE.

so often had chastised. On November 29 he was designated general agent of the Western Associated Press. The news gathering machinery of the country was in a turmoil as the contest began. Both Craig and Simonton transmitted complete reports, day and night, not only to the West but to other clients. The agents of the New York Associated Press in other cities were bombarded first by this faction, then by that. For a month they hardly knew which side they served.

The prophets who had been saying the West was courting destruction in its split with New York soon changed their opinions. Craig had lost none of his old skill. The superiority of his report was apparent almost from the outset. The rank and file of his old correspondents rallied to him and many dissatisfied clients of the New York association came under his banner. The close of his first day of operations found him proudly enumerating the imposing list of papers he was serving:

The leading journals of Cincinnati, St. Louis, Chicago, Louisville, Cleveland, Pittsburgh, Indianapolis, Nashville and Memphis in the West, the majority of the newspapers in Arkansas, Mississippi and Texas in the South-west, every paper in Louisiana with a single exception in New Orleans, all the newspapers in Virginia with but three or four exceptions, four-fifths of the press of Georgia, one-half of the press of Baltimore, all the news-papers of Washington City, eight out of the thirteen Philadelphia papers which publish news by telegraph, two of the three of the prosperous city of Newark, the entire press of Brooklyn, and three of the nine of New York.

New York, pushed suddenly to the wall, fought back doggedly. A shrewd statement was rushed to all members of the Western Associated Press charging that Halstead and White had sought to betray the interests of their fellow publishers at the price of preferential arrangements for their own papers.

Nevertheless, the tide continued strongly toward Craig. The New York State Associated Press debated the wisdom of casting its lot with the rebellious West. The New England association also threatened to desert, and the few clients remaining in the South grew restive. The elder Bennett left his semi-retirement for secret conferences with Halstead and White, who had remained in New York to direct operations with Craig. Then came the first actual break in the solidarity of the New York Associated Press. The *World,* long sympathetic to the insurgents, announced its withdrawal from membership.

It was at this juncture that the shaken New York majority actually ordered all its own news reports withheld from papers using Craig's service. At the direction of Halstead and White, Craig retorted with a broadside notifying his subscribers they could not continue to receive the new Western news budget if they also took service from the New York Associated Press. There was ironic inconsistency in this policy. Halstead and White had been vehement in denouncing just such tactics on the part of the old monopoly. But this was one of those battles in which the better part of valor seemed to be to fight the enemy with his own weapons.

The old association's service began to show a lack of live news, particularly from the Mississippi Valley. Yet New York stubbornly showed no signs of yielding. It redoubled its attacks on Craig, Halstead, and White, revived the old bugaboo of New York's ability to dominate the telegraph, and preyed on the fears of the timid small publishers who feared the split eventually would mean an entire loss of telegraph news. Nor was New York above stooping to sabotage. When Lincoln's successor, President Andrew Johnson, delivered his important message to a hostile Congress that December, trees were felled across the wires being used by Craig to transmit the news.

Although Craig made no effort to conceal his desire for revenge on New York, he demonstrated that he also had the good interests of news gathering at heart by offering to turn over ownership of his United States and Europe Telegraph News Association to its subscribers the moment they organized on a national front. There were no strings attached to the offer and had the opportunity been seized the old monopoly probably could not have survived. Halstead and White pondered the proposal but felt they could not accept without assuming greater responsibility than their Board of Directors had authorized. So the offer was soon forgotten in the rush of other events.

Simonton, the opposing field marshal, meanwhile was laboring to hold together a disintegrating news empire until Wilson could reestablish the association's old dominance abroad. The new general agent placed great store in the importance of Wilson to help turn the tide. The other factor on which he relied was the mounting bill the West was being called upon to meet for the expenses of its adventure in news independence. Despite the forbidding immediate outlook, he was inclined to be optimistic. Already the subtle New York propaganda campaign had begun to bear fruit among the apprehensive small papers in the West. Halstead and White were being called selfish conspirators by fellow members, their authority was being questioned, and there was grumbling about expenses.

Halstead and White were so stung by this sniping back home that

TREES WERE FELLED ACROSS THE WIRES BEING USED TO TRANSMIT NEWS.

they issued an indignant rejoinder, defending their course and denying they had sacrificed the smaller papers to their personal advantage. They realized, however, that eventually their actions of the past feverish fortnight must be formally ratified, and definite plans mapped for the future. They recommended a special meeting and the Western Board of Directors called one for December 12 at Crosby's Opera House in Chicago.

No sooner had the meeting convened than J. E. Scripps, testy managing editor of the Detroit *Advertiser and Tribune*, leaped into the fray. He called upon the association to disavow responsibility for everything Halstead and White had done and lashed the two envoys for their "unwarrantable assumption of power."

Halstead met the attack with a spirited reply.

"The question goes beyond journalism," he declared. "It is a question of importance to every merchant and every man who deals in securities. Every community in the Western country has been robbed of its intelligence by this monopoly, and what we have to do is to break it up—to establish competition. I do not expect to be able to crush the New York Associated Press, but I do expect to be able to release the Western Press from its despotism."

Scripps's motion was thrown out after an animated debate and the chairman recognized Erastus Brooks, who had come from New York to plead for amity. Questions were fired at him from all sides and when asked point-blank if the West would be given a voice in the New York Associated Press, he replied firmly that this could be done only on matters pertaining to its own territory.

Joseph Medill of the Chicago *Tribune*, who had been the leading influence in the foundation of the Western Associated Press four years before, made short work of Brooks's arguments.

First he reproved the smaller papers for distrusting the motives of Halstead and White, and then he charged New York with fomenting such a feeling in order to weaken the West so that the old monopoly could divide and conquer the insurgents piecemeal.

"This New York Association is a monopoly in the worst sense of the word," Medill declared, "the denial of Mr. Brooks to the contrary notwithstanding. It is one of the most pernicious and crushing monopolies that ever existed. It contracts and collects the telegraphic news to suit its own wants and tastes, and then deals out scraps of it to others on such conditions and at such prices as it chooses to affix. What voice have we in that New York association? We are told that we pay but a trifle toward its expenses. I contend that we have paid more than our full quota on all the dispatches we have received. When the cable dispatches were added as a portion to the news of the day, the New York Associated Press apportioned out to the various places their quota of the expenses. Did they take five-sevenths of the cost to themselves? Not exactly. They charged one full third to the association represented on this floor; another third on the papers south of New York; an additional fraction on those west and north of New York, and the residue, if any, they pay themselves!

"I am in favor of confirming the action of the Executive Committee," he continued. "It is necessary for the protection of our interests as Western publishers to carry this action through. Gentlemen, you represent and speak to twelve millions of free people! You speak in the name of twelve states; they in the name of one city! How much longer shall we permit this minority to rule over the majority? Don't be afraid of independence. It is not going to hurt you. It will not take long before these New York birds of paradise will come down from their lofty trees and roost lower. Let us simply be united and all the rest will be easy!"

The meeting voted 21 to 11 to approve the action of Halstead and White. The divorce from New York had been duly ratified.

3

Victory was in the air. Halstead successfully proposed the creation of a three-man committee to correspond with publishers outside of New York City with a view to organizing a United States Associated Press. Then the meeting ended, confident the power of New York had been blasted.

The New Yorkers were not so easily annihilated, however. Wilson's presence in London was giving Simonton the advantage abroad which he had awaited. Now the conflict grew even more expensive for both antagonists. Although cable rates had been reduced from $10 to $5 per word, transatlantic dispatches remained the most costly convenience in newsdom. The fighting factions found their cable bills running over $2,000 weekly, an outlay which threatened bankruptcy if continued. Craig struggled to overcome Simonton's advantage, but it was an uneven contest because Wilson's presence in England made New York's foreign budget superior to that provided the West by European correspondents ignorant of American newspaper practice.

Thus the battle seesawed, with Craig pre-eminent in domestic intelligence and Simonton the leader in the foreign field.

For another fortnight the rivalry continued sharp and intense and then, surprisingly enough, it was the stiff-necked New York majority that finally unbent and made the first real move for peace. As 1866 ended they advanced the suggestion that, if the Western Associated Press would send some of its "old heads" back east along with the "young men" of the Executive Committee, an agreement might be reached. Just when the Westerners might have held out a little longer and perhaps emerged victorious, an unexplained blindness descended. They seemed too preoccupied with the considerations of the immediate present—the fight was proving immensely expensive, Wilson's foreign news report had created a tremendous impression, and the grumbling small papers were sulky in their support of hostilities. At any rate, the Westerners overlooked the past abuses and received the New York overture favorably. They named Medill, H. N. Walker of the Detroit *Free Press*, and Richard Smith of the Cincinnati *Gazette* as the "old heads" to accompany Halstead and White to the eastern metropolis.

A great show of tactful politeness and diplomacy characterized the first several days of the revived conference. New York made numerous efforts to win back the West without making major concessions, but the insurgents sat tight, counting heavily on the apparent friendliness of the New York *World* and *Herald* and the presumed support of both the New England and the New York State Associated Press. Again an impasse threatened. Then the New Yorkers broke the deadlock by resorting to the old divide-and-conquer strategy. Simonton slipped away one night to Boston and negotiated a new contract which brought New England once more under the old standard. Bennett's *Herald* was cozened back and the upstate publishers were persuaded to return.

Robbed of their fancied advantages, the Westerners settled down to earnest efforts to reach an agreement. General Anson Stager, superintendent of Western Union Telegraph Company, was invited to act as mediator. For some reason Western Union had lost its initial enthusiasm for the Craig venture. The company had been hard put to handle the voluminous reports of the rival agencies. Soon a pact was worked out which the Westerners, however mistakenly, considered a major concession. Craig, the veteran of more than thirty years' news gathering, was sacrificed to the agreement and under the terms of the treaty Simonton also was to retire in the interests of harmony. The pact was drawn on January 11, 1867. It contained the following provision, among others:

1. Those papers that left either association during the difficulties are re-admitted.
2. The New York Association is to furnish all its news, for the exclusive use of the Western Associated Press within its territory, to the Western agent in the New York office.
3. The Western Associated Press is to collect and furnish all news of its territory to the agent of the New York Associated Press at Cleveland or Pittsburgh.
4. Delivery of news is to be made as rapidly as received.
5. Both associations agree not to compete for papers in the other's territory.
6. The Western Association is to pay: For general news, $8,000 per annum; for cable news 22 per cent of the expense of obtaining the same, but not exceeding in gross expense $150,000 per annum; for California news, 20 per cent of the whole cost to the New York Associated Press at Chicago.
7. The Western Associated Press is to deliver at Chicago its report for California customers of the New York Associated Press and for customers at other points west of the territory of the Western Associated Press.

Prime, as president, and Beach, as secretary, signed the agreement for New York. H. N. Walker affixed his signature as president for the West.

That same day Walker also signed a contract with Western Union for transmission of news under the new agreement. Buffalo was designated the eastern relay point for news to the West's afternoon papers, and New York for the morning. The day file from Buffalo consisted of a 500-word "early morning report" and a 300-word "noon report." The night report contained the more imposing volume of 3,500 words and went to Pittsburgh, Cincinnati, Indianapolis, Louisville, Chicago, Detroit, Toledo, Cleveland, and Milwaukee. A night "pony" report of 1,500 words, abstracted from the larger report, was filed out of Cleveland to Wheeling, Zanesville, Columbus, Dayton, Madison, Ind., New Albany, and Sandusky.

The local news from all large and small points, aggregating 2,000 words daily, went to the major cities. An additional budget called "River news" was serviced to Pittsburgh, Cincinnati, Louisville, and St. Louis only. The complete Western report averaged 6,000 words daily and for its transmission that association paid Western Union $60,000 a year in $5,000 installments.

To replace Craig, an experienced telegrapher named George B. Hicks was appointed general agent for the West and headquarters were established in Cleveland.

They called it peace, but the settlement left New York still master in the field of news. Although the old organization had lost some prestige, it still retained a tight grip on the highly important cable news, Washington news, and the news of financial New York. Furthermore, it remained in a position to control, if not to dictate, the news output of most of the regional associations.

Besides such psychological advantages as the West reaped, it also won a more satisfactory financial agreement with New York and a limited degree of recognition. But it had surrendered much for these concessions. The loudly urged claim for a voice in the operations of the New York association was quietly jettisoned; the stubbornly asserted right to obtain news from other sources was forgotten, and there were no specifications as to the quality of the news report itself, long the subject of agitation.

Disillusioned and embittered, Craig retired from the news field, but not so Simonton. New York blandly forgot its pledge to eliminate him—the new general agent had proved himself equal to a great emergency.

VIII. BLACK YEARS

I

BY THE time of Grant's inauguration as President, Simonton had settled down in the old New York headquarters, which remained in the same building on Broadway occupied since the days of the first general agent. There was a large force of assistants now and the association had agents in London, Liverpool, Montreal, Quebec, Boston, Philadelphia, Chicago, New Orleans, Washington, Albany, San Francisco, "and in all the principal cities and towns of the United States." News flowed in at the rate of 35,000 words daily. It came by Atlantic cable, by Cuba cable, by land telegraph, by ships from South American ports, by clippers on the China run. Busy copyists with carbon-grimed fingers transcribed it all on the thin manifold sheets, stuffed it into envelopes for delivery to the dozen metropolitan papers, or handed it to waiting regional agents who prepared the reports transmitted to the auxiliary associations.

There was much news for the hard-working copyists during 1869. Wall Street had its famous "Black Friday" when the market went crashing in a cloud of confusion, bankruptcy, and ruin. On Promontory Point, out in Utah, Governor Leland Stanford and Thomas Durant drove the last spike connecting the railroads which first linked the Atlantic and the Pacific. Arthur Cummings was hailed as the man who introduced curve pitching in baseball. Sweating English troops invaded Ethiopia to punish the Lion of Judah. John D. Rockefeller was laying the foundation for his oil empire, and from Europe the rising tide of immigration kept rolling. The country's population was close to 39,-000,000.

Simonton's worries were multiplying. There was a running controversy with the cable company over rates and the priority of press dispatches. Another source of trouble was the emergence of a struggling rival—the Hasson News Association—which was providing unaccustomed competition. Then, too, there were the activities of the Western Union which sold brokers and countinghouses a service of commercial and market news abstracted from the Associated Press report. Such liberties were taken under a vague agreement between the company and the New York association, but there were constant complaints from the West on the ground that the wire concern was invading the regular news field.

Soon the general agent was finding Western Union the cause for more grievous embarrassment. Although close alliance with the telegraph company had undeniable advantages in assuring the best communication facilities, it left the news-gathering organization vulnerable to repeated attack. Throughout the seventies the names of the New York Associated Press and the Western Union were coupled again and again in Congress and denounced as "co-conspirators in building a press monopoly."

In those graft-ridden, ruthless days, Western Union, by controlling the most important telegraph system, held the whip hand and New York was expected not to send out anything inimical to its powerful ally. If necessary the news could be painstakingly selected or colored, and all criticisms by client papers was prohibited. At one stage the president of Western Union acknowledged before a Congressional investigation that the New York Associated Press was under an agreement to use its wires exclusively, and that all papers receiving its reports were forbidden to have any dealings with rival wire systems.

In the face of these incessant assaults, the members who controlled the New York Associated Press maintained an unworried complacency. The harried general agent was left to make such defense as the incidents demanded. Eventually it became necessary that a formal answer to the monopoly charge be made and Congress, after almost ten years of talking, summoned Simonton to appear before a Senate committee. There were six counts in the indictment of the press association's relations with the telegraph company:

1. News associations are compelled by The Associated Press to use only Western Union wires.
2. By their contracts with Western Union, The Associated Press is pledged to oppose other wire companies.
3. The inability of New York Evening Post to use a dispatch from its own correspondent until it has given the dispatch to other members of the New York Associated Press.
4. News originating in New York is sometimes sent to Washington for distribution so that those receiving it will think it originated in Washington.
5. The New York Associated Press censors the papers of the country by cutting off news reports to papers who have criticised The Associated Press.

6. The New York Associated Press is engaged in public business and therefore is amenable to the laws governing corporations transacting public business.

Simonton made a lengthy and vigorous reply, stoutly defended the organization he headed, and did not hesitate to lecture the investigating committee. He said:

The Associated Press is a private business, carried on under the same moral, legal and constitutional rights which permit any one paper, in a country village or in a metropolis, to collect and publish its local news. The charge of monopoly rests upon the single fact that here and there some newspapers, which did not share in the labor or risk of establishing The Associated Press, are not permitted to come in and share its facilities, now that the day of experiment and risk has passed. As well might they demand to force their way into a share of the already created business of any bank or dry goods house, or other mercantile establishment, which, like The Associated Press, had spent thirty-one years in perfecting its plans, securing its customers and their confidence, and creating its opportunities for doing business with profit. The profit of the bank or mercantile business is in cash dividends; the profits of The Associated Press are in the use of the news which it collects, as the profits of the fisherman are in the fish which he captures and takes from the rivers and the sea, just as we take that in which we deal from the great ocean of human events.

He declared that the New York Associated Press was merely a customer of Western Union, denied the association was pledged to fight opposition telegraph companies, and pleaded ignorance of a mutual defense agreement. There were some concessions in rates, considering the large volume of business Western Union received from the association. Were it not for these rate concessions, the general agent said, the New York Associated Press would be unable to continue its liberal practice of supplying news at low cost to the many sections of the nation where populations were sparse and small journals were struggling for existence. His exact words were: "The Press and the telegraph company both agree to give lower rates to the poor and recoup by higher compensation from the well-to-do."

He dismissed the old monopoly charge by pointing out that the auxiliary associations, with few exceptions, made their own rules and determined who should and who should not receive New York's report in the various territories. As to the charge that New York maintained a rigid censorship over the press of the country under the threat of cutting off their news reports, Simonton explained that the so-called censorship in reality was punishment for infractions of rules and regulations. He upheld the association's right to cut off the news report—"our readiest defense"—whenever a subscriber had the hardihood to criticize it in print:

I submit that there is not a gentleman here who would sell dry goods, groceries, or anything else day after day to a man who told him every time he came in, "You are a thief, a swindler and a liar." You would very soon say, "If you can't come in and behave yourself, I do not want your trade and you can get out." That is the sort of censorship we exercise. When papers insist that they have grievances against us and give us an opportunity for explanations, they very often learn that they have been in error. But when papers will persist in abusing us for the alleged grievances in advance of inquiry, we simply say to them, "We do not want to serve you. If we cannot be treated like decent men, you had better get your news service elsewhere."

The general agent recapitulated his testimony in four categorical statements:

1. The Associated Press is not a monopoly. 2. It is a private business. 3. It is independent of the Western Union Telegraph Company. 4. It has no franchise from the government and no legislation within the power of Congress can take from it the tools of its creation.

Simonton acquitted himself well, presenting his organization in the best possible light, and the committee hearings were productive of no untoward results.

2

All these troubles which beset Simonton represented only one side of the picture. It was a period of great news events and the general agent proved himself a capable administrator. He was zealous for the improvement of the report and under his direction it did improve in spite of the handicaps imposed by the structural nature of the organization. His efforts did much to atone for the shortcomings of the service. This was particularly true when the news was not of a controversial nature, and 1871 produced an outstanding demonstration.

That was the year of the most famous bovine in history—Mrs. O'Leary's cow and the lantern she was said to have kicked over. It was half past nine on an October Sunday night when the flames started to race through Chicago before a strong wind. Through seventy-three miles of streets they roared in one mighty, appalling conflagration. Two hundred lives were lost; 98,500 were homeless; 17,500 buildings were destroyed, and some $200,000,000 worth of property went up in smoke.

Together the New York and Western associations brought the country the story of Chicago's disaster. When special correspondents arrived in the stricken city they found telegraph offices would not permit their accounts to interfere with the transmission of the thousands of messages being sent for relief. There was only one exception—The Associated Press—and its dispatches received the right of way. In order to get their stories out, other correspondents found it necessary to send the copy by train to Cleveland.

The next year also there was a great volume of news, including the extraordinary presidential campaign which gave Grant his second term, the malodorous Crédit Mobilier scandal investigation, and a host of other occurrences. Cable tolls alone exceeded $200,000 and special assessments were imposed generally on both New York and auxiliary Associated Press groups.

The mad postwar spree of spending and speculation was over and hard times were beginning to pinch.

William Henry Smith, who had succeeded Hicks in 1869 as general agent of the Western Associated Press, was beset by pleas for lower assessments from his members who protested they could not weather the depression unless the reductions were granted. Occasional evidences of friction cropped up between the West and New York, and the old cry for cheaper telegraph tolls was raised again, though without encouraging results.

Telegraph rates had always been a subject of concern, but in 1872 Simonton was occupied with an entirely different aspect of the association's transmission problems. Always in the past the telegraph company had controlled the wires over which the association moved its news. Simonton wanted to lease a wire outright between New York and Washington to use in moving the heavy volume of news between those two cities and the intermediate points of Philadelphia and Baltimore. He thought it would be more economical and would speed the report. The telegraph company scouted the request as impracticable. Simonton persisted in his campaign, with steadfast encouragement from his young assistant, Walter Polk Phillips, who later became known as the author of the "Phillips Code" of telegraphic abbreviations. The company delayed action for several years, but in 1875 Simonton won and the first leased wire in press association history began operating.

The wire was taken over under a straight leasing arrangement, a practice that grew as the need for exclusive news-transmission facilities steadily increased.

"It was my good fortune as one of the lieutenants of James W. Simonton," Phillips recounted, "to select the men to work that pioneer leased system between New York and Washington. There were eight of them, two each at New York, Philadelphia, Baltimore and Washington." The men Phillips picked were Fred N. Bassett, P. V. De Graw, W. H. C. Hargrave, W. J. Jones, Thomas J. Bishop, H. A. Wells, W. N. Grave, and E. C. Boileau.

This first leased wire was 226 miles in length and was followed by similar lines to Boston, Buffalo, then to Chicago and eventually to the Pacific Coast. The inauguration of the system was one of the great achievements of Simonton's administration.

The same year that brought the leased wire saw the New York Associated Press change its quarters for the first time since 1848. The new home was at Broadway and Dey Street on the eighth floor in the imposing building Western Union had just erected. The flow of news turned into this new center—the famous "stolen" presidential election of Hayes versus Tilden, the expensive Russo-Turkish War, the reign of the "Molly Maguires" in Pennsylvania, and the election of Pope Leo XIII.

History quietly repeated itself that decade, for another great advance in the science of communications passed with scant notice. Alexander Graham Bell's attorney appeared in Washington in 1875 and filed application for a patent on a new device called the telephone. It was several years, however, before the instrument came into general use, even on a small scale, and its quickening effect on news gathering was not immediate.

It was an important year, but the event that caught popular interest was not Bell's invention. A cavalry officer with a reputation for insubordination was riding toward the valley of the Little Big Horn in Montana. And with him and his Seventh Cavalry went a lone newspaperman—an Associated Press correspondent on a nimble gray mule.

IX. STRING CORRESPONDENT

IT WAS May, 1876, and Philadelphia buzzed with last-minute plans for the greatest celebration in the history of the nation—the hundredth anniversary of the Declaration of Independence. The exposition was imposing and the agents of the New York Associated Press who drew the assignment to report the spectacle began sending out their stories telling of the wonders in store for those who planned to attend.

All this was worlds removed from life in the frontier town of Bismarck, North Dakota. On May 14, just four days after the exposition threw open its gates, there was a small gathering in the home of Bismarck's town druggist, John P. Dunn. The occasion was a farewell dinner for the quiet, middle-aged man who had become a close friend of the family in the three years he had been a reporter for the weekly Bismarck *Tribune*. His name was Mark Kellogg and he was preparing to accompany General George Armstrong Custer and his regiment into the badlands westward to punish Sitting Bull and his warlike Sioux. Colonel Clement A. Lounsbury, owner of the Bismarck *Tribune* and a part-time correspondent for the Western Associated Press, had intended making the trip, but last-minute illness in the family compelled him to delegate the assignment.

The Dunn family knew little of Kellogg except that he had moved from town to town along the frontier since his wife died some years before. He was greatly attached to children and he had been attracted to the Dunns by their rollicking youngsters. His presence at the Sunday dinners had become a custom and the entire family looked forward to having him there.

The Dunns lingered as long as possible over the meal because they would miss their friend. He had to leave at three o'clock to ferry the Missouri and join Custer at old Fort Lincoln, so dinner had been served earlier than usual. Mrs. Dunn inquired about his preparations for the trip and he displayed a little black satchel. In it were tobacco pipes, underwear and other pieces of light clothing. There were pencils too, and a supply of paper on which to write his accounts of the campaign against Sitting Bull, for relay by pony across the plains to the nearest newspaper and telegraph offices, many miles away.

Jokingly he told the Dunns that General Alfred H. Terry, commander of the expedition, had assigned him a gray mule. As soon as he arrived at Fort Lincoln the animal was turned over to him. The sure-footed little beast was so small that Kellogg's feet touched the ground, but throughout the campaigning he was able to keep up with the big chargers of the troopers.

The winding blue and yellow column flowed over the Dakota hills. Somewhere over the silent horizon were the upper waters of the Yellowstone where the Sioux were gathered for one last determined stand against the invasion of the Black Hills.

All along the dusty march, Kellogg sent back his dispatches while the expedition pushed slowly across the wild, rugged country. Terry had ignored orders in permitting Kellogg to accompany the troops. The grizzled old general of the armies, William Tecumseh Sherman, was very specific in the instructions he sent from Washington before the expedition started. "Advise Custer to be prudent," he wrote, "and not to take along any newspapermen." But Custer wanted a journalist with him.

The correspondent spent almost a month in the saddle before the column entered the hostile region along the Yellowstone where scouting parties found the fresh trail of the Sioux and their abandoned campsites. On June 21 Terry held a council of war where the pebbly-bottomed Rosebud empties into the Yellowstone River. Custer would push south down the Rosebud with his Seventh Cavalry and circle westward into the valley of the Little Big Horn River where the Indians were believed to be gathering.

He was not to attack from the south, however, until Terry and General Gibbon's forces arrived from the north on June 26. Kellogg had his choice. He could stay with Terry's forces, or he could ride in the advance alongside the impetuous young cavalry leader. Custer's carefree assurance dispelled any indecision and Kellogg went with the Seventh. On June 24 Custer made ready to cross the Rosebud and strike out for the Little Big Horn, so Kellogg sent back a last dispatch describing preparations for the march. He wrote:

We leave the Rosebud tomorrow and by the time this reaches you we will have met and fought the red devils, with what result remains to be seen. I go with Custer and will be at the death.

The next morning commands rattled out and the Seventh went cantering out of camp, some six hundred strong. At the head of the column with the commander rode Kellogg. His little gray mule was comical beside the officers' big chargers, and the black satchel lent a most unmilitary note as it slapped against the mule's flank.

There were thin clouds in the Montana sky on June 25 and the air shimmered with heat as the dust-powdered Seventh pressed toward Little Big Horn. The trail of the Sioux hourly became plainer and Custer studied the signs with impatience. There could be no doubt now. A large concentration of Sioux was at hand. Then the scouts came galloping back with the news that an immense encampment of lodges had been sighted. Custer saw glory and the opportunity to whip the Sioux without waiting for his supporting columns to come up. It would be routine work for the Seventh which had scattered just such hostile bands many times before.

No one ever knew what strategy Custer had in mind that day, but he split the regiment's twelve companies into three detachments. Kellogg knew infallibly that all the color and dramatics would be with the five companies that formed Custer's personal command, so he stayed with the cavalry's beau sabreur. Holster flaps were opened, sabers clattered, carbines were loosened in their boots, and Custer's detachment went swinging forward at a fast trot up the dusty rise that lay between the Seventh Cavalry and the Sioux encampment. Kellogg urged his mule along and the animal struggled to keep up.

They were on the crest now and below spread the valley of the Little Big Horn with its rolling ridges and hills. Custer ordered his adjutant to instruct one of the other detachments to move up immediately with the ammunition packs. A trooper saluted and went galloping off with the order. Then Custer's red-and-blue personal flag with its crossed silver sabers disappeared below the rise and the column rode down into an amphitheater of sudden death.

In an hour it was all over. An officer's charger was the only living thing in the command to escape. But for two days no one knew what had happened in the bloody valley beyond the crest. The other seven companies of the Seventh were too hard pressed elsewhere fighting off the Sioux hordes which surrounded them. Then General Terry arrived with the main column and his troopers found the field of Big Horn silent in the hot sun, with 225 bodies dotting the ridges. They found the body of reckless Custer and they found the crumpled body of the correspondent who had trotted gallantly to death on his small gray mule. Only those two had escaped scalping and mutilation. The red man's code had dictated that the body of the yellow-haired warrior

"I GO WITH CUSTER AND WILL BE AT THE DEATH."

should not be disfigured, and they did not touch "the man who could make the paper talk," as the Indians of Dakota had called Kellogg.

True to his promise, Kellogg had been there "at the death" but the big story of one of news gathering's first part-time, or "string," correspondents never was written.

They found his black satchel where he fell and eventually it was returned to the Dunn family in Bismarck. The motherly woman who had been so solicitous for his comfort the day he departed came upon the pipes, tobacco, and what was left of the blank writing paper.

X. THE LAST TRUCE

I

A NEW decade—the elegant eighties—was filled with trouble for the formidable old New York Associated Press. There was discontent once more in the Western association.

Nevertheless, the tide of news flowed on. The tenth census showed 50,155,783 persons in the thirty-eight states. Boston was ready to celebrate her 250th anniversary, and *Ben Hur* was the literary rage of the season. There were a half dozen marine disasters, and far across the oceans the Boers had begun their mutterings against England. In Germany a wave of anti-Semitism was sweeping Jews from Berlin, and in Ireland the despotic actions of a landlord's agent, Captain Boycott, were about to make his name a new word in the English language.

It was a tired and ailing general agent who scanned the miscellany of changing stories. Simonton's constitution never had been robust and fourteen years at the helm of an ill-contrived organization had left their mark. The general agent was expected to be all things to all men, a symbol of the tenuous union in which all the auxiliary associations were linked.

But, for all its inherent weaknesses, the news-gathering empire Simonton ruled was apparently flourishing and prosperous. In addition to its seven members, the New York Associated Press was serving 343 clients and spending $392,800 annually on domestic telegraph tolls. The foreign service was expanding and the general agent boasted for the association:

Its London offices are never closed. By means of a double corps of agents, the news of Europe, chiefly concentrated at the British capital, forwarded at all hours as rapidly as received. By contracts with the great European news agencies, The Associated Press receives their news collection from every part of civilized Europe, Asia, Africa and South America.

Cable tolls rarely were less than $300 a day and frequently mounted as high as $2,000.

Even the assessments seemed reasonable for the service Simonton

88

had built up. Outside of New York the papers paid from $15 to $250 a week each, and in the metropolis itself from $300 to $1,500.

As the new decade moved forward, Simonton found himself once more with the exacting responsibility of directing coverage of a hard-fought presidential campaign. The Republican James A. Garfield won by the slender popular plurality of 9,500 votes and the cynical speculated on how many of those ballots had been influenced by biased dispatches. Suspicion fixed likewise on the powerful Western Union Telegraph Company which gathered the returns jointly with the New York Associated Press, for it was no secret that the corporation desired a Republican victory.

Inauguration came swiftly on the heels of election, and then only a few months later—on July 2, 1881—a shocking Washington dispatch was thrust into Simonton's hands.

A disgruntled office seeker, Charles Guiteau, had shot and mortally wounded the new president.

Chester A. Arthur, the vice-president, took over the duties of the nation's chief executive and there arose the wild talk that the assassination had been plotted for the sole purpose of putting Arthur in power. The feeling against Arthur grew bitter and editorial tom-toms throbbed to keep it alive. American journalism had not progressed much from the hate-ridden Reconstruction days.

For three months Garfield lingered. Death came on September 19. Like most news stories, however, it was all over in a few days and then, without warning, the publishers in the West were surprised and disquieted by confidential advices from the East. General Agent Simonton no longer directed New York's news-gathering machine.

Inquiries brought assurance that the absence was only temporary and that Simonton would return as soon as he regained his health. Meanwhile Erastus Brooks, of the *Mail and Express*, and James C. Huston had been designated to take direct charge of the New York Associated Press activities. The Westerners did not like the change. They had come to have a sincere respect for Simonton. He could be counted upon to do his utmost to satisfy them and on many occasions he had acted as their friend at court.

2

Simonton's disappearance from the news scene was not the only disturbing factor in 1881. Papers which could not buy The Associated

Press service had been dissatisfied with the makeshift reports they received from a succession of ineffectual agencies, and now a concerted movement was launched to unite all these journals under one banner.

Arthur Jenkins of the Syracuse *Herald* summoned the dissatisfied group to meet in his city. Out of that meeting came the decision to set up another news-gathering agency as a strictly private, money-making enterprise. Thus an organization called the United Press was born and one of its three incorporators was Walter Polk Phillips, Simonton's former aide. Francis X. Schoonmaker was named general agent and the organization got under way early in 1882. This United Press had no connection whatever with the news organization which was to be established in 1907 under the name of the United Press Associations.

The emergence of this new agency and the continued absence of Simonton fed the agitation in the Western Associated Press. The 1866 peace treaty with the eastern monopoly had proved an empty coup in most respects and an unending succession of differences continued. Convinced that it still occupied a position of nominal servitude, the West again debated whether to try wresting recognition from New York or to make one more attempt at a national co-operative service of its own. There were some members who favored preserving the status quo, but the majority wanted action, especially since content of the news report was suffering under the indifferent Brooks-Huston management.

Once more the time seemed propitious for the West to reassert itself. The activities of the new commercial agency had become sufficiently vigorous to cause concern, and again New York was embroiled in a quarrel with Western Union.

The seven members of the New York Associated Press were not long in hearing the rumblings of this new uprising. Realizing that their own position was weak, they sought to catch the West off guard by offering unsolicited minor concessions. The strategy failed, and the New York Board of Directors met to consider the problem.

David Marvin Stone, of the *Journal of Commerce*, who had succeeded Prime as president in 1869, was one of the few who saw the justice of the West's demands. He proposed immediate recognition of their claim for full partnership and the creation of a joint board of control of seven Westerners and seven New Yorkers to administer the combined organization.

This was too much of a surrender for most of his colleagues and Charles A. Dana, now editor of the *Sun*, called for a "more specific and guarded substitute." He suggested an arrangement by which both associations would pool their news under the direction of a five-man executive committee, two members from each association and a chairman chosen by the New York association. Such a plan, he pointed out, still would give the old organization a three-to-two balance of power.

The Dana proposal failed to appeal to the Western Associated Press at its next meeting in October, 1882. Old Joseph Medill, long one of the West's moving spirits, dictated the reply. Flourishing his black ear trumpet, the publisher of the Chicago *Tribune* introduced a resolution which would serve the required notice that the West would not renew its contract which expired that December 31. He coupled this notice with the threat that, unless New York granted equality and sanctioned expansion of the West into certain disputed areas, the organization would strike out for itself again with its own news service.

The gage of battle was flung at the feet of the New York Associated Press. The Easterners were badly prepared for a recurrence of the costly conflict of 1866.

Two new converts to the cause of equality now came forward. The *Times* and the *Herald* fathered a plan which proposed to give recognition not only to the West but also to the other leading auxiliaries. Here, at last, was a definite step in the direction of a truly representative co-operative, but it was far too liberal for the controlling bloc and was decisively voted down.

There was more negotiating between committees representing both associations and presently the New Yorkers learned that, if they would make territorial concessions, the West might be prevailed upon to agree to a union under the five-man joint committee plan advanced by Dana. The New York committeemen seized the chance and offered to surrender considerable territory in the South and West. This made the bargain appear more attractive to the Western committee and a five-year contract eventually was ratified on January 1, 1883.

The New York Associated Press named Charles A. Dana as chairman of the five-man governing committee. Its other two members were representatives of the *Herald* and the *Tribune*.

The Western Associated Press named Walter N. Haldeman, of the Louisville *Courier-Journal*, and Richard Smith, of the Cincinnati *Gazette*, both members of the Western Board and its Executive Committee, as its representatives.

Again the West hailed a great victory, minimizing the fact that the three-to-two committee alignment, carefully stipulated by Dana, gave veto power to New York.

3

The most important result of this latest realignment was the selection of William Henry Smith to fill the vacancy left by General Agent Simonton. The choice was calculated to inspire confidence in the West where Smith's ability was well known. As proof of the new unity in news gathering, Smith also retained his position as general agent of the Western Associated Press. Thus he became the unifying head of the two organizations with the new title of general manager.

Smith was born in upstate New York in 1833, the year the penny press made its first positive appearance with the birth of the New York *Sun*. Before the Civil War he published a small weekly in Cincinnati and by the time hostilities began he was on the staff of the Cincinnati *Gazette*. His newspaper work gave him opportunities for numerous political contacts and he used them to such advantage that in 1863 he was made secretary to Governor Brough of Ohio. The next year he was chosen secretary of state in the same election which seated Rutherford B. Hayes in the governor's chair—first major step in a career which brought Hayes to the White House. Hayes and Smith became fast friends and the close association led political foes to caricature Smith as "the keeper of the governor's conscience." Subsequently he resumed his newspaper work and in 1869 he joined the Western Associated Press in Chicago as general agent.

In his new position as general manager for both associations under the direction of the five-man governing committee Smith soon showed results. He began substituting trained newspapermen for the telegraph operators who had been agents for New York in strategic cities. Most important, he abandoned the old practice of restricting the association's field almost entirely to news that could be picked up from or supplied by member and client newspapers. He believed in a staff of trained reporters who would show initiative in getting news.

If one weakness could be found in his qualifications as general manager it was his political background. In 1876 his old friend Hayes, as President of the United States, rewarded him with an appointment as Collector of the Port of Chicago. It was a political sinecure with a salary that greatly increased the $5,000 a year he then received from the Western Associated Press. In the face of criticism, he held on to the post until he lost it a year before he assumed joint management of the two Associated Press bodies. In his new position, just as in the old, he cultivated his political connections and thereby left the political reporting of the association open to suspicion.

The same months which witnessed the industrious beginnings of Smith's regime saw the further rise of the United Press. Schoonmaker lasted only a short time as its general agent and then a new commander took charge, began improving the service and recruiting new clients. He was the former Associated Press employee, Walter Polk Phillips, and he had the resourcefulness needed.

From his several years of employment in The Associated Press, Phillips was aware of the drawing power of news from abroad. Since the New York Associated Press held exclusive contracts with such foreign agencies as Reuters, Havas, and Wolff, making their reports unavailable to him, Phillips set about under cover to create his own foreign service. He organized a separate agency called The Cable News Company and placed Schoonmaker in charge. Soon this disguised subsidiary was supplying its report not only to United Press clients but also to some of the Associated Press papers.

Phillips ostensibly was the sole guiding genius of the United Press, but actually he was not. His fellow triumvirs, discreetly in the background, were John R. Walsh, financier and part owner of the Chicago *Herald,* and, unaccountably, William Laffan, a dramatic critic who had risen to be business manager of Dana's New York *Sun.*

In the beginning the identity of these latter two remained unknown. In time Walsh's connection could be logically explained, for his publishing partner, James W. Scott, had been one of the founders of the United Press. Moreover, as a financier, he had a finger in numerous business pies. But the caustic Laffan was by all odds the most important of the three, and when his part in the undertaking finally was exposed the anomalous situation presented a mystery. As business manager of the *Sun,* he enjoyed the full confidence and support of Dana, and Dana was chairman of the Joint Executive Committee and kingpin of the renovated Associated Press.

Phillips's disguised Cable News Company continued to expand its list of clients until it had added Medill's Chicago *Tribune.* General Manager Smith quickly called the *Tribune* to task for using a rival's report in violation of regulations. He assailed Cable News as "only an annex to the United Press" and charged it had been organized as a subterfuge by the other news agency in an attempt to inveigle Associated Press members away from their own association.

The *Tribune* confronted Schoonmaker with the charges and he denied them.

"The United Press has no possible connection with the Cable News Company," he declared, "and my special cables are not only beyond the reach of The United Press but, as you will soon see, in hot opposition to their cable service."

When Smith heard this he threatened to cut the *Tribune* off from the report if it did not discontinue the cable service. No epithet was too strong for Schoonmaker; he was a "scoundrel," "the prince of liars," and a news thief who "systematically debauched an employe of the Western Union Telegraph Company to steal Associated Press cables for the benefit of the United Press Association." In the face of Smith's barrage, which he backed by documentary evidence, Schoonmaker finally admitted the Cable News was connected with the United Press, and the *Tribune* dropped the report.

Considering Smith's scathing denunciation, many publishers were amazed in 1884 when this same Schoonmaker quit his Cable News position and was taken into the employ of The Associated Press at a salary of $4,000 a year. Significantly, on that very same date—August 17, 1884—the jointly operated Associated Press itself became a subscriber to the Cable News Company reports—reports which General Manager Smith so recently had described as "bogus cable dispatches prepared by a set of sharpers."

Strange things were going on behind the scenes.

4

The presidential year of 1884 was a poor one for the prestige of the New York Associated Press. The Republican party, after almost a quarter of a century in power, nominated James G. Blaine, "the plumed knight" of Maine, and the Democrats selected Grover Cleveland, the Buffalo bachelor who enjoyed a game of pinochle in the back room of his favorite German-American beer garden.

When news of Cleveland's nomination reached the offices of the usually Democratic New York *Sun*, Dana, the autocrat of The Associated Press, stamped up and down the room.

"It isn't Cleveland . . . It can't be Cleveland . . . It shan't be Cleveland!"

He muttered the words over and over, pounding his palm with his fist, and throughout the campaign the *Sun* fought Cleveland with savage fury.

Dana was only one in the powerful battalions arrayed against Cleveland. Jay Gould, the singular figure of American finance who then controlled the Western Union Telegraph Company, contributed enormous amounts to the Blaine war chest. Other Wall Street operators added to the golden stream, and the Blaine forces spent their funds lavishly. There was uncontradicted testimony that the editor of one inconsequential weekly paper received $60,000 and the disillusioned could calculate the sums spent elsewhere. To bolster their cause further, the Republicans seized upon Cleveland's private life—he was declared the father of an illegitimate child—and dragged his name through the political mire.

While the campaign swept along, the typewriter made its unheralded debut in the newspaper world. Until that year reporters laboriously wrote their news in longhand and telegraphers copied the wire dispatches in their fast scrawl. A few business houses were using the new machine, but little attention had been paid to the invention generally. Then one day word reached the Chicago office of the Western Associated Press that John Paine, the association's telegraph operator at Nashville, was using the newfangled contraption and that the editors there were hailing the cleaner, more legible copy. Addison C. Thomas, the wire chief at Chicago, saw the possibilities and arranged to have all his men supplied. Soon the telegraph companies followed suit and the typewriter played a steadily greater part in the production of news.

The primitive typewriters clacked and as the presidential campaign progressed increasing interest attached to the state canvasses held prior to the November vote. They were looked to as barometers of popular feeling. The Maine primary was held in September and the jointly operated associations reported the Republican majority as 19,739 when it was only 12,082. Again, in Ohio the association's figures were out of line with official totals. Many of the unofficial returns had been gathered by Gould's Western Union; the New York Associated Press and the telegraph company tabulated the votes jointly as they had done for years past.

The cry arose that The New York Associated Press was falsifying returns in Blaine's favor. The Buffalo *Courier* on October 27, 1884, carried a special dispatch from Washington which began pointedly with this quotation:

"Well," said a prominent Blaine Republican tonight, "it does look as though The Associated Press were in our interest."

The story cited the reasons behind the opinion and over another special despatch from the national capital the *Courier* headlined: "The Associated Press Severely Criticized For Its Rank Partisanship." The story stated:

The conduct of The Associated Press in working systematically in the interest of Blaine continues to be severely commented on here by persons having facilities for obtaining inside information. As an illustration of the methods pursued by it during the campaign, the action of the management in employing one of Blaine's stenographers to represent The Associated Press during Blaine's tours is cited. The reports of Blaine's speeches and the incidents of his travels came from this stenographer after careful revision by Blaine himself. This Associated Press agent was in the employ of Blaine for several months preceding and also after his nomination. This is but a specimen of the inner workings of a partisan news agency theoretically supposed to be non-partisan.

Newspapers in the past had been punished with lightning swiftness for much milder criticism of the association. They were as sternly punished for similar transgressions in the future. Yet this time there was no punitive action. General Manager Smith did not attempt a reply.

When Blaine arrived in New York City the week before election the odds were 2 to 1 in his favor. It appeared that New York State probably would decide the contest and both parties concentrated their final efforts there. Although it was his home state, Cleveland labored under a disadvantage. As governor he had estranged the Tammany, labor, and Catholic votes. Blaine's managers, who had been wooing the church vote throughout, assembled a meeting of ministers to greet their candidate and pledge support. It was such a minor campaign function that the local papers did not bother to cover it. Nevertheless, the New York Associated Press sent along Frank W. Mack, a young man of twenty-three.

The Reverend Samuel Dickinson Burchard, seventy-two years old, addressed Blaine on behalf of the assemblage. His speech in the main was newsless until he uttered the dynamite-laden final sentence: "We are Republicans, and do not propose to leave our party and identify ourselves with those whose antecedents have been rum, Romanism, and rebellion!"

Seated in the rear of the meeting place, young Mack saw the sensational importance of Burchard's phrase. His story fanned out over the wires. In many parts of the country "Rum, Romanism, and Rebellion" was a good vote-getting slogan for Blaine, but ironically enough it also was the most deadly ammunition that could have been given the underdog Democrats. They jumped to the attack. Burchard had represented the Republican party inferentially as hostile to Catholicism. That alienated the Catholic support on which Blaine's managers had been counting so heavily. Furthermore, Blaine's mother was a Catholic, and Democratic orators were quick to point out that the Republican candidate had suffered Burchard's oblique slur on her to go unrebuked. In three days the 2 to 1 odds disappeared and Cleveland became a 10 to 9 favorite.

Election day came and in spite of ballot box stuffing, vote stealing and vote buying, the first tabulations showed Cleveland carrying the all-important New York metropolis by a vote of almost three to two. Throughout the country crowds gathered outside newspaper offices to read the hastily lettered bulletins. Cleveland appeared sure of victory and Democrats quickly organized jubilant torchlight parades.

The New York State vote still was in doubt, but Cleveland seemed to have an edge. Dana's *Sun*, which had fought Cleveland so fiercely, surprised everyone by conceding his victory. Then one ominous fact began to stand out. A great bloc of rural New York districts, which normally tabulated early, had failed to report.

Rumors began to fly that Jay Gould's telegraph company was out to steal the election. Crowds outside the newspaper offices grew denser, excitement mounted to a fever pitch, and still the Associated Press-Western Union returns gave the lead to Blaine.

On the day after election the outcome remained in doubt. Blaine wired party chiefs: "Claim everything." The next day came. Most New York districts had reported and a Cleveland victory appeared certain. And still the New York association placed the state in Blaine's column. All day long Blaine leaders conferred with Jay Gould and when the session ended shortly before seven that evening a Gould lieutenant assured waiting reporters: "The state is safe for Blaine."

Almost immediately the wires were carrying a New York Associated Press bulletin stating that Blaine had carried New York State by a margin of more than 572 votes. With thirty districts still missing, the count given was Blaine 555,531, Cleveland 554,959, and the dispatch asserted the unreported districts were staunchly Republican and would swell Blaine's plurality.

In the streets there was a sullen, angry rumble as the throngs read the newly posted dispatch. The rumble swelled into a roar and a mob poured down Broadway toward the Western Union building which housed the offices of both Gould and the New York Associated Press. A great roar went up:

"Hang Jay Gould! Hang Jay Gould!"

Uptown another wrathful crowd, five thousand strong, went surging along Fifth Avenue to storm the Gould mansion. It marched to the same fierce cry:

"Hang Jay Gould! Hang Jay Gould!"

Elsewhere other crowds roamed the streets and as the night re-echoed their cries an editorial writer on the New York *Herald* was writing:

. . . Gould controls the Western Union Telegraph Company. During the last two days Gould, by false reports through his telegraphic agencies, has been executing his share of the plot of preparing Republican partisans for a fraudulent claim that the vote of New York has been cast for Blaine. . . . It is the official returns of the ballot of the people of New York honestly computed, and it is not Jay Gould and his Western Union Telegraph Company that are to determine the electoral vote of this state.

At the Western Union building police action prevented violence. A guard was thrown around the Gould mansion. That night the financier quit the city for the safety of his yacht in the middle of the Hudson.

Soon after Gould had removed himself, the New York Associated Press announced that Cleveland had carried New York State by a scant margin. The official plurality was 1,149, which emphasized how close the contest was and how damaging to Blaine had been Burchard's inept speechmaking. With New York in his column, Cleveland had 219 electoral votes to Blaine's 182. Had Blaine carried the state the count would have been Blaine 218, Cleveland 183.

So the turbulent election of 1884 passed into history. It saw the New York Associated Press accused of complicity in an unsavory election-stealing plot, and yet in contradiction it saw the same organization break the "Rum, Romanism, and Rebellion" story which proved so fatal to the hopes of the plot's beneficiary.

XI. EXPANSION AND DISASTER

I

GROVER CLEVELAND was inaugurated the twenty-second President of the United States on March 4, 1885. Washington had never seen such a jubilant assemblage. More than half a million Democrats flooded the banks of the Potomac.

The size of the Associated Press staff on duty was in impressive contrast to the one when Buchanan took his oath of office in 1857. Only Gobright had been present for The Associated Press to report that story. Now a half dozen reporters were assigned. The recent corruption and fraud charges still were fresh as they knuckled down to write about the colorful occasion, but no subversive influences were interested in the coverage of such a straightforward event.

The reports of the inauguration sped across the country. Although the era of newspaper pictures had not dawned, the Los Angeles *Times* seized upon the occasion to publish a humorous pen sketch of Cleveland mounting the "administration horse." The drawing was jokingly conceived by an artist in the newspaper's office, but the caption accompanying the sketch was an unwitting prophecy of the amazing picture development that revolutionized American journalism fifty years later. The caption read:

This special Photogram to The Times, wired from Washington at enormous expense, is Short (name of the artist who did the drawing) but sweet, and gives a graphic idea of Mr. Cleveland's appearance as he mounted the administration charger. A slight roughness in the lines is due to bumping against the insulators as it came buzzing along on the overland wires.

With the news pulse quickening, reports were pouring into the New York headquarters at the rate of more than 40,000 words daily at the time of Cleveland's inauguration. The dispatches came from a fair-sized staff, yet the names of the reporters themselves never had been identified publicly with any of the work they did. Now occurred an innovation.

Employees of the Missouri Pacific and Iron Mountain Railway were on strike. The walkout, sponsored by the Knights of Labor, threatened a stoppage on other railroads as well. The one man who could point the way to a settlement was Jay Gould, magician of so many business deals. For a long time he could not be found. Then word reached New York that he was in Florida. Charles Sanford Diehl, of the Chicago office of the Western Associated Press, happened to be on vacation there and the formidable task of interviewing Gould was delegated to him.

Diehl finally got the interview and his story contained a statement from Gould which prevented a general walkout. The story was so important, and Diehl presented his information so well, that the association carried his name at the end to indicate it was an exclusive dispatch, obtained and written by one of its own staff men. That was a great departure from tradition, marking the first intentional appearance of a correspondent's by-line in the news report.

Diehl's good work in the past, climaxed by this Florida interview, was responsible for his almost immediate promotion. A short time later, when the Western Associated Press found it imperative to open a division headquarters on the Pacific Coast, he received the assignment. The papers of the Far West were dissatisfied with the service they received and two influential clients had withdrawn. A tactful hand was needed on the scene to hold the others in line and to ensure adequate Pacific news protection.

Diehl was no newcomer to the newspaper business. Born in Maryland in 1854, he was a seventeen-year-old typesetter in Chicago at the time of the great fire. In an attempt to allay the fears of the populace he began printing a handbill newspaper. Later he became a $10 a week reporter on the Chicago *Times* and a month after the Custer massacre the paper sent him into the Northwest to cover the redoubled drive against the Indians. There he operated with the column of General Terry, whose instructions Custer had so tragically disobeyed, and there he learned firsthand the story of Kellogg's end. He was impressed by the part that special, or string, correspondents such as the Bismarck reporter might play in a large news-gathering system. Soon after joining The Associated Press he encouraged the organization of a system of part-time men in the Chicago area and it paid news dividends from the start.

2

When Diehl arrived in San Francisco in May, 1887, he brought energy that was badly needed. The Pacific coast, glamorous and romantic, was also a neglected stepchild. The news budget it received was haphazardly assembled and irregularly delivered. Diehl saw the possibilities and for the first time a detailed report began to appear west of Kansas City, transmitted over regular telegraph lines.

The Associated Press picked the right time to open a Pacific Coast headquarters. Diehl scarcely had established himself and adjusted the complaints of disgruntled editors before the first in a series of important news events occurred in a remote part of his vast territory.

In Hawaii—many miles from communication facilities—revolt overthrew Queen Liliuokalani and her island court. Diehl made special arrangements for a roving correspondent in Honolulu to report the revolution.

The correspondent got his story all right, but he couldn't get it out. Two boats, the *Australia* and the United States revenue cutter *Richard Rush*, were leaving for the mainland the same night. The *Australia* was San Francisco bound and would carry mail, but the commander of the *Richard Rush*, on a shorter run to San Diego, would neither carry the correspondent's story nor permit anyone aboard to do so.

Other reporters decided their only choice was to send their stories by the slower *Australia*, but Diehl's man had different ideas. In the bar of the Royal Hawaiian Hotel he saw a sailor whose cap bore the lettering "Richard Rush." The seaman was quick. A bargain was made. For $75 he concealed a copy of the dispatch inside his undershirt and filed it with the telegraph company as soon as he reached San Diego. In that way Diehl secured the story of the Hawaiian insurrection twenty-four hours before the *Australia* arrived at San Francisco—even before the government in Washington received its official report.

3

While Diehl was organizing the Coast, activities of an entirely different kind were under way in the East. The five-year joint managership contract between the New York and Western associations was to expire at the close of 1887. Its renewal was vital to the furtherance of the secret plans of certain of the five-man governing committee and the undercover owners of the United Press. Therefore, early that year those concerned began to look to the future.

As chairman of the Joint Committee, Dana took steps to see that there was no hitch. The New York Associated Press accordingly proposed a five-year renewal and praised the effectiveness of the existing union. Dana himself urged the Western association to accept it at once. He was seconded by Richard Smith and W. N. Haldeman, who represented the West on the Joint Committee, and the arguments they presented so hoodwinked the Western directors that they ratified the extension six months earlier than necessary.

The decade moved. Cleveland accepted the Statue of Liberty as a gift from the French; the Interstate Commerce Commission was authorized; an ambitious individual completed a trip around the world by bicycle; the phonograph was invented, and the first paper bottles appeared and were laughed at.

In a Baltimore basement a German immigrant named Ottmar Mergenthaler had been trying for several years to perfect a machine suggested by the idea of James O. Clephane, the Washington stenographer who had first thought of the typewriter. His object was to perfect a mechanism that would set newspaper type automatically, thereby replacing the old hand-type method.

His first machine was tried out in the office of the New York *Tribune*. It was christened the Lin-o-type. By 1888 the apparatus was ready for more widespread use and publishers spoke of it as the most significant printing development since the introduction of movable type in the middle of the fifteenth century.

Until the invention of movable type in 1450 printing had been difficult. It was necessary to carve the whole text on a solid block and after that laborious process the block was worthless once it had been used. Movable type made it possible to fashion each letter separately on a small block and these individual pieces could be properly reassembled over and over again as other documents required printing. That was the first major advance in type setting and now, with the advent of the Lin-o-type, the composing rooms of newspapers began a new day of rapid operations.

In the beginning the Lin-o-type was an expensive addition to newspaper equipment; it was several years before it came to be regarded as a necessity. But news could not wait.

4

Out in Samoa in March, 1889, an international controversy had developed over governmental control of the South Sea Islands. Warships of the disputing nations assembled threateningly in Apia harbor.

Diehl, in San Francisco, scented a story of potentially great importance and dispatched a staff man. John P. Dunning drew the assignment. In the absence of cable facilities in that part of the world, he was forced to relay his stories to San Francisco by boat. But it was the violence of nature and not of nations that made the biggest news.

On March 16 the most devastating hurricane ever to strike in that tropical latitude swept the islands with a fury that took many lives and wrecked Samoa and the battleships alike. For a month the world knew nothing of it, and then on April 13 a story running several thousand words reached Diehl. It was from Dunning, by the Australian steamer *Alemada,* and it contained first word of the tragedy. After helping with rescue work Dunning had written his story in the midst of the wreckage. Regular leased wire facilities of The Associated Press still had not reached San Francisco, and Diehl had to feed the big news over the regular commercial lines at a cost of six cents per word.

The eighties, with their wealth of spontaneous news, had made trained newspapermen more than ever conscious of how words could paint a quick picture for the reader. Men like Diehl now were schooling their men to tell all the salient facts in the first inclusive paragraph—later called the "lead"—of any story. It was the real beginning of a modern newspaper style and The Associated Press was beginning to answer, in the first few lines, those five most pertinent questions—who, when, where, why, what.

Dunning's opening sentence on the Samoan disaster was long, but it told the complete story in less than a hundred words. It said:

Apia, Samoa, March 30—The most violent and destructive hurricane ever known in the Southern Pacific passed over the Samoan Islands on the 16th and 17th of March, and as a result, a fleet of six warships and ten other vessels were ground to atoms on the coral reefs in the harbor, or thrown on the beach in front of the little city of Apia, and 142 officers and men of the American and German navies sleep forever under the reefs or lie buried in unmarked graves, thousands of miles from their native lands.

The reporter could have let that paragraph stand alone. The essential facts had been presented. But Dunning went on to the details. He gave the names of the ships and their loss of personnel. Then he returned to the terrifying storm itself, describing its intensity and picturing the great struggle to survive the catastrophe. He told of natives holding up wooden shingles as protection against a rain so fierce that it cut their faces, of the heroic activities of rescuers, and of the valiant efforts at reconstruction.

It was the longest story that ever had moved by telegraph across the continent.

The news editor of the San Francisco *Chronicle*, standing over Diehl's shoulder as the agent edited the copy for the wires, exclaimed: "My God, that is a wonderful picture!" Diehl subsequently said: "If I were to prepare a primer for young writers, not omitting some who are more mature, I would offer Dunning's opening paragraph of a memorable sea tragedy as a code to observe." United States Senator Don Cameron told his colleagues: "When I want to shed tears I read Dunning's story of the heroism of the human race, as it developed in Apia harbor." The New York *Tribune* reproduced the story in pamphlet form to satisfy the requests of readers, and in London the *Times* called it one of the most perfect bits of English ever written.

5

May, 1889, arrived cheerlessly, bringing rains which deluged the eastern states. For three weeks the downpour continued, hampering communications and swelling rivers. The rain was still falling on May 31 when, toward evening, the vague report reached Colonel William Connolly, Associated Press agent in Pittsburgh: "Something has happened at Johnstown."

Telegraph lines and the new telephone circuits were already crippled. There was only one possible way of reaching Johnstown, in the mountains of western Pennsylvania and ninety miles away, and that was by special train. This meant enormous expense, but the Pittsburgh papers and Agent Connolly pooled resources to engage a one-car special.

Before the train pulled out the first shred of news arrived—reports that a flood had taken as many as a hundred and fifty lives. The agent hurried the word off to New York and then with Harry W. Orr, his best telegrapher, set out by train against the advice of railroad officials. The special crept into the darkness with frequent halts while trainmen splashed ahead with lanterns to inspect the track. The water kept mounting until it reached the driving rods and the engineer announced he could go no farther.

Connolly, Orr, and two others—Claude Wetmore, a free lance ordered to the scene by the New York *World*, and a reporter for one of the Pittsburgh papers—plunged into the black water over the roadbed. Three timid colleagues stayed behind. Connolly waded off in

DUNNING HAD WRITTEN HIS STORY IN THE MIDST OF THE WRECKAGE.

search of a farmer who might drive them the remaining miles. While he was away the others were attracted by the dim light of lanterns. They sloshed over to a rickety bridge which spanned the raging Conemaugh River.

The lanterns were being carried by rescuers fishing for human bodies. The workers were using lassos to catch arms or legs as bodies hurtled past in the river. More than two score corpses were piled on the planks and the gruesome work continued.

Several miles up the river from Johnstown a dam had made the Conemaugh a vast lake for many years. The weeks of ceaseless rain had piled up eighteen million tons of water. Late that afternoon the dam had given way and a liquid wall, seventy-five feet high, swept down the valley on the low-lying town. A railroad engineer tied down his locomotive whistle and raced the water toward Johnstown. But he was too late.

Connolly returned presently with a farmer who, for $50, said he would attempt to take the four newspapermen across the mountains. They were six hours covering the few miles and it was seven o'clock in the morning when they reached the south bank of the Conemaugh three miles from Johnstown. No conveyance could go farther. They had to make their own way, slipping and sliding through the muck, slime and water, past half-buried bodies and the hideous jumble of debris. One of the party sickened and turned back. Connolly, Orr and Wetmore struggled on.

Feeling his way along the flooded roadbed, Connolly stumbled over an abandoned cattle guard and floundered into the rushing water. When he tried to get to his feet he found his ankle badly wrenched. The pain was so great he could not even hobble. Orr and Wetmore managed to get him to a farmhouse on a near-by hillside where he collapsed. The injured man, however, refused to let them waste time with first-aid efforts. The only thing that counted was the story of Johnstown's tragedy.

Orr and Wetmore split up, each with the determination to find some way to get out a few positive words. As the representative of a member paper, Wetmore promised Connolly to see that the first news sent out would be to The Associated Press. In the next few horror-filled hours the reporter and the telegrapher slogged through muck, scaled barricades of debris, and brushed past countless bodies of disaster victims. Wetmore had the first luck. He spied a lineman on a pole cutting in on a wire preparatory to sending a message with a pocket

Morse instrument. The free lance begged him to send a dispatch for him.

"Hell, no!" the operator yelled down. "This is railroad business."

But Wetmore was not willing to give up.

"Just a few words," he pleaded. "Ask your superintendent at the other end."

The telegrapher reluctantly consented. A prompt answer came ticking back and the lineman shouted down.

"All right! Get it up to me!"

Wetmore scribbled on a piece of wet paper, found a long pole and passed up his dispatch:

> OVER TWO THOUSAND DEAD. DEVASTATED JOHNS-
> TOWN APPEALS TO THE NATION FOR FOOD AND SHELTER
> FOR OTHER THOUSANDS WHO ARE HOMELESS AND
> STARVING.

Orr encountered Wetmore shortly afterward, and then both were surprised to see Connolly hobbling toward them, supported by two bedraggled farmers. He had not received any medical attention, but was determined to get back to the story. Choosing a vantage point, he found a large board, lay down on his stomach and began to write.

After midday relief trains started to arrive and on their return trips Connolly sent out great wads of copy for relay outside the flood zone. During the afternoon three wire lines were strung into Johnstown. One was set aside for official messages, one for military instructions on troop movements and supplies, and one was given to The Associated Press. Connolly set up headquarters in an abandoned gristmill on the east side of the Conemaugh, and there Orr took charge of the wire, moving Connolly's continuing story directly from the scene.

Unknown to the two staff men, General Manager Smith spent that day and most of the next trying to join them. The flood had caught him near Altoona en route by rail to Chicago. He made his way over the mountains, stopping to report the death of thirteen passengers in a train that had been wrecked by the floods.

Connolly was in a pitiful condition by the time the general manager arrived. He had been working without rest and next to no food for seventy-two hours. His injured ankle was much worse because he insisted on walking. Smith found that part of the Associated Press headquarters had been pressed into service as a morgue. At an improvised

WETMORE FOUND A LONG POLE AND PASSED UP HIS DISPATCH.

desk made of a narrow board on two upturned barrels, Connolly wrote his story and passed it to Orr at his elbow. The rest of the room was a mortuary.

Not long after Smith appeared, Connolly collapsed and the general manager took him back to Pittsburgh, leaving the coverage in charge of Alexander J. Jones, the first additional staff man ordered to the scene. Orr refused to leave his telegraph key. A slight, frail man, Jones was not so vigorous. He could not get anything to eat and twenty-four hours in the nightmare of destruction unnerved him. He called for help from Chicago—the only direct point on the Associated Press wire.

Help arrived, but it was intended for Orr and not Jones. J. Herbert Smythe, a young telegrapher in his twenties, had started from Chicago to act as relief operator for Orr. When he reached Johnstown, Orr broke down after ninety-six hours under pressure and had to be put on a train for Pittsburgh. Jones departed on the same train.

Smythe proved equal to the emergency. Lacking a pair of rubber boots, he tied strings around the bottom of his trousers to keep out the mud and then tackled the story. The first day he sent two thousand words, writing in pencil on copy paper and telegraphing it when he got back to the gristmill. He was meticulous about making corrections if he saw an opportunity to improve the account as he went over it a second time while operating the Morse key. For a while the only food was soda crackers and black coffee. On that diet Smythe turned in a brilliant reportorial performance which won him regular assignment to the news staff.

A few days after Smythe arrived another Associated Press man reached the makeshift headquarters. The newcomer was Lewis from New York, and it had taken three days and nights to wade and flounder from Harrisburg, a little more than a hundred miles away. He had been attending a formal dinner in New York when ordered to the flood zone and the full dress suit he wore was an amazing sight. He had cut the tails off his coat to facilitate his progress. His collapsible silk hat was battered, and his boiled shirt was black.

Johnstown was slowly reviving. The remaining houses on higher ground were crowded with refugees and a small dynamic woman named Clara Barton had taken charge of relief operations for the Red Cross.

Lewis and Wetmore, unable to find any other sleeping place, appropriated some of the boxes that had been brought in by relief trains and stacked near the mill for use by the Red Cross. They lined them with straw and moved them into the windowless building. For the next two weeks, while the full story unfolded, they led a harsh existence, eating what little they could obtain and suffering from the scarcity of drinking water. They slept occasionally—and the boxes into which they tumbled for bed were cheap pine coffins. Smythe was more fastidious. He used a board stretched across two kegs.

From the standpoint of straight news reporting, the Johnstown flood tested the working newspaperman's determination to obtain first-hand information despite all odds.

Although news gathering itself was coming of age, the little handful of men behind the old New York monopoly continued to take liberties with the facts whenever they dealt importantly with politics, the almighty dollar, or any of the other major controversial issues which exerted national influence. Late that same year of 1889 the Montana copper kings spent more than a million dollars to influence voting and once again the association was accused of disseminating biased reports.

XII. FOR THE ALMIGHTY DOLLAR

I

THE country was greedy for quick money as the nation moved into the closing decade of the nineteenth century. Slick promoters and market manipulators lured the small investor and shady financial circles in New York were careful to see that no news leaked out that would disturb the gullible. New states were being admitted to the Union, new industries developed and the magic of a dawning machine age brought the promise of a better future. Legislators were so interested in their own private affairs that enactment of wise regulatory laws was neglected. The entire press was threatened by a news monopoly controlled by moneyed interests.

The period was one of critical transition in the conception of a newspaper's obligations to its readers and in journalism's financial readjustment to the nation's pace. This era of change had begun in the eighties during the most rapid expansion of population and industry in the history of the United States. Until that time the press of the country had been a comparatively small, personalized business. But the development of the telegraph and the cable, the introduction of the telephone, the constantly increasing appetite for news, and the eventual perfection of rapid printing facilities changed the entire complexion of newspapering. Gradually the future of news gathering itself came to be involved. Either it was to become entirely the instrument of forces concerned with profits and special causes or it would emerge as an honest, self-respecting public service.

From Chicago the strongest new figure in the Western Associated Press surveyed the whole uncertain panorama. Victor Fremont Lawson was editor and publisher of the Chicago *Daily News*. He had entered the newspaper field several years before the beginning of this headlong time and had had opportunity to study the pyramiding of the nation's financial structure. He had watched the growth of corporate trusts until they controlled almost every conceivable commodity—whisky, barbed wire, oil, rubber, cordage, even ice and kindling wood. And he had seen the news from financial New York phrased or delayed so that interested men profited to the extent of millions.

Lawson knew how the press could influence the masses. His father had printed foreign-language papers for the large Scandinavian populations of the Middle West, and Lawson continued the business after his father's death. His papers had brought him in contact with the financially unstable Chicago *Daily News,* founded by an old schoolmate, Melville E. Stone. Lawson bought it and gave Stone freedom as editor. It was an effective partnership, Stone with his editorial abilities and Lawson with his idealistic conception of a newspaper's mission, and it lasted until Stone relinquished his position in 1888 because of poor health. Together the pair made the *Daily News* one of the most respected papers in the country. Lawson outlined his views on what the publication should stand for:

Candid—That its utterances shall at all times be the exact truth. It is independent but never indifferent;

Comprehensive—That it shall contain all the news;

Concise—The Daily News is very carefully edited, to the end that the valuable time of its patrons shall not be wasted in reading of mere trifles;

Clean—That its columns shall never be tainted by vulgarity or obscenity;

Cheap—That its price shall be put within the reach of all.

Lawson wondered if these principles could not be applied to newsgathering, where reform plainly was needed.

2

Under the terms of the last truce, the Western Associated Press continued in alliance with the old New York organization and the combined operations of the two were still directed by the same Joint Executive Committee of three New Yorkers and two Westerners which had taken over the dual management at the conclusion of the 1882 hostilities. In the great surge of national development and the wealth of news which followed that rapprochement, there had been little inclination to question the arrangement. There had been complaints, but the West's own William Henry Smith was the general manager of the affiliated associations and the two Western representatives on the Joint Executive Committee had a voice. Superficially this partnership appeared sound. But when the Western Associated Press members gathered for their annual meeting in 1890 there was increasing belief that appearances were deceptive.

For several years the members had watched with misgivings the phenomenal growth of the new agency—the United Press. Publishers beyond the Alleghenies had been worried when this rival first appeared in 1882, but the apprehension subsided with the Western-New York Associated Press realignment a few months later. Now they realized they should have given this upstart organization more attention. It continued to grow stronger in spite of the apparent opposition of the more solidly entrenched Associated Press.

On top of everything else, there was a mystery shrouding both its control and its method of operation. The Westerners had heard rumors that a small clique of financiers owned the United Press, lock, stock, and barrel. In retrospect a few noted that one of the greatest periods of unreliability and distortion in their own news report paralleled the rise of this agency. Most disturbing of all was the suspicion that the United Press had secretly perfected an arrangement to siphon news from Associated Press reports. Some Westerners bluntly charged that such a state of affairs existed and that there was connivance between the shadowy commercial interests and some members of their own Joint Committee.

The Western membership decided at their 1890 meeting on an official inquiry. The investigation was entrusted to Victor Lawson as head of a committee of three.

Lawson himself did not know the extent of his undertaking. His immediate commission was rather limited in scope—to discover what he could about the growth of the United Press and to establish any hidden connection it might have with The Associated Press.

Lawson was assisted by Colonel Frederick Driscoll, of the St. Paul *Pioneer-Press*, and R. W. Patterson, Jr., of the Chicago *Tribune*, among others. During the long months of careful, puzzling research there were repeated attempts to unseat the committee and to discredit its efforts. At one stage I. F. Mack, now president of the Western Associated Press, even attempted to stop Lawson. Others whom Lawson had trusted most implicitly turned out to be among the most culpable. Individuals in high places were involved in the most complicated scheme. Even the majority of the seven members of the old New York Associated Press had not been aware of what was going on.

Lawson made his preliminary report to the regular 1891 meeting and then hurried off to New York to complete his investigation. Interest ran so high that only one member of the entire Western Associated Press failed to attend the special meeting called in Detroit on August 18 of the same year to hear the whole shocking story of betrayal and deceit.

The meeting was stunned by Lawson's revelations.

He presented documentary evidence showing that all of the news-gathering facilities of the country were in the control of a trust dominated by John Walsh, the financier, William Laffan, business manager and publisher of Dana's New York *Sun*, and Walter Phillips, directing head of the United Press.

These men—principal owners of the United Press—controlled all the news by virtue of a secret trust agreement between the United Press and members of the Joint Executive Committee of the New York and Western associations.

They had contrived this agreement with the Joint Executive Committee and they had given stock valued at many thousands of dollars to the committee members privately in order to effect their plan.

Not only was part of this stock held personally by Charles Dana, president of the New York Associated Press and chairman of the Joint Executive Committee, but Richard Smith and W. N. Haldeman, Western representatives on the committee, and General Manager William Henry Smith also had been given large financial interests.

The total holdings of all the Associated Press men involved—until now considered entirely loyal to the best interests of the jointly operated associations—were as follows:

Charles A. Dana, Editor of the *Sun* and chairman of the Joint
Executive Committee ....$ 72,500
Whitelaw Reid, New York Associated Press representative on the
joint committee, in the name of Henry W. Sackett   72,500
W. N. Haldeman, Western Associated Press representative on the
joint committee   50,000
Richard Smith, Western Associated Press representative on the
joint committee, in the name of J. D. Hearne   50,000
William Henry Smith, General Manager of the combined New
York and Western Associated Press   50,000
William M. Laffan, business manager and publisher of the *Sun* ...   72,500

Total $367,500

It took Lawson more than ten thousand words to recount the entire story and his report explained for the first time many mystifying incidents of the past.

3

The incredible situation had its beginning back in 1884 when the rising young United Press in a masterpiece of salesmanship prevailed upon the Joint Executive Committee to buy the bothersome report of its European news subsidiary, the Cable News Company. Ostensibly the move was designed to strengthen The Associated Press's own foreign news service, but there were other shadowy details in the transaction. It was then that the New York Associated Press employed Francis X. Schoonmaker who had been head of the Cable News. Many publishers now recalled that, at the time, they had been surprised by this sudden change of front by General Manager Smith who had previously denounced Schoonmaker as a "scoundrel" and "thief," and the Cable News Company as a purveyor of bogus dispatches.

The Cable News Company proved the entering wedge and for a while the Joint Executive Committee and the United Press worked together privately in the field of foreign intelligence. The first arrangement also called for the New York Associated Press to supply its theoretical rival with news of the New England area, but presently Congressional and Albany reports were added, and soon The Associated Press was supplying its news on a national scale. The news usually was made available to the United Press in New York through a scheme which kept the overt act well concealed.

In return for the news it received from The Associated Press, the United Press exchanged some of the news it gathered, but there was more than reciprocity in the partnership. To cement the union, the men who controlled the United Press presented thirty per cent of their organization's stock to four members of the Joint Executive Committee in 1885. Technically, the committeemen "bought" the stock, but an immediate hundred per cent "dividend" refunded the purchase money. Since the co-operation of the general manager of the combined Associated Press organization was necessary, the two Western committee members reissued one-third of their holdings to Smith.

The theory was simplicity itself. The men who directed the operations of the New York and Western associations would supply the United Press the great bulk of their news secretly and at virtually no cost. The operating expense of the United Press accordingly would be at a minimum and an imposing percentage of its receipts would represent profits—profits to be distributed as dividends to the coterie behind the scenes. Furthermore, the United Press would increase its number of clients by recruiting Associated Press papers to take its report under threat of subsidizing opposition publications in their territories. Thus, in effect, those Associated Press papers which were coerced into subscribing to the United Press would be paying twice for substantially the same news service.

Once the 1885 stock-distributing trust agreement had been ratified, the plan proceeded, successful and surreptitious. In 1887, however, the first five-year contract of the Western Associated Press with New York expired. Failure to renew it not only would cut off the United Press from the news gathered by the West, but also might affect the personnel of the all-important Joint Executive Committee and bring about a change of general managers. That was why the interested parties set about assuring a renewal of the agreement between New York and the West.

All this while the dividends had been rolling in. The returns had surpassed anticipations and carried the promise of even more lucrative operations. The United Press had found itself handicapped by its modest capitalization. As soon as the West renewed its New York contract, Walsh and his group felt free to remedy this deficiency. Accordingly, in 1887 a new United Press was chartered with a $1,000,000 capitalization. The financier, Walsh, as treasurer, immediately bought back the old United Press stock from the Associated Press officials, thereby repaying their initial "investment" a second time.

Then he distributed to them gratis $300,000 worth of the new stock, and the name of William M. Laffan appeared on the list of stockholders for the first time along with those of Dana, Reid, Richard Smith, Haldeman, and General Manager Smith. Dana, Laffan, and Reid each purchased an additional $22,500, so that the total Joint Executive Committee holdings were $367,500. Just as with the 1885 agreement, this stock was pooled with that held by Walsh and a few others to assure continued control of the expanded United Press. Walsh again filled the powerful position of trustee.

With operations on a big scale and the profits mounting, the manipulators realized the need for putting their news juggling partnership on a legal basis. Hitherto everything had been done by informal arrangement. On May 28, 1888, a formal contract was executed and it was Lawson's discovery of this document which started him on the trail leading to all the scandalous revelations.

In the course of his report Lawson told of President Mack's efforts to sabotage the committee's work. He also called for the resignations of Richard Smith and Haldeman as the West's representatives on the joint committee.

Mack took the floor for an explanation of his strange behavior. But the membership rebuked him by electing William Penn Nixon, publisher of the Chicago *Inter-Ocean,* to replace him as the Western president.

Richard Smith and Haldeman entered an extended defense, extolling the progress of news gathering during their ten-year service on the committee. But there was no explaining away the embarrassing possession of stock.

Then General Manager William Henry Smith asked for indulgence to review his twenty-two years in the association. "I have endeavored to be faithful," he protested, "and have given to the work of creating this great and honorable news service the best years of my life." But the members were not to be moved by touching pleas.

The Lawson report was accepted and all its recommendations adopted. Lawson was elected to head the West's reconstituted Executive Committee and the membership referred the whole involved business of the projected trust and the future status of General Manager Smith to that body.

Those members of the monopolistically inclined New York Associated Press who had not known what was going on also were incensed and disillusioned. At last they saw that monopoly, carried to its logical conclusion, meant a national news system operated for the dollar first and news integrity second. The New York majority made some feeble efforts to recoup their former prestige as a news-gathering combination, but they realized that the arrogant association they had so jealously fostered had been virtually stolen from under their noses by a profit-hungry element of their own membership in league with outright commercial interests. The New York Associated Press, historic old trail blazer, was doomed, and they made little attempt to save it.

The day of reckoning had come, but the struggle was only just beginning.

XIII. CHAOS AND CRUSADE

I

THE nation rushed heedlessly along toward a financial debacle and, as the forces of the Western Associated Press left the significant Detroit meeting, the first scattered signs of the panic of 1893 began to appear. The price of silver started its decline, the Treasury's gold reserve was shrinking, there were occasional bank failures, and in some industries the fear of unemployment no longer could be disguised.

It was at such a critical time in national life that Lawson and the other Western publishers started their struggle to wrest control of news from the private money interests. On every side was uncertainty and confusion. Many publishers, still shocked by the scandal which Lawson had unearthed, seemed too dazed to realize the serious plight into which the nation's news-gathering machinery had been maneuvered. There still were strong elements of opposition among some of the publishers themselves. The complexity of motives and the ambitions of selfish interests did not make the future a bright one.

In the next months this clash of interests was bitter. There were many times when Lawson himself wavered and was unsure, but the inevitable fact remained that the men behind the United Press controlled most of the news of the world and were driving resolutely ahead in a determination to control all.

Under such circumstances it behooved the West to compose its own internal differences and strengthen that portion of news gathering which it still controlled. One of the first steps was to employ representatives in many important centers where the Western Associated Press was not already represented. This marked the official introduction of the large-scale string correspondent system into Associated Press coverage, extending the plan which Diehl had instituted in Chicago several years before. Another step was to increase the leased wire facilities. Heretofore the wires had operated only nineteen hours a day, but now began the practice of delivering news to big newspapers around the clock.

The resignation of William Henry Smith as general manager had not been accepted, though there was little doubt that he had lost much of his old initiative and spirit. He kept protesting that the United Press stock in his name actually was the property of Walter Haldeman and Richard Smith, and that he had been incriminated merely for accepting dividends. The administration had become sluggish. The news report suffered and Dana, now in the United Press fold, gloated editorially:

> Those journals of The Associated Press that are distressed by reason of the superior and more accurate news that is regularly supplied by the United Press are hereby informed that there is no necessity for their remaining in such a state of unhappiness.
>
> The United Press is prepared to furnish the news, foreign and domestic, to any newspaper that is ready and willing to pay a reasonable rate for the same; and that without discrimination on account of race, complexion or previous condition of servitude.

There were many factors, however, which made General Manager Smith's continuance necessary. Not the least reason was that a large number of papers in worried auxiliary associations had come to know him personally and to rely upon him for their news.

This was especially true in the South. Adolph S. Ochs, the young publisher of the Chattanooga *Times*, was secretary of the regional Southern Associated Press. He was a stanch supporter of the principles for which Lawson was fighting, and Lawson did not wish to take any step which might alienate so important a block of newspapers.

Lawson's committee set to work to weld the Western Associated Press and its affiliates into a more compact front. It held meetings with representatives of the Southern, New England, and New York State Associated Press organizations in the hope of convincing them that they should all join forces and face the future together.

The full significance of that future was becoming increasingly apparent in Lawson's mind. He saw its inevitable climax must be a finish fight to decide whether control of news should be in the hands of those who gathered it or whether it was to be held by a trust whose primary concern was profit.

2

The first step was to perfect plans looking forward to the transformation of the Western Associated Press into a potentially representative national association. This represented an ambitious undertaking and progress was slow. It was decided, however, to incorporate a new organization under the laws of the state of Illinois. The name of the projected organization was to be The Associated Press of Illinois.

The second step was an exceedingly delicate operation. It involved maneuvering the United Press into a disadvantageous position which would neutralize its superiority in strength and financial resources—an operation which must be performed without arousing suspicion. The United Press still wished to do business with the West and Lawson had suffered negotiations to continue. Now he saw that these negotiations gave him an excellent means to advance toward his second objective. Accordingly, he welcomed the growing anxiety of United Press officials for an understanding. The Laffan-Walsh-Phillips triumvirate had become concerned lest no new working compact be agreed upon before the end of the year, when the one-time secret Associated Press-United Press contract formally expired. They were ready to absorb the legally nonexistent New York Associated Press, and they privately felt it imperative to keep the West quiescent by any sort of concessions until that conquest had been accomplished.

Laffan and Phillips therefore went to Chicago in October, 1892, to expedite matters. The mission had greater magnitude than they realized.

A provisional "unifying" agreement was drawn. Under it the United Press was to retire from the territory of the old Western Associated Press and confine its operations to the states east of the Alleghenies and north of Virginia. The news exchange agreement was to be revived officially, the United Press supplying foreign, eastern seaboard, and Gulf states news in return for the news of the rest of the country, to be furnished by the projected Associated Press of Illinois. The proposed contract, which was to be for a fantastic term of ninety-three years, ostensibly promised a perpetual, peaceful alliance, and at the time the United Press was eager to encourage this delusion. Hence the emissaries agreed readily to an innocently phrased stipulation by Lawson that the tentative contract should not restrict The Associated Press of Illinois to any specific territory in the collection or distribution of news. Colonel Driscoll, of Lawson's committee, summed up the West's attitude: "Bear in mind it was not as though we were treating with honorable gentlemen."

Once the "unifying" provisional agreement had been drawn, Lawson's committee accelerated preparations for the appearance of The Associated Press of Illinois.

The organization they contemplated was a bold and radical

departure from anything ever before undertaken in journalism. It was to be a complete co-operative, making no profits and declaring no dividends. Its sole purpose was to be the collection and distribution of news for its newspapers, which were to be members rather than clients. Each paper was to have a voice in its affairs. Above all, it was to serve the cause of truth in news.

On November 10, 1892, the application was made for a charter of incorporation. The objects were set forth as follows:

> . . . to buy, gather and accumulate information and news; to vend, supply, distribute and publish the same; to purchase, erect, lease, operate and sell telegraph and telephone lines and other means of transmitting news; to publish periodicals; to make and deal in periodicals and other goods, wares and merchandise.

The hastily drawn charter scarcely had been issued before Lawson learned confidentially that at last the United Press had arranged to take over everything that remained of the old New York Associated Press at the beginning of 1893. It was to obtain most of the old organization's members, its excellent foreign report, its wires and news-gathering facilities, its New York and Washington budgets, as well as all the "outside" clients.

That same day the first meeting of the new Associated Press of Illinois was held in Chicago. Sixty-five newspapers were listed as charter members entitled to stockholding privileges. They speedily agreed upon a set of by-laws embodying the revolutionary principle of nonprofit, co-operative news gathering. William Penn Nixon was elected president, and Lawson, Knapp, and Driscoll were named to the Executive Committee. The major business was the question of agreeing to the proposed "unifying" contract with the United Press which Lawson had negotiated. The session was a closed one and the deliberations secret—facts against which indignant United Press officials later inveighed—but before it ended the members ratified Lawson's tentative agreement and authorized the execution of a "general contract" to make it effective.

On December 31, 1892, the old New York Associated Press slipped almost unnoticed from the national scene after forty-four eventful years. As the sabotaged institution passed, it was significant that a majority of its staff—the rank and file of the scattered news army which had made it great in its day—aligned themselves under the standard of the new Associated Press of Illinois. To them the change simply represented a phase of evolution which left the continuity of co-operative news gathering unimpaired and they regarded themselves as the heirs or colleagues of those who had contributed so much to Associated Press history since 1848.

The Laffan-Walsh-Phillips triumvirate counted on the disappearance of the New York organization to leave the outlook serene for the United Press. With the control of all foreign and most eastern news now believed secure, they expected to be free to proceed with the subjugation of the West. Then quite accidentally they learned shocking news which the West had not intended them to know at that stage.

The Associated Press of Illinois, which they had marked for destruction, already was active in a quiet campaign aimed at the destruction of the United Press.

The United Press chieftains made a further discovery which was additional proof of what they immediately termed "double-dealing." At the time the tentative "unifying" contract was negotiated, they had nominated their own general manager, Walter P. Phillips, as the man to administer the revamped affairs of the two associations. With Phillips in this position, future moves against the West would be greatly facilitated. Lawson's committee had received the nomination and the United Press negotiators had departed with the belief that it had tacit approval. Now, to their anger, they learned The Associated Press had no intention of countenancing Phillips in such a role.

On the contrary, The Associated Press of Illinois already had another candidate in mind as its general manager. The man was Melville E. Stone, Lawson's former partner on the Chicago *Daily News*.

Whether or not Lawson and his committeemen were aware that the United Press had all this information, they appeared at the *Sun* office in New York on February 15, 1893, to execute the previously drafted unifying agreement. But it became obvious that the United Press had no intention of going through with it. Laffan, as vice-president of United Press, declined to agree to the contract, promising to make explanations in writing.

The explanations came two days later in an aggrieved letter from Laffan, not to the Lawson committee but to Laffan's fellow triumvir, John R. Walsh of Chicago. Laffan accused The Associated Press of Illinois of bad faith and charged the Westerners had regarded the tentative agreement merely as a "temporary expedient" whereby the United Press should be "belittled, restricted and ultimately destroyed." The committee's motive, he declared, "was to secure our signatures to the agreement and then open their ambuscade upon us when we were no longer in a situation to defend ourselves." The broadside was read to the Board of Directors of The Associated Press of Illinois in the presence of Lawson's committee and went uncontradicted.

The collapse of the contract parley ended all pretense of negotiations. Then in one last attempt at intimidation Laffan boastfully informed Lawson that the United Press had just closed an agreement with the English agency, Reuters, for exclusive American rights to all European news. This dismayed Lawson and his colleagues, who had understood that Reuters planned to deal with them at least on an equal footing with the commercial agency which held the expiring contract between the old New York Associated Press and Reuters.

For several days the outlook for the West appeared gloomy. Then came a turn. Ironically, The Associated Press of Illinois had William Henry Smith to thank. The old general manager, whose loyalty was reasserting itself after his fall from grace, was responsible. As soon as Laffan had announced his negotiation of the foreign contract the thoroughgoing Smith had cabled Walter Neef, former agent in London, asking him to investigate. Neef cabled back on February 21, 1893, that the United Press contract, although discussed with Herbert de Reuter, the European news power, had not yet been executed. The concluding details had been deferred until Laffan could reach London in person. Meanwhile Reuter had heard of the news battle in the States, and it made him adverse to signing any contract which failed to include the co-operative Illinois association. He told Neef that he was willing to treat with the Lawson organization.

Laffan was not due in London for six weeks and Lawson's committee moved warily so as not to betray their valuable information. An agreement must be concluded with Reuter at once. The Board of Directors decided the opportune moment had arrived to bring in Stone as general manager and to send him to London, if necessary, to obtain a contract at least as favorable as any Laffan might get.

Lawson's committee sought out Stone that night and he was with them when they met the next day. It was an important meeting. William Henry Smith received a letter from Neef amplifying the information he had previously cabled. Lawson immediately cabled Neef, appointing him London agent for The Associated Press of Illinois and authorizing him to take steps at once for a contract with Reuter.

Within twenty-four hours the new general manager, too, was on his way to London.

3

Melville E. Stone was born in 1848, the same year which saw The Associated Press founded by the six wrangling New York publishers. The son of a circuit-riding Methodist minister, he was attracted early to newspaper work and at the age of ten he had learned to set type. The family's peregrinations finally brought him to Chicago and there he supplemented a haphazard education in the same public school attended by Victor Lawson. A few years later he became a reporter on the staff of the Chicago *Republican* and at the age of twenty he covered General Grant's nomination for the presidency.

By 1871 reporting temporarily lost its charm and Stone tried to build up a business selling theater seats. The great Chicago fire wiped him out. With the slenderest of resources, he founded the Chicago *Daily News* in 1876. His great ability was strictly in the field of news —the business of operation never appealed to him—and he could not keep his publication on a firm footing. Its financial fortunes went from bad to worse and it had reached the end of the road when Lawson stepped in to save it.

Unhampered by money worries, Stone concentrated on the news department and soon the Chicago *Daily News* won a commanding reputation. It was an exciting life, but in 1888 ill health forced him to sell his share of the paper to Lawson. He spent two years abroad and when he returned he became an officer of a Chicago bank. It was from this post that Lawson's committee summoned him on March 3, 1893. He set forth his motives:

I had a secret longing to return to the printers' craft. And much more controlling than any personal interest was the question of public duty. My friends of the press and I talked it over.

It was quite true that control of the press was wrested from governments at the beginning of our Republic. The first amendment to our Federal Constitution did this. It forbade any attempt in the United States to stop free speech or a free press. But, unhappily, this was not sufficient. Government might not enchain the press, but private monopoly might. The people, for their information—indeed, for the information upon which they based the very conduct of their daily activities—were dependent upon the news of the world as furnished by the newspapers. And this business of news gathering and purveying had fallen into private and mercenary hands. Its control by three men was quite as menacing as that of the governmental autocrats of the ages agone. There could be no really free press in these circumstances. A press to be free must be one which should gather news for itself.

A national co-operative news-gathering organization, owned by the newspapers and by them alone, selling no news, making no profits, paying no dividends, simply the agent and servant of the newspapers, was the thing. Those participating should be journalists of every conceivable partisan, religious, economic, and social affiliation, but all equally zealous that in the business of news gathering for their supply there should be strict accuracy, impartiality, and integrity. This was the dream we dreamed. . . .

4

The new general manager's trip abroad proved largely unnecessary. Neef had carried out instructions with far greater success than Lawson could have hoped. The contract he had concluded was an exclusive one. It was for ten years with an automatic renewal clause. It placed at Associated Press disposal the complete reports of Reuter's Telegram Company, the formidable British organization; the Agence Havas of Paris, its French counterpart, and the Continental-Telegraphen-Compagnie of Berlin, which collected the news of Germany and of middle and southern Europe.

When Stone arrived in London on St. Patrick's Day, 1893, all details had been agreed upon. There was nothing left to do but sign.

But now a tremendous new factor was thrust into the picture. The nation was on the eve of panic. All through the spring of 1893 gold had been fleeing the country and prices melted on the New York Stock Exchange and in commodity markets. It was in this uneasy atmosphere that Grover Cleveland, back in the White House after four years of private life, pressed a button on May 1 to open the Chicago World's Fair.

The fair was expected to be the outstanding event in national life that year, but Wall Street dispatches carried warnings of much grimmer things. There came the resounding collapse of the $10,000,000 National Cordage Company, one of the vast new systems of grasping trusts. Wall Street values toppled under an avalanche of selling, depositors stormed banks, factory after factory suspended operations, frightening rumors flew, and the public nerve was badly shaken. The cataclysm smote the West with crushing force and banks closed in dizzy succession. On July 25, 1893, the Erie Railroad went bankrupt and one of the strongest remaining inland banks failed to open.

The panic became a mad rout and despair settled over the country.

This series of jolting financial blows spread confusion in the ranks of The Associated Press of Illinois. Most of its members were western publishers and their communities were so hard hit that their only thought was to save their newspapers. This was no time for a conflict which would impose severe strain on badly straitened resources. The United Press likewise drew back, although far better buttressed financially. So preoccupied were the opposing associations by the stress of the emergency that hostilities were temporarily suspended.

In spite of the panic, throngs flocked to Chicago. J. P. Morgan strode through the Palace of Fine Arts and snorted that the French exhibit must have been selected by a committee of chambermaids. Crowds filled the Midway to marvel at James J. Corbett, the "gentleman" pugilist who had conquered mighty John L. Sullivan. Blushing women turned their heads when they passed the concession where "Little Egypt" entertained with her danse du ventre.

The fair helped ease the strain in Chicago, but the slight relief did not blind Lawson to conditions elsewhere. News, more than ever, had tremendous importance. But the news most likely to affect the progress of panic—the news of Washington, of the New York money markets, of the industrial East—still was dominated by the opposition agency. The Associated Press of Illinois had not had the time or the resources firmly to establish services out of those centers. Even if it could have done so, the bulk of the country's papers still were under contract to the United Press and received its service. No one could say how much damage had been done by news reports which many people did not trust.

At this disturbing moment the United Press, in violation of the temporary understanding to cease hostilities, began raiding Associated Press papers in the West and elsewhere. The Associated Press met the challenge. Panic or no panic, the long-deferred battle was on.

Fights cost money and The Associated Press soon found itself seriously handicapped by insufficient funds. The United Press, on the other hand, had $2,000,000 in resources on which to draw.

While the United Press boldly extended its lines into Associated Press territory and intrigued with telegraph companies in an effort to embarrass the new co-operative, Stone was improvising a news-gathering system of old New York employees to cover the East and Washington. Temporary New York headquarters were set up in the *Mail and Express* building at Fulton Street and Broadway, but later moved to the Western Union building near by. Stone also called Charles Sanford Diehl from California where he had labored so capably as Pacific Coast superintendent.

The first month favored the United Press. When Stone chanced to meet Laffan in Columbus at the beginning of October, Laffan arrogantly told him that The Associated Press might as well disband and turn over its papers. Stone laughed at him.

Diehl was waiting in Chicago when the general manager returned. He heard the story of the encounter with Laffan and said he was glad Stone had given his antagonist no encouragement.

"You want to fight?" asked Stone.

"No."

"You will have to fight," Stone declared.

Diehl offered no objections.

"Wanting to fight and fighting are two different things," he said. "I have known for ten years we would have to fight."

Stone made Diehl assistant general manager.

Willingness to fight, however, was not enough. Lawson, who had to provide the finances, saw other obstacles ahead. He knew the United Press report generally was inferior, but he knew also how cleverly the enemy had distracted attention from this weakness by spreading defeatist whispers that The Associated Press was on the verge of financial collapse.

Those whispers were all too true. On October 4, 1893, members of The Associated Press of Illinois gathered at Chicago. With the burden of the panic, it did not seem that their new organization could survive much longer. The membership might not be able to make the sacrifices necessary to carry on the campaign. In such a critical moment in their own affairs, it would be easy for them to abandon the new association and beg for peace on whatever terms the United Press might grant.

The financial difficulties already were well known and as Lawson walked through the corridors on his way to the meeting room he saw bigwigs of the United Press lounging about. They had come from New York by special railroad car. Lawson gave them one last look and then went into the meeting.

XIV. THE FIGHT IS OVER

I

VICTOR LAWSON was the man the members waited to hear as their meeting got under way. The chairman of the Executive Committee was grave as he faced them. He had watched the specter of defeat draw nearer and nearer. Since the last meeting the panic had sucked the nation deep into its vortex. Men labored all day for the price of a bowl of soup. Business failures continued and with them suicides, distress, and starvation. In Washington a wrangling Senate kept blocking the repeal of the Sherman Silver Purchase Act which was proving so ruinous to commerce and industry.

Lawson masked his misgivings as best he could and opened his report. The audience sat in sober silence while he presented one blunt, uncontradictable fact after another. The Associated Press of Illinois was facing the end, almost before it had begun to fight. Its news report might be a marked improvement over anything the United Press could offer; the new exclusive contract with Reuters provided an undenied advantage in foreign dispatches, but this superiority had been bought and maintained at a great price. Already there was a deficit. Ensuing months were certain to produce larger ones. The campaign could not continue without better financing.

Lawson had no way of gauging the temper of the members as he looked from face to face.

To carry the fight to United Press strongholds in the East, he said, would require an immediate increase in the association's capitalization from $30,000 to $100,000. This was the first step toward placing operations on a proper basis, and he advocated it strongly.

There was a buzz of conversation at this recommendation and Lawson, hearing it, stopped speaking and sat down, still without mention of the major feature of the war-to-the-death program he had prepared. What he had told them was enough for the time being and he wanted their reaction to this initial proposal before outlining the second essential point which would call for great personal sacrifice on the part of everyone present.

126

"Mr. Chairman!"

The speaker was James E. Scripps, of the Detroit *Tribune*, stormy petrel of so many other meetings. Older members could recall how, as far back as 1866, he had vigorously opposed the first bid of the Western Associated Press for equity with New York. They also remembered that in the past decade he had actually deserted their ranks to become a United Press client, only to return to the fold when he found himself at odds with the aims and administrations of the commercial agency. The appearance of the bearded old scholar on the floor was usually a danger signal.

"Mr. Chairman!"

There was a scraping of chairs and more craning of necks as President Nixon recognized Scripps and he took the floor.

He opened with a résumé of the principles for which The Associated Press was fighting and declared the opposition was seeking to make secure "another Trust even more lucrative than the sugar, the oil, the cordage, or any of the other numerous modern monopolies which have grown fat at the expense of the legitimate trade of the country."

Lawson, intent on all the Detroit man was saying, perceived he was re-stating the case so ably set forth in a recent attack on the United Press which he had mailed to all Western publishers. This was a salutory thing and Scripps was doing it most effectively.

The white-haired publisher warmed to his theme. He told of the evolution of the profit-hungry United Press to its present state of affluence, of the free distribution of stock as "bribes" to Associated Press officials in the past, and of more recent attempts to demoralize the co-operative by private offers to Lawson and others.

"Gentlemen," he declared, "the issue clearly is: Shall the news-gathering business be permitted to fall into the hands of a syndicate of mercenary sharks who will use it simply to plunder the press of the country, or shall the newspapers continue, as in the past, to co-operate in the collection of their own news and to enjoy the advantages of controlling the service and getting it at actual cost? . . .

"It is a dangerous opponent we are confronted with," he continued, "and the more so as the men who dominate the United Press are without question as able as they are unscrupulous. They are not the inferiors in any way of the great schemers who have created previous gigantic trusts and they are not to be met with children's weapons.

"It is a life or death struggle for the great principle of control of the news by the parties most concerned in its purity and cheapness, and to prevent the service from becoming a mere instrument in the hands of unscrupulous and hungry sharks for the thraldom of the press of the nation!"

There was a storm of applause when Scripps finished. Large and small publishers alike were noisily demonstrating one determination— to close ranks and carry on the battle.

General Manager Stone was next and they cheered him as he reported on the extended reconnaissance he had made, seeking out the weak points in the enemy lines. He told of the progress of the hastily improvised news-gathering system in the East.

There was an ovation, too, for Diehl, whom the United Press twice had sought to lure away with tempting offers to double the salary he received. The Pacific Coast papers, he assured them, could be counted upon. Other regional groups, he said, would give their support if they could be brought together and given the entire story. As for the enemy's news service, he pointed his finger at its great shortcoming.

"Their conception," he said, "is that news can be taken out of newspaper composing rooms after somebody else has obtained it and written it. The Associated Press is already procuring and distributing its most important news through its own staff correspondents, and shall continue to do so."

By the time Diehl finished speaking, there was no question regarding Lawson's recommendation for an increase in the association's capitalization. The meeting which had assembled in an atmosphere of apprehension had become an enthusiastic rally.

Lawson took the floor to make a "suggestion."

The fight against the United Press, he reminded the members, was certain to be a series of emergencies. The United Press had circulated reports that The Associated Press was on the verge of bankruptcy. To lay these rumors once and for all and to provide the necessary funds, he proposed that voluntary contributions be made here and now.

"Mr. President," he declared, addressing Nixon, "I am ready to start such a fund with a subscription of $20,000 for the Chicago *Daily News*."

It was a call to arms. In an instant men in all parts of the room were clamoring for recognition. Parliamentary decorum vanished. Subscriptions poured in: $10,000 here, $5,000 there, $20,000 more, and on down the line. Even the smaller papers fought for a place on the list although their pledges of $1,000 represented a tremendous sacrifice

MEN IN ALL PARTS OF THE ROOM WERE CLAMORING FOR RECOGNITION.

in the deepening depression. Before the meeting ended $320,000 had been raised and subsequent subscriptions swelled the total to $550,000.

It was a great profession of faith, for all knew they stood to lose every cent of their subscriptions if the United Press emerged victorious. Nor was that all; the enemy already had threatened that, in the event of victory, it would exact heavy indemnities from the losers to pay the costs. It also promised to punish the conquered further by hiking the rates for the service that all would be compelled to take.

Lawson wasted little time in getting the renewed drive under way. Two days later he was writing to Adolph Ochs of the Chattanooga *Times:*

> By this time you are, of course, fully advised of the magnificent meeting held day before yesterday by the members of The Associated Press and the raising of the volunteer guarantee fund of over three hundred thousand dollars toward any possible contingencies growing out of the present contest with the United Press. If any of our friends on the outside have at any time held any doubt or question as to the purpose and ability of The Associated Press to maintain its rights as against the United Press, I think every one must agree that the meeting this week has definitely and positively settled all such questions. The fight we are making for the preservation of the independence of the American Press is in my judgment substantially won today.

Ochs, prime mover in the Southern Associated Press and long sympathetic to the West, joined The Associated Press of Illinois at once. He stipulated only that the other southern papers should be eligible for admission on the same terms as those given his Chattanooga *Times.*

2

A week later Victor Lawson closed his desk in Chicago and packed his bags. His destination was the East and his purpose was to bring a hundred newspapers then receiving United Press service into The Associated Press. Stone and Diehl had preceded him to open the grand-scale undertaking.

These aggressive tactics put the United Press on the defensive and the enemy captains issued a statement setting forth the financial stability of their organization. It carried an impressive list of signatures, including the names of Dana and many other leading eastern editors. Long held in awe by the struggling smaller papers, these men represented the backbone of United Press strength and many of them publicly acknowledged that private motives prompted their actions.

Throughout the years these leading newspapers had created their own elaborate systems of "special" correspondents, with which no small paper could hope to compete, and it was in their interest to foster no press association improvement which would jeopardize that superiority. The Associated Press of Illinois threatened to do so by making available to all its members, large and small, the extensive news resources previously enjoyed only by the big publications.

Lawson's invasion of the East was audacious. He struck first at the opponent's greatest stronghold—New York City. The key men on three of the papers there once had been connected with the Western Associated Press. John A. Cockerill, formerly of St. Louis, managed the New York *Advertiser*. Horace White, who had been one of the West's emissaries in the 1866 break with the New York Associated Press, was a director of the New York *Post*. The one-time Hungarian immigrant boy, Joseph Pulitzer, had expanded his journalistic efforts from the St. Louis *Post-Dispatch* to include the New York *World*. All three of these men seemed ready to pick sides and it was on them that Lawson and Stone concentrated immediate efforts.

Cockerill was the first convert and he brought in both the morning and evening editions of the *Advertiser*. Aided by Stone, Lawson next laid siege to the *World*, and Pulitzer joined. Then the two Associated Press men walked into the office of the *Post*, where they found Horace White busy on an editorial. Scarcely glancing up from his work, the editor greeted them.

"I am with you," he said. "I do not believe in an association which is controlled by three or four men. The *Evening Post* will join your company. But I am under pledge to make no move in the matter without consulting my friends of the New York *Staats-Zeitung* and the Brooklyn *Eagle*."

Within a few days the *Post, Staats-Zeitung*, and the *Eagle* came into The Associated Press. St. Clair McKelway, editor of the *Eagle*, took occasion to issue an invitation to others.

"The latchstring is out," he said. "Come and toast your tired toes at the family hearthstone."

Two more New York City papers, the *Commercial Advertiser* and the *Press*, transferred their allegiance. Then a number of upstate papers joined and not the least of them was the Syracuse *Herald*, in 1881 the prime mover in the foundation of the now embattled United Press. Lawson shifted operations to Philadelphia and most of the papers in that city became converts.

Diehl was busy in New England. The Worcester *Spy* and the New Haven *Union* joined. It was difficult territory but the important Boston *Herald* set an example others soon followed.

From New England Diehl moved on to Washington. He obtained an interview with Frank B. Noyes, a young man of thirty who shared in the management of the Washington *Star*, of which his father was editor.

The *Star* was served by the United Press. Located outside the territory in which The Associated Press had been making its biggest drive, it had listened to the blandishments of the opposition agency, which had sought to convince Noyes and his associates that the Illinois organization was doomed to failure.

Diehl found Noyes a quiet listener. He began the interview by discoursing on the principles for which the news struggle was being waged, but after some time he realized he had done all the talking— that Noyes had not asked a single question. The young man, nevertheless, seemed to be listening, so Diehl plunged on. He was still plunging on when Noyes interrupted.

"I am convinced of the justice of your cause," he said. "The practical question now has to do with your hope for success."

Diehl spoke of the financial stability of The Associated Press and of the spirit of the men who had made voluntary contributions. He told Noyes that the United Press, rather than his own organization, would collapse. Pulling a pencil from his pocket he listed the papers lost by the commercial agency in recent months, computed the consequent decrease in revenue, and worked out what he believed to be the probable financial condition of the other agency.

Noyes was on the way to New York the next day to call at the elegantly furnished office of the United Press in the Western Union building. Finding Dana and Laffan in conference, he asked a question.

"I would like to know something about the financial condition of the United Press," he said.

Dana attempted to laugh the matter off, declaring such questions should not concern the young man from Washington or any other client of the United Press. But Noyes was insistent and finally Dana instructed that the books be produced.

Diehl was waiting at a New York hotel for the Washington *Star* man to return from his visit to the opposition headquarters. He was certain the figures he had computed on the deficit in the United Press were reasonably accurate, but he was not so sure the commercial agency would permit inspection of its books, or that it might not loose another blast against The Associated Press in an effort to cool the Noyes interest. He waited impatiently. Then Noyes appeared.

"You have told me the truth," the Washington man said, and extended his hand.

Immediately thereafter Noyes convinced his associates that the *Star* should cast its lot with The Associated Press.

Once convinced of the justice of a cause, Noyes was not a man for a passive role. He joined in the campaign and, with Diehl, made a trip to Baltimore. Owing largely to his efforts, the *Sun* and the *American* in that city were quickly inducted into membership, followed later by the Philadelphia *Ledger*.

The success of the whirlwind invasion aroused the United Press. Dana used his editorial page for vicious attacks on Lawson, Stone, and finally Noyes. Damage suits were instituted against deserting clients. A heavy news-war tax was levied on the big New York papers which remained in the United Press and an intensive new drive for customers was launched in the West. But the co-operative lines held firm. Early in 1894, the four Chicago papers which had formed such a strong United Press bloc in the midwestern metropolis shook off the commercial yoke.

In an atmosphere of rejoicing the association gathered for its annual meeting in Chicago on February 14, 1894, and elected Lawson president to succeed William Penn Nixon. The list of eastern papers which had become members since the previous October filled three closely printed pages and Lawson reported that these gains meant a loss to United Press of over $300,000 a year. No one believed the opposition could survive and the Board of Directors congratulated the membership "upon the happy issue of this contest."

But the self-congratulations were premature. The opposition was underrated. For all its reverses, the commercial agency was still backed by many big papers. The conflict continued, sometimes flaring furiously, sometimes lagging. At various times proposals for peace were advanced by some quarters and individual United Press clients made overtures for compromise, but all contemplated a division of territory.

There was no letup in the heavy financial drain on both sides. While Coxey's Army was marching on Washington, hostilities raged through 1894—then on into 1895 as the nation headed into better times. The United Press made frantic efforts to have the strife halted before everything was lost. Pressure was exerted on neutral parties to arrange negotiations with The Associated Press, but Lawson said it would be a mistake to make concessions merely for the sake of hastening the inevitable end.

In the fall of 1895 the United Press had difficulty maintaining its service. General Manager Stone discovered that it was stealing Associated Press dispatches. The membership was notified.

The thievery continued and the general manager saw his chance for a dramatic exposé. One day a dispatch arrived from India telling of a native revolt. Before relay of the story to member papers, Stone inserted a sentence naming the leader of the revolt as one Siht El Otspueht. The dispatch promptly appeared in United Press papers and Stone lost no time in publicizing the fact that the name of the mythical chieftain—spelled backward—proclaimed the galling indictment: "The UP stole this."

Early in 1896 an event occurred in New York which exerted great influence. Adolph S. Ochs of Chattanooga bought the New York *Times*, which had been staggering under a heavy burden, not the least of which was the heavy tax exacted by the United Press. Ochs made no secret of the fact that he intended to bring the *Times* back into The Associated Press as soon as contracts with the United Press could be terminated. To distract attention from this threatened defection, General Manager Phillips of United Press blanketed the country with stories that The Associated Press was prejudiced in favor of the gold-standard Republican party and would distort the news in the feverish presidential campaign about to begin. Only the United Press, he announced, could be counted upon to give equal justice to free-silver Democrats as well as to gold-standard Republicans. It was about this time, too, that United Press enlarged its own name to United Associated Presses. But the change made small impression and the agency remained best known as United Press.

The presidential campaign of 1896, waged on the controversial monetary issue, momentarily eclipsed the prolonged news revolution. On July 6 a 35-year-old congressman stampeded the Democratic convention with his impassioned cross-of-gold speech. William Jennings Bryan shouted: "You shall not press down upon the brow of labor this crown of thorns; you shall not crucify mankind on a cross of gold." It was Bryan for the Democrats and free silver; William McKinley for the Republicans and gold. The victory went to the Republicans, and after the election was over both Bryan and McKinley sent The Associated Press unsolicited letters of commendation for the fairness with which the strenuous campaign had been reported.

Even before McKinley was inaugurated in 1897 The Associated Press announced its readiness to take all eligible United Press clients into its membership provided the battered profit agency would retire from the field. Laffan countered with a proposal to withdraw the United Press in the West if The Associated Press would withdraw from the East. He put on a bold front but the situation was beyond the bluffing stage.

On March 27, 1897, the New York *Herald*, the *Tribune*, the *Times*, and the *Telegram* went over to The Associated Press. In the once formidable stronghold of New York City the United Press had only two papers left—Dana's *Sun*, which had rejected a cordial invitation to become a member, and the New York *Journal*, which had been purchased two years earlier by William Randolph Hearst.

Lawson, his health impaired by the demands of the struggle, had come to New York to take personal command of The Associated Press forces. But, even the wholesale departure of the *Herald, Tribune, Times*, and *Telegram* failed to wring from the United Press any admission of defeat, and Lawson could not help admiring the stubborn determination of his three major foemen—Laffan, Dana, and Phillips. They might be wrong in their cause, but they were as pugnacious as ever and Lawson wondered how much longer they could continue.

There was endless rumors and speculation, and finally—on March 29, 1897—President Dana filed a petition of bankruptcy for the United Press, listing assets of $38,040 and liabilities of $129,415. A receiver was appointed.

Lawson was at his desk all the next day in the cramped cubbyhole of an office on the gloomy fifth floor of the Western Union building where headquarters of The Associated Press were now housed. The office was in shabby contrast to the sumptuous United Press establishment two floors below, with its expensive furniture, rugs, wrought-iron accessories, and stained-glass windows.

But Lawson was interested in what might be happening in those fine offices, not in the fine furniture they contained. What did United Press plan to do next?

His office door was flung open and an editor handed him a piece of paper. He adjusted his pince-nez and read the notice. It was from the elegant offices below, it was dated March 31, 1897, and it was addressed "To Whom It May Concern." It said:

The News service of the United Press will be discontinued after the night of April 7th, at about two o'clock A.M. on April 8th. No news dispatches will be received from correspondents or news agencies or paid for, and the services of all employees will be dispensed with after that time.

XV. REMEMBER THE MAINE!

I

BY THE time the United Press disappeared unmourned from the world of news gathering on April 8, 1897, Lawson's organization was badly battered after four years of conflict. The menace of a gigantic, mercenary news trust had been destroyed; the co-operative, non-profit principle had been vindicated, but the difficulties of reconstruction were many. The fight had cost The Associated Press nearly $1,000,000 over and above the ordinary expenditures necessary to maintain normal news service. That was a staggering sum in days when $50 would buy a first-class passage to Europe.

Lawson and his colleagues, however, considered the success of their crusade worth all the effort and money it had taken.

The organization set about binding up the wounds of war and consolidating its imperfect condition. Although a great majority of the clients who had been with the United Press were taken into membership, the brilliant but aging Dana stubbornly rebuffed all invitations. He announced that the *Sun* would go it alone, relying on the service of a news bureau of its own under the direction of the indomitable Laffan. Dana died a few months later, leaving Laffan in control of the *Sun's* destinies.

There were other papers which could not be admitted on the terms they sought, and they began arrangements to meet their own particular needs. An additional group of disgruntled losers who purposely stayed out of the co-operative threatened to be a future source of trouble.

However pressing the problems of reconstruction, the forces of The Associated Press of Illinois found time to celebrate their triumph. It was, of course, described as a gay and festive occasion when the hundred and eight leaders in the long fight gathered in Chicago on May 19, 1897, for the banquet. There was a huge silver loving cup, brimming with champagne, and each guest drank to a round of applause. North, South, East, and West were represented, and there were toasts, speeches, laughter, and bandinage. In honor of the occasion, a medallion was struck off. Its inscription read: "To commemorate the triumph of the co-operative principle in news gathering."

The year 1897 seemed ideal for "back-to-normalcy" efforts in the news report. The times had a strangely placid air about them, a certain deceptive promise that the world's tomorrows would be serene. In London Captain Ames, the tallest man in the whole British Army, led the Diamond Jubilee procession as the empire paid its extravagant tribute to "the Widow of Windsor."

It was the heyday of the bicycle built for two; "Mr. Dooley" philosophized while his devotees chuckled; Weber and Fields were climbing to popularity, and audiences jammed theaters to hear De Wolff Hopper recite "Casey at the Bat"; music lovers talked of Victor Herbert, and John Phillip Sousa led the United States Marine Band; the biggest beer in town was a nickel, and small boys jeered "Get a horse!" at the first noisy automobiles.

To newspaper readers generally life at home seemed uncommonly good.

2

At Key West on February 15, 1898, it was a quiet night. The cable operator sat at his idle instrument yawning as the minutes dragged by.

Then the sounder on the desk jumped from silence into sudden life like some mechanical cricket. Havana calling Key West—Havana calling Key West. The operator opened his key.

Havana was urgent. The Key West operator decoded the message as it came off the noisy instrument:

THERE HAS BEEN A BIG EXPLOSION SOMEWHERE IN THE HARBOR.

Then the instrument lapsed abruptly into silence and it was minutes before Havana came pounding through again:

THE MAINE HAS BEEN BLOWN UP, AND HUNDREDS OF SAILORS HAVE BEEN KILLED.

While the sounder danced at Key West, F. J. Hilgert, Associated Press correspondent at Havana, already was out in the wreckage-strewn harbor, hurriedly assembling the facts of the disaster which had overtaken the American battleship as she rode at anchor. One after another he questioned dazed survivors. He saw the warship's wrecked superstructure and watched the little fleet of rescue craft scurry about.

Then the Key West sounder started again, spelling out Hilgert's story, and the cable operator bent excitedly over his typewriter, copying the hastily written narrative of the explosion which had taken the lives of 266 men.

Hilgert's story was published throughout the world and the headlines shocked the nation. Although the *Maine's* captain cautioned that "Public opinion should be suspended until further report," a Spanish mine was immediately blamed. War fever swept the streets and in a Broadway bar a man raised his glass and gave the country its battle cry. "Gentlemen," he said, "remember the *Maine!*"

For some years past the United States had been watching conditions in insurrection-torn Cuba, where the natives were waging a seemingly hopeless fight for independence from Spain. Popular opinion was horrified at the rule of General Valeriano Weyler, the military governor who, according to rumor, ruthlessly put down insurrectors and maltreated noncombatants. Americans and their property frequently suffered and for some time William Randolph Hearst and his New York *Journal* had been demanding intervention.

As early as 1896 The Associated Press decided that a staff man was needed in Cuba. Hilgert was assigned to Havana, a post normally filled by a string correspondent. The association took elaborate precautions to protect his identity, and not even to inquiring members would the general manager divulge the name of the man ordered under cover to this dangerous field of news. From the outset Hilgert worked against endless difficulties and at great personal risk. General Weyler forbade all newspaper work under threat of the firing squad, but for two years, by employing all sorts of ingenuity, Hilgert had managed to smuggle out his thrilling, factual accounts of Cuba's struggle. The night of the *Maine's* destruction he threw caution to the winds and used the cable.

As soon as the news was received, Assistant General Manager Diehl saw that quick preparations were necessary. He anticipated a rigid censorship on the Cuban cables. If The Associated Press was to cover a war in the Caribbean, it would be necessary to assemble a flotilla of dispatch boats to carry all news to the nearest neutral cable heads at Jamaica or Haiti. He outlined his plans to General Manager Stone, who was reluctant to approve lest any undue activity by the association inflame an already aroused public. Stone had watched the vociferous efforts of some newspapers to whip the nation into a military frenzy and precipitate war, and he was unwilling that The Associated Press do anything which might set the drums beating louder.

Nevertheless, if news occurs it must be covered. Diehl pointed out that, if war came and found The Associated Press unprepared, press and public alike would charge the management with neglect and incompetence. The preparations he suggested were precautionary and could be carried out without attracting attention.

Stone saw the logic of this reasoning and the assistant general manager was off to Washington to lay siege to official quarters with an audacious request. He wanted permission to place staff men on the flagships of the two American fleets most likely to see active service. Secretary of the Navy John D. Long would not hear of the idea. Diehl presented his case directly to the President. McKinley knew of no precedent for such an extraordinary application and thought to dispose of it tactfully by getting Diehl to acknowledge that such a thing never had been done before. He asked a question:

"Has a war correspondent ever actually been permitted on board a flagship in wartime and in action?"

For the moment Diehl was stopped. Then in some vague corner of his mind a forgotten scrap of information bobbed up.

"Yes," he told the President, "a London *Times* correspondent was on the Chilean flagship *Esmeralda* during the war between Chile and Peru."

McKinley consented without further hesitation.

The war hysteria mounted in the weeks after the *Maine's* destruction, while a Naval Board of Inquiry investigated the explosion. Business and the President were averse to war, but the pressure of public opinion had become almost overwhelming. Theodore Roosevelt, assistant secretary of the navy, lost patience with the hesitation and snorted: "McKinley has no more backbone than a chocolate éclair." He predicted: "We will have this war for the freedom of Cuba in spite of the timidity of the commercial interests."

And already military bands were blaring the marching song of '98—"There'll Be a Hot Time in the Old Town Tonight."

Although Hilgert's position in Havana had become more perilous than ever, he stuck to his duties. In spite of official secrecy surrounding inquiries on the *Maine's* destruction, he learned that evidence gathered by the experts who had examined the wrecked hulk established that the battleship had been blown up "from the outside."

The dispatch doubtless would have been a death warrant if found in Hilgert's possession. Use of the cable was out of the question and so he succeeded in smuggling out his story by mail. Its authenticity was confirmed March 21 when the Navy Board's report blamed the disaster on the detonation of a submarine mine by unknown persons. That report sealed the issue, though its accuracy was later questioned.

Diehl was assembling a flotilla of dispatch boats and a competent war staff. After scouring shipyards along the coast, he chartered five vessels: the *Wanda*, a yacht, and the *Dauntless*, the *Dandy*, the *Cynthia*, and the *Kate Spencer*, all tugs.

The staff included Elmer E. Roberts, J. B. Nelson, Arthur W. Copp, Byron R. Newton, A. W. Lyman, J. W. Mitchell, Howard N. Thompson, H. L. Beach, Harold Martin, A. C. Goudie, G. E. Graham, W. A. M. Goode, H. C. Wright, Albert C. Hunt, J. C. Marriott, E. R. Johnstone, Oscar Watson, R. B. Craemer, and John P. Dunning, the journalistic hero of the Samoan disaster of 1889 and the only American correspondent to cover the Chilean Civil War in 1891.

The preparations were completed none too soon. On April 20— the day before formal declaration of war—Associated Press dispatch boats hurried into Key West, the concentration point for the main American fleet. When Goode climbed aboard Admiral Sampson's flagship, the *New York*, to which he had been assigned, the greeting was not reassuring.

"So you want to come aboard and get your head blown off, do you?" asked Sampson gruffly. "It's foolish."

At daybreak two days later the fleet steamed out, headed for Cuba, and seaman Patrick Walton on the cruiser *Nashville* fired the first shot of the war to capture a Spanish merchantman.

It was the beginning of a conflict such as never had been seen before, nor has been seen since. From the standpoint of news gathering, it was a correspondent's war. The newsboats of The Associated Press cruised at will through the battle lines at sea, maneuvered for the best vantage points regardless of the fire of opposing sides, and scurried back and forth delivering their stories to the nearest usable cable heads. The boats of individual newspapers performed similarly. All sorts of journalistic personalities were attracted and at times the whole fray took on a comic opera complexion. More frequently than not the correspondents risked their lives out of all keeping with the over-all importance of the facts they sought, but there was high interest back home and the news gatherers meant to satisfy it by one means or another.

3

The first big news came not from Cuba or the southern seas, but from the far-off Philippines. Admiral George Dewey with the Asiatic squadron swooped down on Manila harbor on May 1. "You may fire when ready, Gridley," he said to the commanding officer of his flagship, and proceeded to destroy the Spanish fleet without the loss of a single American bluejacket. The news, rushed to Hong Kong by cutter and cabled across the Pacific, did not reach the United States until May 7. The country went wild with rejoicing and almost everyone sported a large celluloid button boasting: "Dewey Did It."

In the preliminary naval operations around Cuba correspondents reported the bombardment of enemy works at Matanzas and later the shelling of the forts at Havana. Besides the men on the dispatch boats and with the fleet, Diehl also had correspondents in sultry Tampa where the army drank gallons of iced tea and groused at repeated postponement of its departure for Cuba.

A big question mark kept the army immobilized at Tampa. The whole country was asking: Where is Cervera? The Spanish admiral, with the main enemy fleet, had sailed from the Cape Verde Islands across the Atlantic on April 29. Then there was no word and the uncertainty spawned nervous rumors. One panicky report had it that he planned to attack the New England coast; another, that he would bombard New York; still another, that his objective was to engage Sampson's fleet off Cuba.

For one staff correspondent this news meant a welcome chance to get to the exciting scene of hostilities. George E. Graham had been assigned to the *Brooklyn,* flagship of the flying squadron commanded by Commodore Winfield S. Schley.

"Can you fight?" Schley asked when Graham came aboard. "We don't allow any loafers aboard a man-of-war, and if a lot of men on this ship are killed during a combat, you'll have to help take their places." To a subordinate he added with a twinkle, "Put him to work with a six-pounder gun crew. He'll be handy."

But Graham had had a very dull time. The flying squadron was kept at Hampton Roads, Virginia, as a precaution against the possible appearance of Cervera off the New England or the Middle Atlantic coast. The news that the Spanish fleet was in southern waters slipped the leash which had held Schley in port and the flying squadron steamed toward Key West to co-operate with Sampson.

But where was Cervera now? More rumors flew as American warships scouted for the elusive Spaniards. Goode, on Admiral Sampson's flagship, was in a position to appreciate how little both Navy Department and fleet commander knew of the enemy's whereabouts. Finally, on his own initiative, he went ashore at Haiti on one of the Association's newsboats and sent cable after cable to Associated Press correspondents, first in the Caribbean-South American area, and then in strategic cities elsewhere. All the messages asked for information on Cervera.

Tense days passed and on May 20 the long-awaited news came in an Associated Press dispatch from—of all places—the Spanish capital of Madrid. Member newspapers published the announcement that Cervera's fleet had arrived in the harbor of Santiago twenty-four hours before. At Washington the Navy Department acknowledged the news by issuing the bulletin: "The Department has information, which is believed to be authentic, that the Spanish squadron is at Santiago de Cuba." And far to the southward Sampson ordered Commodore Schley to Santiago with all speed to bottle up the enemy in port.

Events moved to a more rapid tempo and at 4 A.M. on June 3 Lieutenant Richmond P. Hobson and his crew sank the *Merrimac* in the harbor entrance at Santiago under shell fire from Spanish guns. Before departing Hobson gave Correspondent Goode the only interview he permitted, and as the *Merrimac* dashed for the harbor in the bright moonlight, Graham stood on the bridge of the *Brooklyn* peering through his binoculars for an eyewitness account of the exploit.

No one who saw the young lieutenant and his men set out on their mission expected them to escape with their lives, but late that afternoon Goode was scribbling the news that all had been captured uninjured by the Spanish.

Mauser bullets raked the news yacht *Wanda* on June 9 as she stood by off Guantánamo while the marines went splashing ashore in the first large-scale landing of troops on Cuban soil. Through the surf with them floundered Harrison L. Beach, the first of Diehl's correspondents to get his baptism of fire on land. It was almost a fatal baptism. A Spanish regiment fought the landing in spite of shelling by three American warships and as the marines drove forward a Spanish sharpshooter in the dense chaparral saw Beach before his rifle sights and squeezed the trigger. The bullet tore across the bridge of his nose just below the line of his eyes. Blood streaming down his face, Beach kept

going and the wound was still fresh when Diehl watched him write
his account of the fighting back aboard the *Wanda*.

4

The correspondents on the co-operative's dispatch boats with the
blockading fleet off Santiago were having an equally hazardous time.
When the harbor forts were bombarded, the boats were constantly
exposed to the enemy's return fire. Navigation at night was particularly
dangerous, for all ships had to run without lights, and frequently
American warships opened fire on the dispatch boats, mistaking them for
Spanish scouts.

The news craft had been unwelcome when they made their first
appearance, but this hostile feeling was not long-lived. After a few
weeks the navy was pressing the dispatch boats into service whenever
circumstances warranted, to carry messages and to tow or convoy crippled
warships to port for repairs. On one occasion the Associated Press tug
Dauntless was commissioned to take a captured schooner back to Key
West.

The long-delayed army expeditionary force arrived off Cuba in
thirty transports on June 20 and debarkation began two days later at
Daiquiri, east of Santiago. The *Wanda*, with Diehl aboard, and the
Dauntless were on hand for the preliminary bombardment of the
Spanish land positions, and as soon as the troops started ashore in open
boats, correspondents Lyman, Mitchell, and Dunning were landed to
report the army advance on Santiago. Diehl subsequently reinforced
them with Thompson, Martin, Goudie, and Beach, who still wore a
bandage from the wound at Guantánamo. It was Lyman's last assignment. He contracted yellow fever and died upon returning to the States
after the fall of Santiago.

Four days after the landing at Daiquiri, Dunning was pushing
forward through dense tropical undergrowth with the Rough Riders
of Colonel Leonard Wood and Theodore Roosevelt. A blazing sun
beat down and the sweating troops discarded piece after piece of equipment as they pressed on along the narrow tortuous trail. There was no
sign of the enemy and the tangled mass of trees, vines, high grass, and
chaparral crowded close to the path. Men began to drop under the
intense heat. The trail grew steeper as the column neared Las Guásimas.
Dunning plodded in the van not far from Roosevelt. It was a perfect

place for an ambush. Suddenly from a thicket a Mauser cracked, and another, and another.

"It's up to us, boys!" shouted Roosevelt.

"Deploy, lie down!" Wood called along the line of the Rough Riders, and Krag-Jörgenson carbines began to rattle. It was the regiment's first experience in battle and Dunning saw some men waver as comrades dropped wounded or dying. For an hour the fighting raged. Then reinforcements came up and the whole line swept forward in a charge which routed the Spaniards.

Dunning hurried back to find the army base at Siboney seething with erroneous reports of the action at Las Guásimas. Colonel Wood had been killed. The Rough Riders were being wiped out. Stragglers had brought in fantastic stories. The *Wanda* had just arrived offshore and Dunning got aboard to begin writing his account of the first major fighting of the campaign. By the time the yacht made a fast run to Guantánamo he had four hundred words ready for filing in the section of the Cuba-Haiti cable which the navy had seized. Then the *Wanda* pointed her bow into the teeth of a tropical storm and set out for Jamaica. Through the night Dunning wrote additional details while the sea threatened to engulf the buffeted vessel. The dispatch was ready when they arrived and with it went the only accurate list of dead and wounded published until official reports were released after the war.

Las Guásimas was merely a prelude. On July 1 the American forces began their attack on the blockhouses and outer works of Santiago. Diehl had Beach, Thompson, and Mitchell on the firing line throughout the fighting which added the names of El Caney and San Juan Hill to American military history. The Spanish swept the American lines with a hail of bullets from fortified positions, Cervera turned the heavy guns of the fleet on the advancing troops, and sharpshooters hidden in treetops picked off men like flies.

5

Back in the States newspaper circulations climbed dizzily and the nation reveled in a delirium of flag-waving patriotism. The war brought with it the day of shrieking headlines—nowhere shriller than in New York. Battling to outdo one another, some papers turned front pages into typographical nightmares. Larger and larger type was used until the big block letters were four inches high. When the blackest ink seemed inadequate to scream the latest sensation, drums of red were rolled into pressrooms and even gaudier headlines appeared.

The biggest news of the war, however, was yet to come. On July 3 the blockading American fleet off Santiago prepared for Sunday morning inspection. On the bridge of the battleship *Brooklyn*, Correspondent Graham chatted with Commodore Schley. Off to the east the *Dauntless* and the *Wanda* rose easily in calm seas. With Dunning aboard, the *Wanda* was just back from the Jamaica cable and fortunate to be back at all. Port authorities had threatened to quarantine her for three days because of the prevalence of yellow fever in Cuba. Diehl, alarmed lest his dispatch fleet be tied up, stayed behind to cable Associated Press offices in London instructions to appeal to the British Cabinet for an order exempting his boats from the Jamaican regulations.

It was a perfect Sunday with a blue sky and a hot sun. Graham talked on with the commodore. Then a voice bawled: "The enemy ships are coming out!" The Spanish fleet, bottled up in Santiago harbor for weeks, was steaming out. It was led by Admiral Cervera's flagship, the *Maria Theresa*.

Schley grabbed his binoculars.

"Come on, my boy," he exclaimed to Graham. "We'll give it to them now!"

Orders exploded like a string of firecrackers. Bells jangled.

"Clear ship for action!"

"Signal, 'The enemy is escaping!'"

"Signal the fleet to clear ship!"

With Graham at his heels, Schley went up the ladder to the conning tower. Midway he pulled out a watch—one he had borrowed from Graham a few days ago.

"It's just 9:35," he said.

The guns of the American fleet roared into action. The tornado of sound on the *Brooklyn* almost deafened Graham. Through glasses he could see the harbor mouth choked with black smoke from the enemy's funnels and the brilliant yellow splashes of flame from exploding American shells. The escaping Spaniards turned westward in column. They were going to run for it.

While Graham watched from the *Brooklyn* and a hurtling storm of shot and shell churned the waters, the *Wanda* and the *Dauntless* came steaming into the zone of fire, maneuvering recklessly with the fleet to get the best possible view. So close was the *Wanda* that she was able to save an officer and eight sailors from a Spanish torpedo-boat destroyer which was sinking under heavy gunfire. The rescued officer startled Dunning by kissing him on both cheeks.

Before long Cervera's flagship was disabled and caught fire, and the Spanish admiral himself was picked up from the sea by the U.S.S. *Gloucester*. Dunning boarded her to interview the dripping enemy commander. Although Cervera had lost almost all his clothes, his composure was unshaken and he told briefly from a Spanish viewpoint the story of the battle that still raged.

To the west, at the head of the column, the *Brooklyn* and the *Oregon* kept pouring a devastating fire into the fleeing vessels which had escaped destruction in the terrific first hour of fighting. On the *Brooklyn* Graham stood with several others just in front of the conning tower from which Commodore Schley was directing the action. In the group with the correspondent was a seaman who was taking the enemy's range.

"It's twelve hundred yards, sir," the sailor called to Schley.

Graham heard a thud on the deck beside him and warm blood spattered his face and clothes. Before him sprawled a shapeless heap—the seaman who had been calling out the range a moment before. A Spanish shell had decapitated him.

At 1:15 P.M. that July 3, 1898, the ensign of Spain fluttered down in surrender on the last ship of Cervera's fleet. The *Wanda* came up in time to witness the final act of the victory. Then, after collecting the stories written by the men on the *Dauntless*, Graham on the *Brooklyn*, and Goode on the *New York*, the yacht made her run to the Jamaica cable.

Dunning, who had woven all the accounts into one complete story while en route, stepped ashore at Jamaica at 1 A.M. July 4. Diehl met him with news that the dispatch boat of one of the New York papers had arrived an hour before.

"We are beaten," Dunning said wearily. Diehl thought so too until he learned that the whole Spanish fleet had been destroyed. His dejection immediately vanished. The rival boat had left the battle after only two enemy ships had been sunk.

But that rival correspondent intended to do everything to protect his time advantage on the news of the battle's start. As soon as his first "urgent" story had been cleared, he filed a long unimportant dispatch at low press rates to hold the cable exclusively. Diehl was equal to the emergency. He served notice on the cable company that, if it failed to accept Dunning's story at the "urgent" rate of $1.67 a word as soon as the special's first story had been transmitted, he would sue for damages. The threat was effective and Dunning's complete story

GOUDIE PUT ON PEASANT CLOTHES AND JOINED A CROWD OF REFUGEES.

of Santiago was promptly put on the cable. At the urgent rate, the tolls were $8,000.

6

The naval victory at Santiago virtually ended the war. The city of Santiago surrendered on July 17 and an Associated Press correspondent preceded the troops into the city despite refusal of military authorities to permit newspapermen to enter before the formal occupation took place. The correspondent was Alfred C. Goudie. When permission was denied, Goudie, who spoke both Spanish and French, put on peasant clothes and joined a crowd of Cuban refugees who were being allowed to return to their homes in the city. Carrying a parrot cage on one arm and on the other a baby entrusted him by a tired mother, Goudie passed through the lines without being stopped. Once in the city, he filed three thousand words describing the arrangements for the surrender, the march of refugees, the plight of the city, and the approach of the American forces.

The press corps had been much depleted by that time. Of the two hundred correspondents who had landed with the troops in June to cover operations ashore, only nine remained. Three of them—Goudie, Martin, and Thompson—represented The Associated Press. The vicissitudes of campaigning, the tropical climate, and the peril of yellow fever had driven the others home.

Thompson stayed on for four years, and in 1902, when the American flag was hauled down from the palace in Havana and the flag of the new independent Cuban Republic hoisted in its place he wrote such a brilliant description of the occasion that the Congress of the United States by joint resolution unanimously ordered it printed in the *Congressional Record* as the official history of the event.

With the fall of Santiago, national interest shifted to the final drives against Spain in Puerto Rico and the Philippines, where other correspondents were on the scene.

The guns which started to rumble on other fronts drowned out the navy's parting shots off Santiago. Several days after the destruction of Cervera's fleet the U.S.S. *Potomac* sighted a small craft near the wreck of one of the Spanish warships. The suspicious gunboat opened fire and three shots splashed perilously close to the little target. Then the officers saw the attacked vessel break out her pennant.

The last three "careless" shots of the war off Santiago had been fired at the *Cynthia*—one of the five dispatch boats of The Associated Press.

XVI. THE NEW CENTURY

I

THE second that comes once every hundred years had arrived. It was January 1, 1900, and there was the clink of many glasses and the echo of hopeful toasts. For all the optimism and rejoicing, however, it was a disturbed world that greeted the new century. In the South African veld black clouds of disaster trailed British arms in their war with the stubborn Boers. In far-off China the stage was set for the Boxer uprising. From Berlin came a dispatch saying Kaiser Wilhelm had chosen the first day of the new century to deliver a strident, sabre-rattling speech to his garrison officers.

The turn of the century found The Associated Press of Illinois growing stronger. Nevertheless, the organization was apprehensive over the outcome of litigation which struck at the very purpose and spirit of its existence. One of its own member papers had brought a lawsuit charging that its charter and by-laws were unconstitutional. An adverse decision would destroy the hard-won gains realized after the long, bitter struggle against the peril of a commercial news trust and might so impair the character of the association as to kill it.

Curiously enough, this legal threat was an outgrowth of something entirely foreign to the field of news—the defeated efforts of a Chicago utility magnate to obtain, without adequately compensating the city, a fifty-year extension of his street railway franchises.

Charles T. Yerkes for years had been able by devious ways to obtain whatever he wanted from the corrupt majority of the Chicago city council. But finally the indignant public, backed by all the city's newspapers, rose up in arms to fight him. A citizens' league was formed. In the forefront of the fight was Victor Lawson. His Chicago *Daily News* editorially assailed the corruption which Yerkes had exploited and his checkbook gave support to the forces crusading for honesty in government.

Yerkes realized he could not count upon the venal members of the city council to do his bidding unless they had the encouragement of an outspoken champion. He needed a newspaper to advocate his cause.

With the press of Chicago arrayed against him, there was only one way to get such support. On November 21, 1897, the none too successful Chicago *Inter-Ocean* announced that a "party of Chicago gentlemen" headed by Charles T. Yerkes, had purchased the paper. Equally significant was the statement that George Wheeler Hinman was the new editor. Hinman came direct from the staff of the most implacable of Associated Press enemies, Laffan's New York *Sun*.

The policy of the *Inter-Ocean* immediately changed. At the outset Hinman declared editorially that the twofold platform of the new management was to "oppose the Chicago newspaper trust"—the anti-Yerkes publications—and to advocate the supplying of Associated Press news to any and all papers applying for it.

Hinman quickly singled out Lawson as the one man in the city pre-eminently identified with both the causes the *Inter-Ocean* was attacking. As owner of the Chicago *Daily News* he was the most prominent anti-Yerkes publisher and as President of The Associated Press he personified all that the organization represented. Here was a target and on it Hinman concentrated his fire.

In the beginning the broadsides were against Lawson personally and as a Chicago publisher. There were baseless charges that he sought to profit at the city's expense in a schoolsite land "grab," and Hinman sneeringly dubbed him "Rice Water Lawson" because of the free nursing care which the *Daily News* provided for sick children from tenement districts. Then Lawson's Associated Press affiliations were introduced into the civic tempest, and on December 2, 1897, Hinman wrote:

It is well to remind our readers that Mr. Rice Water Lawson is the soul of the newspaper trust of this city, that the sandbagging methods adopted by him in his editorial capacity have become the methods of the trust, largely through his influence, and that as President of The Associated Press he has striven to bolster monopoly and bolster the boycott, even to the point of dictating the sources of information to which the newspapers of the country shall turn. Do the people of Chicago regard a man of his ways and means as the one to dictate the selection, suppression and manipulation of the news of this great country, city and state?

The next day Hinman, ignoring the fact that the *Inter-Ocean* was a member, further assailed The Associated Press of Illinois and spoke acidly of Lawson, "wrapped in the cloak of religion, exhaling the odor of sanctity." This time Melville Stone's name figured in the diatribe. The *Inter-Ocean* declared:

The leader of the [Associated Press] gang is Mr. Rice Water Lawson; his henchman and accomplice is Melville E. Stone. To suit the personal and financial interests of these two men the news of the country has been misinterpreted, mangled and suppressed.

Abuse and attack, whether directed at him personally or at The Associated Press, left Lawson unruffled. In his judgment, the only intelligent way of dealing with Hinman was to ignore him. Much earlier he had told Yerkes that the *Daily News* would treat him and his utility enterprises impartially and fairly in its news columns. On one occasion he even wrote the traction company head that, if he changed his methods, the *Daily News* would be "quite as ready to commend you as we now are to criticize." Discussing one of Hinman's denunciations, Lawson commented:

The attacks of the Inter-Ocean on The Associated Press are quite consistent with the personal antecedents of the new editor and the personal feeling of the new ownership. I do not imagine that the New York Sun and the Chicago Inter-Ocean can hurt The Associated Press.

The municipal battle continued until April, 1898, and the anti-Yerkes forces emerged victorious. The utilities operator failed to get his franchise extension and soon left Chicago after disposing of his traction interests and his newspaper. Hinman, however, stayed on as the controlling power on the *Inter-Ocean* and there was no diminution of his condemnation of the Illinois association and its president.

Lawson was wrong, however, when he said he did not believe Hinman and his former associates on the New York *Sun* could hurt The Associated Press. He had underestimated the power for discord which existed in the Chicago *Inter-Ocean* by virtue of its Associated Press membership. Hinman's editorial hostility could be ignored indefinitely, but when he carried his fight into the courts the situation immediately assumed a serious character.

The trouble actually began before the elections which ended Yerkes's power. At Hinman's direction, the *Inter-Ocean* had been using dispatches syndicated by the Laffan News Bureau which had continued since the disappearance of the old United Press. During the bitter news war of 1893-1897 the Laffan bureau had been pronounced "antagonistic" to the co-operative, and all members were enjoined against subscribing to it. As soon as the Laffan dispatches were noticed in the *Inter-Ocean*, General Manager Stone pointed out to Hinman that their use was a violation of the agreement under which the paper enjoyed its Associated Press membership. Hinman showed his defiance by contracting for a complete special service.

Such a challenge could not go ignored and the directors of The Associated Press met it by invoking the penalty provided by the by-laws—the suspension of the news report received by the offender. The *Inter-Ocean*, however, had anticipated this action and, before it could be taken, Hinman went into the state courts for an injunction restraining The Associated Press from stopping the news report or enforcing the terms of its contract.

The paper argued the corporate charter of The Associated Press of Illinois was so worded that it made the organization, in effect, a public utility, obligated to give its service without discrimination to any newspaper which sought it. The *Inter-Ocean* maintained further that The Associated Press, by forbidding its members to obtain news from "antagonistic" sources, acted in restraint of trade and therefore unlawfully. In reply, The Associated Press contended it was a co-operative, not conducted for profit, and therefore had a right to limit and govern its membership.

The Circuit Court upheld The Associated Press. The *Inter-Ocean* was suspended from membership and on May 16, 1898, it was declared antagonistic to The Associated Press. But Hinman carried the fight to the Appellate Court, and when he lost there he appealed to the Supreme Court of Illinois. For almost two years the issue went undecided, and the resultant uncertainty colored the outlook in 1900.

2

From the date of the organization of The Associated Press of Illinois—on December 15, 1892—it was inevitable that sooner or later its basic membership principle would be subjected to a rigorous test. There always was the likelihood that an ineligible paper would resort to legal action in an effort to force admission to membership, and there was the other possibility that a member paper such as the *Inter-Ocean*, disciplined for a major violation of the by-laws, might seek to compel the resumption of its suspended report.

Lawson, Driscoll, Knapp, and the others responsible for the evolution of The Associated Press of Illinois believed their theory of organization fundamentally sound. The association was to be made up only of those papers elected to membership and to be governed by those papers. Its news report would stem from two main sources—the mutual exchange of the local news collected by the member papers themselves, and the news gathered by the correspondents of The Associated Press throughout the world. The cost of obtaining and disseminating the report would be borne pro rata by the members, and finances would be administered on a strictly non-profit basis. The purity of the news—such an important factor in the controversy with the defunct United Press and, earlier, with the old New York Associated Press—would be protected by the independence of the active management and by the very diversity of political, social, and religious beliefs among the members receiving the reports.

As with any co-operative, the association would be a defensive and offensive alliance, acting for the benefit of those who enjoyed its privileges, and in this connection certain precautionary measures were necessary. Among these was the right of a member to protest the admission of too many other papers in the same city.

The protest right had a twofold purpose: It served not only to protect existing enterprise but also to exclude financially and editorially irresponsible publications in an era when fly-by-night newspapers were all too common. Many times the Board of Directors wisely overruled protests emanating from selfish motives and admitted desirable papers. A number of times, too, protest rights were sustained, particularly where the paper's financial stability figured in the challenge.

In his attacks Hinman repeatedly denounced the organization as a "monopoly," emphasizing the word which had sinister connotations in the mind of the contemporary public. Lawson realized that nothing could be gained by replying to such charges. The facts spoke for themselves. Far from being a monopoly, The Associated Press was serving roughly one-third of the 2,000-odd newspapers then published in the country. The remainder was supplied by various other news-gathering agencies and most papers appeared quite satisfied.

Under the energetic William M. Laffan, the New York *Sun's* Laffan News Bureau had stepped out boldly after the 1893-1897 strife as a collector of news, serving a sizable list of paying clients. William Randolph Hearst also made arrangements to supply news for his New York *Journal* and San Francisco *Examiner*, as well as others. Still another agency was the Scripps-McRae Press Association, which had for its nucleus four midwestern newspapers owned by Milton McRae and Edward W. Scripps, the latter a brother of the Detroit Scripps so active in the fight against the old United Press.

At the time the United Press went out of existence Edward W.

Scripps had applied for membership in The Associated Press for all his papers. Some of them were in cities in which all available memberships already were taken and Scripps said that, if The Associated Press could not accept all his papers, it could not have any of them. He began the development of his own news service.

Additional services also appeared and, although they were all strictly commercial, operating for profit, their very number provided insurance against monopoly. Moreover, the evolution of The Associated Press had given all the publishers of the country a dependable yardstick by which the truth, accuracy, and cost of any news enterprise could be quickly and honestly measured.

But the courts moved slowly. During the first week of 1900 Secretary of State John Hay made news, announcing completion of negotiations for the "open door" in China. The $35,000,000 contract for New York's first subway was awarded. Then on February 19 the Supreme Court of the State of Illinois handed down the long-awaited decision in the *Inter-Ocean* case.

The decision was a thunderbolt. Hinman and the *Inter-Ocean* won a smashing victory. On every major point the court found against The Associated Press. Its foes were jubilant, but hundreds of papers over the country—non-members of the co-operative as well as members—printed editorials deploring the decision out of which might come another news monopoly. Ignoring the ruling of the Illinois Supreme Court, a similar case in Missouri shortly thereafter was declared in favor of The Associated Press.

However, the court of the association's home state had spoken. The hasty and loose language used in 1892 when the nonprofit co-operative was formed had proved its legal undoing. The sweeping decision cited the fatal portion of the corporate charter which included among the organization's purposes the right "to erect, lease, or sell telegraph or telephone lines." Although this right never had been exercised, the court ruled that it gave The Associated Press of Illinois the nature of a public utility and in consequence the organization was legally bound to supply, without distinction, any persons "who wish to purchase information and news, for purposes of publication, which it was created to furnish." All the damage, immediate and potential, was in that sweeping ruling.

It was of minor importance that the decision also struck at the "antagonistic" section of the by-laws. The court held that provision to be in restraint of trade and declared it null and void.

The Associated Press sought in vain for a rehearing of the case while the victorious *Inter-Ocean* took steps to realize everything it believed the decision guaranteed. The paper applied for reinstatement as a member, sought a receiver for the association, sued for indemnification of alleged losses sustained during the period of suspension, and petitioned for an injunction to prevent dissolution of The Associated Press of Illinois in the event the organization so attempted to escape the result of the protracted court fight. Papers hitherto excluded began to press for admission on the strength of the decision, and legal actions against the co-operative multiplied.

3

It was a disheartened membership that convened in Chicago on May 16, 1900, to hear the formal reports on the stunning setback and to consider what was to be done. Nominally, the members still were masters of their association, but it was debatable for how long. The spirit, concept, and purpose of the organization had been dramatically altered by legal fiat, and it was likely that the mechanics of operation would have to change accordingly.

It was apparent that the membership was unwilling to continue on that basis. All recommendations for the amendment of the by-laws were rejected. Individual publishers said what they thought. They had fought a bitter war to organize a press association free of the evils which had beset news gathering in the past. Many of them had pledged personal fortunes and had contributed unsparingly of time and energy in the struggle. When the hard-won victory finally came, they thought they had earned recognition for the principles they served. Now their gains had been swept away or jeopardized. Some urged the preservation of the spirit and methods of the association, but in the mesh of existing legal entanglements they frankly acknowledged uncertainty as to how that could be accomplished.

When the time came for the annual election of officers, some significant things happened. Victor Lawson declined re-election as president. Melville Stone resigned as general manager. Other officers withdrew their names from nomination. The men who had guided The Associated Press of Illinois through a great news-war revolution had mapped their plans.

Charles Knapp, of the St. Louis *Republic*, absent on account of illness, was elected president to succeed Lawson, and Diehl was name general manager to replace Stone. Writing to Knapp the next day, Lawson hinted of the strategy in preparation:

I understand that certain ex-directors and other people of their kind are pursuing their machinations at this moment within the corporate limits of Chicago with the fell purpose of doing disrespect to our Supreme Court. All of which grieves me much. I am guessing that the developments of the near future will bring us face to face again in New York.

That same week all newsdom knew the steps that were being taken. On May 22, 1900, a certificate of incorporation of a technically new association, bearing The Associated Press name, was filed in New York. It carried the signatures of Stephen O'Meara, of the Boston *Journal*, Adolph S. Ochs, of the New York *Times*, St. Clair McKelway, of the Brooklyn *Eagle*, William L. McLean, of the Philadelphia *Bulletin*, Frank B. Noyes, of the Washington *Star*, and Alfred H. Belo, of the Dallas *News*. So, by coincidence, six papers were represented in this fresh start, as six papers had been represented in the beginning in 1848.

New York had a law applying specifically to co-operative and non-profit organizations and the decision of Lawson and his group had been made to seek incorporation under that statute. This time, however, the legal technicalities received the most thoroughgoing attention. The incorporators were determined not only to avoid the pitfalls which had made the *Inter-Ocean* suit possible, but also to correct the defects and inequities which had manifested themselves in the structure of The Associated Press of Illinois. Great care was taken to make the membership character of the organization so specific as to admit of no contention. The certificate of incorporation, after first describing how newspapers might be elected to membership, stipulated plainly:

No person not so elected shall have any right or interest in the corporation or enjoy any of the privileges or benefits thereof.

Another unequivocal expression of policy was:

The corporation is not to make a profit or to make or declare dividends, and is not to engage in the business of selling intelligence nor traffic in the same.

This phrased a cardinal principle of the new policy—that the members would co-operate in gathering the news of the world for their mutual benefit, each contributing his respective share and each defraying his portion of the total cost; they would not buy their news from the association, but would be part owners, each with an equal voice in all Associated Press affairs.

There were other important changes in the constitution. In the Illinois organization memberships had been divided into two classes of unequal rights and privileges. This distinction was eliminated. The incorporators decided against the issuance of capital stock for financing the association, as had been done in 1892. Instead they substituted first-mortgage bonds, for which the membership might subscribe in varying amounts.

Not unexpectedly, Melville E. Stone was designated general manager and he was soon busy sending out invitations to membership.

4

A special meeting of The Associated Press of Illinois was called in Chicago, September 12, 1900, and by unanimous vote it was decided to disincorporate. The details connected with the dissolution required time, so the Board of Directors was empowered to take the necessary step to close out the business. Significantly, the directors were specifically authorized to dispose of the organization's news-gathering facilities to "such other news association, as, in the opinion of the Board of Directors, it is deemed wise to have relations with." The way was cleared for the legal transfer of the essential working equipment to The Associated Press which was ready to carry on the traditions of the service.

The Chicago meeting was, to all intents and purposes, the actual finale of The Associated Press of Illinois. Legally it continued in existence several months more during which time the directors, among other things, paid $40,500 to the *Inter-Ocean* to satisfy its claims and to effect a dismissal of additional suits brought by that paper and the New York *Sun*.

To lead the transformed Associated Press, the Board of Directors chose as president Frank Brett Noyes, the 37-year-old Washington *Star* executive who had taken such a decisive role in the struggle with United Press and whose influence had helped the reorganization. He was young for this important job, considering the number of older men available. Moreover, some observers considered him too daring because the Washington *Star* printed society and sports news in unprecedented volume. But time proved otherwise.

Quiet, austere, and judicial, Noyes already commanded the respect of the membership at large. They knew he had an unswerving devotion to the best interests of news gathering and that, under him, The Associated Press would scrupulously discharge its mission. Time and again he declared: "News must be non-partisan in its highest sense. It must have no tinge of bias whether political, economic or religious. It must neither advocate nor oppose causes." In view of the public trust which reposed in the press, he believed that no individual had the right to impose any sort of censorship, direct or indirect, upon the free dissemination of public intelligence.

"And," he said, "I don't care whether that man is the nation's ruler, the head of a news agency, or the publisher of an individual paper. Newspapers are business enterprises, and they must make money to survive, but any newspaper that distorts news, or resorts to that even more deadly form of distortion—suppression of essential facts—has no more right to continued existence than any other business enterprise which persistently defrauds its customers."

The Associated Press of Illinois delivered its last news report on September 3, 1900. The next day, over the same wires, the new Associated Press started the first dispatches of the transformed service. The change-over was challenged. Court action was instituted on behalf of some non-member papers, attacking the legality of the transfer to New York. It was some time before the matter was adjudicated, but the verdict upheld the right of Associated Press members to take the course they had followed. The Associated Press of Illinois, the decision stated, was under no obligation to continue when it found it could not achieve its proper purposes under the laws of that state. The association likewise was free to dispose of all its property and there was nothing to bar its former members from incorporating the successor association in New York, which in turn acquired that property.

After years of slow evolution and battle, The Associated Press had reached its goal as the world's only non-profit, co-operative news-gathering organization. The ideal of truth in news had emerged and the association dedicated to that ideal now stood on solid ground.

I. PEACE AND PROPAGANDA

I

BUNDLED in a heavy overcoat, Guglielmo Marconi, then a young man of twenty-seven, moved about giving orders while a huge kite strained at its cord of wire in the high winds over Newfoundland. It was Saturday, December 21, 1901.

There had already been three failures. On Tuesday Marconi and his assistants had flown their first kite but they had not heard signals from the English station at Poldhu in Cornwall. The next day they tried a balloon. Both the balloon and the aerial it supported were carried away in a squall. Then another kite and its aerial were lost, whipped out to sea by the high winds.

By 11:30 that Saturday morning Marconi and his half dozen helpers got a third kite up and the crew paid out the wire until it stretched four hundred feet into the wintry sky. Then they walked back to the barracklike building where a primitive wireless receiving apparatus had been set up. A tense wait began among the jumble of extra supplies—the zinc sheets, gas cylinders, deflated balloons, and spare kites.

For days now, by prearrangement, the experimental station seventeen hundred miles away in Cornwall had been repeating the same test signal—the simplest possible. It was the letter S, three dots in telegraph code.

For almost an hour Marconi sat listening, a single headphone clamped to his ear. The five men watched him. At 12:30 his numbed fingers trembled. The instrument on the table moved almost imperceptibly and the headphone weakly whispered three dots—the letter S! The signal was repeated, once, twice, several times. It was faint but unmistakable.

Marconi was on his feet gesticulating. "Avete sentito? Avete sentito?" he shouted. "Did you hear it? Did you hear it?"

They passed the headphone around and one after another confirmed the signal. Even the fishermen who helped with the kites had their chance to listen. The absence of sending equipment prevented

Marconi from replying. He dashed to the cable office and his jubilant message to co-workers abroad proclaimed that wireless no longer was limited to small distances. It could range the earth!

Marconi's 1901 successes prompted the United States Navy to discontinue the use of pigeons for communications in the fleet and to substitute wireless telegraphy. But before the navy took this step, even before Marconi projected the transatlantic signal test, The Associated Press had employed the inventor and his wireless to report a news event. The story was the first covered by wireless in this country and marked the initial public demonstration of the invention in America. That was in 1899. Marconi had been experimenting in Europe for four years, receiving and sending messages over limited distances. Eager to prove the worth of wireless, he came to America with his equipment stowed in two trunks. At the same time another distinguished visitor arrived. He was the trim, amiable sportsman, Thomas Lipton, here for his first attempt to lift the symbol of international yachting supremacy, the America's Cup.

Marconi had his opportunity to demonstrate wireless in reporting the competition between Lipton's *Shamrock,* and the American *Columbia.* Temporary stations were erected on Long Island and the north Jersey coast, and a fast steam yacht, fitted out with Marconi equipment, was chartered to follow the races. The *Columbia* defeated the English contender in three straight races off Sandy Hook on October 16, 17, and 20, and detailed accounts of the victories were transmitted to the coast stations and relayed by land wires to Associated Press headquarters in New York. The cost exceeded $25,000, a considerable sum in those days for a single story, but the demonstration was highly successful.

A year later Marconi's wireless again assisted The Associated Press in covering the 1900 sailing of the international classic. In 1902, a rival appeared in the person of Lee De Forest, young pioneer of American wireless development. He raised enough money to get from Chicago to New York and offered his services to The Associated Press for reporting the races with equipment he had perfected. General Manager Stone already had contracted with Marconi again and De Forest found employment with one of the commercial agencies.

From a yachting standpoint, the first race went off smoothly enough, but this time the wirelessed news did not fare so well. The Marconi and De Forest boats docked after the finish only to learn that not one understandable word had been received. The two primitive

MARCONI HAD HIS OPPORTUNITY TO DEMONSTRATE WIRELESS . . .

spark sets, operating in such close proximity with their ear-splitting, crackling noise, had set up such a field of interference that they completely jumbled each other's signals.

Later, with Stone's co-operation, the inventor introduced the first regular daily news service on the high seas while conducting experiments on the Cunarder *Lucania*. At the close of each day Stone sent Marconi a summary of important news. Reception was uninterrupted all the way across the Atlantic and the daily news budget Marconi received was posted in the steamer's smoking room.

2

Marconi's experiments during the frigid December days at Newfoundland made 1901 historic in the annals of science, but for America the year marked a national sorrow in President McKinley's assassination on September 6 at the Pan-American Exposition in Buffalo. At the President's side when Leon Czolgosz fired through a handkerchief stood a young string correspondent who had been assigned to cover the reception. The reporter ran to the only telephone in the vicinity and blurted out his story to an editor in the Buffalo bureau. Then, to keep his story exclusive as long as possible, he ripped out all the wires and wrecked the telephone. He thought it an ingenious move until he realized a few minutes later that he had destroyed his own line of communication. It required a full half hour to relay further information from the scene of the assassination.

In 1902 a greater tragedy made the year's big story. The night of May 2 brought the first meager tidings—a telegram from St. Thomas in the Danish West Indies. It reported that Mount Pélee, the volcano on near-by Martinique, was erupting and the town of Saint-Pierre was shrouded in smoke and covered an inch deep with volcanic ashes. All cable communications were broken before The Associated Press could hear from its two correspondents on Martinique, one at Saint-Pierre and the other at Fort-de-France, nine miles away.

Through the night New York headquarters endeavored to devise some way to get the news. Correspondents at St. Vincent, St. Thomas, Puerto Rico, Barbados, Trinidad, and St. Lucia were ordered to send any information which might have reached them, and also to make every effort to reach Martinique. Then Stone discovered that an old newspaper friend, Ayme, was the American consul at Guadeloupe, a small island a dozen miles from Martinique. The general manager appealed to Washington to grant a leave of absence and then cabled the consul to charter a boat for Martinique.

All the way from Guadeloupe Ayme's boat navigated through a thick cloud of falling ashes and cinders. It was a dangerous night trip and when the boat finally reached Saint-Pierre, Ayme was aghast at what he saw. The entire population of the town, some thirty thousand, had been buried under the burning mass of hot ashes, and among the victims was the regular correspondent that New York had tried so hard to reach. Saint-Pierre was a charnel house and even Ayme's long newspaper experience did not immunize him to the horror he found. He began to assemble the story. He was joined presently by the correspondent from Fort-de-France, José Ivanes, who had escaped unhurt, and together these two men worked in the blazing cinders. Ayme pieced the narrative together as his boat dashed back to Guadeloupe.

Stone called the story "worthy of the younger Pliny," who wrote the classic description of the destruction of Pompeii and Herculaneum.

3

The performance of The Associated Press during those first few years of the new century spoke well for the administration of the new organization, but General Manager Stone was dissatisfied with one important phase of the report, the propaganda in and the censorship of European news.

An autumn day in 1902 found him in Paris, walking briskly toward the Quai d'Orsay. The minister of foreign affairs, M. Théophile Delcassé, was expecting him.

With the end of the Spanish-American War, the United States emerged as a modern world power and Stone noticed the heightened interest of Americans in international affairs. Nevertheless, correspondents abroad still labored under great handicaps. In some countries there was the strictest censorship, in others there was unofficial yet none the less rigid regulation, and almost everywhere in Europe there was the hopeless drawback of government-controlled telegraph systems which delayed or withheld America-bound dispatches.

The co-operative had competent American correspondents in some European capitals and in several of the more important cities, but the twin handicaps of censorship and poor telegraphic service had defeated attempts to gather European news at first hand. M. Jules Cambon, the French ambassador at Washington, expressed concern over the need for faster, more adequate news from France and Stone tactfully reminded him of the obstacles France herself interposed. The Republic had no formal censorship, but it achieved the same effect by refusing correspondents access to the news of many of its most important departments. Service of the government-controlled telegraph was so poor that it frequently took a dispatch six or seven hours to get from a provincial city to Paris, and there the story was likely to encounter a like delay before being routed to the United States.

The ambassador's desire to help improve conditions gave Stone his first chance. Cambon forwarded Stone's views and added his own opinion that, if the news of France could be collected and written by unhindered Associated Press correspondents, relations between the two nations would benefit.

Stone's reception at the Quai d'Orsay was cordial. M. Delcassé manifested much interest and appeared well informed. He listened attentively as Stone cited numerous instances when correspondents had filed dispatches only to have them thrown aside by a clerk in a government telegraph office until all government, commercial, even family death telegrams first had been cleared.

M. Delcassé assured Stone he was in agreement that the situation was bad. However, one could understand that it would be an extremely serious matter to make changes. The minister of foreign affairs apologized, but it was something he must first discuss with his confrères, especially with the minister of telegraphs. He would do that immediately and would like Stone to have breakfast with him the next morning so that he might meet the other members of the Cabinet.

The breakfast was served in M. Delcassé's private room in the palace set apart for the Department of Foreign Affairs. Stone's attention was attracted by a piece of furniture in the apartment—an old mahogany table—and he was told that it had played an important part in American history three times. On it three documents had been signed: the agreement by which Benjamin Franklin had obtained financial aid from France for the struggling thirteen colonies; the treaty of peace which ended the War of 1812; lastly, the treaty which brought to a close the Spanish-American War of 1898. The discussion turned temporarily to historical subjects, but when it returned to news, Stone spoke out.

"If The Associated Press is to gather the news of France at first hand," he told the ministers, "then our correspondents must be absolutely free and there must be no attempt to influence them. I understand, of course, that in order to be useful the representative of The Associated Press accredited to any capital must be on friendly terms with the government at that capital, but under no consideration will he be a servile agent of that government. The Associated Press will not surrender the right to free and accurate statement of the news, and anything the association may do in the future must be done with the distinct understanding that the government of France will not attempt to influence the impartial character of the service. If the French government can see its way to expedite our dispatches on the state telegraph system, if it will throw open all departments of the government to us so we can obtain the facts, then I shall be very glad to establish a full-sized bureau in Paris and take all our French news from Paris direct."

Things moved slowly in the Paris of 1902 and Stone saw it would be some time before action, if any, was taken. So he returned to America.

One day less than a month later, a bulky communication reached him in New York. It was from M. Delcassé.

First and foremost, the French government pledged that its officials henceforth would supply representatives of the co-operative with all pertinent information. Officials would answer any questions that might be of interest to the United States and would do everything in their power to expedite the news thus obtained. To eliminate delays, the Ministry of Telegraphs had prepared three special blanks for the exclusive use of The Associated Press. The first, which had "Associated Press" printed across its face in red ink, was for routine stories and took precedence over everything but government telegrams. The second, bearing the inscription "Associated Press, très pressé," was for more important matter and assured transmission immediately after any government message then on the wire. The third, labeled "Associated Press, *urgent*," was for news of outstanding importance and superseded all other telegrams.

4

The success of this system so pleased the French Foreign Office that it offered to assist Stone in the plans he already had in mind to break down the barriers in other countries. During his conferences with M. Delcassé the general manager had mentioned the possibility of treating with Italy and Spain on the same subject. Accordingly, as soon as the reforms were effected in France, the minister of foreign affairs suggested that Stone might find the moment opportune to approach the other two governments. To be helpful, he issued instructions to the French ambassador at the Quirinal to pursue the matter with Italian authorities.

So in 1903 Stone went abroad once again. Italy had been tried by a disastrous Ethiopian War and the assassination of a king since he had been there as a tourist after he left the Chicago *News*. The new monarch, Victor Emmanuel III, and dominant Giovanni Giolitti held the reins of government.

Stone learned that the French ambassador, M. Barrère, had done much to prepare the way for him. The first solution offered was to have correspondents in Italy send dispatches on the government-owned telegraph to the border for relay on the French wires to Paris. That would improve matters somewhat, but there was a better way—sending the dispatches direct from Rome to New York. Stone said so in his conference with officials of the Italian Foreign Office and then came a command to an audience with the King.

The conversation between Stone and Victor Emmanuel was without formality, but it soon reached a delicate point. Rome, in effect, was the capital of two sovereigns—Victor Emmanuel, temporal ruler of Italy, and Leo XIII, spiritual head of the Catholic Church. For years relations between the government and the papacy had been strained—it would be more than a quarter of a century before they were satisfactorily adjusted—and the pontiffs during that period remained voluntary "prisoners" in the Vatican. Stone realized that the man he placed in charge of a Rome Bureau he planned to establish would be in a difficult position because it would be necessary for him to be persona grata both at the Quirinal and at the Vatican.

He voiced his thoughts frankly and Victor Emmanuel assured him that he entertained nothing but the kindliest of personal feelings toward the Pope. Of course, officially, the Quirinal and the Vatican were estranged, but the estrangement should not hamper the co-operative.

A few days after his audience with the King, Stone was received at the Vatican by the ageing Pope who had reigned since 1878. They talked for an hour.

Then he opened the new Rome Bureau, and the man he picked to head it was Salvatore Cortesi, who had been doing part-time work there for The Associated Press since the mid-nineties.

5

A few weeks later Stone was in Berlin. He had met Kaiser Wilhelm's brother, Prince Henry of Prussia, during the latter's visit to the United States in 1902, and he was "commanded" to attend a special Ordenfest given by the Emperor. After the banquet Stone was summoned to an anteroom for his private audience with the Kaiser.

The Kaiser gave the general manager assurances he would issue the necessary orders to place The Associated Press in a satisfactory position in Germany as regarded both censorship and prompt transmission. He turned the details over to Postmaster General Sydow who agreed on a small red label bearing the word: "America." Pasted on a press message anywhere in the Fatherland, it guaranteed the telegram first place on all wires.

That same year the association's new European organization received its first major test. It came almost before Cortesi had become settled as chief of the Rome Bureau and, because of the nature of the event, it caused the Italian government to proclaim a special censorship. In the silence of the Vatican Pope Leo XIII lay dying. At the time of his election as pontiff everyone had expected his reign to be short. He, himself, had jested while being robed on that occasion: "Hurry, or I shall die before you have finished." That was a quarter of a century earlier and he had lived to bury all but one of the cardinals who participated in the conclave which selected him. Now, however, the end was at hand and the Italian government notified all correspondents that no dispatch of the Pope's passing could be transmitted for two hours after his death. This was to permit the Vatican sufficient time to notify papal legates in other lands.

Ever since he had begun work for The Associated Press in the nineties, Cortesi had cultivated sources and contacts in the Vatican. For ten years he had paid weekly visits to Dr. Giuseppe Lapponi, the Pope's personal physician, and the two men had become close friends. He also had made it a point to become acquainted with the Pope's relatives outside the Vatican and as many members of the papal household as possible, until he had a small army of unofficial reporters ready for any emergency.

Leo XIII fell ill during the intolerably hot Rome weather of July. Some of the organization's best correspondents immediately were ordered to Cortesi's aid, among them William A. M. Goode, who had been on Admiral Sampson's flagship during the Spanish-American

War, and Charles T. Thompson, the new chief of the Paris Bureau. They found Cortesi had the situation well in hand. In spite of official silence on what was happening in the sickroom, he was able to report every detail during the eighteen days of the Pope's illness.

The world followed the hourly accounts with anxious suspense. In the United States both Protestant and Catholic churches offered prayers for recovery. To show the importance of quick coverage, Stone cabled Cortesi an account of these services and the correspondent transmitted the message to the Vatican where Monsignor della Chiesa—the future Benedict XV—showed it to Leo XIII. The sinking Pope scanned it with dim eyes and exclaimed: "I die satisfied, as this shows that my idea of the reunion of all Christian churches is not a dream."

Tension increased as the end neared and for weeks Cortesi had been perfecting a plan whereby he not only hoped to have the news promptly, but also—and this was hardly less important—to be able to transmit it to "Melstone, Newyork," the cable address of the general manager.

The last day came. In the little Vatican room a Pope passed away. Then there was an age-old ceremony to be observed. Before the Pope could be declared officially dead, his private physician first must pass a lighted candle before the still lips to show the pontiff breathed no more. Dr. Lapponi stepped into an adjoining room to obtain the candle for the ceremony. It took only a moment to pick up the telephone there and whisper a few words. In the Rome Bureau two miles away, Cortesi heard the few words, wrote down three numbers and dashed out.

Those who braved the blazing heat of that July day stared at the apparently demented man who tore past them in the streets, running for the Central Telegraph Office. He slapped the message on the counter and a perspiring clerk, mystified at the need for such excited haste, read the innocuous words:

```
MELSTONE, NEWYORK
NUMBER MISSING BOND 404
(SIGNED) MONTEFIORE.
```

"Send it all routes," panted Cortesi. "Urgent!"

Nine minutes later The Associated Press in New York learned what no one in Rome and few in the Vatican yet knew. Leo XIII had died at 4:04 P.M. The news was flashed across the United States to San Francisco and from border to border. It went back on the cables to Europe, giving London, Paris, Berlin, even Rome, the first news of the Pope's death.

Stone and Cortesi had prearranged the harmless-appearing code message to circumvent the special censorship. Only the numerals had to be filled in—and the numerals told the precise minute of the Pontiff's passing.

The death of Leo XIII demonstrated the remarkable change which had occurred in the handling of foreign news. When Leo's predecessor died in 1878, only ten lines were carried. On Leo's death the co-operative cabled enough to fill a complete newspaper page, approximately eight thousand words.

6

In America that late summer of 1903 the first automobile crossed the continent in fifty-two days. Joseph Pulitzer gave Columbia University $2,000,000 to found a School of Journalism. Samuel P. Langley failed in his attempt to fly a heavier-than-air machine over the Potomac River. The obstacles blocking the construction of the Panama Canal were at last being surmounted. Nor was news the only thing. Stone's thoughts once more turned toward Europe, this time to Russia.

Up to this time the empire of the Czars had been the despair of news gathering. Every conceivable obstacle was put in the way of correspondents. The censorship was the most stringent in the world. Tolls on the government telegraph were exorbitant and the service itself so slovenly that messages frequently were delayed for days. Until something was done about Russia, The Associated Press could not pretend to supply a complete and accurate news picture of Europe. Previously, however, the time had not seemed propitious to carry the crusade to Muscovy. Now Stone believed the success of his experiment in the other countries would help show Russia the way.

He enlisted the support of Count Cassini, the Russian ambassador at Washington, and also obtained the help of the French and German offices.

It was the dead of winter when he reached St. Petersburg. Bells jingled as droshkies whirled along Nevsky Prospekt. The river Neva was thick with ice and snow blanketed its many islands. An agent whom Stone had met in London had preceded him to the Russian capital so the Czar's ministers might know in advance of the general manager's proposals.

Count Lamsdorff, the Minister of Foreign Affairs, was cordial, but protested he was powerless to give active help. The question of censorship and the telegraph was wholly in the hands of Minister of the Interior Viatscheslav Plehve, who was answerable only to the Czar. Stone met Plehve, who also headed the dread secret police, and his hopes at once suffered a setback. The minister made no secret of the fact that any change in existing conditions might be dangerous in a country harried by assassinations, secret societies, and Nihilist plots to overthrow the government.

"Frankly," he said, "I am not prepared to abolish the censorship. To my mind it would be a very imprudent thing to do. However, I will go as far as I can toward meeting your other wishes."

The telegraph service? The press rate? Plehve promised to make arrangements for dispatches, but of course they could not take precedence over government messages or telegrams from a member of the imperial family. As for the press rate, that unfortunately was not the province of the minister of the interior. Stone would have to consult with the minister of finance.

Shuttled from bureau to bureau, struggling with official red tape and procrastination, Stone's mission seemed hopeless. He talked with the timid foreign censor—who also had time to be government censor of the Russian stage—and found him fearful to pass a single line that might offend anyone.

As the bleak Russian winter grew deeper, Stone slowly began to win a few concessions. Rapidity of transmission first was assured. Next, a satisfactory press rate was negotiated. Then, a little later, two departments agreed to receive the regular correspondent assigned to St. Petersburg. But the citadel of censorship still stood unshaken. Stone was almost ready to confess defeat when, on January 18, 1904, he was asked to an audience with the Czar in the famous Winter Palace.

At the end of a labyrinth of wide halls and endless corridors, lined with guards, functionaries, and attendants, the general manager was ushered into a library to meet the Czar of All the Russias, an unassuming man of thirty-five dressed in the braided white jacket and blue trousers of the navy.

Stone explained the desire of his organization to collect the news of Russia accurately and swiftly and to transmit it to the United States directly from St. Petersburg and not from neighboring nations.

"We come as friends," he said, "and it is my desire that our representatives here shall treat Russia as a friend; but it is the very essence of the proposed plan that we be free to tell the truth. We cannot be the mouthpiece of Russia, we cannot plead her cause, except in so far as telling the truth will do it."

"That," replied the Czar, "is all we could ask of you."

He asked Stone to enumerate the reforms sought.

"It seems to me, your Majesty," Stone said, "that censorship is not only valueless from your own point of view, but works a positive harm. A wall has been built up around the country, and the fact that no correspondent for a foreign paper can live and work here has resulted in a traffic of false Russian news that is most hurtful. Today there are newspapermen in Vienna, Berlin and London who make a living by peddling out the news of Russia, and it is usually false. If we were free to tell the truth in Russia, as we are in other countries, no self-respecting newspaper in the world would print a dispatch from Vienna respecting the internal affairs of Russia, because the editor would know that, if the thing were true, it would come from Russia direct. All you do now is to drive a correspondent to send his dispatches across the German border. I am able to write anything I choose in Russia, and send it by messenger to Wirballen, across the German border, and it will go from there without change. You are powerless to prevent my sending these dispatches, and all you do is to anger the correspondent and make him an enemy, and delay his dispatches, robbing the Russian telegraph lines of a revenue they should receive. So it occurs to me that the censorship is inefficient; that it is a censorship which does not censor, but annoys."

The Czar requested Stone to embody his ideas in a formal memorandum which he might study before issuing any orders. The man's sincerity seemed patent and Stone might have been optimistic had not the monarch been so preoccupied over the crisis in Russia's relations with Japan in the Far East. With the vast empire teetering on the brink of war, Stone knew all too well that his memorandum might be lost in the shuffle.

Little happened that the secret police did not learn and Plehve soon was advised that Stone's memorandum was in the hands of the Czar. Unrelenting in his antagonism to any proposal he considered "revolutionary," he asked Stone to agree to a halfway measure providing for nominal censorship. The suggestion was rejected.

No word came from the Czar and the crisis with Japan hourly grew worse. Stone quit St. Petersburg for a few days in Berlin. There he met the Kaiser again and in a strangely prophetic conversation the German ruler said of Czar Nicholas: "Poor chap. I think he is likely to lose his throne!"

Before Stone got back to St. Petersburg Japan launched a crippling surprise attack on the warships of the Russian Far Eastern squadron at Port Arthur. Two days later the government of the Mikado declared war. Stone foresaw an indefinite wait before he could get a decision from the Czar. He discussed his predicament with Robert McCormick, the American ambassador, and asked him to make inquiries of Count Lamsdorff in the Foreign Office.

The count was surprised when the subject was mentioned.

"Why, the thing is done!" he exclaimed.

"I do not follow you," the ambassador said.

"Mr. Stone left a memorandum of his wishes with his Majesty, did he not? Well, the emperor wrote 'approved' on the corner of the memorandum, and all will be done. There may be a slight delay incident to working out the details, but it will be done."

The news was received with mixed feelings. Stone could rejoice over the victory which the Czar's approval represented, but he was dubious at the mention of "a slight delay incident to working out the details." That might cover a multitude of postponements and give hostile ministers opportunities to circumvent the purpose of the imperial order. But there was nothing to be gained by staying in Russia and Stone had business in Vienna. He departed, leaving the St. Petersburg Bureau in charge of a man he had been training for that assignment. The correspondent was Howard N. Thompson, the same staff man who had won notable recognition for his work in the Spanish-American War and its sequel of Cuban independence.

Stone stepped off the train at Vienna to find a lengthy telegram waiting. It was from Thompson at St. Petersburg and it said:

> I KNOW YOU WILL BE GRATIFIED TO LEARN THAT ON MY RETURN TO THE OFFICE AFTER BIDDING YOU ADIEU, AND BEFORE YOUR FEET LEFT THE SOIL OF ST. PETERSBURG, WE WERE SERVED WITH NOTICE THAT THE CENSORSHIP WAS ABOLISHED SO FAR AS WE WERE CONCERNED. BUT COUNT LAMSDORFF FEELS THAT IT IS A MISTAKE, AND THAT WE SHALL BE CHARGED WITH HAVING MADE A BARGAIN, AND ANY KINDLY THINGS WE MAY SAY OF RUSSIA WILL BE MISCONSTRUED. HE THINKS IT WOULD BE MUCH WISER IF THE CENSORSHIP WERE ABOLISHED AS TO ALL FOREIGN CORRESPONDENTS AND BUREAUS, AND DESIRES YOUR INFLUENCE TO THAT END.

Stone wired back that he was in full agreement with Lamsdorff. The Associated Press had no desire to monopolize this new privilege.

Within forty-eight hours after censorship restrictions were rescinded for The Associated Press, they were rescinded also for all foreign correspondents.

But the world was not standing still. The streets of Tokyo were already resounding to shouts of "Dai Nippon Banzai! Dai Nippon banzai! Banzai, banzai, banzai!" The Mikado's troops were starting for the front, and in Manchuria on the Asiatic mainland the ponderous columns of the Czar were on the march.

Another war demanded reporting.

II. WAR IN THE EAST

I

THERE were strange date lines and strange names on the front pages. Dispatches spoke of Port Arthur, Chemulpo, Chefoo, and the Yellow Sea. Readers struggled with problems of correct pronunciation as they learned about General Kuropatkin, Admiral Vityeft, and the Japanese Kuroki, Nogi, and Togo. The unpredictable limelight of news had fixed upon a new stage and the popular interest of America shifted with it to focus on the clash of Russo-Japanese arms in a distant corner of the Far East.

It was an America of 76,000,000 that read the first scattered war bulletins in February, 1904. The four years that had passed since the transformation of The Associated Press of Illinois into the non-profit co-operative of New York had given the organization time to consolidate its new position. The number of member papers now totaled 648 and the budget for annual operations exceeded $2,000,000. The leased wire network had expanded to 34,000 miles. The news report averaged 60,000 words daily, moving into editorial rooms by Morse at the rate of 35 words a minute.

To General Manager Stone only news of gravity was worthy of notice and he had reproved a youthful member of the Washington staff who made the first slight deviation. Jackson S. Elliott wrote a humorous story about a Congressional fashion plate who had provoked much merriment by appearing absent-mindedly on the Senate floor sporting a tan shoe on one foot and a black one on the other. The story got on the wires while the regular wire editor was at lunch. Although papers from coast to coast seized eagerly on the sprightly piece, Stone called it "too trivial" for the report and issued orders against any repetition. The incident, however, was a straw in the wind.

During Stone's extensive travels for the organization, active command developed on Diehl, Stone's capable right hand. The two men were thousands of miles apart—Stone back in St. Petersburg and Diehl in New York—when the Russo-Japanese War broke, but they were immediately working in unison to complete the mobilization of forces to

175

report the conflict. From the Russian capital, Stone ordered men post-haste to the Far East: Henry J. Middleton of the Paris Bureau, who had done brilliant reporting on the Dreyfus case, Frederick McCormick, Robert M. Collins, Lord Brooke, journalist son of the Earl of Warwick, Kravschenko, an eminent writer who had covered wars in China, and Nicholas E. Popoff, a young Russian who wrote under the name of Kiriloff. To supplement the regular staff, he engaged a number of Russian correspondents to serve as string men for the others. Simultaneously in New York Diehl was issuing assignments which sent another corps to Asia—Paul Cowles, of the San Francisco Bureau, Christian Hagerty, from New York, George Denny, from Chicago, and Richard Smith, who had covered the Boer War.

The power of military censorship made itself felt early, with varying severity. Russia invoked it in the war zone, but its application was not unreasonable and both the men in the field and Thompson in St. Petersburg were able to obtain and transmit their news without difficulties. The Japanese, on the other hand, imposed stifling restrictions. They forbade correspondents with some of the Mikado's armies to send a single line and they hospitably "detained" other newspaper men in Tokyo until the campaigns were well under way.

The focal point of one main Japanese attack was the Russian stronghold of Port Arthur where the Czar's Pacific fleet lay under the protecting guns of the forts. With the Japanese fleet controlling the waters outside the Manchurian port and the first operations all naval in character, it was obvious that some reliable way must be devised to get out uncensored news of the warfare in that whole area. The task fell to Paul Cowles, the Pacific Coast superintendent who had come to the Orient to supervise the news-gathering operations.

A laconic cable gave New York the first inkling of the way Cowles did things. J. R. Youatt, then cashier and later treasurer, blinked when he read the bland message that reached his desk. It was from Cowles:

DRAWING ON YOU FOR $80,000.

This was impossible! Youatt, flabbergasted, went hurrying to Stone, the fantastic cablegram in his hand. Stone, too, exploded.

"The man must be crazy. This is insane. $80,000! Cable him immediately for an explanation. What can Cowles need that amount of money for?"

TO BUY A YACHT.

Succeeding inquiries vindicated Cowles's sanity. Across the Gulf of Pechili—ninety miles from Port Arthur—was the neutral Chinese city of Chefoo where news could be put uncensored on the cable for Shanghai and the United States. Cowles had established headquarters there and he bought the yacht not only to serve as a dispatch boat between Port Arthur and Chefoo but also to provide a means for reporting any naval engagements in that vicinity.

Youatt honored the draft and when the war ended Cowles sold the vessel at a profit.

2

Dispatches from a dozen correspondents gradually brought into outline the strategy dictating the conflict. On land the Japanese aim was a quick decisive victory over the main Russian Army under General Kuropatkin. The Russians were vaguer, delaying decisions until the arrival of endless reinforcements would give them an overwhelming superiority.

But it was apparent that the nation supreme on the sea would be victorious. Admiral Togo had the Czar's Pacific squadron blockaded in Port Arthur, but he was anxious to destroy it piecemeal before arrival of the new enemy fleet which was preparing to come halfway round the world from Europe. The Russian hope was to inflict as much damage as possible without jeopardizing their forces unnecessarily, so that Togo's depleted fleet would be no match for the combined Russian Navy when the new squadron reached Asiatic waters.

After some initial successes, Togo found himself with a foeman of no mean caliber. Admiral Makaroff, a tall, bearded daredevil of a man, took command of the Russian fleet at Port Arthur, and the two Associated Press correspondents there, George Denny and Kravschenko, saw the squadron transformed from a demoralized aggregation into a confident fighting force. Makaroff's torpedo boats harassed Togo, causing considerable losses. Other Russian cruisers, based at Vladivostok, went into action, making the Sea of Japan unsafe for troop transports and shipping. Togo began to sow mines, and Paul Cowles's $80,000 dispatch yacht had to thread dangerous waters between Chefoo and Port Arthur.

Knowing Makaroff's impetuous temperament, Correspondent Kravschenko felt certain that, sooner or later, he would sally forth for a lightning thrust at the enemy when the Japanese fleet was not present in full force. He tried to persuade the admiral to grant him permission to be on board the flagship *Petropavlovsky* when she put out to fight. At first Makaroff was favorably inclined, but he was a quick-tempered person and the two got into a quarrel. The admiral banned Kravschenko from the flagship.

If Kravschenko could not see the action from the bridge of the flagship, he could watch from shore. Golden Hill, outside of Port Arthur, commanded the surrounding waters, and Kravschenko went there on April 10, 1905. For three days and nights he watched distant ships of the Japanese through binoculars. The weather was bleak, with snow squalls and cold winds, and on one night fog was so thick that searchlights of the near-by forts could not pierce it.

It was daybreak on April 13 when Kravschenko picked out a Russian torpedo boat racing for the harbor. Her sister ship had been attacked by one of Togo's flotillas. Makaroff immediately dispatched a cruiser to the aid of the stricken vessel and when another enemy division appeared on the scene, he ordered all available units out against the Japanese. Kravschenko saw them steam out, the *Petropavlovsky* leading the way with Makaroff's flag snapping at the masthead.

In a few minutes guns were roaring and Kravschenko followed the running battle between the two fleets which had closed in to ten thousand yards. He was not alone on the hill now. Grand Duke Boris, his staff, and other officers had arrived to watch the engagement. The Japanese slowly withdrew with Makaroff following. Then smoke, on the horizon told of the approach of Togo's main fleet, and Makaroff, realizing his inferiority to the combined enemy forces, turned for the harbor with Togo on his heels.

Kravschenko's watch said 9:43. The *Petropavlovsky* had reached the protection of the forts and was maneuvering into the harbor entrance. Without warning there were four tremendous explosions. The flagship was ripped asunder, her foremast came smashing down, her bow plunged into the sea, and her stern pointed skyward, propellers spinning in the air. Then she vanished, carrying the intrepid Makaroff and 631 men to death. Togo's mines had done their work well.

On Golden Hill beside Kravschenko Grand Duke Boris fainted when the battleship disappeared. All along the shore officers and men who had witnessed the disastrous spectacle began to weep and pray.

Kravschenko's graphic account of the destruction of the *Petropavlovsky* was one of the most important stories to come out of the Far East during the opening months of the struggle, and American readers read of Makaroff's end the next day.

GRAND DUKE BORIS FAINTED WHEN THE BATTLESHIP DISAPPEARED.

The news was not always so swift. On May 15 the Japanese battleship *Yachima* struck a mine off Dalny, near Port Arthur, and sank. It was not until early June that The Associated Press was able to authenticate the story and cable it to America. Japanese authorities immediately denied the dispatch and insisted that the *Yachima* continued with the fleet. The same authorities, however, officially confirmed the accuracy of the news in November when they formally notified foreign governments of the ship's loss.

3

In Manchuria the opposing armies had come to grips and in April, May, and June the dispatches from Middleton, McCormick, Collins, Kiriloff, Brooke and the others described the Japanese successes at the Yalu River, Nan Shan, and Tolissu. Middleton, a Foreign Service veteran, did not see the campaign through. He contracted dysentery and collapsed. They took him back to a little Red Cross hospital at Liang-chia-Shan, near the squalid city of Liaoyang, headquarters for Russian operations, and there under alien skies, he died a week later— on June 25, 1904.

A Russian firing squad volleyed over his grave when they buried him with full military honors two days later. Three colleagues stood by in silence.

But Liaoyang was not Middleton's last resting place. At Stone's cabled request, the Czar's representative in the Far East, Viceroy Alexieff, had the remains disinterred and sent through the lines. The roar of field artillery ceased and the rattle of rifles stilled as the little procession with the plain wooden coffin left the Russian entrenchments. The warring troops halted in a silent armistice while Middleton took his final leave of the battle front that was his last assignment.

Middleton's death almost cost the co-operative another of its best correspondents. To fill the vacancy with the Russian armies, Cowles picked Denny, who had reported the Japanese assaults on Port Arthur. To reach General Kuropatkin's headquarters at Liaoyang, Denny was compelled to go around the Japanese lines and make a perilous journey through wild country west of the fighting zone. He traveled for days in a jolting cart through territory swarming with Manchurian bandits, and in one encounter he narrowly escaped with his life.

Denny reached Kuropatkin's headquarters safely, but Liaoyang remained unlucky for staff men. Throughout July and August the

Japanese armies kept battering away toward Liaoyang in three converging columns. Everyone was asking: "Will Kuropatkin stand at Liaoyang?" They were answered the last week in August, 1904, when the troops of the Mikado reached the area and found the Russian forces drawn up in strong positions. The bloody six-day engagement began August 29 and the world waited to hear how the troops of the Czar, now greatly superior in numbers, would acquit themselves against a foe that had been monotonously successful.

On a rocky spur in the jumble of heights, ridges, and tortuous valleys surrounding the town, Collins, who was with the Japanese army of General Kuroki, could sweep the whole field of action with his glasses as the ground shuddered under the greatest storm of artillery fire history had yet seen. Wheel to wheel, the Japanese had five hundred guns—many of them captured Russian pieces—hurling destruction into Kuropatkin's lines. Thundering back came the shells of Russian batteries, fully as numerous. The hazy summer air was filled with the ugly orange and red flashes from the mouths of guns, smoke from exploding shells, and the pyres where the Japanese were burning their dead.

All day August 30 the duel raged while wave after wave of Japanese infantry shattered on Kuropatkin's right. Within these lines, Denny, Kiriloff, McCormick, Brooke, and seven others followed the battle. On August 31 the hammer of massed artillery continued unabated. The blazing forenoon saw more ammunition expended than in the whole three days of the Battle of Gettysburg.

Collins could watch from his splendid vantage point, but his colleagues on the other side had a more difficult task, particularly Kiriloff who found himself covering the hottest sector of the Russian front. He was assigned to the corps commanded by Baron Stakelberg—the general who had arrived in the Far East with his wife, her companion, two maids, a French chef, a milch cow, and one hundred and twenty-seven pieces of luggage. It was Stakelberg's division that was bearing the brunt of the Japanese bombardment.

Kiriloff rode out for his second perilous day in the front lines at dawn on August 31. All along the five miles of the Haichong Road he saw the wounded coming back, carts piled with dead, and long ammunition trains moving up. Shrapnel raked the road methodically and there was no lull in the thunder of artillery.

Kiriloff made his way to one of the most exposed spots in the sector, where the field pieces of one battery kept hammering away at the blue Japanese lines below. The position was a shambles. Out of sixty gunners in the unit, forty had been killed or wounded in the first day's fighting. No food had been sent up for twenty-four hours, but the guns kept firing and the piles of empty cartridge cases grew higher.

Kiriloff shared what provisions he had brought along, talked to officers and men, then decided to stay in the shell-smashed emplacement because it gave a view of all Stakelberg's entrenchments. While guns roared and recoiled around him, he found a discarded ammunition box and began to write his narrative.

Time after time he saw the Japanese infantry roll up to the Russian lines only to fall back broken. A storm of protective rifle fire covered the charges and bullets rained about Kiriloff as he wrote.

Thousands of miles away, in the Russian capital of St. Petersburg, Chief of Bureau Thompson matched together the fragmentary dispatches that dribbled in from the men at Liaoyang. Sketchy, inconclusive, they left the outcome of the fighting in doubt. Then the long quiet trans-Siberian wire in the Central Telegraph Office came to life. Kiriloff had filed his story. Thompson edited the account as rapidly as the sheets came to his hand.

"Prudence urged me to leave the spot," Kiriloff's dispatch said, "but I was fascinated."

There it broke off abruptly and Thompson waited for the next "take" to come through. But the "take" was not from Kiriloff. It was signed by a Russian artillery officer. and it said:

```
        KIRILOFF WAS SHOT THROUGH THE RIGHT LUNG
WHILE STANDING BY OUR BATTERY, AND FELL BACK,
SUFFERING INTENSE AGONY.  HE INSISTED UPON
BEING PLACED ON A HORSE, SO THAT HE COULD GET
TO LIAOYANG AND FILE HIS DISPATCH.  IT TOOK
HIM FIVE HOURS AND A HALF TO COVER THE FIVE
MILES TO THE TELEGRAPH STATION.  WHEN HE REACHED
THERE HE WAS SO EXHAUSTED AND WEAK FROM LOSS OF
BLOOD THAT WE GOT HIM TO A HOSPITAL, ALTHOUGH
AGAINST HIS PROTEST.  HE ASKED ME TO COMPLETE
HIS MESSAGE FOR HIM.  I AM A SOLDIER, AND NO
WRITER; BUT I WILL SAY THAT AFTER THE AWFUL
FIGHTING TODAY WE WERE STILL HOLDING OUR POSITION.
JAPANESE BODIES BESTREW ALL THE HEIGHTS.  THEIR
LOSSES MUST HAVE RUN INTO TENS OF THOUSANDS.
WE HAVE LOST FIVE THOUSAND THUS FAR.
```

While this message came into St. Petersburg telling what had happened to Kiriloff, Collins was writing the story of the day as seen from the Japanese side, unaware of what had befallen his fellow correspondent. He had been something of a hero himself that day. A Japanese officer who had become his friend was shot down at the height of the battle. Heedless of danger, Collins dashed into the thick of the fray and carried the wounded man to safety.

The battle went on three days more. The Russians were beaten, hurriedly evacuated Liaoyang and fell back on Mukden.

4

The next big story of the conflict broke, not on the remote battle fronts of the Far East, but on the Dogger Bank fishing grounds off Hull, England. It was news that threatened to plunge Great Britain and Russia into a European war.

For months the Russians had been building an imposing fleet at their European naval base on the Baltic. This fleet was to sail halfway around the world, combine with the Pacific squadron and then give battle to Admiral Togo.

It left on October 14, 1904, with Admiral Rojestvensky in command. Uneasy tension marked the departure. Rumors were rife that the Japanese had torpedo boats in European waters to attack the ships as soon as they were out of the Baltic. Worried officers and men, keyed to the breaking point, sought to guard against the invisible dangers. This psychology made possible the celebrated "Dogger Bank Affair" on October 21.

Nobody knew where the rumors came from, although the French Foreign Office suspected they came from Germany. It was a fantastic business from the start because Lansdowne, the British foreign minister, pointed out it was impossible for a squadron of Japanese warships to have reached the North Sea from Japan without being reported somewhere en route. Unofficially most people who had anything to do with the affair were inclined to agree with Prince Radolin that vodka must have played some part in what Rojestvensky said he saw.

Rojestvensky was steaming through the North Sea that night when one of his repair ships wirelessed: "Foreign torpedo boats are attacking." Vigilance was redoubled. A little later the fleet encountered an indistinct flotilla. Russian guns went into action and several "enemy" boats were sunk or disabled. Later, however, they turned out to be English fishing trawlers, although Rojestvensky maintained to the end that he had sunk a Japanese torpedo boat.

By daybreak the association's cable report was carrying what had happened at Dogger Bank. "English Fishing Fleet Sunk By Russian Guns," headlines announced. Great Britain was incensed. Her navy received orders to be ready for active duty. War was freely predicted, but the Russian government refused to take any steps until it had Rojestvensky's version. For days no one knew what that might be. The limited range of wireless equipment prevented the Czar's ministers from communicating with the admiral, who was steaming for a coaling stop in Spain, totally unaware of the storm. When the crisis seemed at its worst, Associated Press papers were able to print word that calmer counsel had prevailed and Great Britain had agreed to submit the matter to international arbitration.

The situation continued grave, however, in the absence of any statement from Rojestvensky. Then on October 26 the Czar's fleet reached the Spanish port of Vigo and two launches quickly put out for the flagship. One carried the agitated Russian consul-general from Madrid and the other the co-operative's chief of bureau at Paris, Charles T. Thompson, who had hurried to Vigo. Rojestvensky was astounded to learn of the crisis which had arisen from the affair at Dogger Bank. To Thompson he gave substantially the same account he transmitted in his official report to St. Petersburg, and the interview, setting forth Rojestvensky's explanation and defense in detail, did much to relieve the international tension.

The high significance attached to the news was emphasized in Paris the next day when the attitude of the government there was described in this statement:

The French officials attach much importance to The Associated Press interview at Vigo with Vice-Admiral Rojestvensky as giving the most reasonable explanation of the circumstances. The Russian embassy takes a similar view. Therefore the authorities have taken steps to have The Associated Press interview reach the French press, as a means of calming public apprehension over the affair.

5

In the East, Port Arthur, without food and supplies, held out until January 2, 1905. Internal conditions in Russia had grown critical and Denny was detached from the Manchurian front to assist Thompson at St. Petersburg. He arrived in time to help cover "Bloody Sunday," January 22, when troops fired on demonstrators who were seeking political reforms, killing several hundred and wounding nearly three thousand. The "Revolution of 1905" followed.

Then the Japanese decisively defeated Kuropatkin at Mukden in March—and still the war dragged on. Russia had one slim chance. It rested with Admiral Rojestvensky who was leading the new fleet eighteen thousand miles around the world to challenge Togo. Eight months after he put out from the Russian naval base at Libau on the Baltic, he kept his rendezvous with history off the Island of Tsushima in the Korean Strait between Japan and the Asiatic mainland.

Throughout all those months dispatches reported every stage of Rojestvensky's odyssey through European waters, round the continent of Africa, into the Indian Ocean, on past the Malayan Peninsula, and at last into the Pacific. The world knew Togo was waiting and that one fleet or the other would have to be destroyed before the war could be won.

The day that made Japan a major naval power was May 27, 1905. With the strictest censorship in force, Martin Egan, chief of the Tokyo Bureau, cabled the dispatch American papers printed that day. The Russian fleet had been sighted in the Strait of Korea; the whereabouts of Togo was a mystery. But as readers scanned that news, one of the greatest naval battles of all time was being fought at Tsushima, where Togo and Rojestvensky met. In one hour the Russians were defeated, but it took Togo thirty-one hours to destroy them.

Egan had the news in Tokyo the next day but the censor was unyielding. As far as the Japanese government was concerned, the Battle of Tsushima technically continued in progress. Egan might cable that the enemy fleet had entered the Strait of Korea, but any further details were strictly forbidden. Egan thought a moment and wrote the dispatch which gave the first hint that the battle had been fought and that the Japanese had won. He hid the great story in two words—"Historic events"—and the censor passed the harmless-appearing item:

TOKIO, MAY 28, 9 P.M. -- TRANSMITABLE INFORMATION CONCERNING TODAY'S HISTORIC EVENTS IN THE NEIGHBORHOOD OF THE TSU ISLANDS IS LIMITED TO THE BARE FACT THAT ROJESTVENSKY'S MAIN FLEET, STEAMING IN TWO COLUMNS WITH BATTLESHIPS ON THE STARBOARD AND CRUISERS AND MONITORS ON THE PORT SIDE, APPEARED IN THE STRAITS OF KOREA. ALL OTHER INFORMATION IS WITHHELD BY THE JAPANESE AUTHORITIES AND CABLE TRANSMISSION IS REFUSED TO ANY OTHER REFERENCE TO THE MOVEMENTS OF THE RUSSIAN OR JAPANESE FLEETS.

In New York headquarters, the two significant words were a signal that mobilized all the resources of the association to get the story

Egan's cable did not long stand alone. Other dispatches arrived—from Nagasaki, from Chefoo, from Tokyo. In St. Petersburg, Chief of Bureau Thompson gave the Czar and his ministers first tidings of the complete destruction of Russia's fleet. From Washington, Edwin M. Hood supplied the first detailed account of the Russian losses, as reported by American naval attachés in the Orient. When the few Russian warships which escaped reached the safety of Vladivostok, Thompson had a correspondent there for the survivors' stories. From a dozen date lines the story of Tsushima was completed.

6

The disaster was the end of Russian hopes in the Far East. At the invitation of President Theodore Roosevelt, representatives of the warring powers met in a peace conference at Porthsmouth, New Hampshire, early in August, 1905. To report it, General Manager Stone brought Cortesi from Rome, Thompson from St. Petersburg, and James T. Williams and R. O. Bailey from Washington. The three Japanese commissioners, Baron Komura, Baron Takahira, and Baron Kaneko, and the two Russians, Count Sergyey Witte and Baron Rosen, all were personal friends of Stone. He saw them frequently after their arrival in the United States and as the conference at Portsmouth progressed he could not resist the temptation to take the role of peacemaker as well as news gatherer.

The Japanese insisted that Russia pay a large indemnity. Witte and Rosen would not consider it. Both believed Japan had passed the high-water mark of success and was economically unequal to continuing the war. Witte felt resumption of hostilities on a grand scale would bring about the destruction of the Japanese armies in Manchuria.

Stone learned privately from Witte and Rosen that the question of indemnity was causing the deadlock. If that was removed, the Russians could not in good faith reject a peace treaty, for they already had reached agreement with the Japanese on all other questions. Stone went to President Roosevelt. He outlined the terms on which he thought peace could be reached and suggested that the President cable the German Kaiser to use his influence with the Czar to have them accepted.

Ultimately The Associated Press reported that the Japanese were about to waive all claims for indemnity, and other correspondents at Portsmouth were loud in ridicule. That was inconceivable. Everybody knew that when the conference resumed on September 5, Baron Komura would repeat his demands. The Russian commissioners regarded the story as a ruse. Their plans were already made. If the indemnity demands were repeated, as they expected, Witte would leave the conference room and say casually to one of his secretaries, "Send for my Russian cigarettes." That was the prearranged signal for a code message to flash to Manchuria. The heavily reinforced Russians awaited only that word to loose a smashing offensive.

The conference met in strictest secrecy that day. The Associated Press men there knew Witte had set 11:50 A.M. as the hour he would leave the conference room and speak the words which might mean a new deluge of blood in the Far East. Suspense mounted as the appointed time neared.

Promptly at 11:50 the door of the room opened. Witte stepped out. He did not ask for his cigarettes.

"Gospoda, mir," he said in Russian. "Gentlemen, peace!"

III. LEAD WASHINGTON

I

WASHINGTON'S emergence as the news center of America was one of the notable journalistic phenomena in the first decade of the twentieth century. There were several factors involved. The first was the confidence in the nation's destiny which followed the war with Spain and gave Washington significance as a symbol of a united democracy. Second, a period of social consciousness and readjustment had dawned and Washington was the grand arena for its issues, reforms, and legislation. And there was a third major force—the vigorous news personality of President Theodore Roosevelt, who seemed able to dramatize himself or a platform plank with equal ease. For the United States and for other lands, this combination gave Washington date lines a new magic.

To the United States it was the news of social and economic changes which most concerned and affected everyday life. Dispatches from the capital described the stormy progress of pure food and drug legislation, the continued efforts at trust busting, the controversy over railroad rates, the measures for conservation of natural resources, the exposure of graft, and the countless concurrent developments which marked those years.

Newspapers reflected the changes that were taking place, some imperceptibly and some with noticeable swiftness. By and large, discerning journals arrived at a serious realization of the responsibilities which their public character imposed. A more definite code of ethics and standards was established. Many editors and legislators united in a drive on fraudulent and misleading advertisements, abuse of the news columns, dangerous personal notices, and other evils. Revised postal regulations, stricter libel laws, and other statutes implemented the campaign. An increasing number of newspapers began extending a helping hand to the underprivileged—a practice encouraged as early as 1886 when Victor Lawson's Chicago *Daily News* established a sanitarium for sick children from the tenement districts. At last the possibilities of such public service were receiving more widespread recognition and newspaper-sponsored campaigns were helping to provide the needy with free milk, ice, coal, hospitalization, and other necessities. At the same time the papers became aware of the tremendous number of women among their readers, and columns on household hints, menu suggestions, and departments devoted to women's activities were inaugurated.

Things were happening, but the process was gradual. The times moved to a leisurely tempo. It was the day of Spencerian penmanship and Delsarte speakers. Good whisky was $2 a gallon and the British were building the largest steamer in the world—the *Lusitania*.

The chronicle of such a period was not spectacular. The news relied for its significance, not so much on any one outstanding story, or any dozen, as on the great cumulative effect built up month after month. In retrospect the period seemed landmarked more by incidents sidelighting the news and by stories-behind-stories than by anything dramatic or heroic.

There always was "copy" in the President. The hearty New Yorker with the high-pitched voice—"Teddy" to the people, although he despised the nickname—had been on front pages more than ever since his picturesque Rough Riders landed in Cuba in '98. His penchant for phrasemaking caught public fancy and there was applause every time "T.R. got off another one."

2

The man in the street credited the President with "another one" in June, 1904—a fighting one, this time, and the man in the street was wrong. The Republican National Convention had assembled in Chicago for the formality of ratifying Roosevelt as the party's presidential standard-bearer in the approaching election, but newspaper readers momentarily were more exercised over something that had happened in faraway Morocco. A wealthy American, Ion Perdicaris, had been seized and held for ransom by a bandit chieftain, Raisuli. The duty of making the usual diplomatic representations fell to Secretary of State John Hay.

He was completing a draft of his note when Edwin M. Hood dropped in on his customary State Department round. Hood, of the Washington staff, had been reporting the activities of the government for years. He had entree everywhere, was the confidant of many high officials, and once in the early days of the McKinley administration he had been offered the post of assistant secretary of the navy—the office Roosevelt held before the war with Spain. Hay and Hood were old friends and the secretary welcomed an outside opinion on the message.

Hood scanned the document. The message was long, formal, and full of the phraseology dictated by protocol and diplomatic usage. Hood shook his head.

"Well?" asked Hay.

"I'm afraid you're slipping, Mr. Secretary," the correspondent smiled. "If I were you, I'd boil all this down to five words."

He produced a pencil and scribbled five words which reduced Hay's long note to the simplest terms. He handed his suggestion to the secretary:

"Perdicaris alive or Raisuli dead."

Very much as the cry "Remember the Maine!" captured the public imagination, the terse message to the Sultan of Morocco dramatized the "incident." Roosevelt liked the idea so much that he dispatched a copy to the Chicago convention. Although the ultimatum to Morocco bore Hay's signature, everyone said that only the two-fisted man in the White House could be the author of such a laconic line.

The successful Rough Rider President went back to the White House after the election of 1904 with Charles W. Fairbanks, one-time Pittsburgh correspondent of The Associated Press as his vice-president, and the Washington Bureau settled down to four more years of the unpredictable "Teddy."

This was before the day of modern press conferences, and both the President and his Cabinet officers had their own special favorites among the newspapermen. Usually they saved the richest news plums for these reporters. However, the advantage was not always so attractive as it seemed, particularly where the President was concerned. He frequently gave certain correspondents important stories credited to "an informed authority" or some such anonymous source—the President could not be quoted directly—and when public reaction was unfavorable he would disclaim the story and straightaway elect the "offending" reporter to his famous Ananias Club. He didn't call them liars.

One of the best known members of the Washington staff was John Gross. His assignments were diversified, but somehow when a prominent person was dying John Gross invariably drew the deathwatch. Cabinet members, senators, representatives, Supreme Court justices, admirals, generals, and a host of retired officials who made Washington their home all passed on with John Gross keeping patient watch near the sickroom door. Unless John Gross wrote a man's obituary, his political prominence was open to question.

The wife of a former Cabinet officer telephoned one day to say her husband was extremely ill.

"I know you must send someone to the house to get the news," she said understandingly, "but please don't send that terrible Mr. Gross."

The editor who took the call expressed surprise at the request. He said Gross was well liked, tactful, and considerate.

"I know," was the reply, "but people say that whenever Mr. Gross is placed to watch over a sick man, the patient always dies."

The editor assured her again that Gross was the most understanding soul he knew and added that most households found him a help instead of a nuisance.

"Oh, then I have done Mr. Gross an injustice," the lady exclaimed. "Please send him."

Gross got the assignment and the former Cabinet member's wife was so impressed by his consideration that she depended on him to give out all the news of her husband's condition. Everything went along nicely for a few days—and then the patient died.

3

The hard and fast regulations governing both the content of the news report and its preparation sometimes imposed handicaps on the Washington staff. The same strict rules applied to the story of a routine fatality as to important accounts of Congressional maneuvering on major legislation. The precepts ranged from taboos on "all slang phrases" and vulgarity down to admonitions against the use of "phone" for telephone and similar abbreviations. Such regulations encouraged an uninspired style of writing and a sameness of treatment in the daily news budgets.

Exhaustive as the code was, it did not prove equal to all occasions and situations arose where the rules were inadequate or precedent was lacking. Working at top speed and usually too far from headquarters to seek official pronouncement, the perplexed reporter had only one choice in such emergencies—to use his best judgment and trust that the decision was proper. New York would be prompt to let him know if it wasn't.

In 1905 Jackson S. Elliott faced the dilemma. The President was away at the time on a combined hunting and speaking trip through the Southwest and Elliott went along. The tour was without noteworthy incident until the party reached San Antonio, Texas, where state Republican leaders had arranged a banquet in Roosevelt's honor.

The affair was held in the patio of a local hotel and, although there were no women among the diners, the wives, daughters, and friends of many of the men attending listened from surrounding balconies and windows. The toastmaster, a man of political importance, took the occasion to poke sly fun at the President's frequent attacks on the evils of "race suicide." Introducing the chief executive, he made a play on the words of an old nursery rhyme. Originally, he told his audience, the verse had run:

> There was an old woman who lived in a shoe;
> She had so many children she didn't know what to do.

But today, he said, the couplet had been revised in the light of modern conditions to run this way:

> Now there is a young woman; she lives in no shoe;
> She hasn't any children—she *knows* what to do.

Elliott was watching the President, whose dislike for anything off-color was well known. Roosevelt's jaw snapped and his body stiffened. He appeared so indignant that Elliott thought for a moment he intended to interrupt the speaker. Instead, he turned to the guest at his right, opened an animated conversation and paid no further attention. Then, when he spoke, he made no mention of the offending toastmaster beyond deploring the fact that one of the speakers had chosen such an inappropriate occasion to recite a rhyme which he said he hoped was "homemade."

Elliott realized the ticklish story he had on his hands. There was great interest generally in Roosevelt's reception at San Antonio, and member papers in Texas particularly were desirous of a complete account. The turn of events heightened the value of the story, but how was the correspondent to tell it? Elliott cudgeled his brains for ideas on the best approach and the most judicious words. He must not transgress the bounds of good taste which regulations insisted upon, and yet an incident not in good taste was the mainspring of the whole story.

There was no time for extended deliberations, so Elliott solved his dilemma by writing a story based on the President's displeasure with certain unfortunate remarks of a crude nature by one of the speakers. He appended to the dispatch a private "Note to Editors," giving the text of what the offending toastmaster had said. This was primarily for the information of editors, but papers were free to use it or not as they saw fit. In some places the nursery rhyme parody was printed. The policy of the individual member was the determining factor.

4

Member newspapers had widely divergent beliefs and policies and Washington saw countless examples every day. In that period of controversial legislation and much-debated crusades, the task of staff men in the capital was to report events factually, objectively, and completely, without editorializing, without coloring. Member papers might use the material as they pleased as long as they did not change the facts presented. Given truthful news, they could use their individual editorial columns to interpret it, evaluate it, and uphold or attack the issues it set forth.

Frequently there were two or more camps of editorial opinion and they all relied on the same factual dispatches for the arguments and proofs they cited in support of their positions. In the co-operative this multiplicity of political, social, economic, and religious opinion provided a constant guard for the integrity of the report. Every dispatch was subject to endless scrutiny from all sorts of viewpoints.

No one better appreciated the value of such a news report than publicity-seeking pressure groups eager to have a cause presented in the best possible light. Washington swarmed with them and they were eternally besieging members of the staff to include favorable material or to suppress anything unfavorable. Charles A. Boynton, chief of the Washington Bureau, issued explicit instructions on how to deal with such individuals:

If anybody should ever come to you and ask for the publication or suppression of anything on the ground of some alleged acquaintance or relationship with me or with any other official or person supposed to be influential in The Associated Press, throw him out of the window and report the case to the coroner.

Theodore Roosevelt's second term was in full career. Washington date lines were more numerous than ever and the morgue envelopes which preserved the day-by-day history of the President's activities grew fatter as new clippings were added by George Wyville, the librarian in the New York office who kept the files up to date. At the time no one realized it, but the files held one story Roosevelt was to regret politically.

The piece was written the night of his sweeping victory over Alton B. Parker in the 1904 presidential election. Even before the votes had been counted much speculation had arisen as to the course of Roosevelt's political future in the event he won as expected. Some pointed out that he might have three terms without violating the tradition that no man be elected to the office more than twice. They argued that, since his first term had been as successor to the assassinated McKinley, a victory over Parker would mark the first time he had been elected by the people, and therefore he would be free to seek the office again in 1908.

The outcome of the 1904 election was not long in doubt. As soon as returns assured victory, the elated Roosevelt took a few minutes out to write a statement for The Associated Press. The first two paragraphs voiced gratitude to the American people and a promise to serve them well. Then he replied to the 1908 speculation:

On the 4th of March next I shall have served three and one-half years, and the three and one-half years constitute my first term.

The wise custom which limits the President to two terms regards the substance and not the form, and under no circumstances will I be a candidate for or accept another nomination.

Years later he deplored the voluntary promise. Discussing the matter with a close friend and adviser, Herman Kohlsaat, he pointed to his wrist and exclaimed:

"I would cut my hand off right there if I could recall that written statement!"

IV. FLASH!

I

THREE men were on duty in the Associated Press bureau in the Western Union Building in downtown San Francisco at five o'clock in the morning April 18, 1906.

On the main trunk wire to the East, Chief Operator Robert Geistlich sent the signal for "30"—telegraph symbol for "signing off." Then he stretched and pulled on his coat to go home. On the circuit serving California morning papers another operator, Ben McInerney, sent "10" —the sign for the telegraphers' regular ten-minute rest period. He reached for his usual bottle of early morning coffee. Editor John Finlay was in the midst of a ham-and-egg sandwich.

"See you tonight," said Geistlich, nodding to the two others whose tour of duty had not ended.

The hands of the clock on the wall moved to 5:10. McInerney resumed sending on the state circuit, methodically relaying the news which Finlay selected and edited from the trickle of late dispatches.

Suddenly the building rocked and trembled, the walls cracked, plaster showered down, the ceiling light dropped, and the clock crashed, face up, to the swaying floor.

"Earthquake!"

"Bulletin it!" yelled Finlay.

He jumped to his teetering typewriter and pounded out:

"Bulletin: San Francisco, April 18—San Francisco was shaken by an earthquake at"—he took a hurried glance at the silent clock on the floor—"5:15 this morning."

Operator McInerney worked with his state wire. Then he jumped over to the telegraph instrument on the trunk wire east. He turned to the telephone.

"All dead!" he shouted, grabbing the bulletin and dashing for the Western Union office on a floor above.

Pelted by chunks of plaster, Finlay looked out the window at the crumbling city and kept pounding the typewriter keys.

McInerney rushed back into the office and behind him came

THE WALLS CRACKED, PLASTER SHOWERED DOWN . . .

Geistlich, who had dodged the rain of brick and stone to get back to the men he had left a few minutes earlier.

"All telegraph company wires are out!" panted McInerney. "I left the bulletin in case they ever get a wire through."

"All right, let's go!" said Geistlich, snatching the copy Finlay had written. "If we can get to the Oakland ferry, maybe we can get something through on the wires over there."

Geistlich and McInerney raced through a nightmare of demolished streets, clambering over ruins, and making mental note of the devastation as they ran. The downtown area was filling with the panic-stricken. Some were mad with fear that the world was coming to an end. Everyone who could stampeded for the ferry. Geistlich and McInerney jumped aboard the boat just as she was pulling away. By 6:30 they reached the deserted office of the telegraph company across the bay. Conditions there were almost as bad as in San Francisco. All lines were down. They left a copy of the story and headed back to what was left of San Francisco.

2

When the earthquake shook the city, Superintendent Cowles of the Pacific Coast Division was asleep at home. Like thousands of others, he was pitched from bed by the first mighty shock. He finished dressing as he sprinted through the streets toward the bureau. He reached the partially wrecked Western Union building at 5:45. No wires. He hurried to the Postal Telegraph a few blocks away. Swayne, chief operator for that company, was tinkering distractedly with a broken circuit to Chicago.

"Barely possible I can get something through soon," said Swayne.

Cowles wrote a bulletin and stood waiting while the telegrapher tested and tested. The click of the Morse was so faint that it was scarcely audible above the pandemonium outside. The wire refused to work. Cowles called to Swayne to keep trying and made for the Pacific Cable Company office in the same building.

"Your cable functioning?" he demanded.

"Seems to be."

Cowles seized a blank and wrote out a brief message on the disaster, addressing it to The Associated Press in New York.

The attendant shook his head.

"I can't send a cable to New York," he protested. "Our wires are under the Pacific to the Far East."

"Route it around the world!" snapped Cowles.

"Sorry," faltered the clerk, "I'd do it for you if I could, but the company doesn't have any regulations covering such an unusual procedure, and, besides, I don't know the rate."

Cowles exploded.

"Never mind the rules," he bellowed. "I'll pay any rate the company sees fit to charge; but, please, for God's sake, send it immediately!"

"I can't, I can't," the man insisted. "You know I would if I could, but I've got my own job to think of."

"Well, then, send it to Honolulu, at least."

The frightened attendant agreed and Cowles ran back to the Postal office where Swayne still was coaxing the wire to Chicago. Cowles paced the floor. After a long wait the line came to life. Both men hunched closer.

"Got 'em!" exclaimed Swayne.

Then first word of the appalling disaster was swiftly tapped to the outside world.

Cowles returned to the ruined office in the Western Union building, collected the members of his staff who had arrived and shifted the scene of activities to the Postal building. As fast as typewriters could hammer it out, the story was relayed. The lone wire was too good to last. It failed and the fire which had followed the earthquake was sweeping closer. The torn pavement outside was almost melted and the scorching walls made the building like an oven. The Chicago wire eventually was re-established for a brief time, but by eleven that morning it was out again. The heat was so intense the building had to be evacuated.

The flames had not yet reached the abandoned Western Union building, and, for want of a better place, Cowles and his helpers returned there. More members of the staff had reached the old office and Cowles took a mental roll call to make sure all were accounted for.

Morse operators? All present—Harry Collins, Fred Burnell, W. F. Lynch, J. K. Brown, W. Mitchell, and Ben McInerney and Robert Geistlich, who had returned from their dash to Oakland.

Editorial men? There was—Karl von Weigan, the future foreign correspondent for Hearst newspapers, Hershel McDonald, Robert Johnson, E. E. Curtis, and Finlay who had written the bulletin at the moment of the quake.

Where was Jerry Carroll?

No one had seen or heard from him. He might be one of the hundreds who had been crushed under falling walls. Police, firemen, and volunteers already were at work in the ruins. They might find him later. The staff had no time to search for the missing editor. Their urgent job was to find a means for re-establishing contact with the outside world.

Anticipating that troops would take over control of the stricken city, Cowles sent one man to obtain passes from General Frederick Funston, commanding officer for the area. He sent others in search of a launch to transport men and news to Oakland, now that ferry operations had ceased. No launch could be found, but the hurriedly procured army passes induced the captain of the government tug *McDowell* to take Geistlich and Lynch across the bay and to stand by for any help he could give. In Oakland both Western Union and Postal had been busy, and workable wires were set up that afternoon. Official communications swamped the improvised facilities, but Associated Press dispatches were given right-of-way.

Back in San Francisco Cowles assigned others of the staff—operators and editors alike—to each section of the flaming city to obtain every scrap of information and rush it to him for inclusion in the "leads" he began to write.

By one o'clock in the afternoon Cowles was ordered from the shattered Western Union building so authorities could dynamite it in an attempt to halt the fire. He could not wait until his staff returned to headquarters, where all were agreed to meet, so he made his way to the office of the *Bulletin* on Bush Street. There he resumed writing and sent off the copy by messengers to the wire offices in Oakland. All he could do was to hope the remainder of the staff might find him.

Dusk fell and still none of the staff had found him. Just as he was abandoning hope, he looked up from his work and saw a limping bundle of bandages hobbling toward him. He peered at the gauze-swathed features, heard an attempted laugh, and knew that Jerry Carroll had been found. A wall had tumbled on Carroll's home, burying him and his wife under an avalanche of bricks and mortar. Dug out by passers-by, the editor had spent most of the day getting patched up so that he could walk. Then he set out to reach the office. Someone who knew Cowles's whereabouts directed him to the *Bulletin* office. His shoes had been burned and his feet were cut by glass and blistered by the hot pavements.

Carroll received an assignment immediately. Cowles sent him out to write a "color" story of the disaster. Carroll went back into the streets, noting the names of destroyed buildings and the despairing efforts to check the flames, which then were roaring into the Chinese section. On all sides he heard the cries of injured and homeless, and frequently he saw silent rows of blanket-covered dead. In an hour he had the horrible picture and he sat down in a Chinatown doorway to write his story in the light of a fire that was costing a thousand dollars a second.

The Associated Press was the only organization to relay news of the earthquake that day and night. In the twenty-four hours after the first shock the staff wrote and relayed 21,300 words.

3

The San Francisco earthquake served to dramatize the need for a definite method for rushing out the first brief fact on a news event of first importance. In the past the traditional "bulletin" had been considered satisfactory, but in a day of many extra editions newspaper editors required even quicker notice that a story of extraordinary character was breaking. Some old-time telegraphers had developed the habit of tapping out the word F-L-A-S-H before the relay of an out-of-the-ordinary news item. The custom, however, was haphazard and too often abused on cheap sensations.

The Associated Press put the Flash on a hard and fast official basis less than two weeks after the San Francisco disaster. In a general order to all its employees throughout the world these instructions were issued May 1, 1906:

News matter of supreme importance which would necessitate the issuance of extra editions should be sent first as a "Flash" in a message not to exceed ten words, and should go on all leased wires. Such "Flash" must take precedence over all bulletins, must go upon each wire of a double or triple wire system, must be sent instantly upon the development of the news, and must never exceed ten words in length.

Accuracy had been the first watchword. Now speed officially became the second.

V. SURVEY AND CRITICISM

ROOSEVELT would not run again. This was plain from his unequivocal election night statement four years before. Although the 1908 political picture had been complicated by the panic which broke the preceding October, shrewd observers looked for another Republican victory when voting time came. William Jennings Bryan was out for his third nomination as the Democratic standard-bearer and it seemed certain that Roosevelt's mantle would fall either on New York's Governor, Charles Evans Hughes, or on the broad 350-pound frame of William Howard Taft.

While the country at large waited for the campaigns to open, members of The Associated Press met at the old Waldorf-Astoria in New York for another of their annual meetings. Peacock Alley was in all its glory and the sight of fashionably dressed women smoking cigarettes in public shocked more than one inland publisher. There was time for chats with old friends and evenings at the theater. A spirit of camaraderie predominated and the members looked forward to these gatherings with genuine pleasure.

Although the members were proud of the association they had fostered, they were practical newspapermen and experience had taught them the folly of taking things for granted.

With this in mind, the 1908 meeting unanimously voted creation of a special committee of ten members charged with appraising the excellences and shortcomings of the entire report, the possibilities for extension of the service, and the desirability of any changes in the by-laws.

Once the business calendar had been cleared, the members turned to the annual banquet, with its speechmaking, and the traditional loving cup. Each year there had been something about the occasion which caused publishers and editors to remember it.

Two years before it had been the sparkling address of Mark Twain. He said: "There are only two forces that can carry light to all corners of the globe—the sun in the heavens and The Associated Press down here."

Last year it had been the classic story which passed with chuckles from mouth to mouth—the story of Sam Davis, a Nevada string correspondent who interviewed Sarah Bernhardt for the Carson *Appeal*, his own little paper; for the San Francisco *Examiner*; and for the cooperative. The actress liked him so much that, when her train was ready to leave, she put her hands on his shoulders, kissed him on each cheek, and then squarely on the mouth. She said: "The right cheek for the Carson *Appeal*, the left for the *Examiner*, the lips, my friend, for yourself." Davis displayed no trace of bashfulness. "Madam," he exclaimed, "I also represent The Associated Press, which serves three hundred and eighty papers west of the Mississippi River alone!"

And this year it was William Jennings Bryan holding forth in his best oratorical form.

There were endless other topics for informal shop talk. The American Mining Congress considered Associated Press metal market quotations so accurate that it voted them the standard on which all settlements be made in the industry. The news of the birth of an heir to the Spanish throne had been whisked from Madrid to Chicago in ninety seconds—a notable demonstration in swift transmission. There was the celebrated Stanford White-Harry K. Thaw murder case and the dramatic Haywood trial in Montana—the labor leader for whom "T.R." coined the phrase "undersirable citizen."

Much interest centered on Canada where an embattled group of papers had taken first steps in the direction of a co-operative which, molded closely after The Associated Press, eventually became The Canadian Press. And in the United States another agency was entering the domestic field, although as a privately owned commercial enterprise. The Scripps-McRae Press Association, founded in 1897, the Scripps News Association, an affiliated combination, and the Publishers' Press Association joined forces and formed the United Press Associations. The three previously had divided the country between them, covering one another's areas by virtue of a news exchange arrangement. In their discussions editors and publishers saw the consolidation as a development which would supply news to papers ineligible or undesirous of becoming members of The Associated Press. They saw also that the very existence of this agency was irrefutable evidence against any absurd charges that their co-operative had monopolistic inclinations.

BERNHARDT KISSED THE CORRESPONDENT . . . SQUARELY ON THE MOUTH.

2

When the members departed for home, the Special Survey Committee remained behind to work. Headquarters were set up, a program drafted, questionnaires prepared, and one committeeman detailed to tour the country studying bureau operations at first hand.

While another presidential campaign occupied the politicians, the public found some respite in the great to-do which followed the classic "bonehead" play of major league baseball—Fred Merkle's failure to touch second base in the crucial New York-Chicago game that September. For days the pros and cons of the discussion occupied enough wire space to rival developments on the political front, and the word "boner" took its place in the language.

Then the co-operative's committee put the finishing touches on its report and the thoroughgoing study was ready for the Board of Directors on December 1.

The integrity and reliability of the news report was rated "admirable," but the committee called for the cultivation of a more sprightly and concise style and more skillful editing. The report tactfully reminded the members that, since much Associated Press news originated in their own offices because of the mutual exchange principle, the desired improvement, like charity, should begin at home.

A second recommendation called for the appointment of assistant superintendents for each of the six geographical divisions of the service—New England, New York, Washington, Chicago, Denver, and San Francisco. Their principal duty was to keep in close touch with member papers to ascertain their needs or criticisms. The committee saw in these assistant superintendents an opportunity to weld the service into a more coherent whole.

Closely connected with the problem of improving the news report was the widespread demand among the members for greater localization of their service. At the time the association's facilities were divided into three major classifications: There was the main coast-to-coast trunk circuit, which carried only dispatches of general importance. Supplementary to this were the regional wires, which served as the arteries for geographical divisions comprising several states. There also were the few, comparatively recent, "side circuits," operating off the main leased wire or its regional counterpart and serving papers in one state or occasionally two.

Editors in the bureaus controlling these side or state, circuits had been able to anticipate the trend toward a more localized report. Serving a limited group of papers whose interests were similar, the editors of these circuits could prepare a report made up of trunk and regional material which met the needs of the locality and at the same time included more state or bi-state news.

Members who received their news budget only on the main leased wires were not so fortunate. They expressed the need for extension of facilities to provide more localized news coverage, but the committee was not inclined to encourage this agitation, declaring that general news alone was the province of the association. The thorough exposition of this subject, however, served a purpose. It focused attention on the success of the few side circuits in supplying a combination of general and state news, and it raised in some minds the thought that a system of state circuits which would pay more attention to vicinage news might represent the ideal fundamental unit for the organization's future operations.

The committee reminded the members that they were receiving a telegraphic service which, taken as a whole, never had been equaled. "This report," they noted, "has become the cheapest commodity that enters into the making of the daily newspaper." They pointed out that the general news of the entire world was delivered to member papers at a cost less than that of gathering the news in their own circulating areas. Some were assessed as little as 52 cents for each thousand words, while the highest rate was $4.60.

The question of finances likewise was involved in the report. Many of the reforms recommended called for additional expenditures and it behooved the organization to move cautiously in this respect. Since 1900 the association had been oscillating annually from surplus to deficit—a $94,708 deficit for the last half of 1907 was particularly disquieting—and important commitments for the future must be weighed with a practical eye on the extra outlay involved.

3

If an occasional skeptic in the membership ranks was inclined to question the committee's pronouncement on the general excellence of the news service, the staff soon afterward supplied a brilliant demonstration on two of the biggest stories in the opening decade of the century's history.

The first occurred during the 1908 Christmas season. On December 28 there was a convulsive earthquake in the Italian province of Calabria. The earthquake and the accompanying tidal wave took 200,000 lives. Joseph Pierce, the correspondent at Messina, perished before he could get his story through. In Rome Cortesi left a sickbed to write his account of a catastrophe unparalleled in European history. On the first five days he cabled 37,780 words.

Cortesi was Cortesi, and the membership had come to expect superlative work from him. It was not always the front-rank men, however, who were on the spot the moment important news occurred unexpectedly in one place or another. Sometimes it was an obscure correspondent—an ordinary string correspondent such as Jack Irwin on Nantucket Island.

Irwin was one of those restless men never content to stay in one place. An Australian by birth, he had a daredevil disposition which took him to many places in search of adventure. He was in Africa during the Boer War and saw fighting at Magersfontein and Spion Kop. Eventually he came to the United States and was attracted by the wizardry of wireless telegraphy. He settled down for a while as an operator in the Marconi station at Siasconset on Nantucket Island, one of the lonely outposts which gave the first and last greetings to Atlantic steamers. While at Siasconset he became a stringer for the co-operative, occasionally passing along a small story that came his way, but never anything of consequence.

There was no promise of anything of consequence on January 23, 1909, as he sat at his key, keeping the early morning tour of duty. The Atlantic was a thick white wall of fog which came swirling in, blanketing Nantucket. It was 5:40 in the morning.

A thin, faint signal whispered unexpectedly in Irwin's earphones. It was repeated again and again . . . CQD . . . CQD . . . CQD— the international signal for a ship in distress.

Two hundred miles out on the Atlantic Jack Binns, an operator on the White Star liner *Republic*, was desperately sending out the call. The *Republic* had collided with the freighter *Florida* and was sinking.

Irwin at Siasconset was the first to pick up the call from the sinking *Republic* and her 440 passengers. From that moment on, he kept repeating the weak CQD and Binns's subsequent messages, utilizing Siasconset's stronger power to broadcast the calls over a wider area than the *Republic* could cover. Busy as he was, he acted promptly in his capacity as a string correspondent, rushing word of the *Republic's* peril to the Boston Bureau.

For hours the fate of the *Republic* remained in doubt while rescue ships groped through the fog. The White Star liner sank, but thanks to the CQD, only four lives were lost. Irwin continued to relay details of the great drama and the country thrilled to the heroism and courage of the first widely publicized ship rescue by wireless.

4

In the weeks which saw the Calabrian earthquake and the S.S. *Republic* disaster, no group among the members studied the survey of the Special Survey Committe with keener interest and hope than the limited service, or "pony" papers. For many of these small newspapers, published in remote inland towns, the earthquake and ship disaster stories merely demonstrated again an old handicap which plagued them. They could not afford regular leased wire facilities which delivered a large volume of news direct to their offices and the exasperating delays in receiving abbreviated reports over ordinary commercial telegraph lines persisted even when public interest in the news was at fever pitch. The result was that many of these pony members failed to obtain enough news with sufficient speed to make a showing with their readers.

Examining the committee's report, these small members discovered grounds for both hope and discouragement. The committee confessed that it recognized their plight and wanted to do something about it. But the committee could advance no constructive plans to eliminate the delays in news delivery. There was no point in further complaints to the wire companies. Repeated representations in the past had proved futile. The facilities of the wire companies already were burdened with commercial traffic which made impossible the promise of split-second news service to widely separated small papers. Some solution must exist, but it had not been found.

VI. THE AIRPLANE MAKES NEWS

I

THE Associated Press man at Dayton, Ohio, had been inclined to joke when they showed him the Wright family's prepared statement and the telegram which had prompted it:

```
176 C KA CS PAID
KITTY HAWK  N C    DEC 17
BISHOP M. WRIGHT
      7 HAWTHORNE ST

SUCCESS FOUR FLIGHTS THURSDAY MORNING ALL
AGAINST TWENTY ONE MILE WIND STARTING FROM
LEVEL WITH ENGINE POWER ALONE AVERAGE SPEED
THROUGH AIR THIRTY ONE MILES LONGEST 57 SECONDS
INFORM PRESS HOME CHRISTMAS.  OREVELLE WRIGHT
525P
```

"Huh," the correspondent commented. "Fifty-seven seconds! If it were fifty-seven minutes it might be worth talking about."

On the chance that it might be news in some eyes, nevertheless, he copied the message and the statement which old Bishop Wright, father of the sender, had helped prepare. Many editors snorted as they read the dispatch. Perfunctorily it reported that the two Wright brothers claimed to have made man's first successful flights in an airplane. A large number of papers ignored the news as humbug, others poked fun at it, and even some people in Dayton believed it a hoax designed to attract attention to the local bicycle business the Wright brothers conducted.

It was the biggest kind of news, however, and except for two minor errors it was accurate. The commercial telegraph operator who transmitted the message had misread the time of flight, clipping two seconds from the actual performance, and had misspelled Orville Wright's first name.

The dispatch from Dayton was one of the two accounts the co-operative carried that day on the Wrights. The second, an item of some four hundred words, appeared under a Norfolk, Virginia, date line and gave a remarkably good description of the test flights.

People scoffed at those 1903 stories of what Wilbur and Orville Wright had done at Kitty Hawk, and for more than four years few took much stock in the claims that man could navigate the sky in a flying machine. Nevertheless, the Wrights, returning to Dayton, went forward with their experiments and the local correspondent, who had revised his first notions on the subject, kept anxiously after them. Considering the general atmosphere of continuing disbelief, he showed unusual zeal, following their tests and asking questions.

"Any news on the airship today, Wilbur?"

"No, nothing special."

"You and Orville been flying?"

"Just about as usual. Couple of flights."

"How far?"

"Halfway down the field."

"Not so much, eh? Well, you be sure to let me know if anything special happens."

There were stories from Dayton as the months rolled by, yet not until May, 1908, when the Wrights conducted a fresh series of flights at Kitty Hawk did the world awake to the great news that had been happening completely unrecognized.

2

The tardy public recognition of aviation news was accompanied by a realization that the story of aircraft development had international scope. A few months after the Wright brothers returned to Kitty Hawk, cables were telling of aerial experiments along a different line in Germany, where Count Ferdinand von Zeppelin was striving to perfect the dirigible. The 24-hour flight of his LZ4 was an epochal achievement in the history of lighter-than-air craft, even though the cruise ended in misadventure. A staff correspondent, Joseph Herrings, almost succeeded in an ambitious plan to cover the entire 300-mile test flight singlehanded from the ground.

The zeppelin was docked in a floating hangar on Lake Constance. Herrings had been sent to Switzerland to watch developments. No announcement was made, and Herrings's inquiries brought vague replies that the strange cigar-shaped craft would not be prepared to take off for several days. The information sounded unconvincing to the reporter. He arranged for a swift motorboat and the fastest automobile available and then settled down to watch the hangar in case Count Zeppelin decided on an unheralded departure. It was a wise forethought. Early one August morning the nose of the zeppelin poked out of the floating shed.

As soon as he saw the airship being moved out, Herrings tumbled into his motorboat and started across the lake toward her. The zeppelin took off smoothly, circled and headed toward Constance with the motorboat skimming in pursuit on the water below. The dirigible had not picked up speed and the correspondent was able to keep her in sight. While the motorboat rushed along, he scratched off a descriptive account of the LZ4's takeoff. By the time the zeppelin's shadow left the lake at Constance and headed overland, the reporter had ready the dispatch which he hurried to the telegraph office the moment he jumped ashore.

Then the wild part of the day began. He set out in the waiting automobile to continue the breathless chase overland. The LZ4 was cruising at a speed of between 35 and 40 miles an hour and a 1908 model automobile had a hard time keeping up. At towns along the route Herrings stopped to pass hurriedly written copy to open-mouthed telegraph operators.

Other correspondents in places over which the zeppelin passed also had been systematically reporting its progress and across the sea in New York cable editor Harold Martin assembled the dispatches into one co-ordinated story.

All morning Herrings roared across Germany in his reckless chase, and on into the afternoon. He managed to keep the zeppelin in sight until two o'clock when she disappeared beyond a range of hills near Laufen. From correspondents at other points, however, bulletins kept flowing in to New York, telling of the ship's continued progress, her stop for repairs at Nackenheim, her landing near Echterdingen the next day, and her destruction by fire while moored there.

3

Perhaps because distance lent enchantment, aeronautical adventures and misadventures abroad appeared to command greater attention from American newspapers than those at home. Even Wilbur Wright seemed to have greater news value when he went to France to demonstrate his flying machine to the French government. And when Louis Bleriot flew the English channel July 25, 1909, editors in the United States hailed the feat as "one of the greatest news events of a generation."

For a time it seemed likely that aviation would enable man to succeed at last in his long attempt to reach the North Pole. Walter Wellman, newspaperman and explorer, was convinced that an aerial trip to the top of the world was practicable. Using ships and dog sleds, he had led polar expeditions in 1894 and again in 1898. Back from the arctic, he went to work as a Washington correspondent for one of Victor Lawson's newspapers. When he mentioned his daring belief that the North Pole might be discovered by air, he found Lawson interested.

The Chicago publisher discussed Wellman's plans with Frank B. Noyes, president of The Associated Press, and together the two decided to finance the expedition as a private venture on the part of their newspapers.

A dirigible, *America*, was built in Paris, and Wellman made the first aerial voyage over the Arctic Ocean in September, 1907, only to have the weather balk a final dash to the pole. By the time Bleriot was preparing for the celebrated Calais-to-Dover flight, however, Wellman was heading for Spitsbergen and a second attempt to fly to the pole. The flight ended in failure when the *America* was badly damaged after a forced landing among ice hummocks on August 15. One of the *America's* four-man crew was Nicholas Popoff. He was the same Russian who had been shot while covering the Russo-Japanese War under the pen name of Kiriloff.

The possibilities of aerial exploration suffered a temporary eclipse after Wellman's failure, but before a month had passed the North Pole was proving one of the year's biggest and most controversial stories. Associated Press wires carried the first bulletin September 1. From the island of Lorwick, via Copenhagen, came the announcement of Dr. Frederick Cook, a Brooklyn explorer, that he had discovered the North Pole on April 21. The news touched off a rush of reportorial activity. Robert M. Collins, chief of the London Bureau, and R. E. Berry, of the Berlin staff, were ordered to Copenhagen where Albert Thorup, the resident correspondent, waited Cook's arrival.

In New York there was skepticism of Cook's claims and the scientific to-do over the alleged exploration assumed great proportions. The explorer was being lionized, interviewed, and toasted in Copenhagen. And then in New York on September 6 this telegram was delivered.

```
62 NX  B  COLLECT  116P
INDIAN HR VIA CAPE RACE NF 6
   ASSD PRESS  NY

STARS AND STRIPES NAILED TO NORTH POLE.
PEARY.
```

The message immediately created another sensation. The second claim to the discovery of the North Pole within a week? A telegram flashed back to Indian Harbor, Labrador, asking for verification and in it The Associated Press called attention to Dr. Cook's claims.

The answer came back:

```
INDIAN HR VIA CAPE MAY N J SEPT 6
MELVILLE E STONE
    ASSD PRESS  N Y

REGRET UNABLE DISPATCH DETAILS.  MY DISPATCH
STARS AND STRIPES NAILED TO NORTH POLE AUTHOR-
ITATIVE AND CORRECT.  COOK'S STORY SHOULD NOT
BE TAKEN TOO SERIOUSLY.  THE TWO ESKIMOS WHO
ACCOMPANIED HIM SAY HE WENT NO DISTANCE NORTH
AND NOT OUT OF SIGHT OF LAND.  OTHER MEMBERS
OF THE TRIBE CORROBORATE THEIR STORY.  PEARY.
```

The new discovery story splashed across front pages within an hour. Instructions from New York headquarters went north to W. C. Jefferds, correspondent in Portland, Maine, Peary's home town, and to J. W. Regan, correspondent at Halifx. With John Quinpool, another staff man, they had previously received orders to get ready to search for Peary, who had been overdue. The three men hired the *Douglas H. Thomas,* the only oceangoing tug available in Nova Scotia, and set out on their hazardous 475-mile voyage to Battle Harbor. Regan's assistant, W. G. Foster, made a fourth in the party.

Before they started Jefferds delivered the news of Peary's discovery to the explorer's wife, who was at a summer home on an island off the Maine coast. She was skeptical because she thought her husband would have communicated with her at the same time. However, she entrusted the reporter with a message to deliver at Battle Harbor. Her daughter Marie—the famous "Snow Baby" born in the far North on one of Peary's previous arctic trips—was so overjoyed that she hugged and kissed Jefferds. An hour and a half after the correspondent departed the proprietor of the country store on the mainland arrived with a telegram from Peary confirming the news Jefferds had brought.

The Associated Press tug reached Battle Harbor on September 13 and moored alongside the ice-scarred *Roosevelt,* Peary's expedition boat.

Fortunately no communication difficulties hampered relay of the story from Labrador. A low-power wireless station sent out the news to relay points along the bleak mountainous coast. Thence they were forwarded to New York.

The redoubtable Dr. Cook was aboard the steamer *Oscar II*, en route home from Denmark, and Berry of the Berlin staff accompanied him. Controversy raged more fiercely than ever. On special request, the Canadian Marconi Company agreed to transmit Peary's version of the discovery to Cook in mid-Atlantic, and to bring in the stories Berry wrote on the Brooklyn explorer's reaction. When Cook's comment was received, it was relayed to the staff at Battle Harbor for Peary's information and reply.

Although separated by thousands of miles, the rival claimants carried on a stubborn debate and the public read the exchange of statements and contradictions. The four men at Battle Harbor, joined later by Carl Brandebury of the New York staff, had the unique story there to themselves until a steamer arrived with American and Canadian correspondents.

The Peary-Cook dispute made news until a National Geographic Society commission sustained Peary's claims as the true discoverer of the North Pole. Cook's purported proofs were submitted to the University of Copenhagen for adjudication and ruled insufficient.

4

Aviation bounded back into the limelight, and again it was the newspaperman-explorer Wellman who provided a story with no rival for drama and suspense. Early in 1910 he was soliciting financial backing for an unheard-of exploit. He proposed to cross the Atlantic from the United States to Europe in the rebuilt dirigible *America*. Lawson could not resist the lure of the great news such a flight might yield and once more he advanced funds. The New York *Times* and the London *Daily Telegraph* likewise became interested and helped to raise $40,000. In return the three papers received exclusive rights to all details of this first attempt at a transoceanic airship flight.

From the outset the story presented coverage difficulties for the co-operative because Wellman had contracted to give the official information on his venture only to the syndicate financing him. The Associated Press was left to its own devices to get a story which momentarily transcended all others.

Wellman selected Atlantic City as the starting point for the flight and workmen began to reassemble the dismantled dirigible as soon as it arrived by boat from Paris on August 6. Reporters from the New York office wrote reams of copy describing the construction of the

America, the principle of its "equilibrator," and the lifeboat which was to be carried, slung under the car of the airship, well away from the inflammable hull of the ship, to accommodate a short-range wireless set, a stove, and other equipment. Progress in preparing the *America* was slow. August passed. Then September. Many people were calling Wellman a "fake."

At last, on October 12, Columbus Day, the work was finished. Less than sixty hours later, Saturday morning, October 15, Wellman shouted "Let go all!" to an improvised ground crew and the *America* disappeared into a dense fog, Europe bound. She carried a crew of five, a wireless operator, and a mascot kitten, "Kiddo." The wireless operator was Jack Irwin.

Up and down the coast and in cities abroad the association's forces were alert for word of the airship's progress.

Crouched in the lifeboat precariously suspended beneath the dirigible's car, Irwin contacted an Atlantic City station two and a half hours after the take-off and the first wireless messages exchanged between a shore station and an airship were sent. "Headed northeast. All well on board. Machinery working well." Swift bulletins relayed the information. A few minutes later Wellman sent a dispatch in code giving details of the flight up to that point, but it went exclusively to the syndicate financing him.

Then silence descended and for twenty-four hours no further reports came from the ocean fog which held the *America*. Men stopped one another in the streets to inquire if there was any news. From wireless stations all along the coast, from operators on ships at sea, calls went out to the *America*. But there was no answer.

Irwin in his swaying aerial lifeboat could hear the calls, but all his efforts to raise one of the stations failed. His dynamo stopped working, forcing him to switch to batteries and their limited power reduced his signal range. One or two vessels were sighted through the fog, but apparently they carried no wireless equipment. Finally on Sunday afternoon, he got through an "All's well" message to Siasconset—the *America* was then off Nantucket—and Wellman sent a code dispatch to the syndicate enumerating difficulties that were developing. Then the long hours of silence returned.

All Sunday night the airship battled a storm which threatened to destroy her. Irwin flashed CQD after CQD, but the distress signals were never picked up. The "equilibrator," a long metal device towed along the ocean's surface like a huge sea serpent to control the airship's altitude and to compensate for changes in her buoyancy, kept pulling the *America* down toward the crest of the waves. The wind changed and drove the dirigible southward, off her course.

Throughout Monday the battle against disaster went on. Gasoline, oil, supplies, even parts of the motors were jettisoned to lighten ship and keep her from crashing into the ocean. Monday night was the last night. The five aboard realized it as they ate a meal of cold ham, biscuits, and water. They might be able to keep the airship in flight another day, but when the sun set again and the gas cooled, she would plunge into the sea. They would have to risk launching the lifeboat sometime Tuesday, dropping it from mid-air and running the double risk of having it capsize or be smashed by the equilibrator below.

The wireless operator stood watch in the drifting airship until 3 A.M. Tuesday, when Wellman relieved him. Shouts roused him some time later. A steamer had been sighted. Irwin tumbled down into the life boat and started calling, but got no answer.

Seizing a flashlight, he commenced signaling in Morse code, blinking out dots and dashes.

Then, suddenly, the steamer was signaling back by the same method. Irwin asked if they had a wireless aboard and the steamer— she was the Bermuda liner S.S. *Trent*—replied her Marconi man would be routed out at once. In a few minutes Irwin was talking by wireless with Louis S. Ginsberg, the *Trent's* operator, arranging the details of a perilous rescue.

Down came the *America*. The lifeboat's lashings were loosened. The last two release hooks were snapped open and the boat plummeted into the rough ocean with the airship's crew and Kiddo. It almost capsized, righted itself, and crashed into the dreaded equilibrator. Seconds later the *Trent* almost ran them down as she maneuvered and they were in danger of being cut to pieces by the propellers. Lines finally were thrown down and the *America's* bedraggled crew was pulled aboard the *Trent*. The abandoned airship drifted away derelict over the ocean.

Battered and weary, Irwin made his way immediately to the *Trent's* wireless room. Standing beside the steamer's operator the one-time string correspondent stole a march on Wellman by dictating a straightforward report of the *America's* ill-starred aerial odyssey and the rescue 375 miles east of Cape Hatteras.

In a matter of minutes the dispatch reached the New York headquarters of The Associated Press. It was flash news all wires. The two

THEN, SUDDENLY, THE STEAMER WAS SIGNALLING BACK.

American newspapers which had contracted with Wellman for the exclusive story of his adventure got their first tidings, not from him but from the co-operative in which they held membership. Similarly, an Associated Press dispatch, relayed to Europe, gave the London *Telegraph,* the third syndicate member, its first information.

The *America's* wireless operator might have signed his dramatic dispatch from the *Trent* "Irwin," and that would have been sufficient for the news editor who first read it in New York. Apparently he thought more complete identification necessary. After his name he added three words, and the complete signature read: "Irwin, Associated Press correspondent."

VII. A NEW PERSONALITY

I

". . . the revenues for the twelve months of 1910 were $2,728,-888.64 and the expenses $2,742,492.18." This was another deficit, the fifth in seven years.

The Associated Press had celebrated its tenth anniversary as a non-pro-fit co-operative. Its prestige stood high and, as far as externals went, the organization's position was an enviable one. Yet there were danger signals.

The financial condition worried General Manager Stone. For the most part, his efforts had been concentrated on the performance of the association as an impartial news gatherer. The report was the thing by which members and newspaper readers alike judged the organization, and to the report he devoted his genius. Expense, extension of facilities, and costly commitments were no major objects with him when it was a question of maintaining Associated Press pre-eminence. The results bore tribute to his energetic direction and his unusual personality found valuable expression in dramatizing the new principle for which the co-operative stood. Yet the demands of actual news gathering made it difficult for him to turn his notable abilities to less spirited organizational problems. Business details never captured his imagination and he was happier in the midst of a great news emergency than while struggling with the intricacies of a balanced budget.

The difficulty of making ends meet while operating a non-profit organization on the same assessment basis which went into effect in 1900, before the demands of news gathering began to increase, was acute. The basis of prorating expenses during the first ten years was purely experimental. But inasmuch as the formula was based on the population in each member paper's circulating area, there was no chance of revising figures until the 1910 Federal Census became available. At that time Stone and the Board of Directors planned to review the existing scales and readjust wherever necessary. In the meantime the general manager could do little more than refer the recurrent vexations to Treasurer J. R. Youatt for such inconclusive preliminary action as could be taken.

As for savings through a realignment of leased wire facilities—one of the largest items of expense—these possibilities eluded Stone. But he did realize that the question of improving the lot of the harried pony papers was important. This was essentially a news detail because it was necessary that they be served efficiently if they were to remain in membership and contribute the important news of their territories. If he ever did forget the plight of these papers, it was not for long. Day in and day out their messages reached his desk:

"No telegraph budget today until after we had gone to press."

"Today's report not only late but garbled."

"Help. Help. No news telegram today."

"If we can't get news, how can we pay our assessment?"

Spurred by these complaints, Stone ventured into the communications' field to seek a remedy. He sounded out telegraph companies once again on the possibility of an arrangement which would guarantee expeditious commercial delivery without an increase in expense. Company officials could promise nothing.

Then he attempted to arrange for "short-hour" leased wire facilities over which important news could be speeded to the small papers. But wire companies reported this was not feasible except at more expense than the papers could afford.

Just when the pony outlook seemed blackest, help appeared from an unexpected source.

The general manager was at his desk one day shortly before Thanksgiving in 1910, when C. H. Wilson, general manager of the American Telephone and Telegraph Company, telephoned that he was sending over a young man who had some practical ideas about transmitting news rapidly to small papers in isolated places.

The young man was Kent Cooper, from Indiana. Stone promised to see him, but he was not convinced that the solution of the co-operative's problem of delivering world news to distant papers of only modest means could come from such an unknown source, particularly when it was something that had puzzled the best minds in the transmission business. Nevertheless, the general manager had an effective method of dealing with visitors. He greeted them graciously but with his body barring the doorway to his private office while he made tentative appraisal. If sufficiently impressed he could step back in his most cordial manner and permit them to enter. But if not, he could dismiss them without having them suspect that he did not wish to be bothered.

It was in this way that he greeted Cooper.

"I understand you have the solution of the problem of getting news to small papers which cannot afford leased wires," he said with a quizzical smile.

Cooper replied that he believed he did.

Stone still stood in the doorway.

"Well," he said, selecting a point about which a Midwesterner normally would not be expected to have first knowledge, "just exactly what could you do for Burlington, Vermont?"

Cooper thought for a moment.

"You can't serve Burlington economically from Boston, which is your nearest New England Bureau," he replied, "because of the distance."

Stone was surprised that his visitor was that well informed, but the Burlington problem still was not solved.

"So what could you do?" he asked.

"Well," observed Cooper, "why not serve them by telephone out of your Albany Bureau, which is closer? From Albany it would involve only 156 miles of wire as against 233 from Boston, and the cost to deliver 1,500 words daily over this route would be only $16 a week.'

Stone gave the young man another once over.

"Come on in," he said.

2

Stone did not know it then, but Cooper's experience in newspaper work had begun when he was a boy of thirteen—the same year Victor Lawson and his publishing associates started the "revolution of 1893" out of which had come the non-profit co-operative principle in news

The son of an Indiana congressman, Cooper began as a carrier boy and a year later became a fledgling reporter on the Columbus *Republican*. His editor belonged to the school which believed that "names make news" and Cooper's first assignment was to ride his bicycle to the railroad station daily and get the names of all arrivals and departures. In time he came in contact with the resurgent Associated Press and the Chicago Bureau made him a string correspondent at Columbus. He continued this part-time work in addition to his duties on the local paper until he left to attend the University of Indiana. His father died in 1899 and he was forced to leave college to earn his own living.

The Indianapolis *Press* gave him his start at $12 a week. Later he joined the Scripps-McRae Press Association and established its Indianapolis Bureau. Most papers served from that office were small and Cooper came to know the problems which beset them. In 1905 he struck out for himself with a state or vicinage news service of his own, set up with $50 of his own money and a similar amount invested by a friend. He incorporated his enterprise as the United Press News Association and a year later sold it to Scripps-McRae, which merged with two other agencies in 1907 to form the United Press Associations.

Cooper continued as Indianapolis Bureau manager and soon he was experimenting with a telephone talking circuit serving news to several small papers simultaneously. Up to that time the telephone companies had no special press rates but charged on a private-message, point-to-point basis. Cooper convinced them that it was to their advantage to fix a rate which would enable them to compete with the telegraph as a news distribution medium and also demonstrated that the problem of linking a number of papers together on a talking news circuit was feasible.

The idea behind the telephone pony circuit was that a press association employee made up an abbreviated news report in a centrally located bureau and then read it over a long-distance line extending into the offices of small newspapers several miles to hundreds of miles away. In each of the offices the local editor listened into the receiver and copied down the news at it was being read. One appealing feature was that the receiving editors developed the habit of volunteering to the others on the circuit the news of their communities, thus exchanging much neighborhood or vicinage news which ordinarily would not have found its way into a press association report.

In spite of the success of these early efforts, Cooper was not satisfied. He knew of the abuses to which commercially controlled news had been subjected back before the emergence of the non-profit principle in news, and he felt that The Associated Press offered unique opportunity on the side of truthful, unbiased reporting. He was familiar with the practical obstacles which had hindered its expansion into the more isolated areas such as those he had learned to serve by telephone, and so it was through telephone officials that he obtained his introduction to Stone. He began his assignment on December 5, 1910.

3

Although the young Indianian had demonstrated his knowledge of transmission conditions, he still had to convince Stone that news actually could be sent by ordinary telephone to scattered newspapers without losing anything in accuracy—a question about which the general manager had his worst fears.

"You'll have my resignation if I can't deliver stories by telephone more rapidly and with greater accuracy and efficiency than you can deliver them by overhead telegraph," Cooper told Stone soon after he took up his duties in New York.

The general manager accepted the stipulation.

"You are to make your test on two real 'guinea pigs' I'll select for you out in Michigan," he said.

Owing to cumbersome wire systems and the burden of commercial traffic, telegraphed delivery of the association's pony news reports to the Houghton *Gazette* and the Marquette *Journal* had been haphazard and uncertain at best. Their news budgets, prepared in the Chicago office, averaged five thousand words nightly and the long telegraph files were both expensive and subject to frequent garbling.

Cooper lined up his circuit and looked on as the first telephone news report was read to the two papers by an editor in the Chicago office. In Houghton and Marquette, miles away, the two member editors simultaneously copied down dispatch after dispatch as the man in Chicago read the news into the mouthpiece at the sending end. The news not only was delivered more rapidly, but a study of the received copy showed it was completely accurate. Moreover, one telephone circuit linking both papers was less expensive than the double filing necessary to deliver the copy to both papers by overhead telegraph.

Stone was pleased.

"You win," he said. "Now go to work and serve all the papers that have been giving us so much trouble."

He started to wave Cooper away, but on the spur of the moment called him back.

"Tell me," he smiled, "how in the name of the devil did you happen to have the answer on Burlington that day you came to see me? You even knew the exact wire mileage from Albany."

Cooper explained.

"It was very simple," he said. "I studied the situation before I came to see you and memorized the figures on the more isolated places because they were the ones I thought you'd be likely to ask about!"

First in the Midwest, then in the East, the Rocky Mountain area, and other sections of the country, Cooper set up the special telephone pony circuits to supplant the unsatisfactory commercial telegraph transmissions. Before he had been in the service four months thirty-six additional papers were receiving their news over telephone talking circuits and the program had only begun.

VIII. STANDARD OIL

I

WHILE Cooper was improving the lot of the association's smaller newspapers Stone and the Board of Directors were occupied with trouble that was brewing elsewhere.

There were alarming charges affecting the integrity of the news report and the probity of the general manager. The most serious accusation was made by Frank B. Kellogg, the government attorney who later became secretary of state. He had been engaged in prosecuting the Standard Oil Company under the Sherman antitrust law, and during that litigation he wrote:

Melville E. Stone is controlled absolutely by the Standard Oil people. He will not, of course, send out any reports of the testimony that he is not obliged to, at least that is my opinion from all that I have seen. . . . It is astonishing that that concern can control The Associated Press.

John D. Rockefeller's oil empire had been under attack ever since the trust-busting era began in earnest with Theodore Roosevelt's second term in the White House. Roosevelt's vigorous language put the Standard Oil on the defensive in the public eye. The oil company had a bad press editorially, and as early as 1905 some of its people were suggesting that it "start a backfire" to counteract unfavorable publicity. At that time Congressman J. C. Sibley of Pennsylvania, who was interested in Standard Oil, wrote confidentially to John D. Archbold, the corporation's vice-president, proposing a definite plan: "An efficient literary bureau is needed, not for a day but [for] permanent and healthy control of The Associated Press and other kindred avenues. It will cost money, but it will be the cheapest in the end and can be made self-supporting."

No action was taken on Sibley's suggestion and The Associated Press, unaware of the possible schemes of lobbyists and press agents, continued to report news concerning the oil company in an objective, factual manner.

A few years later, however, Kellogg, as government prosecutor, instituted the lengthy proceedings which ultimately brought the dissolution of the parent corporation in the Rockefeller structure, the Standard Oil of New Jersey. During this litigation attempts were made to influence the report in favor of the company. Kellogg was unaware of this when he made his charges against Stone, but it was his accusation that started an inquiry.

At the request of member papers in New York City, the Board of Directors appointed a five-man committee, headed by Oswald Garrison Villard of the New York *Post*, for a thorough investigation not only of Kellogg's allegations but also of any complaints reflecting on the integrity of the news. None of the committee men was a board member and the fact that several of them privately disliked Stone was a guarantee that nothing would be left undone to uncover evidence of collusion.

Kellogg's letter attacking Stone obviously was one of the first points of inquiry. Attempts to have Kellogg appear before the committee proved unsuccessful. The attorney refused and when the Villard committee visited him in a body he denied he had written the letter. The committee confronted him with the original which bore his signature and he reluctantly acknowledged its authenticity. The letter, he said, stated his opinion of the situation as he recalled it. He offered to produce "proof" of the co-operative's failure to carry adequate stories setting forth the government's side of the oil case.

To obtain this proof, Kellogg had his secretary check on Associated Press stories appearing in a single state. Minnesota was the state selected. The survey disclosed that few dispatches on the subject were printed there, and the few appearing had been brief. Kellogg soon found, however, that this survey established nothing except the fallacy of the conclusion on which he had made his charge of bias. There was little interest attached to the Standard Oil case in Minnesota and editors of member papers consequently had made sparing use of the stories they had received. An examination of The Associated Press files disclosed that the case had been reported thoroughly, and a check of papers nationally showed there had been extensive use of the material which Minnesota editors had trimmed down or discarded.

This phase of the investigation had no sooner ended than Villard's committee learned with surprise from the general manager that a correspondent who indirectly covered one phase of the Standard Oil case for The Associated Press had been in the pay of a Standard Oil press agent, Captain P. C. Boyle, of Oil City, Pennsylvania. Unaware of these facts before, Stone volunteered the information as soon as he obtained it from Boyle. Some members of the committee were disposed to be suspicious. It was common knowledge that Boyle, who held membership in the association as publisher of the Oil City *Derrick,* was a friend of Stone.

The investigators sought information on how the Standard Oil case had been covered both in the extended hearings at New York and in the final arguments at St. Louis. It developed that Carl Brandebury, city editor of the New York staff, had been assigned to the case when it opened in New York. He covered forty-four of the ninety-five hearings and was withdrawn only after all the major witnesses had testified. The remaining fifty-one hearings were routine and for coverage on these the co-operative depended on the reports of the City News Association, the local news-gathering agency owned and controlled by the New York newspapers. City News maintained its own staff and supplied the New York papers and The Associated Press with the daily routine and secondary news of the metropolis. Like the co-operative, all but one of the New York papers recalled their staff men after the important witnesses had been heard and relied on City News.

Captain Boyle, appearing before the committee, told of his association with the City News reporter who covered the case. As soon as the oil company hearings were under way, he testified, he felt that Standard Oil was not receiving fair play in the accounts published by the New York papers. He said he felt that the government's case, on the other hand, received too favorable attention. "For accuracy in reporting," as he called it, he arranged with the reporter to give the Standard Oil's side of the controversy "proper" treatment in the City News reports. These, he knew, would go to the local papers, whether or not they had staff men present, and he hoped they might influence editors.

Boyle paid the reporter "never less than $100 a week," although he claimed that the results were so negative that the expense was hardly justified. When it was pointed out to the witness that The Associated Press might have been victimized by misrepresentations in the City News report, Boyle insisted he was thinking only of the local papers when he retained the City News man. He also declared that the reporter was paid to report the Standard Oil side of the case "accurately" and not to distort any facts.

The City News reporter's status changed when the Standard Oil litigation shifted to St. Louis for argument. The involved nature of the case made it desirable that the man covering the argument be thoroughly familiar with all the background, and there was no one in the

St. Louis Bureau so qualified. While Stone was considering the matter of the assignment, the City News man offered his services. He said he had a vacation coming and that he would be glad to utilize the time to cover the brief St. Louis proceedings for The Associated Press. Stone felt that this offered an excellent opportunity to arrange for authoritative coverage since the man was familiar with the case, and so he engaged him. Unknown to Stone, the reporter then got in touch with Boyle and for $500 promised to "look after" Standard Oil interests.

Boyle acknowledged this in his testimony, but again insisted he was aiming at the local press in St. Louis and not at The Associated Press. The local men, he said, would naturally turn to the New York reporter, as one well grounded, to clarify the intricate phases of the case. He denied that the City News man had made clear his Associated Press connection or that this consideration figured in the bargain. He said that he had gone to Stone promptly with all this information as soon as he learned the general manager was under investigation.

These facts established, the Villard committee turned to the news reports to ascertain what effect the secret Boyle understanding had had on the coverage. The findings, however, suggested that Boyle had made a bad bargain. The New York reporter's accounts of the New York hearings had been rewritten by Associated Press men before relay on the leased wires. His stories at St. Louis had contained editorializing in favor of the Standard Oil, but the files showed that Melvin Coleman, vigilant head of the bureau there, had deleted all such references before the copy reached the wires.

Both Boyle and the City News reporter testified that Stone was ignorant of their private arrangement.

After the Boyle conspiracy had been exposed, the investigators turned to less sensational indictments urged against the general manager. Foreign governments had bestowed decorations on Stone in recognition of his efforts to break down censorship. Some of his critics contended that these honors disposed The Associated Press to give preferential treatment to news involving governments which had so honored the general manager.

Another attack centered on the fact that Stone numbered among his social acquaintances such men as J. P. Morgan, Judge Elbert H. Gary, head of the United States Steel Corporation, and others prominent in finance and business. These relations, it was argued, created suspicion that the co-operative was primarily concerned with protecting the interests with which these men were identified. Stone's part in arranging the Russo-Japanese peace at the Portsmouth Conference in 1905 also was criticized as improper activity for a general manager, regardless of his good intentions.

The investigation seemed more and more like a hostile expedition looking for anything to discredit the general manager. Stone found some consolation in the fact that, although the entire membership had been canvassed, no charges had come from its ranks. The accusations, both serious and trivial, emanated from private sources. Nevertheless, the general manager's position became a trying one, for until the committee submitted its findings he lived under a cloud.

2

Under the strained circumstances the service inevitably suffered. Among the things overlooked was the special work Cooper had been doing. His duties had taken him into most parts of the country and his study of wire facilities was bringing to light conditions long unnoticed. In many places he found that the association was paying for wires it was not actually using. In others, mileage could be saved by more direct routing of wires, and in still others the association was paying higher rates than commercial competitors. In numerous instances efficiency and economy could be served by combining or realigning existing wire setups. Cooper discovered, too, that outdated or faulty mechanical equipment was responsible for costly wire delays and that on a number of overtaxed circuits the report should be overhauled.

Individually the potential economies were not always imposing—a few hundred dollars here, a thousand there—but taken together they made a sum of more than $100,000 yearly, no small amount in the affairs of an organization with an annual budget of $2,846,812.

There were the immediate demands of the news report for first consideration—the coronation of King George of England, troubles in Mexico, revolution in China, a Franco-German crisis, and extension of the service into South America. But the Cooper plan soon was adopted with the active encouragement of V. S. McClatchy, of the Sacramento *Bee*, and Adolph S. Ochs, of the New York *Times*. By 1912 the realignment program was in full swing and during a period of recurrent deficits the savings were most welcome. Together with a revision of the assessment schedules by which the expenses of the association were prorated among the member newspapers on the basis of population figures compiled by the 1910 Federal Census, these savings helped the financial affairs of the association return to an even keel.

3

The investigation of Villard's committee entered its closing stages and the Board of Directors instituted action against Captain Boyle as the owner of a member paper. His admissions involving coverage of the Standard Oil litigation had subjected the news report to question. The board termed his conduct "most reprehensible," fined him $1,000, and publicly rebuked him for his actions.

After almost a year of testimony, Villard's committee at length submitted its final report on the whole investigation. Although the language of the report was not friendly to Stone, it vindicated his integrity and the integrity of the news report he administered. The accusations and unsavory insinuations were considered seriatim and dismissed as unfounded. The committee stated that most of the charges against the news report had come from laymen who had jumped to conclusions that The Associated Press had suppressed news on controversial subjects simply because no dispatch appeared in a certain newspaper. In every such instance the committee found that the story had been carried fully and factually on the wires serving member papers.

The investigators termed Kellogg's statement that Stone was "owned" by Standard Oil "inexcusably reckless and unwarranted by the fact," and added:

Your committee is convinced that whatever the individual faults of reporting may have been, or whatever attempts were made by the Standard Oil to color the report, nothing was carried during this long hearing which violated the integrity of the service.

The subsidization of the City News reporter was mentioned at some length, and the committee commented:

It is the best possible testimony to the efficiency and integrity of The Associated Press that his efforts were in vain.

As to charges that Stone's decorations from foreign governments or that his personal acquaintance with influential figures led him to favor their interests, they declared:

. . . it is our judgment that the social relations of the General Manager with individuals in powerful financial circles and likewise his acceptance of decorations from foreign governments without objection from the Board of Directors have, not unnaturally, aroused unjust suspicion of the independence and impartiality of his administration of the news service. Nevertheless, we are convinced that Mr. Stone has not been influenced by these circumstances in his conduct of the business of The Associated Press. On the contrary, we think that he has been indefatigable in developing its services. . . . He is entitled to great credit for the present efficiency of the news organization which has been created largely under his leadership and direction.

The attitude of the committee was that The Associated Press, like Caesar's wife, should be above suspicion. The fact that serious charges had been preferred aroused great concern, even though the allegations had been discredited. It therefore recommended that the general manager and all those connected with the co-operative in future avoid anything that would give even the uninitiated the least grounds to question the honesty of the service. It stated:

We consider that the head of The Associated Press should not only in fact be devoted solely to its interests, but that he should also by his personal conduct and relations give no ground for a suspicion of his independence and incorruptibility as the agent and representative of the Press.

The committee discouraged both the future acceptance of foreign decorations and too great familiarity with individuals who figured in controversial news.

Stone had held his peace. He had welcomed the fullest publicity for all phases of his administration, and he had met all criticisms without resentment. After the official findings had been submitted, he felt free to act. The news report had been vindicated, his personal integrity had been upheld, and he appreciated the wisdom of the constructive suggestions advanced. One thing, however, he said he could not ignore —Kellogg's accusation that he was owned by Standard Oil. He notified the Board of Directors that he intended to sue Kellogg for libel on behalf of both himself and The Associated Press.

Kellogg retracted and apologized. He wrote the general manager:

At the time I wrote that statement I felt I was justified in making it. I have since made further investigation and am now satisfied I was mistaken and was not justified in making the imputation upon the integrity of The Associated Press or of its General Manager.

I wish therefore, in justice to you both, to withdraw the accusation and to express my sincere regret that I was ever betrayed into what I now believe was an act of injustice.

He also repeated his regrets in person.

"I was hot when I wrote this letter," he said, referring to the note which contained the libelous charges. "I thought I was writing it to a personal friend, and I was pretty free in what I said, and I didn't look into it very much."

Stone accepted the apology and the furor of the Standard Oil allegations slipped into history.

IX. HEADLINE YEARS

I

ON the eve of the annual meeting of 1912 the *Titanic* disaster called forth every news-gathering resource to obtain a great story against overwhelming odds, and the next years, with their wealth of drama and excitement, brought still more developments in the methods of news collection and transmission.

The *Titanic* was the largest ship the world had ever known and she was making her maiden voyage.

Far out on the Atlantic three bells clanged sharply in the night. The lookout called to the bridge frantically:

"Iceberg! Right ahead!"

Seconds later the big ship trembled as a knife of ice sliced into her like some gigantic can opener. The time was almost midnight, Sunday, April 14. Many of the 2,201 people aboard did not know what the ship had struck. Blue sparks crackled and hissed in the wireless cabin.

Sitting in the supply room of the Boston Bureau, J. D. Kennedy, a night telegrapher, heard the first electrifying whisper of calamity. It was his lunch hour and he was eating in the supply room so he could tinker with the crude wireless set recently installed for emergency use. He heard the Charlestown Navy Yard station repeat the call and then dashed back to the newsroom, blurting out the story.

From that moment the *Titanic* disaster pre-empted the leased wires. The service was made continuous for both morning and evening papers.

Other calls from the *Titanic* followed the first burst of distress signals. Kennedy and other staff men hunched at the wireless apparatus and strained ears for the meager bits of information that came through the ether.

"Come at once, we have struck a berg."

"It's a CQD, old man. Position 41-46N.; 50-14 W."

"Sinking; cannot hear for noise of steam."

"Engine room getting flooded."

Typewriters rattled out the bulletins. More CQD's, and then the

THE TITANIC . . . "ICEBERG! RIGHT AHEAD!"

Titanic's operator suddenly switched to the newer international call of distress:

SOS . . . SOS . . . SOS . . .

At 2:17 A.M. the signal stopped.

After that there were hours of suspense until the *Carpathia* reported she had arrived on the scene at dawn and was picking up survivors. In New York the Marconi Wireless Company gave The Associated Press the only complete list of those rescued by the *Carpathia* and later offered the co-operative exclusive rights to all the disaster news its facilities could obtain. The general manager felt the story was too big for such an arrangement, however advantageous it might be to The Associated Press.

"It is a thing of such widespread interest that you ought not to bottle it up at all," he told the Marconi man.

All that day the news was fragmentary, incomplete, and often conflicting. Communication with the *Carpathia* was sharply restricted, for its wireless was heavily overburdened with official traffic. Messages late Monday gave the first definite information, and it was not until Thursday night, when the *Carpathia,* with 711 survivors aboard, reached her New York pier, that the whole story became known.

The Associated Press set up an emergency "Titanic Bureau" in a hotel facing the pier. Special telegraph and telephone lines were installed and they carried two widely praised eyewitness stories written for the co-operative by Lawrence Beasley, an Oxford student, and Colonel Archibald Gracie, who leaped from the stern of the *Titanic* just as she made her plunge. Dick Lee, ships news reporter for The Associated Press since 1878, arranged for both accounts after boarding the *Carpathia* at Quarantine. From others among the rescued, Lee also gathered material for a story of his own and produced what was called the best detailed narrative of the disaster.

2

The sinking of the *Titanic* proved the wisdom of the Board of Directors in immediately authorizing what it termed "Extraordinary Occasion Service," which was designated EOS for short. Prior to this time a member paper had not been permitted to publish after its regular morning or afternoon hours of publication, no matter how important the news might be. The board realized there were times when the character of the news was so momentous that, as a public service, all papers should be free to publish it immediately, whether it broke within their hours of publication or not. Thereafter all dispatches of extraordinary importance were designated EOS and that slug told editors that they could publish the news immediately if they desired.

Soon the board took another step in its program of readjusting operation methods to the advanced requirements of news gathering. Recognizing that the organization had become too complex to be administered by one man, it decided to provide the general manager with executive assistance. The administration was divided into three branches: News, Finance, and Traffic. The men picked to head these departments were to direct all activities in their respective spheres, reporting directly to the general manager. Treasurer Youatt was assigned to head the Finance Department, Cooper was the choice for Traffic, and a newly created post of chief of the News Department went to Charles E. Kloeber, who had won his spurs in the Boxer Rebellion.

At the same time the board remedied another managerial weakness by appointing Frederick Roy Martin, editor of the Providence *Journal*, to be assistant general manager, an office vacant since Diehl's resignation a short time before. They were grooming him to succeed Stone. Martin had been one of the five members of the Villard investigating committee and in 1912 the membership had elected him to the Board of Directors. He resigned that position to take up his new duties on September 1.

With organizational and financial troubles largely corrected, the co-operative was amply prepared to cover the famous three-cornered presidential election of 1912 in which Woodrow Wilson was victorious over William Howard Taft and Theodore Roosevelt's insurgent Bull Moose party. Then the news report went on to other things—the ratification of the Income Tax Amendment to the Constitution, another revolution in Mexico, suffragette agitation, floods in Ohio and Indiana, the death of J. Pierpont Morgan, the landing of American bluejackets at Veracruz.

3

The return to a balanced budget made possible another innovation. The report of the Special Survey Committee back in 1908 had taken cognizance of the need for greater concentration on sports news. In the past these stories had been handled by the regular news staff and, while coverage had been fair, it was not in keeping with the rapidly increasing public appetite for detailed sports information. The Sports Page had made its appearance before the turn of the century and the volume of such news expanded with the heightened interest in Major League baseball, horse racing, and prize fighting. The growth of the educational system, the fact that the average citizen had more leisure, the improved standards of living, all contributed.

The game of baseball had been invented back in 1839 and had established itself so firmly that "Casey at The Bat" was a favored recitation well before news gathering itself came of age. Horse racing attracted as well, prize fighting was still illegal in some states, though gaining in popularity, and generally each nationality had brought with it the games of its own homeland during the great surges of immigration. The growth of professional sports and the steady rise of amateur and collegiate activities were assured.

Owing to financial stringencies, the co-operative had been unable to enlarge its routine sports coverage to any noticeable extent at the time the Special Survey Committee made its report. But now the time had come when something could be done. A general sports editor was appointed to co-ordinate and expand the service. The man selected for the job was Edward B. Moss, who had been sports editor of the New York *Sun* for the past eight years.

Moss set about establishing a small staff to assist him and the leased wires began carrying more sports detail—stories on all major events, expanded boxes, summaries of results, and the like.

From the outset, this quick and detailed coverage attracted attention, in such interesting contrast to what had gone before. Until the telegraph and other communications methods had been so highly developed, the physical difficulties of speedy coverage had been great because, by their very nature, so many of the events were held in places where immediate wire facilities were not always available. But there still were a few employes who could remember one classic example of ingenious earlier sports reporting in spite of communications handicaps. It had occurred on July 8, 1889, when prize fighting was illegal in most states. It was the last bare-knuckle championship bout under London prize ring rules and it was between John L. Sullivan and Jake Kilrain. It went seventy-five rounds, lasted two hours and sixteen minutes, and was held in the woods near the little town of Richburg, Mississippi, in an attempt to avoid legal complications.

The nearest telegraph office was in New Orleans, a hundred miles away, and the problem of relaying the result was accentuated by the great public interest in the contest.

Because it was primarily a mechanical problem, Addison Thomas, wire chief of the Western Associated Press Chicago office, was assigned to direct the coverage.

By the time the eagerly awaited day arrived Thomas had made his plans. With the co-operation of The Associated Press papers in New Orleans, he had arranged for a chartered railroad engine and two cars to race the result back to New Orleans ahead of the special fight trains on which spectators flocked to Richburg. It was a train reserved for the exclusive use of Thomas and the representatives of the interested New Orleans papers and it stood with steam up and ready to go on a siding a short distance from the ringside.

But that was not the only preparation needed. Thomas and his associates knew that the excited, shoving spectators would jam the ringside for the long, knuckle-battering contest, perhaps making it impossible for anyone to get away quickly with details to the waiting train. And it was necessary to put the news on the train the moment the fight was over so that the special could get under way ahead of the returning passenger trains.

They met that situation by obtaining hollow balls which were constructed so that they could be opened in halves and then screwed back together. Then, as a quick report was written at the conclusion of each round, they put the copy inside the balls, screwed the halves together and threw the balls over the heads of the spectators to an assistant who caught them on the outside fringe of the crowd. The assistant then could rush them to the train at the conclusion of the bout and the special would be off in a hurry to the waiting telegraph at New Orleans.

The plan operated like clockwork. The loaded balls were tossed over the crowd and at the end of the battle the assistant rushed to the train which quickly got under way.

The plan, however, had overlooked one detail. There were opposition news men present and in some manner they got through the crowds quickly. Before the train had raced many miles they were discovered concealed in one of the two cars of the speeding special. That called for some more quick action.

The Associated Press man hurried up to the engine, cut the two cars loose and left the opposition stranded on the tracks. Then the engine ran full speed the hundred miles to New Orleans.

That had been an exciting and ingenious stunt, but by 1913 telegraph lines could be strung direct to the scene of almost any sports event, irrespective of locale, and the reports written by the new general sports editor and his small staff could go speeding direct to newspaper offices.

4

This step in widespread coverage of still another phase of news had not been under way long before there came other developments in news transmission methods.

The tide of news by telegraph had continued with the years. Facilities had been improved, the Morse clicked into virtually every town in the country, but the old method was the same. Day in and day out, sending operators took dispatches, translated them into the dash-dot of code, and the telegraph keys sent the signals on the circuits at a rate of twenty-five to thirty-five words a minute. In member newspaper offices along the line the Morse sounders clack-clacked busily and receiving operators translated the code symbols back into words, copying the stories in jerky spurts. The news of more than half a century had been handled that way.

For some time, however, Charles L. Krum, a Chicago cold-storage engineer, and his son Howard had been working to perfect an automatic machine which would send the printed word by wire at greater speed without the intermediary of code. They called their invention the Morkrum Telegraph Printer—coining the word Morkrum by combining the inventor's name with the first syllable in the last name of Joy Morton, a Chicago businessman who financed them.

Several other automatic telegraphic devices were being promoted, but Cooper and engineers in the Traffic Department decided Krum's machine held the most promise for their purposes. Tests got under way. In the Associated Press headquarters, which had been moved seven blocks from the old Western Union building to 51 Chambers Street, a sending operator sat at a keyboard similar to that of an ordinary typewriter. As he struck the keys, copying the dispatches before him, the machine perforated a paper tape with a series of holes, each combination representing a letter. The tape fed into a boxlike transmitter which transformed the tape perforations into electrical impulses and sent them along the wires into the receiving machines in newspaper offices. These impulses actuated telegraph relays and set the receiving Morkrum machines automatically reproducing the letters which the sending operators were typing miles away.

The tests demonstrated that the Morkrum could transmit news hour after hour at the rate of sixty words a minute and the copy was delivered clean and uniform. Thus began the slow extension of Morkrum transmission to the whole leased wire system, replacing the "brass pounding" Morse keys. It was a transition that required years and until it was completed both Morse and Morkrum worked side by side in many places.

5

There were faint rumblings of unrest abroad, but in 1913 it was an incident concerning a simple matter of office routine in one of the association's European bureaus that set the year apart for the staff itself and produced a chuckle wherever the story was told.

The story began staidly enough with an action by the Board of Directors requiring the bonding of all chiefs of foreign bureaus who handled funds. Treasurer Youatt diligently mailed out the bonding forms which specified that each bureau chief applying for a bond give two character references well known in America.

Like many other men abroad, Cortesi in Rome seriously wrote his answers to the endless questions. When he reached the place where the character references were to be named, however, a mischievous spirit seized him.

Cortesi mailed the application back to Youatt and forgot it. Several weeks later he had an audience with Pope Pius X and in the midst of their conversation, the Pontiff exclaimed:

"By the way, I have received a letter from an American surety company asking for information about you. Why should they apply to me?"

Bewildered for a moment, Cortesi sheepishly remembered the bonding application and confessed he had tried to play a joke on the treasurer of The Associated Press. He had filled out the reference blank as follows:

NAME	OCCUPATION	ADDRESS
GIUSEPPE SARTO	POPE	VATICAN PALACE, ROME (ITALY)
VICTOR EMMANUEL OF SAVOY	KING	QUIRINAL PALACE, ROME (ITALY)

Pius assured Cortesi that he would give him a good character.

That was in 1913 and the spring of 1914 ran on into a summer that shook the world.

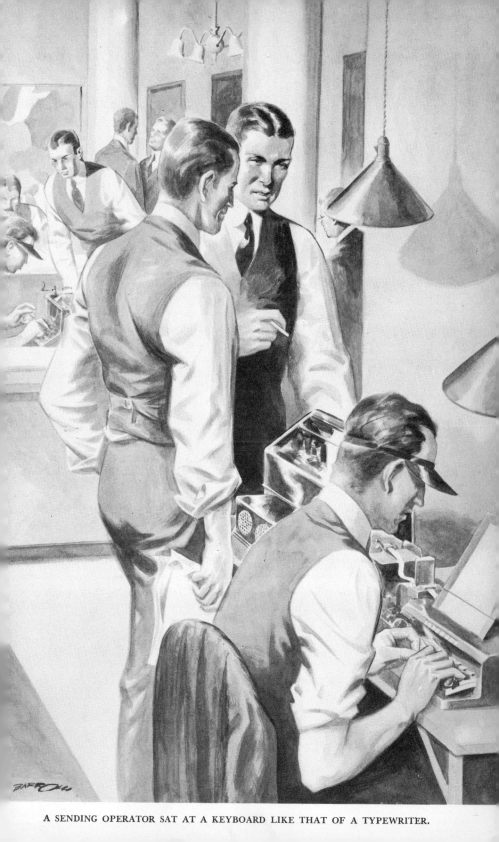

A SENDING OPERATOR SAT AT A KEYBOARD LIKE THAT OF A TYPEWRITER.

6

The chief of the Vienna Bureau, Robert Atter, cabled:

SARAJEVO, BOSNIA, JUNE 28 - ARCHDUKE
FRANCIS FERDINAND, HEIR TO THE AUSTRO-HUNGARIAN
THRONE, AND THE DUCHESS OF HOHENBERG, HIS
MORGANATIC WIFE, WERE SHOT DEAD TODAY BY A
STUDENT IN THE MAIN STREET OF THE BOSNIAN
CAPITAL, A SHORT TIME AFTER THEY HAD ESCAPED
DEATH FROM A BOMB HURLED AT THE ROYAL AUTO-
MOBILES.

IT WAS ON THE RETURN TRIP OF THE PROCESSION
THAT THE TRAGEDY WAS ADDED TO THE LONG LIST OF
THOSE WHICH HAVE DARKENED THE PAGES OF THE
RECENT HISTORY OF THE HAPSBURGS.

AS THE ROYAL AUTOMOBILE REACHED A PROM-
INENT POINT IN THE ROUTE TO THE PALACE, AN
EIGHTH GRADE STUDENT, GARIO PRINZIP, SPRANG
FROM THE CROWD AND POURED A DEADLY FUSILLADE
OF BULLETS FROM AN AUTOMATIC PISTOL AT THE
ARCHDUKE AND PRINCESS. . . .

"Another mess in the Balkans," readers commented. But that dispatch became the lead to a story that beggared anything that had happened before. It saw 65,000,000 soldiers mobilized on battlefields over the world and before the war ended there were 9,000,000 dead and 22,000,000 wounded in armed forces alone. The casualty list of noncombatants was as large, if not larger, and the cost was $337,000,000,000. It was a story that covered both hemispheres and took four years to unfold.

The cables hummed with the ominous overture. Bureau chiefs, staffs and correspondents throughout the Continent worked during the days of tension—Robert Collins, the chief at London; Atter, at Vienna; Roger Lewis, in charge at St. Petersburg; Seymour B. Conger, at Berlin; Elmer Roberts, at Paris; Ed Traus, at Brussels; Cortesi at Rome, and the men assigned with them. At first the story was of Austria's diplomatic moves against Serbia. Inexorably it expanded.

Then came the last week of July and the bulletins flew:

Austria's ultimatum to Serbia . . . Russia Warns Austria . . . Germany Backs Austria . . . Austria Declares War on Serbia . . . Russia Mobilizes . . . Germany Begins Invasion of France . . . Germany Demands Free Passage of Troops Through Belgium . . . Great Britain Protests Violation of Belgian Neutrality . . . Britain Declares War . . .

Armageddon had begun.

As the crisis mounted, The Associated Press rushed some of its best men abroad to reinforce the European staff. George A. Schreiner, who had been covering a revolution in Mexico, was sent to Belgium. Walter C. Whiffen, another of the staff reporting the Mexican troubles, went to St. Petersburg. Robert Berry, day cable editor at New York, took the first boat for France. Charles Stevenson Smith, of the Washington staff, and four others were ordered to London. Assistant General Manager Martin hurriedly embarked for Europe, carrying $20,000 in gold in a leather hatbox to tide foreign bureaus over the financial stringency which accompanied the outbreak of war.

Endless gray German columns swept through Belgium and with them went Conger of Berlin. Covering the hopeless efforts of the Belgians to halt the juggernaut were Schreiner and Hendrik Willem Van Loon, who entered the foreign service in 1906. The stories Schreiner and Van Loon wrote on the destitution and suffering of invaded Belgium were generally credited with providing much of the initial stimulus for the relief funds raised in the United States.

Without official sanction Smith reached Belgium after the British Expeditionary Force—the "contemptible hundred thousand"—and Roberts and Berry followed the French. On the eastern front Whiffen arrived in time to join the Russians for their early battles, while Atter, his colleague from Vienna, reported the same fighting from the Austro-Hungarian lines. On the other side of the world A. M. Bruce used carrier pigeons, native runners, and the wireless to report the Japanese siege of the German fortress of Tsingtao.

America read of Liége, Namur, Mons, Louvain, Rheims, Lemberg, Tannenberg, in lightning succession. Editors and readers alike followed the seemingly irresistible German advance which swept almost to the gates of Paris before it was rolled back in the First Battle of the Marne and the western front settled down to the long months of trench warfare.

X. COVERING THE FIRST ARMAGEDDON

THE immensity of the war assignment and all its attendant difficulties became increasingly clear. The old barriers of censorship returned, more stringent, more unreasoning than ever. Communications were a gamble, what with warring governments pre-empting telephone, telegraph, cable, and wireless facilities for official and military use. Propaganda mills ground out their atrocity stories. Ministries issued communiqués which could not be confirmed. Except on favorable occasions, none of the belligerents welcomed factual, objective, and unbiased reporting. In a conflict that was waged with publicity as well as powder, the integrity of the news report was a prime consideration. The old adage has it that "Truth is the first casualty in any war," and the management labored to find the truth.

The Associated Press obviously could not assume responsibility for the correctness of government statements in formal communiqués and documents. It could and did vouch for the fact that such releases were issued and what official was authority for them. In all practical circumstances, effort was made to have staff men either obtain facts at first hand or confirm them personally.

The war staff had no easy time of it. Fortunately only one of the staff was wounded during the opening months, but even outside the battle zone correspondents were subject to repeated harassment and trouble. One of the London staff was arrested as a spy while covering the hit-and-run bombardment of English Channel towns by German cruisers. That he could read and write German was considered conclusive proof of espionage until higher authorities stepped in. Others were "detained" on different occasions by civil or military authorities. The German occupation of Belgium forced Schreiner and Van Loon out of the country into Holland, where they set up a special bureau to handle the exchange of news between the occupied areas, Germany, London, and New York. Schreiner later was accredited to the Austro-Hungarian armies in Galicia and returned to active duty in the war zone. Ill-health forced Van Loon to resign in 1915.

The belligerents were mindful of the authority which firsthand stories by Associated Press staff correspondents carried. When both French and German High Commands claimed possession of Hartmans-Weilerkopf, an important strategic position in Alsace, Chief of Bureau Roberts went to the sector and reported what he saw. The French War Office, realizing the value of this impartial testimony, issued a communiqué, saying: "The correspondent of The Associated Press visited today the summit of Hartmans-Weilerkopf, which the enemy has not attacked for the last two days." There were similar cases in both England and Germany. When reports circulated that each of those powers had lost well-known battleships during North Sea naval operations, Admiralty officials in London and Berlin invited staff men to visit the vessels in question and report.

2

Abruptly in the spring of 1915 the conflict abroad ceased to be remote for Americans. Until 2:08 P.M. on May 7, the national sentiment was "Keep out of it." Then came the *Lusitania*.

The actual beginning of that story antedated May 7. Six days earlier, copy boys in New York headquarters distributed the first editions of the morning papers. Editors checked their pages for any local news that might not have been included in the report. The attention of several was arrested, not by anything in the regular columns, but by two advertisements on the ship news pages. The first was a single-column display announcing that the Cunarder *Lusitania*, "Fastest and Largest Steamer now in Atlantic Service, Sails Saturday, May 1, 10 A.M." Directly below was another advertisement, with the one-word heading: "Notice!" It was so unusual that a story was prepared, telling how the announcement of the *Lusitania's* sailing that day had been accompanied by an extraordinary warning. The story concluded with its text:

Travellers intending to embark on the Atlantic voyage are reminded that a state of war exists between Germany and her allies and Great Britain and her allies; that the zone of war includes the waters adjacent to the British Isles; that, in accordance with formal notice given by the Imperial German Government, vessels flying the flag of Great Britain, or of any of her allies, are liable to destruction in those waters and that travellers sailing in the war zone on ships of Great Britain or her allies do so at their own risk.

(Signed) Imperial German Embassy
Washington, D. C.

Although Germany had announced in February her intention of waging submarine warfare on allied shipping, the May 1 "Notice!"

went unheeded. General Manager Stone paid as little attention to it as anyone else. His son Herbert was sailing and Stone with his family went down to the pier.

On Friday, May 7, off the Old Head of Kinsdale, Ireland, the unthinkable happened. At 2:08 P.M. Unterseeboot 20, commanded by Leutenant-Kapitan Schwieger, sent a torpedo into the *Lusitania's* starboard side just aft of the bridge. She went to the bottom in twenty minutes. Of the 1,924 persons aboard, 1,198 were lost, among them 114 Americans.

James Ryan, resident correspondent at Queenstown, flashed the first news to London and then, with W. A. Herlihy, the Cork correspondent, went to work on the story. Additional staff men were started for Ireland. In spite of the magnitude of the news, the censors in Whitehall held up the first bulletin fifty-two minutes.

When the bulletin did reach New York, Stone was at lunch with a friend. He hurried to the office. Late that night he knew that his son was lost.

Within a few hours after the torpedoing, the London Bureau, co-ordinating point for the coverage, found the demands of the occasion far transcended the limits of news requirements. Countless inquiries rushed in by telephone and cable from relatives and friends of those aboard the Cunarder. In order that there might be as little confusion as possible, a card index was started, listing both survivors and recovered bodies as they were reported. For days personal inquiries and requests kept coming in from America, asking the bureau to confirm identifications, to verify reports of the lost, to take charge of the effects of the drowned and even to make arrangements for the burial of recovered bodies.

3

The destruction of the *Lusitania* and the diplomatic notes between the United States and Germany that followed put Washington coverage on something like a wartime footing. The policy of the White House assumed tremendous importance and the State, Navy, War and Treasury departments became more vital news sources than ever. Neutrality, contraband, diplomatic representations, emergency legislation, the need for protection of American shipping—subjects such as these took a place in the Washington report.

Among the first major repercussions of the *Lusitania* affair in Washington was the resignation of William Jennings Bryan as secretary of state because of his disagreement with President Wilson's firm attitude toward Germany. Hood, dean of the capital staff, learned on June 8 that Bryan had resigned, but the information was given him in confidence and he could not use it.

Hood walked into a pressroom set aside for the association in the War Department building.

"Boys," he said, "there is a big story here that you have got to get. I know what it is but I cannot say a word more than that it is BIG. The AP has got to break it. You have to get it. Use your heads and your legs."

David Lawrence, Stephen Early, Kirke Simpson, and the two other staff men he was talking to had never seen Hood so excited. There was a dash for the door, each man mentally reviewing the contacts that might give him some clew.

Hood let all except Simpson go. "This is not on your War Department run, Kirke," he explained. "I have got to tell somebody. I can't hold it. Bryan just sent for me to tell me in strict confidence that he had resigned because of the *Lusitania* note. President Wilson has accepted, but Bryan says announcement or even a hint must await White House pleasure. I don't know why he told me, but he did."

"What can I do now?" Simpson asked. "I can't even tap any Cabinet sources because you've tied me up."

"I know," Hood replied, "but you and I are going now to enjoy a rare treat. We are going to stroll about and watch the AP staff work like huntings dogs. They'll get it before night and we'll watch them do it."

Hood and Simpson walked the corridors, watching fellow staffers hurry from office to office. Other correspondents, sensing the suppressed excitement, joined in the blind chase.

Lawrence paused to reason the thing out.

First, he thought of the possibility of a rupture of diplomatic relations between the United States and Germany. He dismissed that because the German note on the *Lusitania* had not yet been answered by the State Department. It must be something else. What else? Then it occurred to him that it might be a story involving Secretary of State Bryan because there had been friction between Bryan and Wilson. Lawrence played the hunch. He sought out Secretary of War Garrison.

"What do you think about Bryan's resignation?" he asked.

Disarmed by the blandness of the question, Garrison told him the story. Lawrence hustled off to the White House, confirmed the President's acceptance of the resignation, and most important, obtained permission to release the news. At 5:26 that afternoon the leased wire network flashed Bryan's resignation.

4

When Germany answered the *Lusitania* note which caused Bryan's resignation, Conger at Berlin transmitted the complete text of the reply to the United States in time for member newspapers to publish it almost forty-eight hours before it was officially delivered to the State Department. Conger's reportorial activities had been hampered during 1915 by the new restrictions German authorities enjoined on foreign correspondents. Newspapermen were barred from the fronts except on officially supervised visits. A summary of war news, giving the High Command's version, was issued three times weekly by the General Staff office in Berlin, and correspondents were held personally responsible not only for the dispatches they wrote, but also for headlines and pictures which might accompany those dispatches when they were printed in America. Berlin officials had been irked by headlines and pictures unfavorable to Germany's cause, and they would make no exception for Conger even though the use of headlines and pictures in member newspapers was, of course, beyond his control.

On the whole, the news during 1915 seemed to favor the Central Powers. On the western front a year of costly French, British, and Belgian attacks had failed to weaken the German positions. In the east the ponderous Russian Army had been flung back almost to Riga. The belated Allied thrust at Gallipoli produced nothing but a casualty list exceeding 100,000. Bulgaria had cast her lot with Germany, Austria-Hungary, and Turkey. The Allied nations in the Balkans were overrun. Italy had entered the war, but her first blows against Austria had been repulsed with the loss of a quarter of a million men.

The staff suffered its second casualty when Whiffen was wounded on the Russian front, which he was covering with D. B. McGowan. Cortesi got his baptism of fire with General Cadorna in the Alps. Schreiner reported successes of the Central Powers at the Dardanelles and in the Balkans, while Paxton Hibben served with the Allied armies that were thrust back into Greece. Thereon J. Damon, the Constantinople correspondent, wrote the story of the Gallipoli campaign and Turkish operations in Mesopotamia. Conger and S. M. Bouton, of the Berlin staff, and men from the London and Paris bureaus cabled accounts of the costly French and British offensives in France and Flanders, where poison gas was used for the first time in modern warfare.

If 1915 had been an epochal year, 1916 outdid its sensations. Abroad there was no slackening in the furious pace and at home the tempo accelerated under the triple pressure of strained relations with Germany, an expeditionary force in Mexico, and the approach of a critical presidential campaign. Editors lived in an avalanche of Flashes and EOS bulletins.

Verdun — the Somme — Irish Rebellion — Jutland — Trentino — Russian Successes in Galicia — Arabia — Pancho Villa — U-boat *Deutschland* in Baltimore — Black Tom Explosion — Washington Warns Kaiser on Submarines.

Jutland was the first great naval battle the association had been called upon to report since Togo blew the Russian fleet out of the water at Tsushima in 1905. The first bulletins, giving the German version of the sea fight off Denmark, came from Berlin by wireless. British accounts arrived later by cable from London, and member papers all over the country scored on "Der Tag"—the day the British Grand Fleet and the German High Sea Fleet should meet in a fight to determine maritime supremacy.

Der Tag, however, proved indecisive; the German fleet inflicted heavier losses, but Britain retained command of the sea. Controversy burst forth immediately and the staffs in Berlin and London set to work to clarify the conflicting claims as far as censorship would permit. For the first time since the war started, Captain Hall, of the Naval Intelligence Bureau in London, permitted the association to quote him in a statement saying that neither the dreadnought *Warspite* nor the *Marlborough* had been sunk as the enemy claimed. Then followed an authoritative interview with Winston Churchill, former first lord of the admiralty, and a naval expert's description of the battle written from Admiralty reports. Most London papers reprinted these exclusive features, crediting them to The Associated Press. The staff in Berlin exhibited similar enterprise. When the German Admiralty refused to withdraw its claim that the *Warspite* had been sunk at Jutland The Associated Press sent a correspondent to see the *Warspite* and interview her captain who declared, a bit superfluously: "I am still commander of the largest warship in the world."

Another of the top-ranking stories that spring was the Irish Rebellion—"Bloody Easter Week" in Dublin. DeWitt Mackenzie arrived in Dublin while the Irish Republican forces still held the Post Office and Four Courts buildings against the artillery, machine guns, and rifles of the British military.

Mackenzie drove into the city after nightfall and the assignment came near costing him his life. Under rigid martial law all civilians were forbidden on the streets after six o'clock and troops were ordered to shoot violators on sight. The British patrol Mackenzie encountered luckily disobeyed instructions and fired over his head. No sooner had the auto stopped, however, than an officer rushed up, cursing the men because Mackenzie and the chauffeur had not been shot.

Hands high in the air and a bayonet against his stomach, Mackenzie tried to convince the officer he was a newspaper correspondent. But the officer thought otherwise. He had already decided that his prisoner was a Sinn Feiner with fraudulent credentials, and he ordered him taken to the barracks. There the rifles of firing squads were cracking as rebels were led out to the barracks wall.

Mackenzie was doing the most persuasive talking of his life. His insistence that he was an American at first did not impress his judges, for some Americans were taking active part in the rising. However, there was the chance of international complications if a wrong man were executed, and the reluctant military finally released him and his chauffeur. Mackenzie's freedom was short-lived. The next day police interned him for the duration of his stay in Ireland and at the end of the adventure he learned with a shock that he actually had carried a death warrant with him that night in Dublin. His taciturn chauffeur, who had let him do all the talking, was a rabid Sinn Feiner.

5

On the Continent the war wallowed on through another year. Frederick Palmer, the only American correspondent with the British Army on the western front, wrote such graphic dispatches on the great Somme offensive and the debut of "tanks" that The Associated Press set a precedent by having them copyrighted. With the exception of Palmer's copyrighted stories, it was optional with a member paper whether any dispatch be printed with credit.

News from the fronts, however, had no unchallenged monopoly of front pages. The slaughter at Verdun dropped to secondary importance when Pancho Villa, the Mexican revolutionist, crossed the border in a night raid and attacked the town of Columbus, New Mexico.

George L. Seese, of the Los Angeles Bureau, was in Columbus when the bandits struck. For several years Mexican disorders had caused the loss of American lives and property and had necessitated the special assignment of staff men in the turbulent areas. When the situation south of the Rio Grande again assumed threatening aspects, Seese was ordered to El Paso in case Villa's activities immediately across the border in Chihuahua became of major significance.

Having seen duty in Mexico in 1911, he knew how to keep informed on Villa's movement. Two days before the raid he received information that the bandit leader's forces were in closer proximity to the border than usual. He promptly moved to Columbus, on the border near the camp of the Thirteenth U.S. Cavalry. Once there, he sent for Edwin L. Van Camp, the leased wire operator at El Paso, to join him in anticipation of a story.

In the early morning hours of March 10 the two men were routed from their sleep by the crash of shots as Villa's raiders descended on the town and the adjacent cavalry encampment. Seese assisted some women and children to safety and sent Van Camp through bullet-swept streets to the local telegraph office while he went out to get the news. When the day leased wires opened Seese and Van Camp had a complete story ready, giving an eyewitness account of Villa's foray, the list of killed and injured, and details of the cavalry pursuit of the raiders into Mexico.

Seese's presence at Columbus for the raid proved too much of a coincidence for army officers on duty along the border. Department of Justice agents tried unsuccessfully to learn if he had had advance knowledge, but he never would tell them how it happened that he was on the exact spot and waiting for the Villa story to break.

On April 18 Morkrum printers and telegraph instruments spelled out the bulletin that the United States had threatened to sever diplomatic relations with Berlin unless Germany abandoned her policy of unrestricted submarine warfare on merchant shipping.

There was an apprehensive wait of two weeks. Then the Berlin Bureau advised that a reply was in preparation and news circuits all over the United States were held fully manned to handle the story when it arrived. The first "take" began moving shortly after 7 A.M. on May 5. It announced that Germany would comply with President Wilson's demands and cease sinking ships without warning. In keeping with the practice it had inaugurated, The Associated Press brought in by wireless the complete text of the 3,000-word note, which temporarily forestalled termination of diplomatic relations.

6

June added the presidential campaign to the heavy roster of continuing stories to be covered for 908 member papers. At St. Louis the Democrats renominated Woodrow Wilson with the slogan: "He kept us out of war." Supreme Court Justice Charles Evans Hughes was picked by the Republicans and the country plunged into the closest national contest of modern times.

As the campaign got under way, the name of an old news-gathering pioneer was restored to its place on Associated Press rolls. The New York *Sun,* one of the six founders of the original organization, returned to the co-operative. For almost a quarter century, ever since the break in 1893, the *Sun* had been conducting a proprietary news-gathering agency of its own. When Dana died in October, 1897, Laffan assumed complete command of the Laffan Bureau, as the service was called, and carried on the undertaking until his own death in 1909. With diminished vigor the agency survived for several years until Frank Munsey purchased the *Sun* on June 30, 1916, and four days later brought it back into Associated Press membership. The rancor and bitterness of the feud started two decades before by other owners of the *Sun* was forgotten, and the paper was welcomed back.

The return of the *Sun* was not the only memorable event that month. The German merchant submarine *Deutschland* appeared unheralded at Baltimore with a cargo of dyes and chemicals. It was an astonishing story and disquieting for those who hitherto had regarded submarine warfare as something possible only in European waters. In less than two weeks San Francisco flashed the Preparedness Day Parade bombing and the name of Tom Mooney first appeared in the report. Then the $22,000,000 munitions plant on Black Tom Island, Jersey City, exploded.

After a summer of war news, political oratory, preparedness speeches, bombings and explosions, readers turned with genuine relief to the approach of the World Series. Debating the relative merits of the Brooklyn Nationals and Carrigan's Boston Red Sox was one way to escape talk of bloodshed and violence. Sports Editor Moss headed the five-man staff assigned to report the series, but it was a Traffic Department triumph which made coverage of the 1916 World's Championship games a sensation in the newspaper world.

Ordinarily the leased wire circuits were broken at strategic points in order that the report might be readjusted for regional needs and relay. Even when the play-by-play story of the World Series took precedence over all other news, this transmission method had been followed. As preparations began for the 1916 edition of the baseball classic, Cooper conceived the ambitious idea of delivering the play-by-play story direct from the baseball park to every point on the main leased wire system without any intervening relay or delay.

Nothing of the kind had ever been attempted before in either news or commercial transmission. Cooper's Traffic Department, however, set out to make telegraphic history by arranging for an unprecedented single circuit, 26,000 miles in length, to operate from the ball parks in Boston and Brooklyn into the office of every leased wire member newspaper. The plan worked flawlessly. When John A. Bates, the chief operator assigned to the World Series staff, tapped out the play-by-play story dictated by Moss, operators in member offices across the country received the Morse code signals simultaneously.

Members were impressed by the feat, but one of the greatest expressions of praise came from an inventor:

```
KENT COOPER
      TRAFFIC AGT AP NY

      THE ASSOCIATED PRESS MUST BE WONDERFULLY
WELL ORGANIZED TO BE ABLE TO ACCOMPLISH WHAT
WAS DONE IN THE BALL GAMES.  UNCLE SAM HAS NOW
A REAL ARTERIAL SYSTEM AND IT IS NEVER GOING TO
HARDEN
                        EDISON
```

The World Series opened in Boston on a Saturday and hundreds of operators began copying the play-by-play account. The first inning and a half had been played and Bates in the press box at Braves Field was sending evenly:

```
      BOSTON, OCT. 7 - SECOND INNING, SECOND
HALF: LEWIS UP.  BALL ONE.  FOUL.  STRIKE ONE.
BALL TWO.  BALL THREE.  LEWIS WALKED.  GARDNER
UP.  GARDNER BUNTED SAFELY -
```

Just as Gardner bunted safely the smooth flow of signals was interrupted. Then:

```
      F-L-A-S-H

      NEWPORT, R.I., OCT. 7 - A GERMAN SUB-
MARINE HAS ARRIVED HERE.
```

Frank M. Wheeler, string correspondent at Newport, had tried vainly to reach the Boston Bureau by telephone with news that the U-53, flying a German man-of-war ensign, had just put into Newport harbor. In desperation he ordered the operator at the Newport *Herald* to break in on the play-by-play with a flash and bulletin. This was no *Deutschland,* such as had turned up at Baltimore, but a fighting submarine. Wheeler was positive of his facts; he had confirmed them with Rear-Admiral Austin M. Knight and the U.S. Engineers' office in Newport.

Once he had crowded all the information he had onto the special World Series wire, he put out in a motorboat to the U-boat's anchorage, exhibited his credentials and was the first person permitted on board. Leutenant-Kapitan Hans Rose, her commander, gave Wheeler the story of the transatlantic trip, explained that he had entered the port "to pay his respects," and asked the reporter to post a letter for him to the German embassy at Washington. He said he planned to sail again in a few hours.

It was not pure chance that gave the association immediate information on the U-53's arrival. Conger at Berlin had confidentially advised headquarters some weeks earlier that another transatlantic submarine voyage was likely and correspondents along the coast had been instructed to watch.

Wheeler followed the U-53 well out to sea by motorboat and was the only newspaperman to report the halting of the American freighter *Kansan* off Nantucket Lightship. Although the *Kansan* was permitted to proceed, the news served warning that Leutenant-Kapitan Rose had a definite mission off New England. Day and night staffs, twenty men in all, were mobilized. All shipping in the danger zone was charted so accurately that the Boston staff figuratively watched the liner *Stephano,* first of the U-boat's victims, steam toward her doom.

The submarine's torpedoes sent five ships in all to the bottom, some of them within sight of American shores, but outside the three-mile limit. Utilizing wireless stations, marine observers, ships at sea, the British Atlantic squadron, American destroyers, shore correspondents and staff men, Boston covered the U-53's daring raid with a 10,000-word budget in the Sunday night report and 14,000 words on Monday. Staff men went miles offshore in fast motorboats to meet rescue vessels and get the stories of the survivors.

Editors called the U-53 the biggest story to develop this side of the Atlantic in connection with the European war. It brought the terror of submarine warfare into American waters, revived the public indignation that had smoldered since the sinking of the *Lusitania* and imposed a further stress on the government's policy of neutrality.

In this uneasy atmosphere the nation looked ahead to the climax of a presidential campaign in which the war had been a major issue.

XI. "HE KEPT US OUT OF WAR"

I

ON THE New York Curb Exchange the odds were 10 to 7 that Charles Evans Hughes would be the next president. The Republican National Committee confidently claimed 358 of the country's 531 electoral votes. Political soothsayers prophesied certain defeat for Wilson. The air was full of partisan clamor through the final week of electioneering, and even a second American trip of the submarine *Deutschland* failed to displace politics as the top story of the day.

The zero hour was the closing of the polls on the night of November 7, and The Associated Press had been four years preparing for it. The co-operative's new election service, devised and directed by Wilmer Stuart of the New York office, faced its first real test on a national scale. For months Stuart had traveled all over the country, setting up the machinery by states and instructing bureau staffs on how the service was to operate. It was painstaking and undramatic work, stressing accuracy first and then speed in the collection and tabulation of the vote.

Until Stuart began his survey, election coverage had little uniformity in plan or in method. The organization first undertook to report a presidential election with some independence in 1888. Before that time the management had relied unquestioningly on the returns collected by commercial telegraph companies. The ugly charges provoked by the famous Cleveland-Blaine contest in 1884 led The Associated Press to cover the next national election, as far as possible, on its own resources. The procedure was improvised and experimental, varying from state to state and often changing between one election and another. All the elections covered in this patchwork way were decided by comfortable margins; only this kept attention from the inherent weakness in election service operations.

State by state Stuart examined the existing machinery. In some the association depended on returns compiled by county clerks or secretaries of state, and the vote totals, while accurate, were likely to be extremely slow. In others, notably the Solid South and traditional Republican territory, the reports of the dominant party were utilized, the figures gathered by the minority party providing the basis for a reasonable check of accuracy. Then there were a few states in which member papers pooled resources to set up election services of their own and the returns, as tabulated, were made available to the co-operative. Stuart also found that returns in any election were zealously compared with the vote polled by the party in the same district in the previous election to determine the gain or loss. This made for a cumbersome and confusing procedure, but politicians and editors generally were firmly convinced that election returns without these comparative figures were worthless.

After much study Stuart evolved a system, and in the 1904 Roosevelt election, using New York State as a guinea pig, he subjected it to its first limited test. The county was made the basic unit of the machine. A correspondent or member newspaper was instructed to collect the returns directly from every precinct in the county by telephone, telegraph, messenger, or other means. These were reported cumulatively to a central bureau where a special force of accountants and calculators added the votes to those being received from all the other counties in the state. The voting results were thus obtained not only swiftly, but also with remarkable accuracy. Stuart introduced the system experimentally into several other large states for the 1908 and 1912 elections, and again it functioned with smooth and accurate efficiency, justifying a thoroughgoing test on a major scale. The 1916 election offered the first opportunity.

Long before the campaign ended Stuart had perfected the machinery for the service in almost thirty states, among them all those with large electoral votes and those which surveys listed as doubtful.

The time-honored practice of carrying the comparative vote of the preceding election was discarded—much to the horror of those who believed there was no way like the old way—and the association decided to report the election on the principle that the votes spoke for themselves, regardless of how rival parties had fared four years before.

2

On November 7 the election army swung into action. The East came in rapidly. By 6:03 P.M. New York was definitely in Hughes's column. Maine, Massachusetts, Rhode Island, Vermont, Connecticut, New Jersey, Pennsylvania were going Republican also. New Hampshire, too, had Hughes in the lead, but by a surprisingly small figure

The first scattering returns from the nearer Midwestern states began to trickle in with Hughes ahead.

By eight o'clock two New York papers which had supported Wilson conceded his defeat. Others followed suit. A number of wire services flashed a Republican "victory" and bragged of being so many minutes ahead of competitors in announcing the result. Presses spewed "extras" that carried editorials on the Democratic downfall. Opposition cables from abroad gave Europe's reaction to the Hughes "triumph." Wilson, who had returned to New Jersey to vote, heard the reports with dejected resignation. Theodore Roosevelt said: "It appears Mr. Hughes is elected." In the suite on the eighth floor of the Hotel Astor, Mrs. Hughes embraced her husband and exclaimed: "Mr. President!"

All the while 65,000 miles of Associated Press wires carried the returns as fast as they were compiled. There were no flashes that the election had been decided. No "overwhelming defeat" bulletins. Just facts and figures as they materialized. State by state the report carried the number of districts counted, the total number of districts involved, and the vote. As Democratic chairmen and pro-Wilson newspapers in state after state conceded, stories recorded only the facts.

The storm broke. Messages poured in from member papers, demanding an immediate story on the election's outcome. The Associated Press was a laughingstock! Everybody was conceding a Republican victory! One news agency after another had flashed the Hughes landslide! The Associated Press was pro-Wilson and too stubborn to admit its man had been beaten! The sheaf of angry telegrams on the general manager's desk grew larger and the telephone jangled insistently.

Stone talked with Stuart and together they studied the incomplete electoral jigsaw. The East, of course, was clearly Republican, except for New Hampshire where a nip-and-tuck fight was in progress. Wilson led in Ohio and Minnesota, but the greater part of the midwest appeared safe for Hughes. Even with such a commanding bloc of states assured, however, the Republicans were still short of mathematical certainty. Returns from Rocky Mountain and far western states were too meager to be conclusive, and an abrupt change in the tide there could throw everything into doubt.

Women were voting for the first time in many of those states and they were an unknown political quantity. Furthermore, the Progressives were strong in this area and their support could be decisive. A check of available returns showed that Wilson had a nest egg of 157 electoral votes, largely contributed by the Solid South.

"The Associated Press will make no statement on the outcome of the election until the result has been definitely decided," the general manager said after his conference with Stuart ended.

In the early morning hours the picture began to change. Missouri and Kansas plumped for Wilson. The tide was running strongly to him in the Rocky Mountains and the Northwest. And California, which the Republicans claimed by 40,000, had started to report.

California, 1,264 out of 5,917 precincts: Wilson 60,734; Hughes 59,000 . . . 1,557 precincts: Wilson 79,136; Hughes 78,849 . . . 1,784 precincts: Wilson 106,445; Hughes 107,846. . . .

By 3 A.M. Wednesday the vote, contrary to all expectations, was running so unbelievably close in California, Minnesota, West Virginia, and New Hampshire—states where clear-cut Republican victories had been generally anticipated—that Stuart's faith in the accuracy of his machine faltered momentarily. Urgent instructions were wired to the staff to recanvass every district already counted and verify the totals. The rechecks left the figure unchanged. Only in California did a difference occur and it was a mere 20 votes.

The "landslide" ceased to be a landslide.

Toward dawn papers which had been on the street with headlines blazoning Hughes's election issued new extras that the result was in doubt. Editorials which had been written on the "new president" were thrown out and noncommittal substitutes inserted. The enthusiasm of "victory" celebrations gave way to misgivings and pay-offs on election wagers halted abruptly.

All Wednesday the suspense and doubt continued. Wilson's original lead of 10,000 in Minnesota melted away and Hughes crept out in front by 803 votes. Hughes went ahead in New Mexico by 258, and in West Virginia by 1,538. In California Wilson's advantage varied erratically. In the afternoon it climbed from 1,538 to 2,945, then to 4,694, and then slumped back to 1,490. By 2:30 A.M Thursday, with 5,347 out of 5,917 precincts reporting, the count stood: Wilson 439,896; Hughes 438,486. Another lead from San Francisco stressed that most of the returns were from an area where the Democrats could hope for the greatest support. Very little had been heard from southern California or from the northern section of the state. A bloc of more than a hundred precincts in Los Angeles, where Republicans hoped for gains, had been locked up for a second night.

3

The staff in New York labored on into Thursday, poring over the latest batches of returns. Wilson started the day in California with a lead of more than 3,000 votes, but before noon additional returns from Los Angeles and from Alameda County whittled it down to 500. Hughes pushed farther in front in Minnesota and New Hampshire flopped back into his column. Wilson was ahead in North Dakota and, by the narrowest of margins, in New Mexico. It was obvious that, without California, Wilson would lose.

In southern California men on horses and mules went out into the isolated areas to get news of how the vote had gone. Where storms had interrupted makeshift communications with back counties, correspondents set out on foot to bring in the delayed tabulations.

With tension at the breaking point, the day wore on. New Hampshire swung back to Wilson. Hughes edged out in front in New Mexico, but then the substantial Democratic votes from the back settlements arrived—by all manner of conveyances—and Wilson was never again headed.

Before long the outstanding California districts began to come in, at first slowly and then at a quicker pace. District after district from southern California served only to strengthen Wilson's lead. By nightfall the belated votes of northern California were being tabulated and the bulletins flew along the leased wires to the offices of 911 member newspapers. Northern California was sustaining Wilson's advantage. More districts in. More counties complete. Figures for two-thirds of the state were back-checked and found correct.

But still the election hung in the balance. There had been so many lightning changes in the two days since the polls closed that anything still might happen. The hours dragged by. More missing districts were reported during the evening. In New York Stuart and Stone waited. Nine o'clock. Ten o'clock. Eleven o'clock. Eleven-twenty . . .

"FLASH!"

The operator manning the main transcontinental wire yelled it across the newsroom and began to copy the sudden fast burst of signals. Men fell over chairs and wastebaskets to crowd around him as the type bars of his machine flipped out the rapid words:

```
SAN FRANCISCO - WILSON CARRIES CALIFORNIA
AND IS REELECTED.
```

On the heels of the Flash rode a bulletin giving the vote: Wilson, 465,194; Hughes, 462,224. A few minutes later another bulletin— Chester A. Rowell, Republican state chairman for California, reluctantly conceded the state to Wilson "on the face of the returns as compiled by The Associated Press."

The news was rushed to the special wire which had been strung to the President's temporary residence in New Jersey and when Joseph Tumulty, his secretary, read the first brief report he seized The Associated Press operator and waltzed him around the room in a boisterous whirl of jubilation. Wilson had left on the presidential yacht *Mayflower* to keep a speaking engagement in New England, so Tumulty dispatched a wireless message.

Toward midnight, while Wilson's staff rejoiced at Long Branch, an editor in New York picked up a telephone to break the news to the man the nation had hailed as the next president only two days ago. Someone in the Hughes suite at the Hotel Astor answered the call.

"The President-elect," he said officiously, "has retired for the night and cannot be disturbed."

That was too much for the patience of the editor.

"Well," he replied, "when the President-elect wakes up in the morning, tell him he isn't President-elect any more."

It was several days before every precinct in the country was accounted for and the verdict of sixteen million voters confirmed. The electoral vote was: Wilson, 277; Hughes, 254. California represented the difference between victory and defeat. Had Hughes carried the state, he would have had one more electoral vote than the number necessary for election. Political experts, trying to explain away their bad guesses, blamed the loss of the state on Hughes's failure during the campaign to make peace with Hiram Johnson, the Republican candidate for the United States Senate in California, who carried the state by the enormous majority of 296,815.

The 1916 election was a triumph for the efficiency of Stuart's service. In several states the pluralities were only a few hundred votes and the smallest percentage of error in tabulating the count would have given a totally inaccurate result.

The machinery which had proved so efficient at a time when others were busy "electing" the unsuccessful candidate was continued, expanded, and refined for other national elections. It became the only service of its kind in existence, the only one to operate on a nation-wide scale, and the government at Washington placed so much confidence

MEN ON HORSES AND MULES WENT . . . TO GET THE NEWS OF THE VOTE.

in it that it accepted The Associated Press returns as conclusive proof of the election of one candidate or another weeks in advance of the completion of the official count.

"He kept us out of war," had been Wilson's 1916 slogan but within weeks after his re-election the war clouds became blacker than ever. The campaign slogan had been phrased in the past tense.

XII. THE UNITED STATES AT WAR

I

Front pages carried staggering news on the morning of March 1, 1917, and from that date events marched to the climax.

There had been some confidence as the new year began. Wilson formally appealed to the belligerent powers "on behalf of humanity" to cease the slaughter and agree to a lasting peace. That was on January 22. Nine days later the White House knew the futility of the proposal.

Tumulty brought the disillusioning information to the President's private office. The Washington Bureau had just rushed a bulletin from Berlin to the Executive Mansion. Tumulty laid the slip of paper on Wilson's desk and watched him as he read it.

The President's face turned gray and when he looked up he said: "This means war. The break that we have tried so hard to avoid now seems inevitable."

The Berlin bulletin announced that Germany would begin absolutely unrestricted warfare on all sea traffic to Europe within twenty-four hours. When Ambassador von Bernstorff delivered the formal note later in the day, Washington already knew its contents.

On February 3 Wilson went before Congress to announce severance of diplomatic relations with Germany and a few minutes later von Bernstorff was handed his passport. The big question everyone kept asking was: "What next?"

The experts of the State Department decoding room got the first astounding hint of the answer on February 24 and before the month ended Hood of the Washington staff learned what the closely guarded messages contained.

Secretary of State Lansing called the reporter at six o'clock the night of February 28 and asked him to come to his house. Hood realized that something was in the air, for Lansing pledged him to secrecy even before their talk got beyond greetings. Then the secretary of state proceeded to give Hood one of the most amazing stories of the reporter's career—a story which, had it not been backed by documentary proof, Hood certainly would have branded as outright propaganda although it came from a high government source. Coming from Lansing under the circumstances it still may have been propaganda, but it also was authentic news of a most sensational nature.

The administration, Lansing explained, had obtained a copy of a coded German communication from Dr. Arthur Zimmermann, the Kaiser's foreign secretary, to Count von Bernstorff, ambassador at Washington, for relay to von Echardt, the German Minister in Mexico City. The message, the secretary said, was dated January 19 and stated Germany's intention to resume unrestricted submarine warfare twelve days later, regardless of Wilson's peace moves then being discussed.

But all that was merely incidental. Zimmermann's coded note directed von Echardt to propose to Mexico secretly that she ally herself with Germany and make war on the United States if the nation failed to remain neutral. Germany would supply financial support and Mexico's reward would be the states of Texas, New Mexico, and Arizona, the territory she lost back in the dim, forgotten days when James Gordon Bennett and David Hale were co-operating on the pony express shortly before the formation of The Associated Press in 1848. The final point in the plan was that Japan should be persuaded to forsake the Allies and join in the attack on the United States.

Lansing produced proof that the information had been in the hands of the administration for four days and that its authenticity had been established beyond question. How the cipher message was obtained and decoded was something that could not be divulged at the time, but the secretary in the strongest possible language pledged his word that it was genuine.

Lansing thereupon told Hood he could have the story, but that its source could not be disclosed. No administration official could be quoted and the origin of the news must be vigorously protected at all costs. Lastly, it even might be necessary for the State Department to deny knowledge of the document after the story had been published. An official release had been considered, but Lansing had advised against such a course because it might appear that the government was using the news to bring pressure on recalcitrant members of Congress, then fighting the administration bill for arming American merchant ships against U-boat attacks.

Hood debated. For The Associated Press to carry such an explosive story solely on its own authority was contrary to regulations. Nevertheless, this news was too big to wait on precedent.

"I think we can use it," he said.

Immediately upon leaving Lansing, Hood called Jackson S. Elliott, his chief of bureau, and repeated the information he had obtained. Elliott weighed the facts, reflected on the responsibility The Associated Press would assume by carrying the story, and made his decision.

"Go ahead. I'll be right down," he said.

Hood promptly telephoned Lional C. Probert, news editor at the bureau. Realizing his own regular assignment to the State Department would prove a fatal clew if word leaked out that he had anything to do with the preparation of the story, he requested Probert to take it over. He told the news editor that Lansing had promised to have the text of the intercepted note ready later in a sealed envelope.

It was a heavy news night, with a dying Congress grinding out its final grist in a late session preparatory to adjournment and Wilson's second inauguration. Probert looked around the room. Byron Price was needed on the desk. The night editor, Horace Eppes, already had his hands full. David Lawrence was busy.

Probert saw young Stephen Early.

"You're to go to Secretary Lansing's home on Eighteenth Street," he instructed, "and bring back whatever Lansing gives you. Then you're to forget you ever saw the secretary tonight. That's all. No questions."

Early got to the old red-brick house in record time. A servant ushered him into a reception room and left him to catch his breath. Presently Lansing came down the stairway. Reaching inside his long dressing robe, he drew out a big, unmarked envelope.

Probert had the envelope the minute Early came back into the office. Shirt-sleeved, an uptilted cigar clamped between his teeth, he hustled Lawrence, Eppes, and Price into an inner office and plumped down before a typewriter. There were a few moments of discussion with Elliott on the form and wording to be used in the opening paragraphs of the story. Then Probert began typing in his one-finger newsroom manner.

2

It had been decided not to start the dispatch on the wires until very late that night so that other correspondents would be unable to check government officials once the news was out. For that reason the need for haste was not pressing. The facts were there and Probert went to work on them. He made no effort to heighten the story by emphasis— the material itself was too sensational. Hammering away at the keys, he turned out a straightforward, factual story which marshaled every fact that could be printed without exposing the source. As Probert's typewriter rattled, Price prepared a detailed "Add" which reviewed past difficulties with Mexico and the known facts on German activities south of the Rio Grande.

Elliott went off in search of the secretary of state. He wanted to talk to Lansing before the story was actually released, particularly in view of Lansing's statement that he might have to deny the news after it appeared. Elliott found the secretary at a diplomatic reception and they retired to an anteroom.

"You feel, Mr. Secretary, that because of circumstances you may have to deny all knowledge of this Zimmermann story?" the Bureau chief asked.

Lansing nodded.

"Yet you agree for us to carry it?"

"Yes."

"Then we'll do it on one condition. You will be asked all sorts of things about this story at your press conference tomorrow. I don't care how you reply. The Associated Press man will ask you three questions. We will carry the story if you will answer those questions as I request."

Lansing hesitated until he heard the questions, then agreed.

It was almost midnight when Probert walked into the newsroom of the Washington Bureau with the wad of copy in his hand. He had written more than two columns. A confidential note had just been sent to all member papers notifying them that news of surpassing importance would be transmitted shortly. A clear wire and a ready telegrapher were waiting.

Probert dropped the pages before the telegrapher:

```
                BY THE ASSOCIATED PRESS

        WASHINGTON, D. C., FEB. 28-THE ASSOCIATED
PRESS IS ENABLED TO REVEAL THAT GERMANY, IN
PLANNING UNRESTRICTED SUBMARINE WARFARE AND
COUNTING ITS CONSEQUENCES, PROPOSED AN ALLIANCE
WITH MEXICO AND JAPAN TO MAKE WAR ON THE UNITED
STATES, IF THIS COUNTRY SHOULD NOT REMAIN NEUTRAL.
        JAPAN, THROUGH MEXICAN MEDIATION, WAS
TO BE URGED TO ABANDON HER ALLIES AND JOIN IN
THE ATTACK ON THE UNITED STATES.
        MEXICO, FOR HER REWARD, WAS TO RECEIVE
GENERAL FINANCIAL SUPPORT FROM GERMANY, RECONQUER
TEXAS, NEW MEXICO AND ARIZONA-LOST PROVINCES-
AND SHARE IN THE VICTORIOUS PEACE TERMS
GERMANY CONTEMPLATED. . . .
```

Paragraph after paragraph the story went out over the wires, and with it the text of the document which is now known as the Zimmermann Note. In scores of member offices editors read the dispatch. As unbelievable as the story was, they were even more astonished at the fact that The Associated Press, on its own authority, was making such statements. It was the first time member papers had been asked to take momentous news on nothing more than the co-operative's word, but they did have that word, for the story was accompanied by a confidential note saying the facts had been thoroughly authenticated.

No sooner had the story appeared than telephone and telegraph wires began to hum as commercial agencies and individual newspapers flooded their Washington offices with insistent queries. Unable to confirm the news anywhere, other correspondents called the whole thing a fraud.

The next morning a hundred newspapermen jammed Lansing's office to find out about this Zimmermann Note. There were shouted questions. Lansing parried and sidestepped. He said he knew only what had appeared in the papers. A murmur went through the room:

"The Associated Press has stubbed its toe!"

Lansing managed the interview deftly. Just as he was about to bring it to a close, The Associated Press man stepped forward and quietly posed the only questions asked that day by the co-operative.

"Mr. Secretary, did you know The Associated Press had this story last night?"

Lansing studied for a moment.

"Yes."

"Did you deny its authenticity?"

"No."

"Did you object to The Associated Press carrying the story?"

"No."

With that Lansing stepped through the draperies which hid the door of his private office and the press conference ended.

Confirmation was forthcoming later in the day. The Senate, aroused by the disclosures, called upon the President for whatever information he had. Wilson answered by transmitting a memorandum from Lansing that the Zimmermann Note was authentic and had been in possession of the administration for several days. But the most convincing proof of all came when Chief of Bureau Conger cabled from Berlin that Zimmermann, the foreign minister, volunteered the admission that he had sent the note. As though to justify himself, Zimmermann ingeniously stressed that "the instructions were to be carried out *only* after declaration of war by America."

The story of how the United States government obtained the text of the Zimmermann note was not made public until years later. The British Intelligence Service had intercepted a copy of Zimmermann's instructions to von Bernstorff and it was turned over to Admiralty experts for decoding. The contents were so astounding that the information was given to the American ambassador at London on February 24, and he immediately cabled it to the State Department. The State Department later said that the necessity for concealing Britain's knowledge of German codes was a major reason why Lansing withheld from Hood any facts on how the Zimmermann message came into the administration's possession.

3

The United States entered the World War on April 6, 1917. President Noyes and General Manager Stone called on Wilson and the subject of wartime censorship was discussed. They suggested that any American arrangement include provision for competent newspapermen on the censorship boards so that the people would be assured of receiving all the news the publication of which was not actually injurious to the country's interests.

Army and Navy officials, they pointed out, were instinctively disposed to suppress almost everything and might automatically forbid dispatches which obviously were of value to the people at home. Wilson agreed and to a great degree the suggestion was incorporated in censorship methods.

The declaration of war touched off a great surge of patriotism. Seen from the headquarters of the association, however, the outlook was hardly as bright as orators painted it. Private advices, the reports of men on furlough from the front, and what could be read between the lines of closely censored dispatches gave a dark picture. Britain's spring offensive in Artois had been a costly failure, and the French thrust in Champagne had been hurled back with such terrific slaughter that sixteen army corps mutinied and refused to attack. The news from Whiffen at Petrograd was no less disquieting. The Czar had abdicated in the face of revolution and a shaky coalition of moderates were struggling to keep Russian armies in action. On the seas submarine warfare was taking an appalling toll of shipping. Allied fortunes were at a low ebb.

America's entry redoubled the importance of news coverage abroad.

The general manager started the first contingent of additional staff men to Europe and selected others to sail as soon as troop movements started. Overseas the continued collection of news of enemy nations was a definite problem. The expulsion of staff men made neighboring neutral countries the substitute channels for obtaining the news of the Central Powers, and reporters regularly assigned to key neutral centers were brought to New York for special instructions.

Ulrich Salchow, for years correspondent in Stockholm, was one of those recalled. When he was ready to embark from Brooklyn to return to Sweden, he had trouble boarding his boat. A crowd of Russians jammed the pier, listening to a fiery speech from a man who harangued them in their native tongue from the ship's rail. Salchow, who understood Russian, was surprised by what he heard, yet the police and secret-service men present made no move to interfere.

"I go to Russia to help the revolution," he was yelling. "Russia will make peace with Germany. We will see to that, and we will end the loss of Russian lives in a war in support of capitalism. I shall be back, my comrades, to join you in the destruction of the capitalistic system in America. England, France, Italy will fall before our cause. Communism is the call for the world revolution."

Salchow struck up an acquaintance with the speaker when the boat left port and told him he marveled that he spoke so plainly in the presence of the police.

"The officers of the law are idiots," the Russian said. "They did not know what I was saying."

The British Intelligence, however, learned what had been said. When the ship touched at Halifax two days later the Russian was arrested and taken ashore. Unperturbed, he promised Salchow: "I shall charm these fools and I will see you in Stockholm."

Three weeks later the Russian walked into Salchow's office in Stockholm.

"How in the world did you make it?" asked the correspondent.

"Easy," the visitor replied. "I merely told them how I was going back to Russia to end the revolution and throw the force of Russia back into the war wholeheartedly against Germany. That assurance was all they wanted. They not only released me, free to take the next ship, but they furnished me some funds as a bon voyage."

The Russian was Leon Trotsky.

4

America's first shot of the war was fired April 19, the anniversary of the Battle of Lexington. A naval gun crew on the American liner *Mongolia* opened fire on an attacking U-boat in British waters and sank her. Captain Rice, the *Mongolia's* commander, gave the co-operative an eyewitness account as soon as the ship reached port—an account which was such big news that commercial competitors pirated it as soon as it appeared.

By this time piracy of news had reached such proportions that the association instituted legal action against the major offender, Hearst's International News Service. The piracy demonstrated the need for having the association's dispatches regularly credited, instead of leaving the matter to the discretion of individual members, for pirates could always offer the defense that they did not know an uncredited item was Associated Press news. Accordingly, on April 26 the Board of Directors issued orders that all Associated Press matter should be credited and that all members should daily carry printed notice of the paper's affiliation with the co-operative.

Besides the problem created by piracy, the association, like so many enterprises in different fields, encountered operation difficulties as staff men left to join the colors. The Traffic Department suffered heavily. The Signal Corps was in need of trained telegraph men and within the first months a hundred of the six hundred and sixty regular telegraphers had joined. A number of the men were in France three weeks after their enlistment. Some two hundred others, unable to serve because of age or disability, devoted spare time to the instruction of Signal Corps recruits.

The editorial staff also was involved. Seventy-five men joined the armed forces and others volunteered for Red Cross and Y.M.C.A. units overseas. Washington lost three front-rank men when Steve Early, Byron Price, and W. F. Caldwell enlisted, and other bureaus suffered in proportion to their size.

The first drawing of the draft imposed a tremendous burden on wire facilities, already hampered by government demands on communications. At 9:49 one summer morning, in the public hearing room of the Senate office building, Secretary of War Newton D. Baker drew out the first draft number—258—and a minute later it went out over the news network. To the men numbered 258 in each of 4,500 draft precincts it was notice they had been chosen to fight. In all, 10,500 numbers were drawn in the two days of the draft lottery, and the report carried every one of them. To handle the story which meant so much personally to the able-bodied men of the nation, four special parallel trunk wires were set up. From 9:50 A.M. one day until 2:18 P.M. the next, the numbers streamed across the continent, until the last one was flashed ten minutes after it had been drawn. One Traffic man, John Mooney at the Scranton *Republican,* stayed on duty twenty-six hours and fifteen minutes. At 8 A.M. the second day one number ticked off the sounder that made Mooney grin—it was his own.

5

The first troops—Regular Army units—sailed for France a few weeks after General Pershing's arrival in England in June, and Stanley W. Prenosil, from the Boston Bureau, made the trip in one of the transports. The news of troop departures was suppressed as a military measure, but when the first transport reached France with Prenosil aboard, he cabled a story that touched off unbounded enthusiasm throughout the United States. Phillip Powers of the Paris Bureau also sent a story on the landing of the troops on French soil. These dispatches were the only ones that came through.

Then a tempest burst. The wartime Committee on Public Information criticized the association for carrying the stories, It charged that the news had been sent in defiance of censorship regulations through the bribery of a telegraph operator. Publication of the dispatches, it said, gave the enemy information which jeopardized the lives of troops still in the danger zone at sea on other transports.

Stone instituted an investigation. Prenosil and Powers were instructed to forward sworn statements regarding the charge that they bribed an operator to violate censorship regulations, and a request was made to the Intelligence Section of the American Expeditionary Force for any information its inquiry uncovered.

Developments proved that the exclusive stories were exclusive only by virtue of an accident. Censorship orders had, in truth, been issued, directing that all dispatches dealing with the arrival of the first American units in France be withheld for simultaneous release after the last of the transport fleet docked. The Intelligence section reported:

. . . the fault was not with any correspondent, but with some one who permitted these telegrams to go through to London before the word of release was given.

No retraction of the charges came, however, and in less than two weeks an even wilder teapot episode occurred. On July 3, after all ships of the first transport fleet had safely reached France, The Committee on Public Information released in the name of Secretary of Navy Josephus Daniels a stirring story of two battles between the troopships and destroyers under Admiral Graves and enemy submarines. The attack, the release said, "was made in force, although the night made impossible any exact count of the U-boats gathered for what they deemed a slaughter." On the authority of the wartime information czar, the Daniels story was carried, but it aroused the doubts of staff editors informed on submarine warfare. Since U-boats were blind when submerged, they traveled alone to avoid the dangers of collision and no one had ever heard of an attack in flotilla force.

A copy of the story was relayed to London and Frank America, one of the staff there, sought comment from British naval experts and at the European headquarters of the American naval forces under Admiral Sims. Two days later New York headquarters received the following:

JULY 5, 1917. LONDON. THURSDAY CONFIDEN-
TIAL FOLLOWING AMERICAS NAVAL BASE PASSED FOR
PUBLICATION USA ONLY QUOTE PRIVATE ATTITUDE
OFFICIAL CIRCLES HERE THAT DANIELS STORY MADE
OUT OF WHOLE CLOTH THERE NO SUBMARINE ATTACK
WHATEVER NO TORPEDOES SEEN NO GUNFIRE FROM
DESTROYERS STOP OUR DESTROYERS DROPPED EX-
PLOSIVE CHARGE AS PRECAUTION BUT NO SUBMARINE OR
WRECKAGE SEEN STOP EXPLAINED DESTROYERS FRE-
QUENTLY FIRE AT LOGS OR ANYTHING WHICH MIGHT
PROVE PERISCOPE STOP OFFICIALS HERE THEREFORE
DECLINE PERMIT AFTERMATH STORY FROM THIS END.

To the general manager and the news editors alike the preliminary phrasing of the dispatch proved puzzling. It was marked "confidential" but it also bore the censor's release: "Passed for publication USA only." After discussion, the conclusion was finally reached that the London Bureau had labeled the message confidential because of doubt that the censor would permit its transmission for publication. As long as the British censor had passed it for publication, they reasoned, there was nothing to prevent its use. In a matter of minutes the story was on the wire, exploding the original story of submarines attacking in fleets.

Washington questioned Secretary Daniels about the London dispatch, and Daniels, whose newspaper, the Raleigh (N. C.) *News and*

Observer, was a member of The Associated Press, immediately called Stone by long-distance telephone. He asked that the story be killed quickly. The request was an official demand from the wartime government and Stone had no alternative. A mandatory notice to kill the story went out immediately, but in most places the dispatch was in print.

Once more the Committee hurled its charges. The London dispatch was damned as "a cruel lie . . . the work of a correspondent in search of a story, and the British Court of Inquiry branded him a liar and expelled him from the fleet." President Wilson was so incensed that he said he never again would speak to Melville Stone. Daniels was too philosophical to quarrel, but he told Stone that Admiral Gleaves, like Wilson, would never forgive him either. Stone expressed his regrets, but explained that the story had come from a staff man and The Associated Press believed it.

Another investigation was ordered and while it was in progress Stone attended a reception in honor of one of the Allied missions which had arrived in New York to help co-ordinate war efforts.

"Mr. Stone," said a voice at his elbow, "is there any reason why you and I can't have a cocktail together?"

The general manager found himself facing Admiral Gleaves, who had just returned from convoying the first troopships to France.

"Mr. Stone," said the admiral, "I owe you a debt that I never can repay. I mean for denying that silly story given out from Washington respecting two fierce battles with submarines. I am a plain common sailor and not given to that kind of statement. I could not be responsible for the hysterical rhapsody. Of course, the order to all our boats was that if anything like a periscope appeared to fire at it, and that was done. The officers on the individual boats saw evidences of periscopes and torpedoes and took a shot at them. That was the whole story."

The investigation abroad upheld the truth of Frank America's dispatch. He had obtained the information from officers at Admiral Sims' base, where convoy destroyers frequently took on supplies. Publication of the story in the United States, however, was a mistake. America had meant the information to be confidential, but the censor's stamp, "Passed for publication USA only," which should not have been transmitted, was incorporated as part of the cabled message. As for America himself, the British Admiralty exonerated him and he continued welcome at Admiral Sims' headquarters.

6

Not long after the submarine episode the general manager went to Europe to supervise arrangements for the increased news demands that would arise when American troops began active fighting. He toured the lines, sloshing through muddy trenches with a sergeant of marines as his guide. The costly British Passchendaele offensive was bogging down in the quagmire of Flanders. Bled white by heavy casualties, the French had reverted to defensive tactics, and on the eastern front the last fitful Russian drive flickered out under the hammering of German counterattacks.

Shifting his men to meet the war situation as it existed, Stone sent Charles T. Thompson to the Italian front. Because of the growing acuteness of affairs in Russia, Charles Stephenson Smith, correspondent at Peking, was ordered to Petrograd to relieve Whiffen. Robert T. Small, with the British in Flanders for some time, was transferred to Pershing's headquarters where he was later reinforced by Norman L. Draper.

Just before his reassignment, Small almost lost his life in the Somme during the limited advance which took Péronne. Crossing a ruined bridge he plunged through a camouflaged section into the river. A party of British engineers rescued him.

Small's successor with the British and Belgian forces was DeWitt Mackenzie, the only American correspondent to see what was happening in the Egypto-Arabic theater of war. Captain John Yardley, D.W.O., one of England's World War heroes and then aide-de-camp to the British commander in chief in the Near East, said of his work:

It was well known to us at General Headquarters that Mackenzie's dispatches, not only from Egypt, but from other theaters of war, were the most potent written, for they lifted the veil, and revealed to the American public the true facts.

As the autumn waned, William Gibson, an operator, was killed in London during an air raid and Frank America had a narrow escape when a zeppelin bomb burst so close that he was knocked down and covered by falling debris.

In London Stone devoted himself to a firsthand study of the chaotic cable conditions which were playing havoc with efforts to get news to the United States promptly. Government messages took precedence and their volume was extremely heavy. "Urgent" rates no longer existed, so the association began filing a large number of dispatches at the full commercial rate of 25 cents a word. This boosted cable tolls to $2,000 a day, but failed to improve conditions materially. Western Union declined to guarantee delivery of any press messages in less than forty-eight hours, and the French cable company refused newspaper dispatches because it was unable to provide satisfactory service.

Stories sent at the full commercial rate often took from seventeen to fifty-two hours in transmission. Frequently dispatches filed at the slower 17-cents-a-word press rate arrived in New York long before full-rate stories. Communications with Russia were wholly unpredictable. Some stories never reached New York at all, and many times instructions from New York never reached Petrograd. One message from the Russian capital to New York was sixty-two days in transit. Throughout the remainder of the conflict the erratic cables destroyed many clean beats and on any number of occasions gave scoops to dispatches which normally should have been hours behind.

7

Back home in the United States, the nation was trying to forget its war worries momentarily by reading of the World Series, and again Cooper lined up his 26,000-mile circuit to report the Chicago White Sox-New York Giants games direct from the ball parks. Despite the keen competition of other news, the baseball classic could still command position on American front pages, and it had one less story to contend with that October, thanks to one of the co-operative's staff.

Upheavals in Mexico no longer made the stories they once did now that America was embroiled in Europe, but Pancho Villa continued active in Chihuahua and was anxious to impress the United States by defeating President Carranza. An attack on the federal-held town of Ojinaga seemed to offer a good opportunity, and Villa laid plans for an assault early in October. Just as he finished preparations, Norman Walker, a staff correspondent, reached his camp. Villa had known the reporter during several years of assignments south of the Rio Grande, and therefore confided his plans to Walker and asked if he considered the date propitious.

Smiling, Walker told Villa he could not have chosen a worse time. The World Series, he pointed out, was just starting and what space American newspapers had for news other than baseball would be preempted by war dispatches.

"If you wait until after the World Series," Walker said, "you might make the front pages."

Villa waited, and when he finally took Ojinaga he did make the front pages.

But there was far greater news that October than the 1917 World Series or a postponed Mexican battle. On October 24, in a thick fog intensified by snow and rain, a spearhead of six German and nine Austrian divisions smashed through on the Caporetto sector and the entire Italian front collapsed. Thompson was caught in the rout which streamed back toward the River Piave in confusion. The second day of the swift Austro-German advance found him on the crumbling front at Gorizia, which was being mercilessly pounded by massed enemy artillery. He had mounted the highest available rampart to get a better view of operations, when a shell burst near by, burying him and several companions under an avalanche of earth and mud. Rescuers dug out the party. Thompson was the only one wounded; a piece of shrapnel had hit him in the head. The wound was dressed at a first-aid station and he returned to his task of reporting the offensive which hurled the Italians back more than sixty miles and at one time threatened the utter destruction of their armies. As it was, General Cadorna lost 800,000 effectives.

On the heels of the Italian breakdown came the black news from Russia. For weeks the cables that got through from Whiffen, Chief of Bureau Smith, H. L. Rennick, and other members of the staff at Petrograd or at the Russian front had been alarming. They told of rioting, unrest, demonstrations for a separate peace and the ugly atmosphere pervading the country. The report began to mention the unfamiliar names of Nikolay Lenin and Leon Trotsky, Salchow's shipboard companion of a few months earlier. When Associated Press dispatches described how Russian troops were shooting their officers and parading under red flags to shouts of "Down with the war!" the State Department at Washington felt sufficiently concerned to issue a counterstatement that diplomatic advices from Russia indicated no grounds for worry and that full confidence continued in Russia's loyalty to the Allies.

The bloody Russian Revolution which broke on November 7 proved how well the Petrograd staff had been reporting true conditions. Throughout the Red Terror the men daily took their lives in their hands when they got their news and arranged for its transmission. Smith saved an American consular official from being bayoneted by a berserk soldier and was promptly felled by a clubbed rifle. Soldiers pounced on him and beat him up badly. Another member of the staff was shot in the knee by a sniper. But the news came out—the spread of the revolution, the conclusion of an armistice between the Central Powers and Russia, and finally on December 27 the full text of the treaty of Brest-Litovsk, first Teutonic peace terms formulated since the beginning of the war.

Just as the Board of Directors opposed carrying the by-lines of staff men, it likewise vetoed any wartime relaxation in the hard and fast rules governing the handling of cabled dispatches. The policy was to carry nothing under a foreign date line which did not come by cable, and the board ordered that this regulation continue to be strictly observed. Even when half of a story arrived in the day report and the other half at night, there was to be no rewriting of the previously published portion so that the night report might have a slightly different lead from that carried on the day wires. The practice was sharply at variance with that of commercial agencies and individual newspapers, for many regularly rewrote and expanded the cables they received, incorporating matter the original dispatches did not contain, drawing conclusions from war maps, and giving the stories a literary polish not likely to appear in copy written in haste under fire.

The only concession made to the war was the introduction of Undated War Leads, written in New York, which rounded up all information into one comprehensive story. Undated Leads subsequently became the approved newspaper method of handling any major story involving a multiplicity of date lines and developments.

8

General Manager Stone returned from Europe late in the year to an America which had settled down in earnest to the serious business of being at war. New York was singing "Over There," "Tipperary," and "Oh, How I Hate to Get Up in the Morning," a catchy air written by a Camp Upton sergeant, Irving Berlin. The advertising signs along Broadway were darkened by order of the federal fuel administrator. People joked about wheatless Mondays, meatless Tuesdays, sugarless coffee, and coalless furnaces. Herbert Hoover had become the nation's food czar, and wartime Prohibition was around the corner.

The war moved on into 1918. The collapse of Russia had freed thirty German divisions from the eastern front for service in France.

"WAIT UNTIL AFTER THE WORLD SERIES," THE CORRESPONDENT TOLD VILLA.

Every sign pointed to a gigantic struggle for a decision on the western front. Charles Kloeber, chief of the News Department, had relieved the general manager in Europe as active director of the staff, and Cooper, the Traffic Department head, went abroad to attempt improvement in the erratic cable conditions. American troops were almost ready for battle lines and once they went into action there would be an additional heavy burden on the jammed cables.

Early in March confidential advices began to trickle into New York headquarters that a German drive on the western front was imminent. Soon after the first advices there came a publishable cable: The German High Command had invited neutral correspondents to start for the west "to witness the German offensive." The dispatch aroused little attention. Military authorities in Washington expressed the opinion that an Allied offensive was more likely, and the public looked on the story as a Teutonic ruse. Nevertheless, Jackson Elliott, who had been brought from Washington to command the News Department in Kloeber's absence, took all precautions and ordered preparation of a background story outlining the exact military situation in France so that it would be ready for use if the Germans unleashed their drive.

The advance information from neutral sources proved all too correct. At 9:30 A.M., March 21, the leased wires hummed with a bulletin from Mackenzie telling of the pulverizing German bombardment on the sixty-mile Arras–Cambrai–Saint-Quentin front. Other cables added further details: The enemy was hurling a force of approximately half a million men against the British. An hour and a quarter after the first bulletin there came further confirmation of the importance of the offensive. From Amsterdam Correspondent Thomas Stockwell forwarded a dispatch quoting the Kaiser as saying: "We are at the decisive moment of the war, and one of the greatest moments in German history."

The tremendous drive was the beginning of Ludendorff's March break-through and the sagging British lines were thrust relentlessly backward. As Ludendorff hammered out an ever-deepening salient into the Somme sector, the cables on March 23 brought from Roberts in Paris something so improbable that news editors in New York hesitated to use it. The story stated that a heavy siege gun had been bombarding the French capital throughout the forenoon, firing at fifteen-minute intervals. What made the news almost incredible was the fact that the office war maps showed the nearest German lines to be twenty-six miles away—a far greater distance than the range of any known artillery piece.

The dispatch was withheld and a hurried check made through Washington with War Department ordnance experts. They called the story absurd. To bombard Paris from such a distance a gun would have to hurl its projectile at least twenty miles into the air, and no such weapon was known to exist.

Stone was in St. Louis at the time and Elliott passed the dilemma to him. The story gave Stone pause. If the news were not true, he realized that the consequences would be most serious. On the other hand, he knew Roberts was not a man to lose his head. The times given in the dispatch showed the correspondent had waited five hours after the start of the bombardment before filing his story, and that was evidence he had not acted on the spur of the moment. Lastly, the cable had been passed by the French censor. Stone made his decision:

"Release Roberts story. We'll stand pat on it."

The appearance of the news that day provoked an outburst of scorn and disbelief. Commercial agencies ridiculed the notion of such a siege gun, calling it an "absurd invention" and a "plain blunder."

At a dinner that evening Stone was publicly twitted.

"Well," he said good-naturedly, "back in New York I have a friend, the Reverend Dr. Minot J. Savage, who holds with a Cape Cod farmer that the religious faith of the Evangelical Christian is 'believin' in the thing that you know ain't so.' Such is my position. I believe this story 'that I know ain't so,' because The Associated Press says it."

For forty-eight hours the co-operative "stood pat," and then the critics, military and journalistic, belatedly discovered that the facts set forth were correct. Not airplanes, but a monster long-range gun had been bombarding Paris.

Cable tolls more than doubled as the German March offensive smashed forward forty miles before Mackenzie and Roberts cabled that the break-through had been finally halted. From the Paris Bureau came equally significant news: Ferdinand Foch had been appointed to co-ordinate Allied operations, his first step toward becoming generalissimo a few weeks later.

There was little respite for Mackenzie. Hardly had Ludendorff's offensive been checked on one sector than Germany loosed a new drive at another part of the British-held front and shook eleven divisions into the clear in an April break-through which menaced the vital Channel ports. It was then that the report carried General Haig's famous order:

"There must be no retiring. With our back to the wall and believing in the justice of our cause, each one of us must fight to the end."

American divisions by this time had taken over three front-line sectors, mostly quiet in character, and four correspondents were assigned to cover them—Norman Draper, John T. Parkerson, Samuel F. Wader, and Philip M. Powers who had served at one time or another on every front in Europe except the Dardanelles. Wader wrote the story of the first real engagement of American troops on April 20 at Seicheprey, when the Germans took the town and held the position for half a day before they were dislodged. It was a month before cables told of the capture of Cantigny, which served to atone for the initial reverse of United States arms at Seicheprey.

9

While the British were battling desperately to halt the year's second "big push" by Ludendorff and conditions in France grew more critical, the members of The Associated Press convened in New York for the annual meeting. This was no routine assembly. Melville E. Stone, now seventy, had completed a quarter of a century of service as general manager and they gathered to fete him. The aging Victor Lawson was there to pay him tribute, and there was praise, too, from Adolph Ochs, Noyes, and others of the group that had fought with him in behalf of honest news gathering during the turbulent 1890's. Stone spoke of the testimonial celebration as "a fine funeral," but even this attempt at levity could not conceal how deeply he was touched.

The war seemed far away during the festive celebration, but before many weeks had passed Stone was packing his bags to resume direction of the report in Europe. Matching their March and April drives, the Germans broke through again in May, this time on the French Chemin des Dames front which Berry covered, and the gray tide rolled on toward Paris as it had in the crucial autumn of 1914. Philip Powers and Burge McFall, formerly of the Washington staff, accompanied the Second Division at Château-Thierry and Belleau Wood early in June when United States regulars and marines dramatically stopped the German left at the Marne. The brilliant counterattack of the Second Division marked the debut of large-scale American action on the western front and the cables carried every word censors' blue pencils permitted to go. By the time Stone arrived in Europe the May break-through had been completely halted, more American divisions were going into the lines and the stage was almost set for the Second Battle of the Marne.

The association's entire attention, however, was not focused on France. Much closer to home a covert bloodless war was being waged by the Central Powers in South America, and in it the name of The Associated Press had suffered.

Immediately upon the outbreak of hostilities in 1914, Germany had invaded the Latin-American nations with a government-subsidized propaganda service which masqueraded as a news agency under the name of *Prensa Asociada*—Spanish for Associated Press. Supplied to South American papers more or less gratis, the news was strongly pro-German and the directors of the service cultivated the belief that the dispatches actually came from The Associated Press. Until the United States entered the war, the propaganda was directed against the Allies, but in April, 1917, the service extended its operations to minimize and deprecate America's part in the conflict.

The tardiness of The Associated Press in expanding into South America was due primarily to an old agreement between the major news-gathering organizations of the world. It dated back to the days of William Henry Smith. Under this pact the Reuter Agency had Great Britain, her colonies, Egypt, Turkey, China, and the countries within Britain's sphere of influence. The Havas Agency of Paris took for its territory France, Switzerland, Italy, Spain, Portugal, Central and South America. The German Wolfe Bureau was given jurisdiction over the Reich, Scandinavian countries, Holland, Russia, Austria-Hungary, and the Balkans. The Associated Press had the United States. Foreseeing that closer relations between the United States and South America were essential, Stone declined to agree in 1912 to a long-term extension of the agreement, but the war in 1914 interrupted plans for a definite program.

Havas, therefore, continued to serve South America, although its war news was almost as one-sided as the German Prensa Asociada. Controlled by the French government, Havas carried no news of enemy successes, enemy communiqués, or similar material. When South American papers, desirous of getting both sides of the story on an important event, demanded American Associated Press dispatches, Havas representatives in New York abstracted the required copy from the co-operative's report, in contravention of the existing agreement, and relayed it to Havas men in South America. Except for these occasions when actual Associated Press news was demanded, South American papers were largely dependent on Havas and Prensa Asociada. Furthermore, Havas was interested solely in distributing news in South America and not in gathering South American news for the rest of the world. To get anything approaching adequate coverage, The Associated Press had found it necessary to assign its own staff men to the continent.

With Prensa Asociada redoubling its efforts after America's entry into the war, it was obvious to the Board of Directors of The Associated Press that they could not combat such an agency through the medium of Havas. The State Department, concerned over the influence wielded by the German propaganda service, urged The Associated Press to give the nation's Latin-American neighbors factual news both about the war and the United States. Notice accordingly was served on Havas that the co-operative would terminate its agreement, and on June 8, 1918, Cooper sailed for South America.

News of Cooper's coming preceded him. When he reached Valparaiso, the first person to seek him out was an agent of Prensa Asociada. The man came to the point at once. He wanted to negotiate a contract that would give Prensa Asociada exclusive South American rights to the name of The Associated Press and distribution of its news report. He named an attractive figure. Cooper told him Prensa Asociada might multiply its offer a thousand times, but neither that sum nor any other astronomical amount could buy The Associated Press.

Cooper spent three months in South America. He found the important newspapers anxious to obtain a genuine Associated Press report. They were disgusted with both Havas and Prensa Asociada and they had lost reliance in the accuracy of one American commercial agency because of such major blunders as the reporting of the fall of Soissons thirty days before the city actually fell. Cooper left behind a discredited Prensa Asociada which collapsed a few months later.

10

In the busy cable room in New York the flood of cables was endless. On July 15 Ludendorff launched Germany's final bid for victory in a great Friedensturm, or "peace offensive," on the Marne. Burge McFall, James P. Howe, Norman Draper, and Samuel Wader were with the A.E.F. divisions which helped turn the tide. Roberts and Berry were on the French front to the American left, and in Paris Stone himself could hear the thunder of artillery in the battle that was the beginning of the end.

After the second Marne the tide flowed back, and in France alone, from the North Sea to Switzerland, operations became so continuous that no one man, however capable, could hope to cover them adequately. The story called for a tried and co-ordinated staff, each man contributing his part to the broad sweep of a narrative that pounded toward its climax. As the repeated Allied counterblows beat Ludendorff staggering back, only those in the cable department in New York knew from day to day which of the men on the front did the outstanding work in any one twenty-four hours.

Dispatches from Stockwell in Holland and Bouton in Sweden gave added significance to the German retreat when they told of seething unrest on the home fronts of the Central Powers, mutinies in the German fleet, the insistent demands for peace. And there were many more —reports of the Central Powers' reverses in the Balkans, Whiffen's stories on the White Army in Siberia, Smith's cables from the turmoil of Petrograd, the news Rennick sent from the Allied anti-Bolshevik forces at Archangel, Frank King's dispatches from another Allied command at Vladivostok, and all the rest of the heavy transoceanic tide of copy.

The pins on the map moved.

American First Army Destroys Saint-Mihiel salient . . . British Take Nazareth . . . Hindenburg Line Broken . . . Bulgaria Surrenders . . . Argonne Forest . . . Germany Asks Peace Terms . . . Kaiser's Abdication Demanded . . . Italians Crush Enemy on Austrian Front . . . Ludendorff Resigns . . . Americans Take Sedan . . . E.O.S. Bulletin . . . E.O.S. Bulletin . . .

In France, McFall and Powers "captured" the German stronghold of Stenay, entering the town alone well before the advancing troops they had accidently outdistanced. In Belgium, Mackenzie appealed directly to Field Marshal Haig when no transportation was available to enable him to keep pace with the rapid British gains. To his bewilderment he got not one but seven touring cars. From a temporary post in neutral Denmark, Bouton slipped across the German frontier and started on his risky way to Berlin. And to the southward W. C. Hiatt followed the fleeing, disorganized Austrians in a strenuous race to be the first newsman to reach Vienna.

The general manager returned to the United States November 3, two days before Germany was informed that the Allies had designated Marshal Foch to receive delegates and communicate armistice terms. The pins kept moving on the big cable department map. On the 53,000-mile leased wire network 1,033 newspapers were waiting around the clock.

XIII. FALSE ARMISTICE

NOVEMBER 7, 1918.

The lunch-hour crowds flowed tranquilly along Broadway and Park Row. Then suddenly everyone seemed to go mad in a frenzy of hysterical noise. With incredible speed the tidings raced through New York. Church bells clanged, whistles shrilled, and a storm of ticker tape and paper swirled down.

They could see all this happening from The Associated Press windows at 51 Chambers Street. Below, City Hall Park swarmed black with people. Crowds were climbing on top of surface cars, stalled in the pack of humanity which jammed Broadway to the right and Park Row to the left. Urchins scaled the scrubby trees behind the Post Office, waving flags which had materialized from nowhere. Office buildings disgorged an elbowing tumult of men and women into the bobbing sea of heads.

The men who looked down from 51 Chambers Street wore worried expressions. They knew what had touched off the explosion of noise and emotions, and with that knowledge had come a hopeless, sinking feeling of defeat. Even before the jubilant clamor shattered Broadway's lunchtime serenity, a dumbfounded editor tore across the newsroom with the message which told the story. Inarticulately he thrust it into the hands of Elliott, chief of the News Department.

Just five words which had come pounding through from an alert bureau:

UNITED PRESS FLASHING ARMISTICE SIGNED.

Elliott frowned, unbelieving. In a trice another urgent message was on his desk—"Opposition Has Armistice"—and the wires were buzzing with a dozen more. They all were the same.

The Associated Press was beaten on the biggest story of the war!

The moment of sick paralysis ended in an instant, and then there was Elliott's voice, tense but unexcited:

"Get cables after London and Paris! Full rate!"

"Open a line to the State Department! I'll talk to Frank Polk!"

"Bring me a map!"

He kept rapping out instructions to check every possible source. An oppressive silence descended on the newsroom like some physical weight, magnifying the staccato of the Morkrum battery, the importunate voices of the men working telephones, the monotonous rattle of Morse keys. In the Cable Department tight-lipped editors hung over every incoming news wire. A staff man, back from lunch, burst into the office, hurrahing that the Armistice had been signed, but the look on every face smothered his jubilation.

Elliott sat grimly at the desk which had become the focal point not only of the office but of the entire domestic service. By leased wire and telegram a storm of complaint and criticism was rolling in.

Why didn't The Associated Press have the Armistice? Badly beaten here . . . The Associated Press is pro-German—withholding the news . . . Resigning our membership as soon as possible . . .

The stacks of outraged communications grew with the minutes. The telephone clamored repeatedly and Elliott listened to the abuse and imprecations which members near and far shouted into his ear.

To all verbal inquiries, he gave the same stock answer, repeating it quietly, almost by rote:

"We have no news that an armistice has been signed. Our men abroad are on the job. The State Department has made no such announcement. When The Associated Press gets the news, we will carry it, but not before!"

All the while the clock hands crept onward, and the thunderous roar that beat in from the sunlit early afternoon was an incessant reminder that deepened the gloom of the newsroom.

One by one, each source failed to provide the story. Elliott talked with Undersecretary of State Polk: the State Department knew nothing . . . Collins in London could not confirm . . . Still no word from Paris . . .

The chief of the News Department bent over the large-scale map spread on the desk. Around him was a knot of intent men—L. F. Curtis, Elliott's assistant; Harry Romer, day cable editor; Harold Martin, news superintendent for the Eastern Division; and M. A. White night general editor. With a pair of dividers Elliott measured off miles on the map while Romer thumbed through a thick file of cable dispatches, meticulously checking time elements or facts concerning the projected visit of German plenipotentiaries to Foch to negotiate an armistice.

The opposition flash had stated flatly that the armistice had been signed at 11 A.M., yet the big map emphatically told the group at

Elliott's desk that it was impossible. Romer produced his cables. At 12:30 that morning the German High Command had wirelessed Marshal Foch the names of its emissaries and requested that he designate the point along the front where they would be permitted to enter the Allied lines. Foch's reply, sent at 1:25 A.M., informed the enemy that the party would be passed through the French outposts near the Chimay–Fourmies–La Capelle–Guise road. While this exchange occurred, and for at least three hours longer, the German emissaries were known to be still at German General Headquarters in Spa, Belgium. Moreover, the latest advices, although without specific timing, had the general Allied advance smashing forward unchecked.

The map gave the rest of the story. The air-line distance between Spa and Foch's headquarters in the forest of Compiègne was roughly 105 miles. By road it would be almost half as far again, and a speedy automobile trip was the remotest of possibilities. Heavy shellfire and aerial bombardments had been smashing the roads behind the German front, and those in any sort of repair were clogged with troops, supply lorries, and great quantities of equipment the Germans were trying to save.

Elliott shook his head.

"It couldn't be done," he said. "The Germans could not have reached there from Spa in time to sign an armistice at that hour."

The clocks kept moving, the bedlam of noise from the streets beat against the windows, and the tension of uncertainty tightened. It couldn't be true, it wasn't true, yet . . .

2

The general manager had been at lunch with President Noyes when the first report flew through downtown New York. They battled their way through the delirious crowds to reach the office. Stone's first question was on the story.

"How did we make out?" he asked Elliott.

"We didn't, Mr. Stone. We don't have the story."

"What?"

"No, Mr. Stone, and I'm convinced the story is wrong, that no armistice has been signed."

Elliott quickly sketched everything that had been done since first word had come of the opposition's flash. Stone nodded as he heard the exhaustive check made in all conceivable quarters and was impressed by the evidence found in the map and in the hours of the Franco-German exchange of messages early that morning.

"What have you put out on the wire?" the general manager demanded.

"Nothing, sir."

"H-m. We should carry an informative note giving members the status of this thing as we know it."

He thought a moment.

"Put out a Note to Editors at once, and one every half hour until we get to the bottom of this. I want to see all copy. Go ahead."

The informative message hit the wires as soon as Elliott finished writing it. In member offices people read:

```
                    NOTE TO EDITORS
        AT THIS HOUR THE GOVERNMENT AT WASHINGTON
    HAS RECEIVED NOTHING TO SUPPORT THE REPORT THAT
    THE ARMISTICE HAS BEEN SIGNED AND WE HAVE RE-
    CEIVED NOTHING FROM OUR CORRESPONDENTS ABROAD
    TO SUPPORT IT.
        STREET DEMONSTRATIONS ARE TAKING PLACE IN
    NEW YORK, AS IS PROBABLY THE CASE IN OTHER
    CITIES, BUT WE ARE NOT REPORTING THEM UP TO
    THIS MOMENT BECAUSE WE HAVE BEEN UNABLE TO
    CONFIRM THE REPORT ON WHICH THEY ARE BASED.
```

By that time even the man in the street had come to know that The Associated Press had not carried any news of an armistice. In some cities this failure acted as a brake on demonstrations after the first spontaneous outbursts.

In San Francisco, Mayor James Rolph, addressing an exuberant crowd which descended upon the City Hall, said: "The United Press has been informed that the armistice has been signed. I have received no confirmation of this from The Associated Press, and until I do I suggest that celebration plans be suspended." A few minutes later speaking to the San Francisco Bureau by telephone, he declared: " will wait until I hear from you before giving the order for any peace celebration."

In New York, however, the reaction assumed an ugly character and an angry phalanx of demonstrators marched on 51 Chambers Street. The cry of "Damned Huns" went up to the windows and fists were brandished when one bibulous patriot shouted: "Come on, let's clean out the rats." Upstairs, Elliott told a reporter to call police headquarters and arrange for a detail to guard the building.

THE BEDLAM OF NOISE FROM THE STREETS BEAT AGAINST THE WINDOW.

Still no word, and still no halt in the succession of heated telegrams, messages, and telephone calls. Not even the Hughes-Wilson
election had provoked such a violent outpouring.

Then the suspense snapped. For more than an hour City Editor
Carl Brandebury had been sitting with an ear glued to a telephone
receiver on the line which had been kept open to the State Department in Washington. Undersecretary Polk had promised word as soon
as any definite information came from abroad, and the department was
working the cables unsparingly. Brandebury watched the clock hands
tick toward 2:15. The receiver clicked in his ear.

"Elliott!"

The shout brought Stone to the door of his private office.

"Polk will be on here in a second!"

Everyone watched Elliott's face as he jammed it close to the
telephone mouthpiece to shut out the noise of the room. Everyone
watched his pencil fly across a piece of copy paper.

"Bulletin! All Wires! Bulletin!"

Telegraphers waited, ready fingers hovering over suddenly idle
keys.

Copy boys scrambled across the room.

Filing editors grinned with relief.

Morse keys vibrated and the sounders chorused:

```
                B U L L E T I N
            (BY THE ASSOCIATED PRESS)
        WASHINGTON, NOV. 7 - IT WAS OFFICIALLY
  ANNOUNCED AT THE STATE DEPARTMENT AT 2:15 O'CLOCK
  THIS AFTERNOON THAT THE GERMANS HAD NOT SIGNED
  ARMISTICE TERMS.
```

All other events that day were anticlimactic. It did not even seem
important that Elliott and his aides had their dinners interrupted the
same evening in Whyte's Restaurant and were hurried through a back
door to save them from attack by a bellicose group of drunken revelers
who brandished water carafes.

The end came four days later. Everyone knew then that the German emissaries were conferring with Foch. Everyone knew that the
long-awaited news was only a matter of hours. When the regular
"Good Night" was given on leased wire circuits at 2:30 A.M., November
11, operators remained at their keys, lights burned on in newspaper
offices, and composing room crews waited in readiness. It might come
any minute.

From Washington. Two words. 2:46 A.M.:

```
F-L-A-S-H   F-L-A-S-H
ARMISTICE SIGNED
```

Then the first bulletin:

```
B U L L E T I N
(BY THE ASSOCIATED PRESS)

    WASHINGTON, MONDAY, NOV. 11 - THE ARMISTICE
BETWEEN GERMANY, ON THE ONE HAND, AND THE ALLIED
GOVERNMENTS AND THE UNITED STATES, ON THE OTHER,
HAS BEEN SIGNED.


    ADD BULLETIN

    THE STATE DEPARTMENT ANNOUNCED AT 2:45
O'CLOCK THIS MORNING THAT GERMANY HAD SIGNED.


    ADD BULLETIN

    THE WORLD WAR WILL END AT 6 O'CLOCK THIS
MORNING, WASHINGTON TIME, 11 O'CLOCK PARIS
TIME.


    ADD BULLETIN

    THE ARMISTICE . . .
```

The first whistles started to shriek. Bonfires flared. Gongs clanged. Cannon boomed. And papers slithered in a damp flood from the whirling plates.

Extra . . . Extra . . . Extra . . .

Washington functioned with the smooth precision of a highly geared machine. Before sunset that day the bureau poured 11,582 words onto the leased wires. Treading on the heels of the first Washington bulletins came the rush from abroad which swept in on the Cable Department. Paris. Berlin. Amsterdam. Hohenzollern in Holland. Rome. Vienna. The Front. A.E.F. . . .

The emotional jag of November 7 was a mere rehearsal for the paroxysm of jubilant celebration which took the country by storm. This time it was real. This time it was authentic. This time there was no question of the facts.

As the cheering, screaming throngs took possession of the streets once more for a hysterical holiday of triumph and relief, telephones jangled in a thousand editorial rooms. Readers who had been misled November 7 wanted to know if they could trust this latest news.

At a desk in the office of the *Tribune Herald* at Rome, Georgia, J. D. McCartney sat before a telephone, answering the endless queries.

"Yes, madam, it's right this time. . . . Yes, it's correct. . . . It's all in the extra that's on the street now. . . . Oh, no, no doubt whatsoever. . . . Yes . . . Yes . . . Yes . . ."

It was a boring job when everyone else was out celebrating.

Another call. A staid, elderly woman by the tone of her voice.

"Who says the Armistice has been signed?" she asked briskly.

"The State Department at Washington," intoned McCartney for the hundredth time.

"Oh, pshaw!" the voice exclaimed impatiently. "Does The Associated Press say it?"

XIV. "BACK TO NORMALCY"

I

WITH twenty-five miles of delirious noise New York welcomed the first troops home from France on December 23, 1918. That same day Mr. Justice Pitney in Washington delivered an opinion of the United States Supreme Court. The case of The Associated Press versus the International News Service had been in litigation for two years before the decision was handed down.

Back in the rough-and-tumble days of early nineteenth century journalism when Hale and Hallock were outdoing the New York harbor news combine, competitors regularly filched news from the *Journal of Commerce*. Bennett and, later, Greeley both suffered at the hands of news thieves, but in that era the tendency was to look upon piracy as an oblique compliment. Some editors even boasted in print that rivals found it necessary to steal their news in order to keep pace. "We rather like it," Greeley acknowleged.

This attitude did not long survive the period of individual journalism. Although outright news piracy came in time to be looked upon with disfavor, the practice continued uncurbed and for a long while no consistent efforts were made to stop it.

As newspaper production methods speeded up and transmission facilities improved, the operations of the pirates assumed more damaging proportions. Editors saw their news, gathered at considerable effort and expense, regularly pirated by agencies of various types which made no comparable attempt to cover the world. Most of these agencies were short-lived in spite of their wholesale appropriation of dispatches, but the evil remained. At first individual publishers hoped that the national copyright laws might be extended to protect the contents of a daily paper. Congress, however, showed no disposition to oblige, and the bill died in committee.

Ignoring previous failures, The Associated Press in 1899 designated a special committee to investigate the possibility of having a news copyright law enacted. The committee's work proved ineffectual.

The World War tremendously stimulated the activities of the

pirates. Without an extensive news-gathering organization abroad, it was impossible for some agencies to cover the conflict adequately or promptly, so the appropriators of news began to prey more than ever on the reports of The Associated Press. If the news thefts were to be stopped, the organization would have to strike at the practice itself and not at the devices by which it was carried on.

Late in 1916, because of what it termed "continued garbling of messages and breach of faith," the British government debarred International News Service from securing any news in Great Britain or from using cable lines running from Great Britain. France, Canada, Portugal, and Japan followed suit. The actions were based on the publication in the United States of stories purporting to be International cable dispatches which contained statements not appearing in the cables passed by the censors. The prohibitions became effective November 17, and after that date the agency was denied the opportunity to obtain or cable the news from any one of the five countries. Despite this, International continued to supply this news regularly and promptly as if it were being normally received by cable.

A discharged employee of the International News Service at Cleveland confided to Traffic Chief Cooper that an editorial man of the Cleveland *News* was selling the Associated Press war news to the commercial agency at so much per week. Cooper went to Cleveland, got written statements, and dictated affidavits to which the signatures were affixed. He returned to New York and told Stone: "Here's the basis for your legal test of the property right in news."

Armed with these affidavits, The Associated Press took its case into the Federal District Court at New York on January 4, 1917, and petitioned Judge Augustus N. Hand for an injunction restraining International from further piracy.

International News Service contested the action, disclaiming all guilt of pre-publication piracy.

An injunction granted by Judge Hand, as modified by the Circuit Court of Appeals, covered all points raised by The Associated Press. International News Service then took the fight before the United States Supreme Court. There the contest centered on a single issue: Whether the commercial agency had the right to appropriate Associated Press dispatches once these items had been printed. The Supreme Court held that it did not, thereby establishing the property right in news.

For The Associated Press in particular and for news-gathering enterprise in general, the decision was a major triumph. The Board of

Directors spoke of it as a victory that "may well be celebrated." A mutual, permanent injunction was obtained.

As a supplementary action the Board of Directors renewed its insistence that all Associated Press news be properly credited, so that no pirate could plead ignorance of its origin. Accordingly all members of the co-operative began to credit the news, either with the established line, "*By The Associated Press*," or with a logotype—(*AP*)—which could be carried in the dateline of each story. The logotype became the more popular method and in time The Associated Press came to be known universally as "AP."

2

General Manager Stone learned of the Supreme Court decision in Paris where he had gone December 3 to organize the special staff being assembled to cover the most momentous peace conference of modern history. The conference was not to open until January, but already delegations were foregathering to study the intricate and complex problems left by the war.

The Paris Peace Conference proved an unparalleled assignment. The subject matter presented a distinct departure from the accepted range of news in prewar days. There were questions of economics, ethnography, geography, history. Experts collated masses of material on Mandates, Demilitarization, Self-determination, War Guilt, and Reparations. The place of a League of Nations in postwar civilization was envisaged and discussed.

The fact that secrecy shrouded so much of the negotiations imposed a heavy handicap on all efforts to obtain complete, accurate, and honest accounts of what was happening. The world-wide interest was tremendous, for mankind looked hopefully to the peace conference to lay the foundations for a new era of international order on the wreckage of "the war to end war."

For all its surpassing importance, however, the conference was merely a news island in a troubled Europe. At Rome, Thomas Morgan heard members of the Italian Parliament sing the "Red Flag" and hiss the King. Bouton and Enderis in Berlin had days of street fighting to report as Communists and Independent Socialists loosed a determined effort to seize the government. W. S. Hiatt, the correspondent with the most luxurious mustache in the service, led a peripatetic existence from Warsaw to Prague, back to Poland, to Galicia, and then to the Ukraine as the news currents shifted. The virtual state of war in Ireland sent

Guy Moyston and Thomas W. Morris from London to join W. H. Brayden, resident correspondent at Dublin. Nor was that all. There were the armies of occupation along the Rhine, the patient watch at the gates of the Kaiser's refuge in Holland, the luckless campaigns of White Russian armies, the revolt in Hungary, and the ferment in the Near East.

In the Cable Department at New York the expectation had been that, with the end of the war, European news would gradually revert to the proportions of the days of 1914. On the contrary, before the Peace Conference was well under way it became apparent that Europe had assumed a new and vast importance in American affairs. The multicolored pins on the big Cable Department map moved as frequently as they had before the Armistice. The staff abroad was greater than at any time during the war years, and still growing.

In recognition of this great development, the general manager appointed Charles T. Thompson to assume immediate supervision, under the chief of the News Department, of the service from Europe and Asia. In spite of the costly burden of all the extensive war coverage and the even heavier expenses of the exacting postwar period, however, the co-operative could boast that it had been able to deliver an outstanding report to member papers without once raising assessments. Commercial agencies, on the other hand, had found it necessary to levy additional charges on clients for the reports they furnished.

In all, war coverage expenses totaled $2,685,125.12, and meeting that bill without assessment increases was quite an achievement for an organization with an annual income from all sources of approximately $3,000,000. Foreign Service costs for 1913, the last prewar year, were $225,543. From August 1, 1914, when the war broke out, until the end of the year—a matter of only four months—expenses were $258,-551. In 1915 the figure was $518,875, or more than double. The bill for 1916 was $541,935; for 1917, $564,604. Large-scale American participation in 1918 boosted costs for the final year to $801,157—or almost one-third of the entire annual news budget.

Owing to the war, the domestic branch of the service had been in temporary eclipse, but by 1919 it was resuming its place. The greatest immediate expansion occurred in the Southern Division with extension of wire circuits, enlarged bureaus, and reorganized facilities. The return to something approaching a peacetime footing was accelerated by the return of editorial and traffic employees who had left their desks or telegraph keys to join the armed forces.

3

Like the draft drawing of 1917, the news of the home-coming troops in 1919 provided a succession of stories which intimately touched the lives of millions of readers. So numerous were special coverage requests that The Associated Press in co-operation with the War Department worked out a detailed system to handle the service. Each day the report carried a cumulative abstract of the homeward bound troops, giving the names of the transports, dates of sailing, ports of embarkation, the number of troops on each ship and their units, the ports of debarkation and the names of the camps to which the men were to be sent before departing for demobilization centers. Two staff men from the New York office were assigned to meet the incoming ship and one of them was Stanley W. Prenosil, who had sailed with the first A.E.F. transports for France two years before.

The general news of the domestic scene had a tenor of unrest and uncertainty. Labor disturbances were widespread, and the curve of unemployment mounted as industrial production was sharply slashed from the peaks of wartime pressure. Boston had its celebrated police strike which projected Governor Calvin Coolidge into the national limelight. The high cost of living added to distress, and there were endless items dealing with arrests, speechmaking and legislative action concerning the postwar "Red scare."

From a coverage point of view, the Boston police strike showed all the difficulties which arose in so many of the labor controversies that year. Feeling ran righ and contending forces read every line of news with hypercritical eyes. When the strike ended, James H. Vahney, counsel for the policemen's union, in an unsolicited statement, praised the Boston Bureau for "utmost fairness," and Governor Coolidge wrote his appreciation of the "efficient and faithful" manner in which the news had been treated.

Men who returned to their positions with The Associated Press that year after the war found that a forward-looking step had been taken in their absence. The Board of Directors had established a comprehensive system of employes' insurance, pensions, disability and sick benefits. Heretofore only commercial and industrial corporations with large financial resources had undertaken to set up such a plan for the welfare of employes, and the introduction of the idea into the field of journalism on an extensive scale aroused considerable comment.

Until the evolution of the organization into a non-profit co-operative, the lot of men who made news gathering their career had been a precarious one. The precursors of the modern press association gave scant thought to the welfare of employes. Sickness or disability was looked upon as an individual's private concern. Long and faithful service was of little help to men whose value had been impaired by age. As for death, it was a calamity survivors had to meet with such savings as the deceased had been able to build up from salaries which never had been extravagant.

Under President Noyes and General Manager Stone the co-operative began to recognize the association's responsibility toward employes. In spite of the deficits and financial stress of the first decade of the century, the board made numerous individual provisions for pensions, sick pay, and disability allowances. Adolph Ochs, of the New York *Times*, consistently advocated the most liberal attitude. There was no well-formulated, universal policy, however. Each case was considered separately on the special set of facts involved.

When the association's fortunes became financially stabilized shortly before the World War, the board gave more thought to the establishment of a workable plan. Traffic Department Chief Cooper, who had been an advocate of such a system since his second year in the service, began a study of various actuarial plans and devised the program which the board put into effect on July 1, 1918. Besides sick pay and disability allowance, the plan provided for pensions for retiring employes and death benefits to surviving families. By the start of 1920 the plan protected 1,038 employes, editorial, clerical, and traffic alike.

In April, 1920, Melville E. Stone relinquished active duties as general manager to take an extended leave of absence at his own request for reasons of health. The Board of Directors appointed the assistant general manager, Frederick Roy Martin, to be acting general manager in Stone's absence, and the next day brought further administrative changes. Cooper was promoted to assistant general manager; Jackson Elliott became general superintendent in immediate charge of the news report; Milton Garges succeeded Cooper as chief of the Traffic Department.

4

And so it was 1920. The war was done, peace treaties had been signed, but the man in the street summed up the times with a rare aptness when he used the new slang phrase, "the cockeyed world." National Prohibition was ushered in. New England buzzed about Ponzi's extravagant financial manipulations. The Ku Klux Klan rode again. Douglas Fairbanks and Mary Pickford got married. F. Scott Fitzgerald wrote of the younger generation. A mysterious explosion rocked Wall Street, killing thirty-eight. And a cause célèbre began with the arrest of two Italian workmen, Nicola Sacco and Bartolommeo Vanzetti, for a fatal Massachusetts holdup.

Abroad the turmoil never slackened. Gabrielle d'Annunzio seized Fiume, the port denied Italy in the peace settlement, and Morgan of the Rome Bureau buried himself under the coal of a locomotive tender to get into the city and obtain the first authentic news. Germany battled through another revolution, the Kapp uprising, and automobiles placarded. "The Associated Press of America" were passed through the lines by both rebel and government factions. An amazing Red army smashed the Poles back to the very gates of Warsaw, and James P. Howe found himself with a 350-mile front to patrol. In the Near East Allied armies occupied Constantinople, and Charles Stephenson Smith saw Turkey's new man of destiny, Mustapha Kemal.

The Black and Tan terror was loose in Ireland, and four staff correspondents carried on in the face of unconcealed hostility from both Crown and republican forces. At Amerongen in Holland Rennick and Berry alternated in the patient wait for a moment that never came— the opportunity to interview the secluded ex-Kaiser. Experts struggled with the question of what reparations the Central Powers should pay, and Correspondent Kloeber in Vienna found himself covering Sir William A. Goode—the British reparations commission for Austria but the same "Billy" Goode whom Diehl had assigned to Admiral Sampson's flagship back in the days of the Spanish-American War. Monarchist uprisings in Portugal, maneuvers for King Constantine's return in Greece, the White Armies in the Ukraine, agitation in Italy, plebiscites in the Balkans—the bulky log ran on from day to day.

The only sustained break in the heavy character of the news came with the Olympic Games at Antwerp where Correspondent Salchow of Stockholm doubled in brass by winning the world's figure skating championship on the ice and serving on the four-man sports staff which covered the events.

Throughout the year in Europe the coverage of Russia's news remained a continual source of concern. Since the enforced departure of the Petrograd staff late in 1918, the association had no regular correspondents in the vast country, except for those with the Allied forces operating against the Bolsheviks. Attempts to reach some agreement with the government encountered a succession of failures. Maxim Litvinoff, commissar of foreign affairs, refused to grant visas to any correspondents not "of known sympathy" with Soviet rule. This imposed an impossible condition for The Associated Press. For a time an improvised service of fair regularity was maintained by a special undercover correspondent, Mrs. Marguerite Harrison, but eventually she was imprisoned and the news halted. Thereafter the association was forced to rely on staff correspondents assigned to strategic spots along Russia's borders and such news as could be smuggled out of the country from time to time.

America was again preoccupied with the concerns of a presidential year. The bitterly debated League of Nations issue, the disillusionment which accompanied postwar reaction, and the temper of political feelings gave the contest an unusual character and placed a premium on accurate, factual reporting.

The conventions were the first Stone had missed as general manager since the McKinley-Bryan nominations in 1896. Acting General Manager Martin took charge of the staff first at the Chicago gathering, which selected Warren G. Harding, and then at the Democratic convention in San Francisco, where James M. Cox was chosen. But he was not the familiar figure that the old chief had been. The fact proved embarrassing to J. C. Godfrey, one of the operators on the traffic force at the Chicago convention. Arriving early in the press section the opening day, he found a man sitting quietly there, apparently a spectator who had wandered into the wrong benches. As Godfrey tested and checked the telegraph wires, he ordered the stranger about casually, telling him "ease over here," "slip over there," and "you'll have to move." The spectator obliged without comment. Then Godfrey began talking by wire to the Chicago Bureau where the convention hall circuits fed onto the news network.

"Any AP man there?" asked the bureau.

Godfrey turned to the man sitting near by.

"You happen to be an AP man?" he asked.

"Yes, sir."

Impressed by the politeness, Godfrey messaged the bureau:

"Yes, one fellow here. Guess he's a reporter."

He turned to the man again.

"This guy wants to know your name," he said with a gesture toward the Morse key.

"I'm Mr. Martin," said the acting general manager of The Associated Press.

Before the electorate cast the ballots which produced the great Coolidge-Harding landslide in November, the country—or at least the part of it that read the sports pages—was shocked by the sensational Chicago "Black Sox" scandal, which exposed the "throwing" of the World Series baseball games between Chicago and the Cincinnati Reds the previous autumn. Charlie Dunkley and Don M. Ewing of the Chicago staff "broke" the story that Eddie Cicotte and Joe Jackson, two of the best known Chicago players, had confessed, and it was Ewing who witnessed the moving scene outside the criminal courts building where several hundred small boys loyally waited for their idol, Joe Jackson, to appear after testifying before the grand jury.

Ewing left with Jackson and as they made their way through the hushed crowd, one tiny youngster timidly stepped up to the outfielder and tugged at his sleeve.

"Say it ain't so, Joe," he pleaded.

Joe Jackson looked down.

"Yes, kid, I'm afraid it is."

The crowd of little fans parted silently to make a path.

"Well, I'd never thought it," gulped the youngster. "I'd never thought it."

The Chicago story of Joe Jackson's disillusioned admirer and the pathetic "Say-it-ain't-so-Joe" entreaty that became a national expression were typical of the humanizing sidelights which were appearing occasionally in the report. Not yet numerous enough to be considered essential, they indicated a definite trend.

Superintendent Elliott summed up the record in the accounting of operations submitted to the Board of Directors a few weeks before 1920 passed into history. Discussing the march of events, he said:

A notable feature of our news service of late has been the large number of remote and rather inaccessible points, far removed from the old news centers, which seem to have developed into important news field—Athens, Constantinople, Warsaw, Fiume, Lucerne, Geneva, Riga and Dublin. This has given an exceptional diversity of datelines, and has led to the more general use of AP dispatches from the outlying points, as individual newspapers have their staffs concentrated at the old centers—London, Paris and Berlin, and are dependent on The AP when important news breaks elsewhere. . . .

This general policy of covering news from the scene of action is a transformation from the old system of covering practically all news largely from

London and Paris. Editors no longer want news filtered through the old capitals. They want it direct from the scene.

To the man in the street the news was still of a "cockeyed" world. In Chicago a staff correspondent eluded a cordon of guards and interviewed the legendary John D. Rockefeller in his long underwear. The first Prohibition agent was slain in New Jersey. Cortesi watched the rise of a black-shirted Fascist party recently founded by a prewar Socialist named Mussolini. And in the beer halls of Munich a former corporal harangued crowds, denouncing the Versailles Treaty, the French, the Jews, the capitalists. Handbills identified the speaker as Herr Adolf Hitler.

President-elect Warren G. Harding only recently had coined the phrase: "Back to normalcy."

XV. THE ORDER CHANGES

I

AROUND the long conference table, members of the Board of Directors were discussing the possibility of increasing employes' insurance benefits when Stone entered the room. He was almost seventy-three, yet he seemed almost as alert and commanding as ever.

"At my time of life," he said, "it must be obvious to anybody that in the comparatively near future my career must be over. I should be a fool if I hung on here as general manager like the Old Man of the Sea until an hour when death thrust someone suddenly into my position.

"That is why I asked for a leave of absence last year so it could be determined whether the personnel that I had gathered around me was capable of running the service. Not alone whether they were capable of running it, but whether the Board of Directors felt they were capable of running it. And not alone that the Board of Directors felt that, but the membership of the association.

"Now I have purposely avoided going to the office. They have consulted me from time to time. I have the very warmest regard for the personnel here. The responsibility is upon you. It must be you who exercise the judgment, but my own feeling is if you agree with me that Mr. Martin has shown a capacity, that these other gentlemen have shown a capacity to carry on the work, then I think it is due Mr. Martin that he be made, not the acting, but the real general manager. I should like to resign."

In a few minutes the thing was done. Melville E. Stone ceased to be the general manager of The Associated Press. But the board was not willing that resignation should sever all his ties. President Noyes proposed that the office of counselor be created and that Stone be appointed to fill it. There were some feeble attempts at levity which did not quite come off.

"The title of counselor suggests a fountainhead of wisdom," objected John R. Rathom of the Providence *Journal* with mock seriousness.

"Mr. Stone is not rejecting that," smiled Noyes, and the resolution was unanimously adopted.

Henceforth it would be Counselor Stone.

That same day, April 29, 1921, Frederick Roy Martin was appointed general manager. Theoretically, the assignments of the executive family lapsed with the naming of a new general manager, but Martin immediately reappointed Assistant General Manager Cooper and Traffic Chief Garges, and within two weeks Jackson Elliott was raised from general superintendent to be a second assistant general manager.

Like Hale, Hallock, and Craig, Martin was a New Englander by birth. A man of independent means, he had devoted himself to newspaper work since his graduation from Harvard in 1893—the same year Stone, his predecessor, took the helm of The Associated Press of Illinois. For six years Martin worked in Boston. Then he joined the Providence *Journal* and presently became its editor and treasurer. During his administration the paper's prestige, circulation, and finances advanced materially and Martin's reputation gained such influence that in April, 1912, he was elected to the Board of Directors of The Associated Press.

The most immediate administrative problem of the new general manager was the steady loss of able and experienced staff men. The wartime development of propaganda had been an object lesson to business, big and small, in the possibilities of publicity, and trained newspapermen were eagerly sought as press agents. Most attractive salaries were offered—sometimes double what a man earned with the co-operative—and some men on the staff were sorely tempted. In a period when the cost of living soared to uncomfortable heights, it was difficult to refuse the commercial propositions, in spite of the fact that so many of the positions were obviously transitory.

Martin, Stone, Cooper, and Elliott brought the matter to the attention of the board and urged that the management be given a free hand to readjust salaries in order to anticipate or at least meet the bids of commercial enterprises for staff men. The point carried and the raids on the personnel were checked to a degree. Another aspect of publicity's development, however, continued a nuisance. The postwar crop of press agents utilized all sorts of artifices in their attempts to get publicity stories on the leased wires, and endless vigilance was required to keep the report free from advertising matter skillfully disguised as news.

The character of contemporary news, moreover, left no space in the report for anything not essential. Even the humanizing little features had to compete against a welter of prime dispatches. Congressional debate on a soldiers' bonus and tax legislation kept Washington busy. Sports had the "Battle of the Century" when Jack Dempsey and Georges Carpentier met at Boyle's Thirty Acres. Rum Row set up business off the coast. The depression which began in 1920 sagged toward its low, with 5,735,000 unemployed. The demand for economic, business, and financial news continued without abatement, necessitating further expansion in that department of the report. A number of members were especially insistent that the association enlarge its Wall Street coverage to include stock and bond quotations, together with a longer list of other markets.

2

The story, however, which made 1921 so memorable for the news report belonged to Kirke L. Simpson of the Washington Bureau.

But for the impressive solemnity of the occasion, Simpson's assignment might have been considered routine. The nation was bringing its Unknown Soldier home from France to a final resting place in Arlington National Cemetery, and Simpson was assigned to write the stories on the final obsequies for the nameless man whom the country paused to honor.

Simpson was only one of the scores of newspapermen—many of them journalists of reputation—who stood under the sodden skies in the gray, chilling rain at Washington Navy Yard on November 9 when the *Olympia*, Admiral Dewey's flagship at Manila Bay, slowly swung up the Potomac bringing the dead Unknown home from the wars. Minute guns boomed in salute.

Simpson wrote the first of his seven Unknown Soldier stories that afternoon. The next day he described the steady tide of humanity which flowed in silence past the catafalque under the vast rotunda of the Capitol. Then on the third anniversary of the Armistice there were the final ceremonies at the Unknown's tomb on the wooded ridge high above the Potomac. Simpson's first story read:

Washington, Nov. 9.—(By The Associated Press).—A plain soldier, unknown but weighted with honors as perhaps no American before him because he died for the flag in France, lay to-night in a place where only martyred Presidents Lincoln, Garfield and McKinley, have slept in death.

He kept lonely vigil lying in state under the vast, shadowy dome of the Capitol. Only the motionless figures of the five armed comrades, one at the head and one facing inward at each corner of the bier, kept watch with him.

But far above, towering from the great bulk of the dome, the brooding

"UNKNOWN BUT WEIGHED WITH HONORS AS PERHAPS NO OTHER AMERICAN."

figure of Freedom watched too, as though it said "well done" to the servant faithful unto death, asleep there in the vast, dim chamber below.

America's unknown dead is home from France at last, and the nation has no honor too great for him. In him, it pays its unstinted tribute of pride and glory to all those sleeping in the far soil of France. It was their homecoming to-day; their day of days in the heart of the nation and they must have known it for the heart beat of a nation defies the laws of space, even of eternity.

Sodden skies and a gray, creeping, chilling rain all through the day seemed to mark the mourning of this American soil and air at the bier of this unknown hero. But no jot of the full meed of honor was denied the dead on that account. From the highest officials of this democratic government to the last soldier or marine or bluejacket, rain and cold meant nothing beside the desire to do honor to the dead.

The ceremonies were brief to-day. They began when the far boom of saluting cannon down the river signalled the coming of the great gray cruiser Olympia. The fog of rain hid her slow approach up the Potomac, but fort by fort, post by post, the guns took up the tale of honors for the dead as she passed.

Slowly the ship swung into her dock. Along her rails stood her crew in long lines of dark blue, rigid at attention and with a solemn expression uncommon to the young faces beneath the jaunty sailor hats. Astern, under the long, gray muzzle of a gun that once echoed its way into history more than twenty years ago in Manila Bay, lay the flag-draped casket. Above, a tented awning held off the dripping rain, the inner side of the canvas lined with great American flags to make a canopy for the sleeper below. At attention stood five sailors and marines as guards of honor for the dead at each corner and the head of his bier. . . .

They were simple stories, unpretentious in style. The exigencies of wire conditions kept them comparatively short and they were written with the haste news usually dictates. Yet for all that, Simpson's accounts of those three solemn days seemed to catch the spirit of all that lay in the tributes to the Unknown Soldier. The restraint, the emotion, the sincerity with which he wrote made his words a fitting commentary.

Not in a long time had any news story made such a deep impression on millions of Americans. The co-operative's general offices were overwhelmed by the outpouring of praise. Editors, public officials, clergymen, professors, schoolteachers, former staff men, average newspaper readers, wrote in to express appreciation. From all sides came inquiries as to the identity of the author—the stores carried no by-line—and so insistent was the demand that the general manager, relaxing the age-old rule of anonymity, disclosed Simpson's name. To meet numerous requests, The Associated Press published a special booklet containing the seven Unknown Soldier stories. In Illinois and other states superintendents of public instruction issued a similar brochure for classroom use. Permission was granted for republication of the series in school readers. From pulpits ministers extolled the simple beauty of the work, and students in public speaking learned the sentences by heart. The requests for copies continued for the next eighteen years.

Simpson's brilliant handling of the Unknown Soldier assignment was formally recognized when he was voted the Pulitzer prize, the first press association man ever to receive the award.

3

The day after the Unknown Soldier was entombed, the International Arms Limitation Conference called by Secretary of State Hughes met in the capital and Simpson was one of the twelve-man staff organized for its coverage. The conference made diplomatic history when Hughes proposed a ten-year naval holiday and the scrapping of sixty-six capital ships in the interests of world peace.

The heart of the Hughes proposal was that the foremost naval powers—United States, Great Britain, and Japan—"freeze" their navies at the ratio of their existing strength, one to the other. For several days news writers generally groped for some terse expression to describe the formula, which provided for fleet equality between the United States and Great Britain, and a Japanese navy of 40 per cent less strength. A number of different phrases were tried but none proved apt.

Simpson was specializing in the technical aspects of the conference and on November 18 he talked over the American proposals with Rear Admiral Sir Ernle Chatfield, chief British technician. In the course of that talk Chatfield referred offhand to the Hughes' "big three" formula as the "50-50-30 ratio" plan. Simpson, writing his story that night, simplified Chatfield's chance description by eliminating the zeros. The paragraph in which the well-known phrase first appeared read:

It is certain that British naval experts regard their country as already committed, through Mr. Balfour's speech of acceptance, to what might be called the "5-5-3 ratio" of naval strength as between Great Britain, the United States and Japan. That is regarded by both British and American experts as the heart of the matter.

The expression, "5-5-3 ratio," was invariably used thereafter. Other correspondents picked it up and soon it appeared also in the official press statements released by the conference itself.

The basis on which Japan ultimately agreed to the Five-Power Navy Treaty negotiated at Washington was described in the report weeks before the conference got under way. When the Japanese delegation sailed for the United States, it was accompanied by Joseph E. Sharkey, chief of bureau at Tokyo. One night, as the boat fought its way through a typhoon, Admiral Kato, Japan's chief plenipotentiary, sent word to Sharkey that he would like to see him.

"I am disposed," began the admiral when Sharkey reached his cabin, "I am disposed—if you fancy it has news value—to tell you the basic principle of the Japanese policy at the Washington conference."

Sharkey fancied it would have news value.

"All right," said Kato. "Here it is in a few words: Japan will agree to negotiate an arrangement concerning capital ships, provided the United States agrees not to increase the fortifications of her possessions in the Far East."

There was a little more, but that was the crux of the story. It created a stir in Washington. Many congressmen commented that the condition was utterly impossible of acceptance, but eventually it was incorporated in the naval and political accords reached at the conference.

4

Sharing interest with the disarmament conference were the negotiations in London looking to the end of the bitter warfare in Ireland between the Sinn Feiners and the military forces of the British crown. For the better part of three years the men on that assignment had worked under nerve-racking peril and difficulty in an atmosphere of ambushes, raids, killings, and reprisals.

Like so many of his colleagues, Guy Moyston, of the London Bureau, led a hectic life the many months he spent in Ireland. Mistaken for an English agent one night when he arrived late in a rural town, he was awakened to find himself blinking sleepily into the muzzles of Sinn Fein rifles and revolvers. On another occasion a British patrol arrested him and hustled him off at bayonet point to Bridewell prison in Cork. Information found in his possession on the attempted assassination of the commander of the crown forces in Southern Ireland gave rise to the suspicion that he was a rebel dispatch bearer. His arrest turned out to be a fortunate happening, for upon his release he encountered a talkative constable who supplied him with additional details of the assassination attempt the British wanted to suppress.

Moyston sought for weeks to arrange for an interview with Eamon De Valera, the President of the Irish Republic who, like so many active in the rebellion, was "on the run." Negotiations were highly dangerous. They involved secret meetings with outlawed members of the Irish Republican Army whom the Black and Tans were ready to shoot at sight, and the men with whom he dealt would not have hesitated to kill him on the least suspicion of treachery. The efforts to arrange the interview seemed foredoomed to failure, but Moyston kept trying.

Another meeting was arranged. Moyston found two men in trench coats and low-pulled caps waiting for him at the rendezvous. In a trice he was blindfolded, bundled roughly from the house, and thrust into a waiting automobile which set off at breakneck speed. Moyston could feel the bulky shoulders of his two guards against him as the car careened along. Many an informer and government spy had been taken out like this and his body found later with an I.R.A. death warrant pinned to his coat. There was no quarter in the fierce warfare and there was no assurance that the men in the automobile had not decided that Moyston was a secret agent with fraudulent credentials. One bogus correspondent had fled Dublin just in time to escape execution.

It was a torturing ride until the swaying automobile eventually skidded to a stop. Hands gripped Moyston's arms and hurried him stumbling along an unseen path. He tripped through a doorway and into a room. There the blindfold was whipped away and he found himself standing before a spare, scholarly figure.

The man was De Valera and it was only then that Moyston knew for certain that the brusque handling to which he had been subjected was all incidental to obtaining his long-sought interview.

A truce halted the fighting during the negotiations at London which led to the establishment of the Irish Free State. The co-operative had a staff of thirteen men, Moyston among them, covering the various phases of the conference which led to the signing of the Anglo-Irish Treaty, a highly controversial subject even in the United States. The story on the signing of the agreement was complete enough, but it by no means spelled the end of extraordinary staff arrangements in Ireland. The treaty created a schism in Irish ranks and the country plunged into a civil war which made the task of coverage just as hazardous as ever.

5

Throughout the year leased wire facilities were steadily enlarged to cope with the burden of news which assumed heavier proportions.

The cable report approximated 6,500 words each twenty-four hours, and a survey showed that the co-operative brought in an average of fifty-eight foreign items daily as compared with eleven for commercial agencies. Although the service from the Orient increased considerably, Europe remained the major continent in the foreign report, what with the nightmare of German inflation, the beginning of the Fascist regime in Italy, the crushing Greek defeat at the hands of Kemal, the League of Nations, and the perennial maneuverings of Old World diplomacy.

The domestic report had its own sensations with the bloody Herrin mine war, New Jersey's spectacular Hall-Mills murder case, and the beginning of the grim gang wars which marked Prohibition. The pattern of news was unpredictable—flappers, the crystal radio set craze, dawn of the night club era, Gallagher and Shean, and *Abie's Irish Rose*.

The year saved its greatest journalistic surprise until the last weeks when it made a 4,000-year-old Egyptian king the most exceptional news carried in many a day. The tomb of King Tutankhamen was found December 1 near Luxor, Egypt. Experts termed it "the greatest archaeological discovery of all time," and so closely did people follow the story that reference to "King Tut" cropped up daily in ordinary conversation.

A syndicate headed by the London *Times* had paid $100,000 to the British archaeologists excavating at the tomb site, and the contract carried exclusive rights to all news and photographs. No other correspondents had the right to enter the rockhewn royal tomb while the scientists were cutting through the wall which was believed to separate the richly furnished anteroom from the actual mortuary chamber where they hoped to find the sarcophagus and mummy of the King who ruled in the fourteenth century before Christ.

As far as the archaeologists were concerned, Valentine Williams was merely one of some forty correspondents who had no choice but to wait daily in the blazing heat outside the hidden tomb and laboriously piece stories together from such scraps of information as could be coaxed from secondhand sources. All firsthand news went to the London *Times* syndicate.

That the archaeologist expected any day to broach the rock wall into the mortuary chamber ceased to be news; it only served to deepen the gloom which pervaded the press corps. On February 16, 1923, Williams was racking his brains for some forlorn plan to circumvent the syndicate's monopoly on the story. He happened to notice an Egyptian official who had just emerged from the vault.

Paying no attention to the newspapermen at the tomb entrance, the Egyptian walked over the sands to a water cooler set up about two hundred feet away. Williams recognized him as one of the party which had entered the excavation with the archaeologists more than an hour earlier. He watched the man for a moment and decided that he, too, needed a drink of water. Casually he strolled after the Egyptian without attracting the attention of rival correspondents.

Williams smiled disarmingly and the Egyptian nodded. They had a drink of water together. The desert heat made one thirsty.

"Excuse me, sir," said Williams idly, "a controversy has arisen as to whether you found one coffin or two coffins inside the tomb. Can you put me straight on it?"

He drew another drink of water.

"Two coffins!" exclaimed the official. "Why, no. Of course not. We found only *one coffin!*"

"Oh," said Williams innocently. "The coffin of King Tutankhamen?"

"Yes," said the unsuspecting Egyptian, "we believe it is. The royal seal on the coffin is still intact and the sarcophagus bears the hieroglyphic cartouche of Tutankhamen."

Williams nodded understandingly.

"And you believe the coffin contains the mummy of the King?"

"Yes, we have every reason to think so," replied the unwitting official, describing the scenes within the tomb.

"Oh, thank you very much," Williams said politely.

As soon as the Egyptian returned to the tomb, the correspondent was racing over the Theban plain in a small automobile to the nearest telegraph office.

In a matter of minutes London had the flash:

TUTANKHAMEN'S SARCOPHAGUS AND MUMMY FOUND.

The news shot over the cables into New York. Long before the archaeologists emerged from the tomb to prepare their official communiqué, member papers had the story of how, for the first time in history, a royal Egyptian sarcophagus had been discovered intact and unprofaned by thieves or vandals.

6

Although it captured popular imagination to an unusual degree, the news of King Tutankhamen's tomb provided little more than a diversion in the news log of the months immediately preceding the

"EXCUSE ME, SIR," SAID WILLIAMS IDLY, "A CONTROVERSY HAS ARISEN."

1923 annual meeting. Of more significance were the dispatches from James P. Howe, Thomas Topping, Walter Hiatt, and Clifford L. Day when French and Belgian troops occupied the highly industrialized Ruhr Valley to enforce German reparations payments. Joseph Sharkey, assigned to the League of Nations at Geneva, reported the efforts of the Lausanne Conference to conclude a lasting peace for the turbulent Near East. And at home the Lick Observatory announced that it had confirmed Professor Albert Einstein's theory of relativity.

Looking behind the externals of the news service, the members could gauge the extent of the association's postwar expansion. The leased wires crisscrossing the continent totaled 92,000 miles, with an operator at every eighty-five miles along the circuit. The threads of the vast web linked 1,207 members with the fifty-five domestic bureaus which served them and, by cable, with the twenty-seven American-manned bureaus abroad. Employes numbered almost two thousand, annual expenditures exceeded $6,000,000. Member papers published in every one of the forty-eight states, in Alaska, Hawaii, the Philippines, Puerto Rico, Cuba, Mexico, Central and South America, and the news appeared in English, French, Spanish, German, Portuguese, and Japanese. Telegraph keys, Morkrum machines, telephones, cables, and wireless sped the general report, totaling 75,000 words daily, over more than a hundred different channels.

The Board of Directors had an impressive statistical summary to marshal in the annual report presented to the 1923 meeting of the membership. President Noyes, who had just returned from a round-the-world tour, told of the firsthand study he had made of news conditions, particularly in China and Japan. Then President Harding addressed the gathering on national and international affairs.

Two months after Harding spoke at the annual luncheon he left Washington for a trip to Alaska. The country was singing "Yes, We Have no Bananas" that summer, talking about marathon dances, or discussing Rudolph Valentino's latest movie. Few, even among the informed, knew definitely the proportions of the political scandals brewing in the Veterans' Bureau, the Interior Department, and other governmental quarters at Washington. Perhaps Harding had a feeling that all was not well. Stephen Early and E. R. Bartley, the staff men assigned to accompany the party, remarked how weary the President seemed.

The first four weeks of the trip were humdrum. The special train rolled across the country, the President made set speeches, audiences applauded politely, and nothing unusual happened. When Alaska was reached, Harding seemed to grow more tired and dispatches spoke of concern over the President's health. The concern deepened on the return trip when Harding was stricken at Seattle, July 27. His physician attributed the attack to ptomaine poisoning. The President insisted that the journey be resumed, however, and the party arrived in San Francisco on July 29. There Harding took to his bed and his condition failed to improve over the weekend.

Early and Bartley understood the gravity of the situation. Harding's condition had not yet become critical, but the circumstances warranted preparedness. Paul Cowles, superintendent of the Pacific Coast Division, cut short his vacation. Members of the San Francisco staff were assigned to work with the Washington men, and a special wire was looped to the seventh floor of the Palace Hotel, ten feet from a private back stairway leading to the presidential suite on the floor above. The coast traffic chief, Percy Hall, took charge of the telegraphers at the improvised headquarters. "Never leave the wire unmanned for a second," were his orders. "The man who leaves this room without permission leaves the service."

On Monday night Harding's condition took a turn for the worse. Bronchial pneumonia developed and Early, keeping watch outside the sickroom, saw worried doctors come and go. On Tuesday the President's heart weakened and fears for his life became acute. Telegraphers ate their meals while they kept Morse keys clicking off the news. Every minute of the day and night someone was on duty at the chief executive's bedroom door.

Dispatches Wednesday were better. The President had shown "remarkable improvement." By the afternoon Dr. Joal T. Boone, one of the White House physicians, announced the crisis had passed. The ranks of reporters assigned to the story by individual newspapers began to dwindle.

For The Associated Press, however, Superintendent Cowles was not at all satisfied. Even after the encouraging bulletins Thursday afternoon, he thought it wise to consult San Francisco physicians for their private opinions. They told him that any patient with symptoms similar to those described in the presidential bulletins was far from out of danger. Any reduction in staff precautions was out of the question after Cowles received that information.

Thursday night Early waited at his post a few feet away from the

President's door. Many members of Harding's party were out attending social functions in the city. The last word from the sickroom had been reassuring and most correspondents had not yet returned from dinner. On the Pacific Coast it was about seven-thirty.

Just then the door of the room flew open and Early saw Mrs. Harding's white, distraught face.

"Call Dr. Boone; call Dr. Boone!" she was crying. "Find him and the others quick!"

Attendants scurried to find the physician, and Early, after confirming what he sensed had happened, went racing down the back stairway to the seventh floor. Standing over the operator, he rapidly dictated a series of bulletins which told that the President's condition had taken a sudden turn for the worse. It was the first intimation that the President's life was in danger.

A few minutes after the first rush of bulletins, Early was back again in the wire room, breathlessly dictating:

```
FLASH - FLASH
SAN FRANCISCO - PRESIDENT HARDING DEAD
```

The flash gave official Washington the shocking news. In the confusion at the hotel in San Francisco those in Harding's party forgot to send any notification to the capital. Vice-President Coolidge was away, vacationing at his father's home in Plymouth, Vermont.

But Plymouth had not been neglected in the association's precautions. Days earlier, when Harding had been stricken, W. E. Playfair, night editor in Boston, had been sent to the Coolidge homestead with instructions to remain close to the vice-president in case an emergency arose. He found two of Boston's string correspondents, Arthur Granger, of Rutland, and Joseph H. Fountain, of Springfield, Vermont, already there, and they worked under his direction as Plymouth's importance waxed, then waned with the tenor of the bulletins from the San Francisco sickroom. The little farming hamlet had no telephone or telegraph lines, and to get out the news it was necessary to go to Rutland, the nearest leased wire point, or eleven miles to the slightly nearer communities, Bridgewater and Ludlow, where telephones were available.

It was a telephone call to Ludlow from the Boston Bureau that told Playfair of Harding's death and started him over dark country roads to the Coolidge farm. The vice-president had gone to bed and Playfair gave his news to the elder Coolidge who seemed awed by the gravity of the moment. Other reporters started to arrive, among them

Granger and Fountain. The backfire of automobiles shattered the still of the night. Coolidge and his wife came downstairs.

"Good morning, Mr. President," someone said.

Coolidge did not reply.

"Is this information authentic?" he asked.

Technically still vice-president, Coolidge issued his first statement as the nation's leader:

Reports have reached me, which I fear are correct, that President Harding is gone. The world has lost a great and good man. I mourn his loss. He was my Chief and my friend.

It will be my purpose to carry out the policies which he has begun for the service of the American people and for meeting their responsibilities wherever they may arise.

For this purpose . . .

As soon as the statement was issued in the hushed farmhouse room, Playfair left for Ludlow to telephone it to Boston. Granger remained behind to gather additional details. Then he was off to Bridgewater. Other correspondents departed in haste to get their own stories in, but Fountain remained behind. Coolidge had not yet been sworn in as president and it was Fountain's assignment to stay there until he was.

At 2:43 A.M. on August 3, 1923, by the light of a kerosene lamp, Calvin Coolidge took the oath of office as President of the United States, repeating the words as his father read them. Seven persons witnessed the ceremony. The only newspaperman among them was Joseph H. Fountain.

7

Harding's death was the forerunner of a freshet of big news which continued until the end of 1923. George Denny, the veteran of the Russo-Japanese War who had replaced Sharkey as bureau chief at Tokyo, covered the earthquake which struck Japan on September 1, taking almost 100,000 lives. There also was the Dempsey-Firpo fight, one of the early events in the so-called "Golden Age" of professional sports. The six-man staff was directed by a new general sports editor—Alan J. Gould, who had been appointed to the post in March when Moss resigned. Two days after the fight interest centered on the New York pressmen's strike which left the metropolis without its regular papers for a week. Then Washington took first place in the domestic report with the startling disclosures of the Teapot Dome scandal investigation, and in the cable news there were dispatches from Elmer Roberts at Munich describing an abortive beer-hall Putsch to

BY THE LIGHT OF A KEROSENE LAMP . . .

overthrow the government in Germany. The uprising lost its news value after one of its leaders, Adolf Hitler, was sentenced to five years' imprisonment.

With the coming of the new year the association's headquarters was moved from downtown New York, where so much bygone journalistic history had been made, to larger offices at 383 Madison Avenue, in the midtown area. The transfer of operating equipment, the change-over of wire circuits controlling the leased network, and other details of the move presented a complex problem, but the new quarters were occupied on March 2 without interruption in the service.

The presidential campaigns and election called for the dominant news-gathering efforts in 1924 when the country, swept along by the tide of increasing prosperity, rallied to the call: "Keep Cool with Coolidge." The convention staff had it lengthiest assignment in history at the marathon Democratic sessions in Madison Square Garden, where Alfred E. Smith lost his first bid for the nomination in an atmosphere of bitterness and acrimony. The leased wires flashed the November verdict: a landslide for Coolidge and his running mate, Charles G. Dawes.

As the headlines of 1924 told their stories, an important administrative change was brewing in the co-operative. Vague intimations reached some of the staff and the better informed members late in the year. Confirmation came on the eve of the 1925 annual meeting. Frederick Roy Martin submitted his resignation as general manager, effective the end of April. Private publishing opportunities had presented themselves, and Martin also had other interests which demanded greater attention. With a tribute to his service, the board accepted the resignation which closed the shortest administration since the days of Alexander Jones in the middle of the previous century.

The unanimous choice of the board, Kent Cooper stepped in as the new general manager. Frank B. Noyes, whose twenty-fifth anniversary came the same year, later said of the appointment: "No chronicle of my connection with The Associated Press would be complete without a record of the fact of the importance of my service in bringing forward and encouraging the energies of Cooper through a long series of years, of my recommendation that he be made general manager and of my profound satisfaction at his subsequent fulfilment of my every hope."

Under ordinary circumstances such an important administrative change might have been expected to monopolize the attention of an annual meeting, but 1925 was not an ordinary year. Since it was Noyes's twenty-fifth anniversary, the uppermost thought of the publishers who attended in record numbers was to memorialize the occasion.

8

For a quarter of a turbulent century the quiet, distinguished-looking publisher of the Washington *Star* had guided the destinies of the organization. Year after year with unfailing regularity he had been re-elected. Managerial changes occurred, directors came and went, but Frank Noyes continued. There were many among the membership who could not remember a time when he was not president of The Associated Press, and there were others who had come to consider him an indispensable personality in the life of the association.

Of medium stature, military in bearing, he was outwardly a stern but nevertheless benevolent leader among his fellow publishers. In an even, well-modulated voice he could parry distasteful questions or sudden stabs of wit. At annual meetings he spoke in conversational tones and his words flowed with an ease that frequently confounded some of the more fiery and excitable members. His opening lines frequently gave listeners the impression they were in for a deadly serious discourse, yet within minutes he was quietly employing a sense of humor that was as compelling as it was unexpected. The fund of stories from which he drew to illustrate any pertinent point were so apt, his selection of words so precise, that any utterance, no matter how impromptu, assumed a quality of polish that invariably left listeners in open admiration.

Yet active as Noyes was in the inner councils of the association, well known as he was in high places, he studiously avoided any public act which conceivably might be construed as reflecting a viewpoint of the nonpartisan news-gathering agency he headed. He diplomatically abstained from speaking on controversial subjects, and on only one occasion during his entire regime was a member of his own craft able to obtain a headline from him.

On that occasion Noyes was vacationing in Florida and one of the local papers sent around a cub reporter—an inquisitive little lady who charmingly peppered him with questions on politics, world affairs, and his own personal preference in the fields of music, the arts, and the sciences.

"My dear child," he said, "I am sorry, but I really can't talk on any of those subjects."

The young reporter was determined. She asked her questions over and over again until finally, in an effort to have her understand fully why he felt he should not express opinions for publication, he tried again to state his position.

"You see," he explained, "as head of The Associated Press I try to maintain a detached neutrality on all public matters because ours is a factual organization and anything I say personally might be open to misconstruction."

He paused, mentally framing a definition, and then there was a barely perceptible twinkle in his eye.

"Because of my position," he smiled, "I suppose that for the past thirty-five years I have been somewhat of an intellectual eunuch."

The young interviewer heard him through, graciously thanked him for his kindly reception, and made her departure. Noyes thought no more about the incident until shown a copy of the reporter's paper the next day. There on the front page was the young woman's story, one sentence of which read:

"The president of The Associated Press says he is an intellectual UNIT."

One of Noyes's greatest contributions during that first quarter century was the way he maintained the association's stability in the inevitable conflicts of interest which arose between the large and the small papers making up the membership. He said:

There have always been two schools of thought as to the membership makeup of The Associated Press. One has held to the desirability of having a large membership consisting of a great number of small papers and a small number of large papers.

On the other hand, there were those who believed that the membership should be confined to the larger papers.

The Board of Directors almost unanimously has believed in the theory of the large organization, and has consistently and scrupulously sought to conserve the interests of the smaller units of the membership.

The annual meeting was held April 2, 1925, and applause swept the room when Ralph H. Booth, of the Saginaw (Mich.) News-Courier, on behalf of the membership, presented the president with a golden bowl to commemorate the anniversary.

The cheering of several hundred members failed to drown the voice of Victor Lawson, calling for the floor. The old fighter had lost much of his vigor, but he still could command attention.

"An ideal is the very essence of any great endeavor inspired by a sincere purpose," Lawson said, addressing Noyes. "The conception of an Associated Press as a national co-operative news-gathering and distributing agency, charging itself in the conduct of a business enterprise with the high responsibility of a great public service in the preservation of the sources of public information and opinion free from the pollution of selfish commercialism and political ambition, depended for its permanent realization upon a loyal and continuing devotion to the common good. This high conception of public duty has been from the first the common bond of the membership of this association, and in response to which you have accepted and discharged the constant and exacting duties of your leadership."

He paused, then added:

"You have served a great and righteous cause, the cause of Truth in News, and served it faithfully."

Visibly touched, Noyes for once found it difficult to phrase his feelings.

"This is indeed for me a day of fulfillment," he said. "I would not, even if I could, conceal how deeply I am affected by what has been said here and by those outward and visible signs of your friendship and good will. While no one realizes better than I do that much that has been said by my dear friends who have spoken applies to the sort of president that I should have been and not to what really I have been, still the words of over-appreciative friendship and tenderness are very dear to me—precious beyond any words of mine to express. . . ."

To the right of the dais the stenographer, who was keeping the usual transcript of the proceedings, listened to the spontaneous outburst which broke loose as Noyes concluded, and conservatively entered in his notes:

"Great applause."

1925

I. SPEED AND PROSPERITY

A QUARTER of a century of tremendous progress had transformed the newspaper world into a marvel of high-speed efficiency. Dispatches were turned into type with amazing rapidity. The total circulations of American newspapers mounted close to 40,000,000 daily and the income of newspaper enterprises topped $900,000,000 annually.

The afternoon papers, which assumed during the World War a position they had never held before, continued to advance in the ensuing years. Sunday editions grew thicker. Chain organizations extended their holdings and consolidations strengthened the publishing field.

In content and appearance the majority of papers strove to be as attractive as possible. The development of photo-engraving processes made good news pictures possible. Typography and format style received a larger share of attention in the interests of reading ease, and increased departmentalizing added noticeably to newspaper appeal.

Day-to-day news continued the essential commodity and its volume kept increasing as the world turned. If anything, the swift march of mechanical progress had made news a more perishable commodity than ever. In keeping with the pace of newspaper manufacture, communications moved toward greater perfection. The enormous expansion of telephone systems brought many previously remote regions within the periphery of speedy news gathering. Technical advances had given both telegraph and cable lines higher standards of reliability and efficiency. Radio, that comparative newcomer in the communications family, provided still another channel. Even such a pedestrian department of news dissemination as the mail services found a brisker gait, for postal deliveries were quicker and air mail could be enlisted whenever haste was essential.

The advent of this high-speed day produced a series of opportunities and needs which The AP had been tardy in realizing. Many of its members felt there had been a failure to catch the complete significance of all the changes taking place in the newspaper world. In the past the news had been the only important thing, regardless of its presentation. Now editors and readers were critical of the manner in which a story was told. They wanted their news written in the most interesting, vivid style, not only on isolated occasions but as a regular thing. There was redoubled insistence that the brighter and curious side of life be reported; the fads and foibles of an era were as much a part of its history as were its politics or perils. The long predominance of foreign news on front pages had diminished, and as balance returned neighborhood news came back to its own—and the automobile had given neighborhoods a wide area. Not only had people become picture minded but they also liked diversions, as the interest in feature material testified.

2

It was at this time that Kent Cooper took over as general manager. He was loyal to the principles for which the nonprofit co-operative stood in the field of news and he already had declined offers by commercial news agencies which would have brought financial rewards many times beyond what he ever could hope for with The AP. Now that he had been given his opportunity, he stated his creed:

I believe there is nothing so fascinating as the true day-to-day story of humanity. Man, what he feels, what he does, what he says; his fears, his hopes, his aspirations. And, as truth is stranger than fiction, nothing can be more engrossing than the truthful portrayal of life itself. The journalist who deals in facts diligently developed and intelligently presented exalts his profession, and his stories need never be colorless or dull. On the other hand, the reporter who resorts to the rouge pot to make his wares attractive convicts himself of laziness and ineptitude. The head of another press association once said that it was always proper to qualify the news with color in order to stimulate reader interest. This I deny. Artificiality and superficiality in news writing not only are unnecessary, but ultimately must have a baneful influence on the reader. Simple honesty and good business demand from the newspaperman an uncolored tale of what is. That is my creed.

Zealously adhering to the principle of factual reporting, nevertheless Cooper had little patience with the old myth that impartiality postulated drab, tedious writing. The official drive for livelier, more interesting presentation of the news was a foregone conclusion. That definite part of the staff was ready for such a change was demonstrated by the promptness of the response. The stiff and sometimes stodgy writing habits were not to be rooted out overnight, but the process had been started and it continued without relaxation as part of the fundamental policy of the new regime.

The second emphasis concerned itself with extending the variety in the report. Human-interest stories ceased to be regarded as decorative and were given due, if belated, recognition. One of the first manifestations of the new trend was the special daily wire feature called "Flashes of Life." It was a series of brief items side-lighting the humorous and the unusual in everyday existence.

At the outset, these departures did not meet with universal approval. One publisher warned tartly: "We will soon be devoting ourselves entirely to trivialities." The Board of Directors thought differently, encouraging the trend until the proportion of humanizing stories in the report had risen to a respectable level.

The transformation attracted so much journalistic attention that papers commented editorially, among them the Kansas City *Star* which said:

The AP Reports The Human Spectacle

Until recently The Associated Press has conceived its field to be restricted to the chronicling of serious and important news. From its standpoint, a catastrophe, an election, a congressional debate, the death of a distinguished man, an important trial, pretty much exhausted the topics of human interest.

Until recently. An attentive reader of The Star must have noticed a change in the last few months. The Associated Press by-line now is appearing over dispatches that are gay as well as grave. . . . The Associated Press has begun to live up to the Greek philosopher's saying that nothing human is alien to him. It has not lowered its standards. It has simply enlarged the field of its interests. It is striving to report every phase of the human spectacle.

The transformation has been due to the vision and imagination of Mr. Kent Cooper.

This "vision and imagination" was by no means an overnight development. The disclosure of the idea of humanizing the news report went back to 1916 and a flagman's shanty along a railroad right-of-way between Utica and Syracuse in New York.

Melville Stone was general manager then and, together with Cooper, he had entrained one winter night to attend a meeting of Canadian Press members in Toronto. While the two men sat reading in a smoking compartment the train came to a stop between the two upstate cities. The older man and his young assistant speculated on the cause of the stop and soon Stone closed his book with the suggestion that they alight and determine the trouble.

They climbed down the steps into a cold rain and looked up and down the tracks. There was nothing in sight but a lighted flagman's hut and Stone suggested they go there to inquire. Inside they found three railroad employes around a stove. From the gruff greeting there was no doubt but that the two passengers were considered intruders. But the cool reception did not abash Stone. A man of exceptional personality and charm, he observed that one of the men was chewing tobacco. The general manager did not make a habit of tobacco in such form, but he nevertheless asked if he might borrow a chew. The plug was grudgingly offered and he bit off a sizeable piece.

Stone then stood chewing his wad and conversing lightly with his newly made acquaintances. Within a few minutes he had the three railroad employees and Cooper so engrossed in his humorous anecdotes that the train was pulling away unnoticed.

Stone and Cooper hurriedly swung aboard and in the corridor of their car they met a former Canadian premier who was an old acquaintance of the general manager. The next ten minutes were given over to a serious discussion of international affairs—the World War and the probability of conditions at its termination. The discussion with the one-time Canadian official was totally unlike that in which Stone had just indulged with the tobacco-chewing workers in the stove-heated shanty, yet the general manager seemed equally at home with what interested each, talking in a language both could understand.

Stone and Cooper resumed their seats in the smoking compartment and the assistant then took over the conversation. They laughed over the shanty episode and Cooper ventured a thought.

"These two little incidents I have just witnessed have a direct bearing on what I think The Associated Press news report should be," he said. "I think it should be at home and welcome in both such circles as you yourself have been welcomed tonight."

The two men discussed the suggestion late into the night and as the general manager said good night he turned to Cooper.

"Well, if I were a younger man I might try your idea as an experiment," he observed. Then he added with a wry face:

"But that certainly was strong tobacco!"

Cooper little thought that within a decade he himself would be trying to make all the news completely at home to both such circles on a world-wide scale.

3

Reporting the human spectacle, however, sometimes brought humorous repercussions. On one occasion the cables carried a short on the fact that soup was disappearing from the menus of many European hotels. Widely used, this harmless enough little piece aroused the indignation of one large soup manufacturer who protested that the co-operative was attacking the soup industry.

From the long-range point of view, Cooper's most significant decision perhaps was to concentrate on the development of state services. A number of factors were involved, notably recognition of the future of vicinage news, the consequent extension of news-gathering facilities, and a shift in the basic operating methods of the co-operative.

Although it represented a logical step in the modern co-operative, State Service development had been slow. When member papers showed considerable desire in 1908 for a more localized report—something possible only through the creation of State Services, or "side circuits" as they then were called—the Special Survey Committee that year discouraged the idea, holding that the co-operative's sphere was news of general interest only. Nevertheless, the success of existing side circuits helped to keep the idea alive.

The movement took on fresh vigor in the postwar years and no difficulties were placed in the way of the members in some areas who expressed a desire for the development of state services to supplement their general report. On the contrary, there seemed reason to believe that the projects received enthusiastic, if unofficial, help from some members of the management's staff.

By the time he became general manager, Cooper found Noyes and others on the Board of Directors sympathetic to the State Service-vicinage news trend and soon the possibilities were receiving the active stimulus needed. The state was made the basic unit of domestic operations, and in each a strategic bureau was designated to serve as the control point. These bureaus siphoned off dispatches of general importance from the regular report and used this material in conjunction with news of more local origin to build up a special report for the state circuits they operated. Bureau chiefs were appointed to supervise activities and to act as the general manager's personal representative in each of the states. The enlarged scope of operations necessitated a corresponding increase in staff personnel.

The full development of the state services had a salutary effect on the attitude of members. Where the organization as a world-wide enterprise might be too vast to encourage active interest or personal enthusiasm, the more compact state organization represented something tangible and close to home. Members showed interest in the betterment and success of these smaller units and one manifestation was the general introduction of periodical state meetings at which members gathered to discuss news in terms of the circuits which served their newspapers.

For the General Service, considered in its strictest sense as a budget containing only the most important news, the strengthening and the extending of state services had an obvious advantage. If each unit covered all its own news thoroughly, from small events to great ones, there was little likelihood that the General Service would fail to receive promptly any important news with an interest that transcended state lines.

4

Another innovation was the appointment of a science editor to specialize in the news to be found in laboratory research and experiment. The new general manager had been impressed by the possibilities in this field for news gathering, not in the random manner of the past when a single important discovery or invention momentarily attracted popular attention, but rather in a regular day-to-day manner. He talked of the possibility to the president of Stevens Institute of Technology.

"People even sleep better because of the scientific study of bed-springs," he said. "Don't you agree there is a field for science news in language all newspaper readers will understand?"

"Yes," said the professor, "but you'll need a scientist as a reporter." Cooper considered that.

"No," he decided; "instead of trying to make a reporter of a scientist, we'll make a scientist of a reporter. We'll get a man who is smart enough to know science, but who also knows how to write for the average newspaper reader."

The appointment of a science editor followed. John Cooley did pioneering work and, after him, Coleman B. Jones. The science editor responsible for the development of the new department to full stature was its third editor, Howard W. Blakeslee, a man with a wide range of experience in all phases of the service. He developed into a science specialist of top rank, winning university degrees and a Pulitzer prize.

Coincident with the expansion of the scope of the news report, the new general manager made another departure from precedent. He began the practice of using "by-lines" over stories of unusual interest and importance. In the past the writer of any AP story had been anonymous, but Cooper felt there was advantage to both The AP and the staff to have the man identified with the work he did. The practice applied only on outstanding cases and the papers receiving the by-lined stories could carry the name of the author or not, as individual policy dictated.

5

In the midst of all this activity, planning, and improving, The AP lost one of its great figures. On August 19, 1925, Victor Lawson died. If David Hale could be called the father of The Associated Press, then Victor Lawson was its foster father, for without him the co-operative principle never would have been preserved. The membership and the newspaper world at large mourned him as one of the foremost figures ever produced by his profession.

In the ranks of the staff, too, old familiar figures were disappearing. Dick Lee, ship news editor for forty-seven years, died within a few weeks after illness forced him out of harness. A legendary character, he always insisted on working seven days a week and until the end he refused all offers of assistance.

The younger staff men who were replacing such older hands as Lee experienced a hectic summer in 1925, particularly in the sweltering heat at Dayton, Tennessee, where the Scopes Evolution Trial made the strangest news of the year. The epic legal battle between Clarence Darrow and William Jennings Bryan, the Bible's champion, kept four staff correspondents busy from dawn until midnight or later. W. F. Caldwell, news editor of the Southern Division, who was credited with being the first newsman to see the possibilities of the story when Scopes was arrested, supervised the coverage, assisted by Brian Bell, W. B. Ragsdale, and P. I. Lipsey. Bell, who had been on the story even before Scopes' indictment, became so well known that when the trial ended in a flood of oratory Judge Raulston called on him for some expression for the court record.

"Mr. Bell," he asked, smiling toward the AP table, "won't you say a word?"

"No, sir, judge," was the good-natured reply.

There was no dearth of provocative material in the record the times produced. There were the navy air disasters: the *Shenandoah* and the rescue of Commander Rodgers from the navy airplane PN-9-No.1 after his attempted flight to Hawaii. Florida was having its fabulous land boom and the Miami *Daily News* printed the biggest newspaper yet in journalistic history—504 pages. Crossword puzzles had become a national mania, and football fans chanted the praises of that "galloping

ghost" from the University of Illinois, Red Grange. There was the
S-51 submarine disaster off Block Island, the great anthracite coal strike
in Pennsylvania, Germany's entry into the League of Nations, and the
passing of baseball's immortal Christy Mathewson.

6

The report itself was feeling a new exterior pressure and by 1926
it became serious. Postwar disillusionment, moral relaxation, the Prohibition era, and the cult of ballyhoo had generated influences which
were producing deleterious effects in American journalism. One mani-
fest tendency was the dramatization of cheap heroics and the sensa-
tionalizing of crime. Old standards of delicacy disappeared in some
published accounts of unsavory scandals. Some newspapers began hippo-
droming events out of all proportion to their objective news value.

To preserve the balance and sanity of the report in the midst
of such an atmosphere required ceaseless care. The Board of Directors
and the general manager reiterated the standing instructions against
the glorification of criminals. The norm of good state was reaffirmed for
all stories whenever the subject matter transgressed the limits of common
decency. Artificial sensations were ruthlessly dealt with and hysterical
sentimentality got short shrift from staff editors. Some members, who
preferred the gaudy, theatrical trappings of the journalistic moment,
may not have been pleased with the attitude of the administration, but
the vast majority considered it a levelheaded stand.

When the nineteen-year-old Marion Talley made her operatic
debut on February 17, the Metropolitan broke tradition by permitting
the installation of a special news wire. For the first time in the history
of the opera the clicking of a telegraph key mingled with coloratura
arias. The wire was set up in the conductors' room on the stage level
across a narrow passage from the wings. S. A. Dawson wrote the story
of Miss Talley's performance and reception. Ethel Halsey, the first
woman reporter on the New York staff, obtained interviews with Mrs.
Talley and later with the young opera star.

Unknown to the glittering audience of 4,100 which jammed the
opera house and the crowd of 5,000 gathered outside, it was Charles
M. Talley, the star's father, who started the story of the debut onto
the leased wires. A former Associated Press telegrapher, he returned
to the Morse key and tapped out the first story.

As the news beginnings indicated, it was to be a year of infinite variety. "Daddy" Browning, fifty-one, wed "Peaches" Heenan, fifteen, and Germany elected General von Hindenburg president. Swimmers conquered the English channel and Joseph Stalin was rising to power in Soviet Russia. President Coolidge's father died in Vermont and a New York jury heard all about the nude chorus girl in Earl Carroll's bathtub. Mabel Walker Willebrandt directed the newest federal drive for enforcement of the Volstead Act, and the Charleston dance craze seemed likely to stay.

May produced, among a welter of other things, the biggest story from England since World War days—the British General Strike. Harry H. Rober, of the New York cable staff, happened to take a European vacation that spring and it turned out to be a busman's holiday. He landed in England on May 3—the day the first of 4,000,000 workers walked out—and within an hour he was busy in the London office. The bureau chief, Charles Stephenson Smith, mobilized a staff of twenty-five for the emergency which turned Great Britain upside down, brought troops in full field kit into the streets, and put volunteers to work manning the nation's vital services.

Assigned to labor headquarters, James P. Howe, the former A.E.F. war correspondent, bought out a little notions shop in order to have exclusive use of the nearest telephone. The small bewhiskered shopkeeper sat behind the locked front door, waiting to pull the bolt and admit Howe the moment he appeared.

Bureau Chief Smith and Frank King were at No. 10 Downing Street on May 12 for the meeting between Prime Minister Stanley Baldwin and the Council of the Trades Union Congress which ended the strike. Bowler hat and notes in one hand and the inevitable London umbrella in the other, King won the race to get first word to the wires.

7

Before the echo of the General Strike died, news exploded on another European front. Marshal Josef Pilsudski staged the swift coup d'état which made him undisputed master of Poland. When Pilsudski's forces seized power on May 15, Louis Lochner of Berlin was ordered to Warsaw to assist the residential correspondent, Marylla Chrzanowska, who was in the midst of the fighting which accompanied the coup.

Flying to the Polish frontier, Lochner got a foretaste of the difficulties surrounding the story. Not only had the strictest military censorship been invoked, but the border itself was closed. Lochner smuggled himself across the frontier and by various means made his way to the Polish capital, which was swarming with Pilsudski's troops. It was Sunday, May 16.

All that day Lochner and Miss Chrzanowska pursued the grizzled old marshal. Pilsudski remained inaccessible. Guards watched every approach to his headquarters. Soldiers surrounded his car as he hurried from one place to another. Secret police pounced on anyone who dared approach too close to the prime minister's palace, another center of activity.

By nightfall the palace had assumed greater importance than ever. In spite of the secrecy, Miss Chrzanowska had ferreted out the news that the first meeting of the new Cabinet was in session, with Pilsudski presiding. Lochner and the resident correspondent succeeded in talking their way into the palace. There they encountered fresh obstacles. Palace flunkies declared they were responsible with their lives for Pilsudski's safety. Furthermore, no foreigner could be tolerated in the building. The newspaper pair found themselves back on the street.

Lochner's companion remembered another entrance and they tried again. Their exit was hurried and unceremonious. The supply of palace doors had not been exhausted however. The pair entered the third time, the fourth, the fifth, and the sixth, only to be ejected. The guards were becoming ugly.

The two weary correspondents happened to encounter a director of the Polish Telegraphic Agency whom they knew. He offered to get them back into the palace—for the seventh time.

For two hours Lochner and Miss Chrzanowska sat in the palace rotunda. Presently there was a commotion. The guards started disappearing through a swinging glass door leading to the right wing. Pilsudski must be leaving. The two correspondents dashed after the guards. In a few more seconds the opportunity would have been lost.

"Please, Mr. Marshal," Miss Chrzanowska was pleading in Polish, "don't refuse just one little request by my American colleague."

"My dear lady," Pilsudski said, "I'm extremely tired. I want to sleep, sleep, and sleep again. For three days I have not been to bed."

He looked haggard and worn as he stood there in the loose-fitting blue-gray uniform of a Polish legionnaire.

Lochner spoke up.

"But America takes the liveliest interest in Polish events and is anxious to know the truth."

"You must understand," Pilsudski replied, "that I must consider what I say, and in a moment like this I'll either say something stupid or pronounce an aphorism. I'm a specialist in aphorisms, you know. Sometimes I can roll off aphorisms one after another, but today I'm too tired even for aphorisms."

Lochner persisted.

"May I know for my American readers whether you are of the opinion that stable conditions will now result for Poland after your coup d'état?"

An animated light came into the dictator's eyes.

"Why, that's been the purpose of all this. That's what I've been working for all this time—and I've accomplished it. In fact, I'm quite surprised we succeeded so quickly. Everything went like a stroke of lightning."

It was because of that final phrase that the brief chat became known as the "lightning interview."

"Just one final question," urged Lochner, walking briskly at Pilsudski's side as the marshal hurried from the palace. "May I say, as coming from you, that you consider the country pacified and further ructions unlikely?"

Knitting his shaggy brows and snapping his jaws, Pilsudski answered with a single English word.

"Yes!"

Telephone communication to points outside Poland was still suspended. There was no doubt the censor would hold up the story. Lochner left immediately for Germany, got across the frontier and telephoned to Berlin the only statement Pilsudski made for publication in the first five days of the coup.

8

Competing with the London and Warsaw date lines were dozens of top-flight stories. Sinclair Lewis created a domestic furor by refusing the Pulitzer prize for his novel *Arrowsmith*. The dirigible *Norge* reached Alaska after carrying the Nobile-Ellsworth-Amundsen across the North Pole from Spitzbergen. The *Norge's* flight gave the co-operative a barren territory of some 4,000,000 square miles to watch. Aimee Semple McPherson, the California evangelist, announced that she had been kidnaped and held for ransom in Mexico. Philadelphia opened its Sesquicentennial Exposition. And in Morocco Abd-el-Krim, the Riff rebel chieftain, surrendered after his long, amazing war on the French and Spanish armies.

During these busy months the service also was developing stories which could not be classified as spontaneous news, yet were important or unusual enough to command preferred positions in newspapers. Cooper himself took the lead in developing these stories, arranging for a series of notable interviews. The first was with Golfer Bobby Jones. Of greater historical value, however, were the extended interview with Mussolini and the much-discussed story on Calvin Coolidge.

White House precedent was against an interview quoting the President of the United States and Coolidge at first was against it. Nevertheless, Cooper set to work.

Invited to lunch with the President, he ended by spending the day. He found the so-called "silent New Englander" engrossing. He had the assistance of Mrs. Coolidge and the presidential adviser, Frank W. Stearns, but it finally became evident that the trio were not making much progress in their attempt to show the President he would be performing a service to newspaper readers generally by permitting an extended interview. Cooper pointed out that few actually knew the President of the United States and still Coolidge smoked his cigar and was adamant. Cooper tried one last time.

"Mr. President," he smiled, "do you know that all sorts of stories are going the rounds about you—that they are going the rounds because people don't really know you."

He glanced disarmingly across at the President and asked:

"Would you like to hear one of the latest?"

The President hunched slightly forward in his chair.

"Yes," he said.

"Well," Cooper began, "they say that a raw young congressman called on you and said: 'Mr. President, the folks back home don't know much about my job here. They think you and I are great buddies, that we rub elbows every day and that you call me in for advice whenever you have a problem of any sort. Of course, that's not the case, but it would help me no end if I could have some memento or souvenir from you to show them when I go back for the elections.'

"So, Mr. President," Cooper continued, "they say that you asked what he would like and he replied: 'I don't want anything very valuable, Mr. President, just a band off one of your cigars would do.'

"With that, Mr. President," Cooper concluded, "the story is that you pulled out your big box of cigars, carefully removed one of the bands and handed it to the young congressman. Then you put the cigar back in the box and put the box away—that you didn't even give him the cigar!"

Coolidge pondered and for a fleeting moment the usual mask of seriousness appeared to drop. Then he was in character again.

"Well, Mr. Cooper," he said, smiling faintly, "that congressman only asked for the band, not for the cigar!"

The Coolidge story appeared in the co-operative's report a short time later, authored by Bruce Barton at the request of Cooper. It filled five columns in the New York *Times*, was used in virtually every member paper, and in editorial circles it created a sensation. It gave the country a picture of the Coolidge so few knew—his home life, his philosophy, and the human side of his official character.

9

In the field of spontaneous news Florida produced one of 1926's biggest emergencies. On September 18 a tropical hurricane roared up the east coast, smashing a score of communities.

The first stages of the storm were reported in dispatches which flowed northward to divisional headquarters at Atlanta. Then one after another the Florida wires began to fail. The last bulletins gave Atlanta an inkling of the story's proportions—scores dead, hundreds injured, thousands homeless, and vast property damage. The final wire went out as the full force of the hurricane struck. At Atlanta the south circuits were silent.

As the hurricane slashed through Florida, staffers were already pushing their way into its wake to get the news. In the state and outside its borders, the association threw every available resource into the breach. At the first warning, Chief of Bureau O. S. Morton at Jacksonville ordered men at once into the region and Atlanta started additional reinforcements by airplane, train, and automobile. Traffic Department crews tackled the complicated task of restoring shattered wire facilities. No one knew what had happened to Correspondent Mitchell at Miami.

Mitchell was all right, struggling to get out his story. When the hurricane tore out the last wire to Miami on that disastrous Saturday, he and telegrapher Howard Switzer braved the storm to search for an automobile to carry them north. Luckily they secured a truck, and Reese T. Amis, telegraph editor of the Miami *Daily News*, joined them as they set out.

Progress was slow over the flooded, debris-littered roads. Rain-whipped darkness added to their difficulties. Many times the truck was forced to leave the highway and crawl through fields or woods. Water sloshed over the running boards. Each hamlet they passed showed increasingly greater damage. Pressing doggedly on past Hollywood, the party found the highway blocked by a barricade of trees snarled with telephone and telegraph wires. The truck mired down at midnight in a ditch six miles from Fort Lauderdale and the trio struck out on foot in the heavy rain.

While Mitchell, Switzer, and Amis were trying to get north from Miami, R. S. Pickens and M. B. Alexander of the Atlanta staff were flying south through the turbulent edges of the storm. Their goal was Miami and they made a pact to stay with the plane "till she crashes."

Alexander never forgot the wild ride.

"Through crosscurrents, air pockets, and up and over storms' edges we went until the big one near Lake City, Florida," he related. "There in a semicircle ahead was the blackest cloud we ever saw. White streaks of wind-driven rain were illuminated by vivid flashes of lightning and suddenly the little plane quivered, dipped, dropped, and then under the pilot's masterful handling righted herself and climbed. We fought varying degrees of tropical hurricane for over two hours and finally won out when the wind changed and headed for Pensacola to continue its work of destruction."

The daredevil pilot brought the ship down in a water-covered pasture bordering a swamp. The men waded to a highway and pushed on to Miami. They found streets blocked by trees, fallen timbers, and ruined homes. The stench of dead fish made the air nauseous. Searching parties looked for bodies. There was no safe drinking water and the food was impossible.

Miami was merely part of the story. At Moore Haven alone 110 had been killed. Stephen Early, who had been sent from Washington, and A. R. Bird, correspondents at Orlando, worked toward the wrecked community from different directions.

After many detours, Early's automobile got within five miles of the town, and there the road vanished under water. He drove on cautiously through the black, stinking liquid that concealed the highway. The posts near the road edges were the only guides to keep the car from plunging into the drainage ditches along the sides. The engine finally quit and the reporter found a truck, which eventually splashed its way into town.

The return trip was a nightmare. A mile after the start, the truck swamped and there was no choice but to wade through the dark to higher ground. Early thought of saving his already bedraggled clothes. Before plunging from the truck, he bundled them up, and stood there in shirtail and underwear. The truckman handed him creosote and coal oil to smear on as protection against insects and the foul water. Not long after Early left the truck he lost the clothes he thought of saving. For four miles he labored through surging waters and finally reached the automobile he had abandoned hours earlier. The balky engine started and Early drove back to Sebring where wire facilities were being restored.

All that week the staff worked to bring the nation the news of a disaster which took 372 lives, injured 6,281, and left 17,884 families homeless.

II. PICTURES ARE NEWS

THE co-operative could no longer ignore the fact that spot news represented only a part of the content of the modern newspaper. Features and spot-news pictures were important. If the association expanded the scope of operations to include supplemental services in these auxiliary fields, its value to member papers would be greatly increased.

In both prewar and postwar newspapers, extensive use of feature material marked a definite journalistic trend. Editors had come to the conclusion that it was no longer enough for newspapers to be informative. They must entertain and divert as well. At first only the larger publications had money and facilities for experimenting, and they did most of the pioneer work. The development of feature syndicates was a logical sequel. One of the earliest, in the modern sense of the word, was organized by George Matthew Adams in 1912 at the suggestion of Victor Lawson, and a mushroom growth in the field followed. By the mid-twenties commercial companies were supplying papers generally with budgets ranging from comic strips and popular fiction to picture matrices and personalized columns of comment by leading writers. With a large clientele, the syndicates, for a given price, could supply subscribers with quantities of feature material which no average paper could duplicate.

A goodly portion of the budgets furnished by these commercial syndicates duplicated in subject matter, although not in treatment, the material carried in the co-operative's General Mail Service, which for years had been sent to members as a supplement to the wire report. There was this difference, however. Instead of appearing on dreary mimeographed paper, the commercial features were presented on neatly printed proof sheets with headlines already written. And most important, the features were accompanied by attractive pictures, line drawings, or layouts, all designed to make them as visually pleasing as possible.

This illustrated material was popular from the start. The syndicates were profit-making ventures, and the greater the margin of profit the more satisfactory the business. There was no rigid rule of thumb governing the prices charged for budgets. Some salesmen, working on commission, often charged any price they could get. When any feature became valuable to a paper, prices were frequently raised and a publisher had the choice either of losing a circulation-getting attraction or of paying more money.

As these practices grew, members who had been victimized began to wonder if their co-operative could not enter the feature field in a thoroughgoing way and produce just as good a budget on a non-profit basis. If this could be done, they realized, it would give them good supplemental material at actual cost and would protect them against arbitrary withdrawals of features once they had been established. Strangely enough, however, they did not seem to recognize that in the General Mail Service the association possessed the complete ground-work for an efficient feature department. All that was lacking was the vision, initiative, and the modernizing touch to effect the transformation.

2

Cooper, as an assistant general manager, saw the great possibilities. But he knew that the association at that time had not sufficiently adjusted itself to postwar conditions to develop the plan. He stopped in at the Chicago Bureau one day during the course of an inspection trip. A young editor was busy preparing an issue of the General Mail Service. Looking over his shoulder, Cooper saw the stacks of mimeographed copy paper.

"Looks pretty dull, doesn't it?" he commented.

The editor shrugged. Single-spaced typewriting, mimeographed on coarse paper did not, after all, make an exciting appearance.

Cooper examined several sheets and dropped them back on the desk.

"Well," he said with characteristic directness, "what would you think of illustrating it?"

"I'd think very well of it."

The assistant general manager ventured a prediction.

"Before long you will be doing it."

Shortly after this incident Cooper became general manager, pressed the matter with the board, and was directed to proceed. One of his first steps was to bring the mail editor from Chicago to organize the Feature Department. The young man was Lloyd Stratton, a Kansan who had

joined the service in 1920. His earlier newspaper experience had been
in the Middle West except for a wartime interlude in France where
he drove an ambulance until it was hit by a shell, sending driver and
wounded alike to the hospital.

The first Feature Service release—printed proof sheets and matted
illustrations—was mailed to 1228 members without assessment. The
package contained a letter from the general manager, explaining the
plan on which the service would operate and the assessment base for
its financing. The assessments were nominal as compared with the
prices of commercial syndicates, which ran to many dollars a week
in some cases. The maximum assessment for the proof sheets was
fixed at $6 a week for papers published in areas of more than 100,000
population. From the maximum, the charge scaled down to $1 a
week for papers in cities of less than 20,000. The assessment for
mats of illustrations, an optional part of the service, was eventually
fixed at $3.50 weekly for all.

Editors on member papers opened the package containing the first
release and promises of support poured in to the general offices. Of
the entire membership, only 78 papers declined to participate.

3

Like the history of news gathering, the development of pictorial
journalism had its own story. Benjamin Franklin made the first attempt
to provide illustrations with reading matter when he printed his famous
cartoon in the *Pennsylvania Gazette* in 1754. War with France was
rumored, and to heighten the effect of his editorial appeal for a united
common defense Franklin inserted a cartoon showing a snake cut into
eight parts. The parts represented the various colonies and the caption,
"Join or Die," dramatized the need of the moment.

The value of the cartoon impressed other colonial editors and they
copied the idea, using Franklin's snake with variations. When the
Boston Massacre occurred in 1770 Paul Revere made an engraving of
five coffins to illustrate the Boston *Gazette's* account of the funerals for
the victims.

Since the first cartoon was employed to reinforce editorial opinion,
it was perhaps natural that editors came to look upon such illustrations
solely as an editorial medium. On a few occasions they purported to
represent a news event, though the emphasis was always on editorial
connotations.

James Gordon Bennett was probably the first to use a real news illustration. In 1835 he published a picture of the old Merchants' Exchange which had burned down in the great fire of that year. Mechanical difficulties with the presses of the day made for poor, smudgy reproduction and often the identity of the rough illustrations could be determined only by reference to the printed caption. Indeed, when the *Herald* appeared with a supposed drawing of General Jackson's funeral, in 1845, rival papers pounced on Bennett, charging that the same engraving already had done duty as an illustration for Queen Victoria's coronation, the funeral of General William Henry Harrison, and the Croton Water Celebration.

While Bennett's efforts may have been worthy of some note, the real pioneering work in depicting spot news occurrences was not a newspaper enterprise. The credit belonged to Nathaniel Currier. As a boy of fifteen he began his apprenticeship with a Boston firm of lithographers in 1828, the same year Hale and Hallock were making news-gathering history in Manhattan. Currier came to New York and set up a small shop in Printing House Square, the journalistic heart of the city. The newspaper atmosphere had its influence and when the steamboat *Lexington* burned with heavy loss of life on Long Island Sound in 1840, Currier tried an experiment. A theatrically graphic picture of the disaster was drawn and three days later Currier had prints for sale on the streets. They were snatched up eagerly.

The 1840 steamboat disaster decided the future of the Currier lithographing establishment. Illustrations of spot news became its specialty. Currier recruited a staff of artists who rushed to the scene of any news event in the vicinity, sketched the general details, and afterward completed the more careful drawings from which the lithographs were made.

Currier was joined by James Merritt Ives and the firm's name became Currier & Ives. For the next three decades they flourished as printmakers to the American public. Pictures were sold by direct mail, by representatives in the principal cities, and by peddlers who hawked them through the streets. Prices ranged from 6 cents for a small print to $4 for a large picture in full color. Prints on spot-news events were usually available in New York a day or two after the news appeared in the papers. The success of the firm gave unmistakable proof of the great popular appeal of pictorial reporting.

Even before young Currier began issuing his dramatic news-picture prints, Daguerre's experiments in photography had produced the first unheralded examples of the pictorial reporting process which ultimately exerted such a profound effect on the concept of complete news presentation. Although Samuel Morse and a few others later became interested, the possibilities Daguerre opened up were not apparent when the Frenchman announced his discovery in 1838. By the time of the Mexican War in 1846, however, photography had advanced sufficiently to produce the first actual pictures of a major news story. Although the few daguerreotypes taken of American staff officers and troops had no particular spot-news value, they were part of the history of pictorial reporting.

So few people saw the Mexican War daguerreotypes that they made little impression on the journalistic consciousness of the day. The accepted pictorial record of the war was a series of illustrations prepared at the direction of George Wilkins Kendall, the only reporter to accompany the American Army.

4

The undeniable popularity of news illustrations encouraged the appearance of illustrated weeklies in the next decade. *Frank Leslie's Illustrated Newspaper* was founded in 1855 and *Harper's Weekly* entered the field as a competitor in 1857. The weeklies covered a wide range of subjects—"current events of interest and importance, art and story illustrations, portraiture, the humor and comedy of social life, and foreign and domestic politics." The illustrations were all line drawings, and both publications maintained large staffs of artists and wood engravers.

When the Civil War came, the artists of the illustrated weeklies did the pictorial reporting for the country at large. Their "on the spot" sketches were scanned almost as eagerly as newspaper dispatches, and army officials regarded the artists as an integral part of the press corps. The weeklies continued to be the sole publications which attempted to provide news pictures. The only initiative demonstrated by newspapers was in presenting maps of major battles and campaigns. One wood engraver on the New York *Herald* was considered phenomenal because he was able to turn out a half-page war map in twenty-four hours, but sometimes as many as twenty men worked on a single map to complete the engraving in half the time. Cartoons disappeared almost entirely during the Civil War and were not restored generally as a regular feature until the New York *World* revived the idea in the 1880's.

The most important single event of the war years was the performance of photography as a vital medium for recording news. The work of Matthew B. Brady in compiling a photographic history of the conflict remains one of the greatest achievements in the annals of photography. Although these photographs made a vivid record for posterity, the pictures had comparatively small circulation at the time. Very much as Currier & Ives lithographs had been sold to supplement the current news, prints and stereographs made from the Brady negatives were offered for sale to the general public.

Newspapers generally continued to regard illustrated news as something alien to their activities. However, the New York *Daily Graphic,* the first American daily to use illustrations regularly, appeared in 1873. The paper's existence was bedeviled by mechanical and financial difficulties arising from printing problems. Illustrations were black-and-white line drawings exclusively, for no practical process had been discovered to make possible reproduction of the intermediate tones found in photographs.

Stephen H. Horgan, a photographer in charge of the *Graphic's* engraving and mechanical equipment, made the experiments which led to the appearance of the first halftone photograph in an American newspaper. The *Graphic* printed the picture on March 14, 1880, but Horgan's successful employment of the screen process failed to clear the way for regular use of pictures generally.

When Joseph Pulitzer acquired the New York *World* in 1883 he transplanted the illustrated weekly technique to daily journalism. He engaged two artists and they depicted the day's important news in drawings. The pictorial departure had a magic effect on the *World's* circulation, but Pulitzer feared large use of pictures tended to lower the paper's dignity and he ordered the woodcuts gradually eliminated. The order was rescinded quickly when circulation declined proportionately.

The effect of Pulitzer's experiment attracted attention and other large papers imitated his methods. Stone borrowed a member of the *World's* mechanical force to help him introduce the idea in the Chicago *Daily News.* Victor Lawson saw a great future for such a news medium, but Stone was skeptical.

"Newspaper pictures are just a temporary fad," he remarked, "but we're going to get the benefit of the fad while it lasts."

The fad was far from temporary and before long many papers were printing black-and-white line drawings of important events. Photography meanwhile had made tremendous strides and by the end of the eighties action pictures were an established reality. Various difficulties, however, continued to delay the wide employment of the halftone process.

5

In theory there was little difference between the collection and distribution of news pictures and the collection and distribution of written news dispatches. The AP was in a position to gather news pictures as well as news, but the membership as a whole showed no great interest at first. The prevailing opinion seemed to be that news pictures, for some obscure reason, did not represent a proper field for the co-operative. Many publishers held to this view, even though they felt that news pictures were a necessity for their papers.

When a News Photo Service was first suggested at an annual meeting it was decisively voted down. The agitation continued. Most larger papers were indifferent, for they already had their own picture arrangements, but the smaller papers needed some sort of service. Commercial picture syndicates had entered the field and the news-picture situation had become similar to that governing the operations of the commercial feature syndicates. Prices were high and the attitude of the syndicates frequently was one of arrogance and independence.

Cooper wanted to extend the work of the co-operative to pictorial reporting. He saw that the news photo had scarcely begun to come into its own and he was convinced that there had been a change in the majority opinion that pictures were not properly a press association concern. More than anything else, he wanted to extend the non-profit co-operative principle into this increasingly important phase of news gathering.

"It is my feeling," he told the Board of Directors in 1926, "that The Associated Press should do anything that is a proper news activity —whether it be in pictures or in written news."

Nor was that all. He added:

"I visualize the day when we will be sending pictures over our own leased wire system, just as we now send the news."

That seemed much too visionary at the time, but the board agreed that a mail News Photo Service should be established. President Noyes saw the possibilities.

"We are going to recognize frankly," he said, "that the whole trend in newspaper work is toward making the picture a news medium.

There will be developments all along and we ought to be prepared to meet them."

It was with this view that the management approached the task of building up the AP News Photo Service as an integral part of the co-operative's broadened news-gathering activities.

III. LINDBERGH APPEARS

I

THE News pattern was spoiling for a change. Crime, scandal, and ballyhoo had been writing a lopsided amount of top news of the twenties.

The spring of 1927 produced one forceful demonstration of this popular preference in news. It was a story which came out of Paris—a story that in itself had a most unusual background and was destined to go down in any serious history of the times.

Smith Reavis, a member of the Paris staff, had a note on his datebook showing that April 6, 1927, was the tenth anniversary of America's entry into the World War. In charge of the news desk, it was his job to plan the daily report from the French capital. He noted the penciled memo a few days in advance and decided to try for a message of peace from Foreign Minister Aristide Briand for relay to member papers in the United States.

He sought out the foreign minister and outlined his conception of the sort of message that should appeal to the public of America. M. Briand listened and at length promised to prepare something.

Sitting at his desk on the morning of April 6, Reavis found the promised statement in his mail. He hurriedly scanned the message and came upon this significant paragraph:

"If there were need of it between the two great democracies [France and the United States] in order to give high testimony of their desire for peace and to furnish a solemn example to other peoples, France would be willing to enter into an engagement with America mutually outlawing war, to use your [Reavis's] way of expressing it."

The dispatch Reavis wrote that day was credited with laying the groundwork for the famous Kellogg-Briand Pact to outlaw war. But so preoccupied was the country that the story was little more than a lost chord in the whole blatant symphony of national interest. It found its way into State Department files, however, and months later President Coolidge started a series of representations which quickly developed the idea of a world-embracing peace treaty.

Though time proved it just another scrap of paper, virtually every civilized nation signed the pact that was evolved. Secretary of State Kellogg received the Nobel peace prize and the French government, in a book outlining the background of the treaty, officially gave the AP correspondent credit for the idea.

Reavis's story was big news, but at the time many people were reading about something else.

That "something else" was the sordid drama of the Snyder-Gray murder case—a crime which received greater space and display in American newspapers than the sinking of the *Titanic*. Hordes of curiosity seekers descended on Long Island City for the trial, and "special" writers turned the court proceedings into a Roman holiday. In this hippodrome atmosphere the co-operative's responsibility was to report the case as completely as its news value warranted and yet preserve the proper balance of decency. Brian Bell's handling of the trial, in which so much testimony was unprintable, brought praise from thinking editors.

2

The Snyder-Gray trial ended on May 9, but the news spotlight remained focused on Long Island. At Roosevelt Field two planes were awaiting favorable weather to take off in quest of the $25,000 prize which Raymond Orteig had offered back in 1919 for the first non-stop flight between New York and Paris. There was the *America* with Lieutenant Commander Richard E. Byrd and an expert crew. There was also the *Columbia* piloted by Clarence Chamberlin and Lloyd Bertaud.

Another story in the making, but no one seemed particularly excited about it.

Then suddenly things changed. On May 12 the *Spirit of St. Louis* flew in unheralded from the Pacific Coast. Charles A. Lindbergh was at the controls. No one had ever heard of him, his chances seemed slim, but there was something about him that captured the imagination of a public wearied by the tawdry series of sensations of recent years. Almost overnight he became the symbol of something new.

From that point on the story was "made." The uncertainty as to which plane would be the first to take off whetted popular interest. There was the spice of great danger. The French aces, Nungesser and Coli, had been lost on a Paris-New York flight for the Orteig prize. There was high adventure. And there was Lindbergh.

Bell and James MacDonald kept the vigil at Roosevelt Field.

There were days of rumors and reports, but weather conditions kept delaying the starts and heightening the suspense.

At dawn on May 20, Lindbergh glanced apprehensively at the water-splotched runway and studied the weather reports. Rain had been falling and there was a murky sky. It seemed a poor day to start, but reports said the unfavorable weather was only local in character. The flier was not long in making up his mind.

"This is the day," he said.

Five hundred people had waited through the night on the chance that one flier or another might take off. MacDonald and Bell were at Lindbergh's elbow as the tall flier prepared to climb into the cockpit. Commander Byrd arrived to wish his rival well.

"Good luck to you, old man," Byrd said. "I'll see you in Paris." The crowd milled round.

"Are you only taking five sandwiches?" someone asked.

"Yes," smiled the flier. "That's enough. If I get to Paris I won't need any more, and if I don't get to Paris I won't need any more, either."

At 7:52 A.M. Lindbergh lifted the *Spirit of St. Louis* into the air. In a hangar near the end of the runway Bell dictated the flash which went out over the wire. For tense seconds the fate of the flight hung in the balance. The plane, loaded with 458 gallons of gasoline, rose sluggishly, fighting for altitude. The crowd waited to see if the ship would be able to clear the string of telegraph wires which skirted the far edge of the field. Then there was a gasp of relief.

Bell stood beside his special wire describing the beginning of the flight:

```
        BULLETIN E.O.S NEW LEAD
ROOSEVELT FIELD, NEW YORK, MAY 20, AP - CHARLES
A. LINDBERGH COMMA QUOTE CAPTAIN UNQUOTE TO
THE MISSOURI NATIONAL GUARD COMMA BUT QUOTE
SLIM UNQUOTE TO HIS BUDDIES COMMA SET OUT TO
DAY ON AN UNMARKED AIR TRAIL FOR PARIS PERIOD.
```

MacDonald kept feeding Bell additional information. The dictation continued:

```
        ADD NEW LEAD LINDY
        THE MISSOURIAN COMMA WHO PLAYS A LONE
HAND COMMA HAD NO ONE TO SHOW HIM THE WAY AS
HE HURLED HIS RYAN MONOPLANE COMMA THE SPIRIT
OF ST. LOUIS COMMA INTO THE MUGGY AIR OVER
ROOSEVELT FIELD A FEW MINUTES BEFORE EIGHT
O'CLOCK THIS MORNING  EASTERN DAYLIGHT TIME
PERIOD.
```

MacDonald shouted:

"He's cleared the trees and is disappearing into the northeast!"
Bell's story flowed on.

```
       ADD NEW LEAD LINDY
       AT THE VERY LAST COMMA HIS PLANE COMMA
WEIGHTED BY A LOAD OF FIVE COMMA NAUGHT FIVE
FIVE POUNDS COMMA BARELY CLEARED A STRING OF
TELEGRAPH WIRES PERIOD A FEW SECONDS BEFORE IT
HAD ALMOST STRUCK A ROAD SCRAPER AS HE WAS
ATTEMPTING TO GET IT OFF THE GROUND PERIOD
PARAGRAPH THREE TIMES COMMA THE PLANE STRUCK
ROUGH SPOTS AND BOUNCED INTO THE AIR COMMA
ALWAYS COMING BACK TO EARTH AND FINALLY
STRAIGHTENING OUT PERIOD.
```

After 7:52 that morning Lindbergh was the only news the nation
wanted. The whole country was gripped by a common emotion.

In the New York office George Turner, the city editor, working
with W. W. Chaplin, logged the flight on a chart designed to show
hour by hour the plane's position if it kept to its course. Boston reported
the first stages of Lindbergh's progress as he headed north through
New England, and then The Canadian Press followed him up the
coast until he passed Newfoundland and headed out to sea.

The world waited in vain that night for some further word. In
the Yankee Stadium forty thousand boxing fans at the Sharkey-Maloney
fight rose in silence when Joe Humphreys, the veteran announcer,
asked prayers for Lindbergh.

A few hours later in the New York office Tom O'Neil, the early
report editor, was casting about for some fresh, vivid phrase that would
do justice to the flier who was somewhere out over the sea. Finally a
thought came to him and he typed out the words: ". . . the Lone
Eagle."

The second day wore on toward noon. Along the coast of Ireland
at thirty-six strategic points correspondents watched for the high-wing
monoplane bearing the license markings NX-211. Each man was
instructed to telephone London as soon as he sighted and positively
identified the *Spirit of St. Louis*. The precautions proved worth while.
When Lindbergh made landfall at Dingle Bay, County Kerry, Stephen
Williamson called London, and within minutes after the plane had
been sighted the leased wire network in the United States hummed with
the flash that Lindbergh was over Ireland.

The bulletins came faster after the *Spirit of St. Louis* passed over
Dingle Bay.

Lindbergh flying high over Plymouth, England . . . Lindbergh makes French coast at Bayeux . . . Lindbergh reported passing Cherbourg . . .

Then:

```
F-L-A-S-H

PARIS - LINDBERGH LANDED 5:21 P.M.
```

3

For Paris the Lindbergh story had begun days before the flier hopped off from Roosevelt Field, but most of the background never found its way into print. The loss of Nungesser and Coli on their Paris-New York flight on May 9 had shocked the French people. As hope for the rescue of the two popular aviators dwindled, the fantastic rumor began to circulate that they had been killed by Americans in order to keep them from stealing the glory from the fliers poised at Roosevelt Field. At first it was whispered by French housewives and servants as they did their marketing. Then it spread in ever-wider circles, stirring up an undertone of resentment and animosity. Parisians manifested an ugly feeling for American tourists and on one occasion a crowd forced the newspaper, *Le Matin*, to take down the United States flag displayed at the building.

In some quarters the temper reached such a pitch that it aroused Myron T. Herrick, United States ambassador to France. He feared for the safety of any American flier who might reach Paris. He telephoned the AP bureau and asked John Evans to cable a story so emphatic that it would arouse the government at Washington to cancel all permission for the projected flights.

Evans listened. He was familiar with the wild rumors and mention of them had already been made in the bureau's cable dispatches. An unqualified story of the type Herrick proposed, however, would violate service regulations. Evans offered to prepare a story quoting the ambassador's strong language, but Herrick seemed unwilling to commit himself that far. After discussion, he authorized a carefully guarded statement which failed to throw any new light on the situation.

At Le Bourget Flying Field outside of Paris, Evans and the six-man staff assigned to cover Lindbergh's arrival found Herrick's anxiety had not diminished since the telephone conversation a few days before. The ambassador was present ostensibly to greet Lindbergh, but Evans learned that he privately feared his real task would be to protect the flier from rough treatment at the hands of a hostile crowd.

Evans, however, had noticed a distinct change in popular feeling since Lindbergh headed out over the ocean from the North American continent. Little by little animosity gave way to grudging concessions of admiration and then to worried solicitude for Lindbergh's safety.

There was only a small knot of people at Le Bourget when Evans, Tom Topping, Hudson Hawley, Edward Angly, Sam Wader, and George Langelaan arrived in the afternoon, but by nightfall 25,000 were on hand. There was only one public telephone at the airdrome, but one of the men had been able to arrange for the use of a direct line from a private office in the administration building.

All the while Evans kept his fingers on the pulse of the waiting people, and the reports he got from the men he assigned to circulate among the throngs left no doubt in his mind as to the popular feeling. All hostility had disappeared. There was admiration now and genuine hope that nothing would stop the flier short of his goal.

Then the drone of a motor was heard. Landing lights flooded the field and once more the searchlight swept the sky, groping until it picked out a swift silver monoplane.

In an instant the plane disappeared from the searchlight's glare, but not before eyes caught the license markings—NX-211.

Lindbergh!

Evans flashed the word to Paris that Lindbergh was over Le Bourget and dictated two hundred words describing the scene. Then the telephone line suddenly went dead. The minutes that elapsed between the time Lindbergh was sighted and his landing were frantic for Evans. A tremendous story was breaking and his line of communication was gone. Luckily, the erratic telephone came to life again a few minutes later and Evans picked up with the flash of Lindbergh's landing and a running account of the frenzied welcome.

Lindbergh's New York-to-Paris flight ushered in a whole new cycle of news. The headlines belonged to aviation and there seemed no end to the stories. There was Byrd's flight to Ver-sur-Mer, France, and Chamberlin's long hop to Germany. Brock and Schlee, of Detroit, made a fifteen-stop air jaunt from Harbor Grace to Tokyo. Ruth Elder was rescued at sea near the Azores when her Paris-bound plane was forced down. In the Pacific, Maitland and Hegenberg flew nonstop from Oakland to Honolulu. The Frenchmen, Costes and Le Brix, spanned the South Atlantic to Brazil. There were altitude flights, endurance flights, speed flights, and stunt flights. The volume of aviation news carried on the leased wire system set a record that was not surpassed for years.

IV. "MORE MARGIN, MORE MARGIN!"

I

THE nation had reached the threshold of a fabulous era, but there was no hint of anything startling on August 2, 1927, when President Coolidge held his regular Tuesday press conference at Rapid City, South Dakota. The conferences had produced nothing noteworthy in the seven weeks the chief executive had been vacationing in the Black Hills.

Between occasional puffs on a long cigar, Coolidge discussed the threatened failure of the Arms Limitation Conference at Geneva, the encouraging business conditions, governmental problems, Walter Johnson's twentieth anniversary in baseball, and a number of other subjects.

"If the conference will reassemble at twelve o'clock I will have a statement," he concluded.

That announcement caused no stir. Francis M. Stephenson, the staff man assigned to Coolidge, thought the President probably had something to say which would be of interest to the financial world. There was a three-hour time difference between Rapid City and New York, so any Coolidge announcement at noon would not reach Wall Street until after the markets had closed at 3 P.M.

Promptly at noon Stephenson and his colleagues returned to the school building in which the President had set up summer headquarters. Coolidge waited for them in a classroom which served as his private office. In his right hand he held a bunch of paper slips.

"If you will pass in front of me," he told the reporters, "I will hand these to you."

The slips, Stephenson found, had been folded twice so that their message was not visible. He opened his and read it:

I DO NOT CHOOSE TO RUN FOR PRESIDENT IN NINE-TEEN-TWENTY-EIGHT.

There were exclamations of surprise. The question of Coolidge's standing for re-election had been discussed in some quarters, but without particular urgency because his term had a year and a half to go.

"Is there any other comment, Mr. President? Any amplification?"

Coolidge shook his head.

"None."

Stephenson dashed for his wire. The bulletin he sent touched off a rush of activity. There were "follows" from a score of cities. Washington reported that political leaders now regarded Secretary of Commerce Herbert Hoover as a leading contender for the Republican nomination in 1928. And in his California home Hoover cautiously told a staff man:

"It is too soon to discuss it. I must think over the President's announcement."

2

While the country speculated over the proper interpretation of the phrasing of the President's statement, W. E. Playfair of the Boston staff, the same man who had covered Coolidge the night Harding died, kept watch over a far more contentious story. It was the case of Nicola Sacco, the shoemaker, and Bartolommeo Vanzetti, the fish peddler. Playfair had been assigned to the story in 1920 when Sacco and Vanzetti were arrested on a charge of complicity in a fatal holdup. Then it was just another crime story, of little interest beyond New England. Killings in payroll holdups were not uncommon. Sacco and Vanzetti were convicted on a charge of murder and the long fight to save them from the electric chair saw their case become one of the most controversial and highly publicized in the history of American jurisprudence.

Playfair was at the State House in Boston early on August 3 Governor Alvan T. Fuller, who had conducted a final investigation of the case with a special advisory committee, had promised to give his decision during the day. Some expected that he would announce clemency, or even pardon. There was world-wide interest in the decision and on the floor above the Executive Offices the gallery of the Massachusetts House of Representatives had been converted into a pressroom

It was nine o'clock when Playfair took up his watch at the governor's offices. The day dragged along and night came. Still no announcement from the governor. More hours of waiting.

It was almost 11:30 when the governor's secretary, Herman Mac Donald, appeared with sealed envelopes containing the long-delayed decision. Playfair took one of the first and ran to the press gallery o the floor above. A telegrapher was ready.

F-L-A-S-H

BOSTON - GOVERNOR UPHOLDS SACCO-VANZETTI
DEATH SENTENCE.

The decision had world-wide repercussions. There were bombings in New York and Albany. The American flag was burned before consulates abroad. A protest strike was called in Czechoslovakia. Appeals for clemency poured into Boston. There were attempts to picket the State House. The men were to die at Charleston Prison at midnight of August 12.

Prison regulations limited the press to one representative at the execution—and that assignment had been given Playfair in 1921 when Sacco and Vanzetti were convicted. Ever since Massachusetts took executions from the hands of county sheriffs in 1901 and turned them over to the warden of the state prison, the warden's practice had been to invite an AP man to be the newspaper representative in the death chamber. The custom had the approval of the state's newspapers and the only condition the wardens imposed was that the AP man supply, without reservation, all the details of executions to other reporters assigned to the stories.

It was through Playfair's eyes that the whole world watched the condemned men go to the electric chair. But they did not die the night of August 12. At 11:12 P.M., less than an hour before the time set for the electrocutions, a circuit court judge intervened and a ten-day reprieve was ordered. The news reached the prison at 11:25, just as Playfair was about to start for the death chamber with Warden William Hendry.

The reprieve brought no relaxation of tension. The Sacco-Vanzetti defense organizations opened a new series of desperate legal efforts to save the two men. One by one their forlorn hopes shattered.

Playfair found Charlestown Prison a veritable fortress the night of August 22. All near-by streets were roped off, searchlights cut swaths through the darkness, tear gas and machine gun squads stood ready. An uneasy feeling pervaded the prison. The dispatches which had come into Boston that day were disquieting—street fighting in Paris and in Geneva bomb threats.

Warden Hendry ordered all newspapermen to be on hand by ten o'clock. For almost two hours there was nothing to do but wait in the Prison Officers' Club which had been converted into a press and wire room. All windows had been nailed down, and the room was stifling in the August heat. Then Playfair left with a guard for the death house.

Sacco was the first to go. He walked the seventeen steps from his cell to the chair in silence. As they strapped him in, he cried out in Italian: "Long live anarchy!" Then in broken English he spoke again:

"Farewell my wife and child and all my friends." There was a moment's silence. The executioner was ready. "Good evening, gentlemen," said Sacco. He was pronounced dead at 12:11 A.M.

A messenger brought Playfair's bulletin on Sacco's electrocution to the pressroom. It was for all the other reporters, as well as for the co-operative. In the death chamber Playfair was listening to Vanzetti's farewell words: "I wish to forgive some people for what they are now doing to me." Then it was all over.

3

The schoolroom at Rapid City and the death chamber at Charlestown Prison made news, but they did not indicate the fantastic days ahead. As conditions changed, the co-operative had to prepare itself better than ever to separate the wheat from the chaff. It was a difficult task because too frequently events that seemed legitimate news were more artificial than spontaneous, and already in one field the fabulous days had come.

One month after the Sacco-Vanzetti executions there occurred at Soldier Field, Chicago, an event quite unlike anything before. Some 150,000 persons paid in a gate of $2,650,000 to watch Gene Tunney and Jack Dempsey battle for the World Heavyweight Championship. At the ringside, the association had the largest staff ever assigned to a sports event—General Sports Editor Alan Gould and a dozen other sports and feature writers. Ten people died of excitement while listening to a radio broadcast of the fight, and for days thousands debated the pros and cons of a referee's decision allowing Tunney a "long count" because Dempsey had neglected to retire to a neutral corner after the knockdown.

Perhaps the so-called "golden age" of sports, with its hysterical following, its parade of heroes, and its incredible gate receipts, was a good advance indication of the dizzier golden age of prosperity which followed. At least it hinted at the strange psychological ferment at work.

In Wall Street during the autumn of 1927, although business generally appeared to be losing headway and the rediscount rate was lowered to assist agriculture and industry, the market developed a buoyant trend upward. Motor and radio stocks seemed to catch the public fancy. The AP Financial Service recorded the day-to-day fluctuations without comment or editorializing, letting the facts speak for

IT WAS THROUGH PLAYFAIR'S EYES THAT THE WHOLE WORLD WATCHED

themselves. By the closing months of the year the association's average for sixty selected issues on the New York Stock Exchange—a quick index of market conditions—stood in the vicinity of $70.

When the moderate rise began, the Wall Street Bureau was considered equal to any predictable emergency. Stanley Prenosil, financial editor, headed a staff of eight specialists, and George A. Wyville directed the work of the tabulators, checkers, and operators who prepared the quotations of the stock, bond, and other markets for transmission. Until late in 1927, three-million-share days on the New York Stock Exchange had been rarities, but as the market pushed higher that trading mark was passed and the Wall Street staff felt it was working under abnormal conditions.

"What," someone asked, "would ever happen with a four-million-share day?"

Nothing better demonstrated the absorbing public interest in industrial news than the debut of the new Model A Ford in December, 1927. During the months when Ford was developing the automobile which was to replace the old Model T, people devoured every rumor on the forthcoming car. So tremendous was the pressure that the news report carried a description of the new Ford and the price list as soon as the information was released.

. Under any other circumstances, such material would have been barred from the wires as advertising, but the strange alchemy of the times made it news of national interest. In New York an estimated one million people tried to get into a showroom for a glimpse of the automobile the day it was first displayed. In Detroit, Cleveland, Kansas City, and other cities police reserves were called out to control the crowds which fought to see the car.

4

By early 1928 papers considered stock market fluctuations an essential part of their news report. The general manager was urged to enlarge the size of the Wall Street staff and to develop further the entire financial and commodity market service. The Traffic Department wrestled with the problem of arranging wire facilities so that a heavier list of daily quotations could be delivered with a minimum of delay. Financial writers were assigned at Washington, Chicago, and San Francisco to supplement the Wall Street Bureau.

The new year brought scattered warnings that the market's advance was too swift. The news wires told of the $500,000,000 increase in brokers' loans, but from Washington came other stories quoting President Coolidge as saying that he saw "nothing unfavorable" in this enormous use of credit for "natural expansion of business."

There were 1,228 members receiving AP service as 1928 began. The leased wire web which linked them covered 160,000 miles, and an average of more than 300,000 words of news was written and delivered each twenty-four hours. The staff had increased 33 per cent in three years.

In the supplemental Feature and News Photo services there had been sustained progress. The Feature Service had been expanded to include a special budget in Spanish for Latin America. The Photo Service had started its own corps of photographers—Berk Payne, at Washington, and N. B. Harris, at New York, were the first two staff cameramen engaged—and news pictures were made available to the smaller members through inauguration of a matted news photo service.

If the management had one major problem in the general report, it arose from the welter of crime news, much of it linked with Prohibition. Advocates of the Eighteenth Amendment protested whenever the news showed Prohibition in an unfavorable light. Similarly, anti-prohibitionists grew angry every time they felt the case against Prohibition was not presented in the strongest possible way. Every questioned item was investigated as a matter of course and it was invariably established that the criticism came from those who felt that the story should have taken the side for which they stood.

All signs indicated that the problem of Prohibition and crime news would increase rather than lessen, and the approach of a presidential campaign served warning that the Prohibition issue would add to the difficulties in the heat preceding a national election.

The stock markets kept advancing claim to recognition as big news. Members of the Wall Street staff, who had wondered what a four-million-share day would be like, found out in March. Trading exceeded that amount and made Stock Exchange history. Brokers' loans continued to climb, and some papers which had ignored quotations in the past began to print the lists of stock prices to meet the public demand. Before the World War five hundred words a day had sufficed to describe gyrations on the Exchange. Now it was a dull day when the Wall Street Bureau produced less than five thousand words, and on "big days" the total climbed to eight and ten thousand.

The record of the first months of 1928 was as varied as any other period which the service had taken in stride. There were the Snyder-Gray electrocutions and the exile of Leon Trotsky from Russia. Sports fans discussed Heavyweight Champion Gene Tunney's interest in literature, music, and other fine arts, and the annual aviation fever began with the conquest of the North Atlantic by two Germans and an Irishman in the Junkers plane *Bremen*.

At the annual meeting of the co-operative that spring, the most important business was the unanimous action to arrange the voting power of the membership more equitably by a better distribution of the association's bonds. An additional bond issue was authorized so that all members might subscribe in proportion to the amounts they contributed in weekly assessments. The bonds carried voting privileges in election of directors. One of the reasons why an inequitable distribution had arisen was the fact that the Board of Directors had felt itself without authority to redistribute bonds held in the treasury after being redeemed because of membership consolidations or other reasons. Thus, until the change was voted, newly elected members were unable to participate in the bondholding privilege. As far as the actual operation of the co-operative was concerned, the change was largely technical in its effects and the administration continued along established lines.

5

The Republicans nominated Herbert Clark Hoover for president at Kansas City and the Democrats selected Alfred E. Smith in the June heat at Houston. At both conventions Byron Price, the chief of bureau at Washington, headed a specially chosen staff of seventy-five. As the campaign got under way, two men and one woman were assigned to each of the presidential nominees, and one reporter to each of the vice-presidential candidates.

It was not long before the usual criticisms and complaints began to reach Cooper from both sides. Republicans charged The AP either was purposely making Smith seem more interesting, or that the reporters assigned to his party were more able than those with Hoover. The critics were not mollified when it was pointed out to them that Smith talked freely with correspondents and permitted the use of question and answer quotations while Hoover imposed a strict regulation that nothing he said was to be quoted without specific permission. One member of the Board of Directors said of this type of criticism:

"It's the Republicans' fault if Smith is making more news and delivering more speeches."

In the heat of the campaign, however, the Smith adherents were just as vociferous as their Republican foes. They charged the co-operative with aiding Hoover's candidacy by reporting the slang Smith used or quoting his words and expressions when they were not polished. The whispering campaigns, the religious issue, the activities of the Ku Klux Klan, all contributed to the difficulties which attended a fair, accurate, and unbiased account of the contest.

The campaign ended November 5. The air rang with the slogans on the prosperity and Prohibition issues—with catchphrases such as "a chicken in every pot, two cars in every garage."

Thirty-six million Americans cast their votes and in New York on election night the Board of Directors room was transformed into a special election headquarters where a picked staff, working under the immediate supervision of Price and Assistant General Manager Elliott, tabulated the returns and prepared the election leads.

Cooper, studying the figures as they were brought to his office, was leafing through a fresh batch of returns when his door opened. Looking up, he was surprised to see the white-haired figure of Melville E. Stone.

"Well, I just couldn't stay away," the former general manager explained apologetically.

For a while the two men sat talking. Then Stone took his leave. He stood for a few minutes on the busy news floor and made his way to the board room where the election staff was hard at work. His entry passed almost unnoticed and he found a chair in the corner of the room. Elliott saw him and nodded a greeting. For a long time the old man watched the scene. Finally he motioned to Elliott.

"Isn't this beautiful, Elliott?" he exclaimed. "Here is the staff of The Associated Press doing the same work that has been done in our organization in preceding elections over a long period. The staff is made up of new blood, young men whose faces are new to me, and yet nothing is changed. It is just like every preceding election staff—an efficient group carrying on without fluster or bluster."

He studied the room again and nodded his head.

"No," he repeated, "nothing is changed, nothing is changed."

A few months later Stone died and messages of condolence poured in from the world's great and near great who had known him. He was buried in Washington Cathedral in the crypt set aside for the nation's distinguished dead. He had said he wished to be buried as a plain citizen, but the cathedral's trustees offered his family the privilege of having him entombed there, alongside the vaults of Woodrow Wilson and Admiral Dewey.

6

The Wall Street Bureau was the first to feel the effects of the Hoover landslide. Markets bounded upward at the opening bell on November 7 and stories of the broad advances competed for preference on leased wires already crowded with election material. The "prosperity bull market" had begun its spectacular career. Before the month ended, trading on the "big board" reached the unprecedented daily total of 6,900,000 shares, and transactions in other markets mounted accordingly.

It was only a beginning, but on December 1 the bureau's files showed how great the gains had been since the last day of trading in 1927. Montgomery Ward, which sold then at 119, had skyrocketed to 434. Radio had soared from 90 to 382, General Motors from 138 to 211, Wright Aeronautical from 81 to 263, Adams Express from 185 to 390. Other issues followed these bell-wethers with large gains. Brokers' loans, an index of speculation, exceeded $6,000,000,000, an increase of approximately $2,000,000,000 in the space of eleven months. Call money rates had climbed as high as 8 and 9 per cent.

Economists and Wall Street spokesmen told reporters that 1929 would be a most prosperous year. Financial analysts expatiated on the "new business cycle." Sports reported the death of Tex Rickard and the mass funeral service for him at Madison Square Garden, where his last "gate" was a big success. The Philadelphia Bureau reported that the National Association of Merchant Tailors, in convention assembled, gravely decreed that the well-dressed man should have at least twenty suits, a dozen hats, eight overcoats, and twenty-four pairs of shoes. And in her New York night club, Texas Guinan sounded one ironic keynote for the year when she hailed patrons with the rowdy greeting: "Hello, sucker!"

So the great news year of 1929 began. The foreign report told of Mahatma Gandhi's passive resistance campaign in India, the War Reparations Conference at Paris which was drafting the Young plan in an effort to remedy Germany's financial problems, and the signing of the Lateran Treaty at Rome, ending a half century of estrangement between the Vatican and the Italian government. The cable dispatches shared front pages with domestic stories of Anne Morrow's engagement to Colonel Lindbergh, Chicago's St. Valentine Day massacre, and the skyward progress of securities and commodity markets.

Through the spring and on into the summer the Wall Street Bureau chronicled the sustained advance of security prices. The booms of the past seemed insignificant by comparison. Public participation in the market had never been so tremendous. From the Atlantic to the Pacific, ticker tape quotations had become the symbols of sudden and easy wealth. Where once people had bought newspapers to read of politics, war, achievement, or disaster, now they looked first for the closing prices.

As the market soared upward, a handful of experts sounded stern warnings that the orgy of speculation was headed for disaster. These represented the other side of Wall Street's amazing story, and the report carried them just as it did the counter forecasts of bankers who saw boundless prosperity ahead.

The scattered warnings went unheeded. A few of the more vigorous ones caused the market to sell off—the Wall Street euphemism for such recessions was "technical reaction"—but they had no lasting effect. The market broke sharply in March when the unprecedented total of 8,246,740 shares were traded in one day and call money catapulted to 20 per cent. Recovery was swift, however, and prices soon poked back into higher levels. After that, public and professional confidence in the future of the market was stronger than ever. It survived a sinking spell in May, and then once more pushed upward resolutely to greater peaks.

On September 3, 1929, The AP average of sixty selected stocks reached an all-time high of $157.70, more than double the $70 level of late 1927. Sales that day were a mere 4,438,910 shares. By mid-September the co-operative's average began to drop and by October it was sliding several dollars a day. The Wall Street staff was unable to find any genuine alarm in brokerage circles. The slow decline was regarded as a repetition of the March break which the market had soon overcome. Brokers realized that the drop in prices was eating away the slim margin on which billions of dollars' worth of stocks were held, but the consensus was that the technical reaction could not possibly go much further. The report quoted their views.

On October 24—"Black Thursday"—a torrent of liquidation hit the market and hammered stocks down $5,000,000,000. One issue plummeted 96 points. The trading floor was a bedlam and tickers fell far behind transactions, adding to the confusion as the Wall Street Bureau

. . . BROKERAGE CLERKS DEMANDING, "MORE MARGIN, MORE MARGIN!"

struggled to keep abreast of the selling. Trading smashed all previous records with a total of 12,894,650 shares and it was nightfall before the last quotations were cleared on the special financial wires.

Five days later came the deluge which completely swamped wire facilities and all but engulfed the staff in its effort to report what was happening. Tickers were useless, grinding out prices which were hours behind actual trading. On the Stock Exchange transactions totaled 16,410,030. Curb sales exceeded 7,000,000. Out-of-town and foreign markets were demoralized.

The crash began as soon as the Stock Exchange opened on October 29 and it quickly became apparent that the regular Wall Street staff could not cope with the collapse. Claude A. Jagger, acting as financial editor, recruited reinforcements from the New York city staff and assigned them throughout the financial district. Men were stationed in the office of J. P. Morgan, in all the big banks and brokerage offices, with the regular members of the Wall Street staff working in key positions at the various markets. Jagger, a seasoned financial writer, did the main story of Wall Street's biggest day. He alone wrote 8,000 words before the day finished.

Those 8,000 words told the story of collapse which wiped out billions of dollars' worth of open market values and swept prices down in panic. They told of wild scenes on the Stock Exchange floor as huge blocks of stock were dumped on the market; of the tense, white-faced customers in board rooms watching paper fortunes melt away; of the solemn conferences of bankers and stock exchange officials; of the sober crowds which gathered in the streets of the financial district; of brokerage clerks at telephones demanding "More margin, more margin!"

V. INTO THE DEPRESSION

I

THE big story was a thousand stories. Some were columns long, some a few sentences. The date lines were legion. The basic subject matter was, monotonously unvaried—a deepening world-wide depression. The domestic report told recurrently of fresh lows in security and commodity prices, of tobogganing earnings, of bank closings, mounting unemployment and distress. The news by cable added other details—Europe's precarious financial condition, slackening of industry, the destruction of world markets, and the intricate problems of international indebtedness. Individually most of the dispatches had no surpassing significance; collectively their weight was staggering.

During 1930, as the world slid deeper into the economic morass, the report was studded with accounts of political unrest. In South America an epidemic of revolutions kept correspondents working under pressure and peril. When the Vargas rebellion broke out in Brazil, E. M. Castro of the Rio de Janeiro staff, raced through the bullet-splattered streets to flash the beginning of the insurrection. Paul Sanders, the bureau chief, was routed from his typewriter by a fusillade of shots which peppered the office walls. A zealous Boy Scout, intent on rescuing the Brazilian flag on the building, had climbed up past the office window in human-fly fashion, drawing the fire of a rebel detachment in the street. Censorship added to difficulties, as it had in Peru, the Argentine, and other South American countries.

Chief of Bureau Morris J. Harris at Shanghai had the upheaval of China's civil war to report, and in India there were the violent disorders of Gandhi's civil disobedience campaign for national autonomy. In Germany Hitler's National Socialist party made tremendous gains in the September election, becoming for the first time a powerful bloc in the Reichstag. There were reports of impending revolution. The uneasiness subsided after Chief of Bureau Lochner obtained from President von Hindenburg a statement affirming confidence in Germany's continued stability and discounting the possibilities of a radical dictatorship.

Although member papers were feeling the pinch of economic conditions—smaller publications had been complaining as early as the autumn of 1929—there was no suggestion that service be curtailed. The insistence was that the report be maintained unimpaired. This was particularly true of the financial service, even though the market collapse had robbed security and commodity prices of their 1929 circulation-building magic.

The daily ledger of the depression made a drab background, but the report had colorful contrasts. The most picturesque copy in many months came from Addis Ababa where Haile Selassie, "Conquering Lion of Judah, the Anointed of God, and the Lord of the World," was crowned Emperor of Ethiopia with barbaric ceremonials and splendor. The extraordinary coronation in Africa meant a change of scene for Jim Mills, roving correspondent of the Foreign Service. After five years in the Balkans, he had been sent to Moscow as chief of bureau in 1924 for a three-year tour of duty during which he covered all parts of the Soviet Union. Then he came back to Middle Europe, once more as chief of bureau at Vienna, with Austria, Czechoslovakia, Hungary, Yugoslavia, Albania, Greece, Bulgaria, and Rumania for his territory. During this period he secured interviews with King Constantine of Greece, King Boris of Bulgaria, King Alexander of Yugoslavia, Queen Marie and King Carol of Rumania, and King Zog of Albania. After two years in the post, he was reappointed to Moscow and was finishing his second year there when he was ordered to Africa for the coronation of Haile Selassie on November 2, 1930.

The ceremonies, which lasted a week, were an ordeal, even for a seasoned reporter like Mills. The rites began at four in the morning and the heat in the small, stuffy cathedral became unbearable as the day wore on. The air was foul with the smoke of mutton-fat candles, the nauseating odor of strange incense, and the overpowering stench of Ethiopians, greased from head to foot with rancid butter and animal fat. American and European guests needed surreptitious recourse to flasks of brandy in order to stand the torture. But Mills survived.

2

Early in 1931 the foreign report produced one of those teapot tempests which demonstrated the scrutiny to which dispatches were subjected by editors and public alike. The news was the address of Pope Pius XI during ceremonies dedicating the Vatican radio station, HVJ. An international hookup of 250 stations had been arranged to carry the Pontiff's message of peace and good will to all parts of the world.

Andrue Berding, the new bureau chief at Rome—Cortesi had just retired—was at the Vatican for the dedication and the papal broadcast. After the Pope had begun his talk, Berding hastened to the Vatican telegraph office with a copy of the speech. The Pope made his address in Latin, but the prepared copies were in Italian. Berding translated the text into English and filed it page by page at the telegraph office. Presently he came upon a Biblical quotation. There was no time to rush around the Vatican looking for a Bible, so without hesitation he translated the passage into simple, direct English.

The story did not end there, however. Soon Berding received a sheaf of letters from Catholics in the United States, saying, in effect: "You have made the Pope quote the Protestant version of the Bible!" Accompanying the letters was the general manager's request for an explanation. Embarrassed by the complaints the bureau chief checked on the Biblical passage the Pope had used. He consulted the Catholic version of the Bible, then the Protestant version. The critics were wrong. The quotation, as Berding had translated it, did not appear verbatim in either. It was his own version, and he wrote the general manager that he felt it was as good as either of the other renditions.

All this while the many-sided story of economic distress kept unfolding. The news was even gloomier than in 1930. Big corporations announced pay cuts, hunger marchers paraded, Treasury statistics showed an alarming increase in money hoarding, the army of unemployed grew larger, bank failures averaged almost a hundred a month, and the price of wheat in the Chicago grain pit sank to the lowest levels since 1896. From South America cables brought tidings of fresh revolutions. Madrid reported the overthrow of King Alphonso and the setting up of a Spanish republic. Dispatches from London, Berlin, Vienna, and other European centers set forth the unchecked development of the financial crisis which menaced the Old World.

On June 20, 1931, the report announced a proposal by President Hoover for a one-year moratorium on all payments of war reparations and intergovernmental debts—the administration's effort to avert a catastrophe, inevitable if financial collapse occurred in Germany and Central Europe. The next day Washington quoted Secretary of State Henry L. Stimson as saying a personal appeal from President von Hindenburg of Germany had figured importantly in Hoover's decision. The contents of Hindenburg's letter, however, were not disclosed. Hoover regarded them as confidential and all efforts to obtain the document proved unavailing.

Failing in Washington, the association turned to Berlin. Cooper cabled Lochner to secure the text of Hindenburg's appeal. Lochner afterward called the assignment the most difficult he had ever received.

He sounded out Foreign Minister Julius Curtius.

"As far as I am concerned," the Cabinet official said, "there is no objection to giving publicity to the letter. But the letter is addressed to President Hoover and international courtesy demands that your American President, rather than we, give it out. Besides, this is really a matter which, so far as Germany is concerned, only President von Hindenburg can decide."

Lochner went to the presidential palace, but got nothing there. After days more of trying, he gave up hope. He received instructions to accompany Chancellor Heinrich Bruening and Foreign Minister Curtius to London for the Seven-Power Conference on the financial woes of Europe.

The departure for London was only three hours distant when Lochner met a government official just back from vacation. There were a few words of greeting, and then the official said enthusiastically:

"That was certainly a great message your President Hoover addressed to the world on the moratorium. I read about it when on leave, but now I must find out just how it came about."

Lochner listened with a poker face.

"By the way," he interposed idly, "I have never seen President von Hindenburg's appeal to Hoover published anywhere, yet I understand it is a deeply moving document. Can't you have a copy made and send it to me at London? It seems to me your president should get some credit for the part he played."

To Lochner's joy, the German did not summarily reject the idea.

"I'd rather not send you the text direct because it might be misconstrued," the official said. "I'll simply address an envelope to your wife here in Berlin, and when she opens it she will find the text."

Several nights later Lochner was at a typewriter in the London Bureau tapping out his story on the progress of the Seven-Power Conference. The telephone operator told him Berlin was calling.

It was Mrs. Lochner with the 500-word German text of President von Hindenburg's letter.

Quitting London with the German delegation two days later, Lochner picked up an English newspaper. It carried a dispatch from New York saying The AP had succeeded in obtaining for exclusive publication the text of President von Hindenburg's letter to President

Hoover. The paper reprinted most of the message. Mischievously, Lochner passed the paper over to Curtius and indicated the article.

"Herr Reichminister," he said in tones of injured innocence, "that's what happens when you and I leave the country!"

In spite of the Hoover moratorium, Europe's economic condition failed to improve. Germany's difficulties became so acute that the government was forced to close all stock exchanges and banks. Heavy withdrawals of gold from London by frightened Swiss, Dutch, and Belgian bankers impaired England's financial stability, and on September 21, 1931, the country abandoned the gold standard. The cables were heavy with the story and its international repercussions.

3

Because of its sheer magnitude, its endless ramifications and baffling complexity, the depression produced no one dominant figure who dramatized the tremendous story. It was another field of events which gave the report one of the period's most vivid personalities—Mahatma Gandhi. The graphic dispatches of Jim Mills, who had gone to India from Africa, were in part responsible.

Mills managed to win the confidence and respect of the homely little 62-year-old Hindu. It was his reportorial treatment of Gandhi as an intensely appealing human character, rather than as a fanatic or freak, that won the holy man's trust. Gandhi informed him in advance of every move he planned to make, and the co-operative was able to supply its members with prompt and complete coverage on all important developments in India's struggle for independence.

Mills traveled throughout India with Gandhi, reporting the progress of the civil disobedience movement, riots, and bloodshed. When Gandhi went to London in September, 1931, for the India Round Table Conference, Mills went with him. The conference failed and Mills was forewarned that Gandhi's return to India would be the signal for a spirited resumption of the civil disobedience campaign.

The British authorities in India moved swiftly to meet the new challenge and on January 3, 1932, Gandhi confided to Mills that he expected to be arrested again. Seated at a spinning wheel in the tattered tent he had pitched on the roof of a Bombay tenement, Gandhi predicted that a reign of terror would follow his imprisonment.

Jim Mills was there when the police arrived at three o'clock the next morning.

"They are coming! They are coming!" the leader's disciples cried.

Gandhi, roused from sleep, was told the police were outside. "Usher them in," he said sleepily. "They are welcome."

A few minutes later the Mahatma repaired to another part of the roof where he prayed silently with his followers and wrote a few notes of farewell. Then, spying Mills, he motioned him to approach.

"I do not know when, or whether ever, I shall see you again," he said in a low voice. "The Associated Press has reported the political situation in India as no other news organization in the world has covered it. Therefore, on the threshold of prison, I give you and The Associated Press a farewell message. It may be that I shall die in prison. It may be I shall never see you again. Therefore, I want to thank you and The Associated Press for the thorough and impartial way in which you have always reported my activities and the progress of the Indian Nationalist movement.

"I hope that after I am gone The Associated Press will continue to inform the American people of the exact situation in India, telling them what we as Indian Nationalists are trying to do to emancipate India. But at the same time I would ask you to do the fullest justice to the British side of the controversy. For I do not wish to hurt as much as a hair on any English head."

With that, Gandhi placed himself in the hands of the police who whisked him by automobile to the Yeroda Prison at Poona, seventy-five miles away.

On this occasion, while the events of an outside world crowded one on the other, the Mahatma remained in jail for months. There was great secrecy when he was unexpectedly given his freedom. To avoid attention the release was effected after midnight and Gandhi, with his pots, pans, and goat's milk, was taken by car to a distant railroad station. He reached the platform, squatted down, and pulled his clattering possessions about him. Peering into the darkness, he discerned someone approaching. With a toothless smile, he recognized a familiar figure.

"I suppose," said he, shaking his head in mock resignation, "when I go to the Hereafter and stand at the Golden Gate, the first person I shall meet will be a correspondent of The Associated Press."

4

To the general public the news-gathering activities of The AP at any given time represented the sum total of its operations. Outside of journalistic circles, few knew in 1932 that the Board of Directors and the management faced an acute administrative problem which directly involved continued news gathering. Two years of depression had sharply reduced the financial resources of the member papers, and the member papers defrayed the cost of the entire service. Some had been forced to suspend publication, a few had consolidated, and a number were barely able to meet their weekly share of the association's expenses. The board and the general manager were fully aware of the distress and knew the papers looked to them to do everything possible to ameliorate the situation. The gravity of matters could not be exaggerated. Unless members were able to meet their weekly assessments, the association would not have sufficient funds for news operations, and hundreds of employes would be without jobs.

One publisher, thinking to be helpful, approached the general manager with a suggestion for a flat 20 per cent reduction in all assessments. It required a lot of explanation to convince him there was no such easy short cut to a lightening of the financial burden.

In the first place, the member learned, more than 60 per cent of all the association's expenses went for domestic wire charges. Of that amount, at least half was obligated under unexpired contracts and could not be touched. The remaining wire costs could be slashed to effect the desired assessment decrease, but this would entail an arbitrary curtailment of the leased network.

The next major budget item was the 20 per cent spent on the Foreign Service and incoming news. Here again, the member found himself unwilling to urge retrenchment. He knew that if the co-operative diminished the outlay for the foreign service it would jeopardize its position in that field. Similarly, if the reductions were made at the cost of national and state news, papers might get slightly lower assessments but, on the other hand, they would be forced to spend several times the amount saved to supplement an incomplete report.

The only other sizable item on the balance sheet was 11 per cent for salaries and all administrative and office expenses. Obviously not even a 10 per cent assessment reduction was possible here, without virtually wiping out all payroll, office maintenance, and administrative costs. During the discussion on the subject of salary cuts, it was pointed out to the member that if all salaries in the service were reduced 20 per cent, the decrease would range from 10 cents weekly in small places to $10 or $15 in the largest cities.

The publisher who came to New York to suggest an easy way to lower assessments was a much better informed man when he left. As far as he could see, the books held no promise of any major savings. For the first time, he appreciated the tremendous problem with which the board and the general manager were grappling.

After a study of the problem, the Board of Directors delegated General Manager Cooper to devise, if possible, a retrenchment program which would permit a minimum monthly refund of 10 per cent on assessments. The assignment was the most formidable administrative task Cooper had undertaken since 1912 when he turned a threatened deficit of $50,000 into a $100,000 saving.

No department, domestic or foreign, escaped scrutiny in the search for economies. Wherever possible, transmission facilities were realigned or rerouted so that each mile of wire delivered the maximum of service and linked as many papers as practicable. This was a start.

The greater portion of transmission savings, however, came from the duplexing of existing wire circuits. Duplexing was a communications development whereby one wire could carry two sets of signals simultaneously, without interference. This, in effect, made one wire do the work of two, for the impulses which actuated either Morkrum printers or Morse sounders were transmitted in separate harmonic channels, rendering the wire, for practical purposes, almost the equivalent of a double circuit. This increased the cost of each wire, but the amount involved was less than the price of two outright wires.

Quite apart from the immediate retrenchments realized, the thoroughgoing survey of wires and transmission equipment led to one development of long-range value. W. J. McCambridge, a man who had come up from the ranks to become chief of the Traffic Department in 1928, got to thinking of the advantages a research and experimental laboratory might yield. The more he considered the idea the more it impressed him. The possibilities, he saw, were endless. In all likelihood, a laboratory could work out a number of mechanical refinements to meet the present need for economies. McCambridge knew how pressing that need was. Equally important, however, was the fact that the cooperative would have a unit constantly seeking to invent and perfect equipment for the future.

McCambridge had no trouble in getting approval for his idea. His department contained many men of high scientific and technical ability, and from among them he recruited the nucleus of an able laboratory staff. Laboratory enterprise on the part of a press association was something quite novel, yet the experiment attracted scant attention.

The economy hunt went on. An additional necessary saving was effected by a 10 per cent reduction in the salaries of the entire personnel. Cooper authorized the cuts reluctantly. He always had thought staff salaries were lower than he would like to have them, and only the emergency compelled his consent to a decrease in the existing scale. It was the only reduction ordered during the whole depression period. Cooper, incidentally, was the first to have his salary reduced. Before directing action on the staff payroll, the Board of Directors reduced the general manager's salary by a like percentage.

Further decreases in operating costs were worked out by a one-year postponement of the annual allotments to the Emergency Reserve Fund, the Employes Benefit Fund, and the fund set aside for amortization of telegraphic and traffic equipment. All three reserves were in sound financial condition and payments could be suspended temporarily. Economies ran from pencils, paste, paper clips, and paper towels up to bigger items. Typewriters which ordinarily would have been replaced were made to last a little longer. Office furniture which had seen its best days continued to do duty. Telephone and telegraph tolls were watched relentlessly and even the outlays for postage were challenged.

The program was helped by a sizable personal contribution from President Noyes. For several years it had been the custom of the board to vote him annually an honorarium of $10,000 in appreciation of the amount of time and money he spent in discharging his duties as the unsalaried head of the co-operative. From 1932 on Noyes declined the award.

Member newspapers received the benefits of the economies in two ways. Assessments generally were adjusted downward—although in most cases the 1930 census figures actually called for increases—and, retroactive to January 1, 1932, a part of these lowered assessments was returned to members in regular weekly refunds.

In the first thirty-three months of the emergency budget's operation, the membership received $1,391,066.78 in cash refunds and $1,184,220.48 in outright assessment reductions.

The emergency depression measures wisely did not ignore adequate provisions for the association's expansion and growth. Arrangement was made for the continued support of two new subsidiaries—The Associated Press of Great Britain and The Associated Press of Germany—news and photo organizations which had been set up abroad in 1930.

In spite of the steps that had been taken, some members were unable to weather the economic collapse. Others found it necessary to substitute pony reports for leased wire service.

The big story that was a thousand stories went on through the months and the dispatches kept adding somber footnotes.

Unemployed demonstrators converge on Washington . . . Farmers' Holiday movement spreads . . . Bankruptcies . . . "Frozen" credits . . . Currency hoarding . . . Depression . . .

VI. KIDNAP

I

IN THE Newark Bureau it was the quietest night in months. Against one wall a battery of four Morkrums droned along. The last top items of news had been cleared on the New Jersey wires much earlier. The best story in the report seemed to be the by-lined account of Morris J. Harris on the fierce fighting at Shanghai in the undeclared Sino-Japanese War. The state budget offered nothing better than a fire at Pennsgrove.

At the filing editor's desk, Gregory Hewlett sifted through a thin pile of secondary material edited for relay on the double circuit which served the state's morning papers. At the state news desk, the night editor, W. A. Kinney, relaxed in his chair. His desk was clear, all the night report stories were up, and the few early report items had been written. Dull nights like this were few and far between.

The Morse wire clicked off a message. Hewlett read it and pushed it across the news desk.

"The nightly Lindbergh rumor," he announced.

Kinney glanced at the message. It was from the Atlantic City *Press*.

"Hear Lindbergh in accident near Hopewell," it read. "Anything?"

The night editor did not bother to comment. Ever since Colonel Lindbergh had taken up residence in the state, the bureau had been plagued with requests to check reports that this or that had happened to the famous flier. After two years of that, another query did not cause a great stir. Lindbergh's unlisted telephone number was in the card index —as a matter of fact, it was only within the past week that the number of his new estate at Hopewell had been substituted for a temporary Princeton one—but the office order was that the colonel must not be bothered in checking such reports. The telephone number was for extraordinary emergencies only, and there never had been occasion to use it.

The time was almost 10:40. The Morse operator, George Williamson, copied down another message and passed it to the filing editor.

"Here's another one," Hewlett called over to Kinney, now on his way to the telephone booth which shut out the drumming noise of the

364

Morkrums. "Paterson wants to know if there's anything to Lindbergh being in a crash somewhere."

The night editor went into the telephone booth and picked up the receiver.

"Market 2-5400," he told the operator.

That was Newark Police Headquarters. If anything important was happening in the state, they invariably knew it there quickly.

Headquarters listened patiently.

"No. Nothing tonight. Switch you to the teletype room, but if they had anything we'd know before this. Hold on."

The teletype room, where police communications were received, had no information.

"The only State Police stuff we've had in the last hour has been routine—stolen cars and a few alarm cancellations. They'd have had anything like that before this. Yes, a couple more phonies, I guess . . . Wait, there's something starting to come in on the State Police printer now."

Then the detective's voice exploded in Kinney's ear.

"My God! Listen, AP! Here's the State Police alarm. The Lindbergh baby's been kidnaped!"

The editor listened as the detective read the text of the alarm and then bolted out of the booth. Pulling up a typewriter, he yelled at the top of his voice.

"Bulletin!"

He didn't think of a flash. Just get the news out. A straightaway bulletin. Hang it right on the State Police flier.

The typewriter banged out the words:

```
BULLETIN
     NEWARK, N. J., MARCH 1 - (AP) - THE
STATE POLICE TONIGHT BROADCAST THE FOLLOWING
TELETYPE ALARM:
     "COLONEL LINDBERGH'S BABY WAS KIDNAPED
FROM LINDBERGH HOME IN HOPEWELL, N. J., SOME
TIME BETWEEN 7:30 AND 10:00 P.M. THIS DATE.
BABY IS 19 MONTHS OLD AND A BOY.  IS DRESSED
IN SLEEPING SUIT.  REQUEST THAT ALL CARS BE
INVESTIGATED BY POLICE PATROLS."
```

Hewlett ripped the paper out of the machine as soon as the last typebar hit, and Kinney darted back into the telephone booth, fumbling hurriedly through the card index for Lindbergh's private number. In a moment Hewlett joined him, and sat down at the other telephone.

"I'll get after Breckinridge and Hopewell police," he said.

When Kinney finally got through to the Lindbergh home, he heard a voice filled with both hope and anxiety. He recognized it immediately. He had covered Lindbergh on numerous assignments before.

"Colonel Lindbergh, this is The Associated Press in Newark. We hesitate to bother you at such a moment, but we've just received the State Police alarm that your son has been kidnaped."

The colonel interrupted.

"I have no statement to make at this time," he said.

He didn't say it the unworried way the editor had heard him say it often before at the airport. There was time for only a few other quick questions before the conversation ended, but by then the Newark editor was convinced the kidnaping report was true.

Hewlett called Colonel Lindbergh's attorney, Henry Breckinridge, and got positive confirmation of the story. Then the Hopewell police were reached. An officer had been sent up to the remote white house in the gloomy Sourlands, but until they heard from him there was no further information.

Hammering away at typewriters, the two men pieced out the story as fast as they could.

As the story began to roll, Newark raised the other New Jersey bureau, in the State House at Trenton, so that staff men there could be started for Hopewell, which was much nearer that city than Newark.

In Trenton Sam Blackman hustled over to State Police headquarters. The lieutenant on duty told him that Colonel Lindbergh personally had called in the report of the kidnaping, but that was all they knew. Troopers already were at the estate in the Sourlands. Blackman started for Hopewell with Frank Jamieson, the correspondent in charge at Trenton. Jim Lawrence was assigned to the police headquarters and W. F. Carter manned the State House Bureau so that the men could relay their news through Trenton in case Newark's telephones were busy.

To know that Jamieson and Blackman were racing toward Hopewell gave a lift to the men in Newark, but it might be an hour before the first word was received from them.

Hewlett remembered a young woman who happened to be a friend of Anne Lindbergh's sister. Maybe she had heard something. The call woke her. Hewlett started to tell her.

"Oh," she exclaimed, "and Anne is expecting another baby!"

Things like that kept happening.

Another try at the Lindbergh telephone number produced a quickly interrupted few words with the state trooper who answered, but the brief seconds developed that an unspecified ransom had been asked, and a note found.

Newark then called the estate of Mrs. Lindbergh's mother at Englewood and told Mrs. Morrow that The AP felt it might be helpful in the search for the stolen baby if she would supply a description of the child for immediate nation-wide distribution. She agreed and expressed her thanks for the suggestion.

2

The Lindbergh house in the Sourland mountains was a difficult place to find that dark, blustery March night, but Jamieson and Blackman had the experience of two previous trips over the winding, bumpy road. They had written stories of the flier's isolated estate before he took up residence.

Whateley, the butler, answered the door. He recognized Blackman but the smile of other visits was gone.

"What about the baby being kidnaped?" Blackman asked.

"All we know," the servant said sadly, "is that the baby isn't here. Colonel Lindbergh is out on the grounds, but you can come in and wait."

Jamieson went off in search of the police. Blackman started back toward Hopewell looking for a telephone. By the entrance to the Lindbergh estate, about a half mile from the house, he found the home of a baker. None too happy at being roused from bed at midnight, the man grumblingly permitted the use of his party-line telephone. Blackman talked to Newark—Whateley's few words proved to be the first positive statement obtained from a member of the Lindbergh household—and then started back up the dark muddy lane.

From the blackness of the estate's entrance four figures emerged.

"Are you troopers?" Blackman hailed.

A tall, hatless man answered him.

"I'm Colonel Lindbergh."

"I'm Blackman of The AP."

The aviator shook his head.

"I'm sorry, Blackman, but I can't say anything now."

Accompanied by two of the troopers, Lindbergh strode on up the lane toward the house. Blinking flashlights marked the progress of the three men. Then the reporter became aware that one trooper had remained near the gatehouse.

"Let's see your police card," the officer asked.

His electric torch flickered briefly as he examined the credential. Then he flashed it for a moment on Blackman's face.

"O.K., AP, I'll tell you the story, but you don't know where you got it."

While Blackman scribbled notes, the trooper told what had happened, filling in numerous gaps in the story which Newark had so quickly assembled by telephone.

He told how Betty Gow, the nurse, had found the child's crib empty at ten o'clock. He told of the discovery of the $50,000 ransom note and its cryptic signature, of the mud tracks on the nursery floor, of the footmarks in the soft earth below the window, and of the three-piece wooden ladder and the chisel which had been abandoned near the house.

Blackman sprinted back to the baker's house. He told his story over the telephone to Newark where the two men, working in relays, rushed a New Lead onto the wires with Blackman's by-line. It was not until two hours later that the State Police held a press conference at which some of the details of the kidnaping were disclosed.

3

Overnight, Hopewell, a quiet country town, became the news center of the world. The shocking story aroused universal anxiety and horror, not only in the United States but in foreign countries. To cover developments at the scene, the co-operative assembled a special staff. New Jersey contributed Jamieson, Blackman, Lawrence, and Kinney. New York sent Robert Cavagnaro, Morris Watson, Lorena Hickok, and Katherine Beebe, as well as cameramen Joe Caneva, Tom Sande, and Walter Durkin.

In reality, those at Hopewell represented only a small portion of the news force which had a part in the story. No one knew in what part of the country, or even in what part of the world, the next "break" might occur. Every staff man considered himself assigned to run down any lead which might have a bearing on the case. Hundreds of date lines supplemented the stories from Hopewell. There were dispatches on the reaction of foreign capitals, on official activity in Washington, on

WHILE BLACKMAN SCRIBBLED NOTES, THE TROOPER TOLD WHAT HAPPENED.

police operations in a score of cities, and on the epidemic of crank "clues" which began almost immediately.

At Hopewell it soon became apparent that the story would be extremely difficult to cover accurately and promptly. State Police surrounded their activities with secrecy. Silence shrouded every development detectives thought important. The police issued official communiqués from time to time, but the information was carefully selected and usually dealt with exploded clues or secondary detective work.

For every line of news written there were hours of wearisome, unproductive digging. Men were kept on duty at the gatehouse of the estate, watching the mysterious goings and comings of uncommunicative officers. Endless time was spent on hopeful amateur detective work in the vicinity. And there were the frequent wild rides over back roads at breakneck speed to run down "hot tips" which never survived investigation.

But there was real news somewhere behind the barriers which police had raised, and the job was to get that news for the report. The New Jersey members of the staff had numerous contacts because of their service in the state and these were quietly canvassed in the hope that some reliable channel of information could be found.

Correspondent Jamieson in particular had built up a long list of confidential news sources during many years of reporting governmental and political activities. Enlisting the co-operation of an official not connected with the state government, he ultimately was able to improvise a roundabout but effective and trustworthy way of learning what was happening behind the scenes.

He reported the receipt of additional ransom notes, the entrance of Dr. John F. ("Jafsie") Condon as an intermediary in negotiations with the kidnaper and Colonel Lindbergh's personal activities in the hunt for his stolen son. His sources of information varied, and the news might come at any hour of the day or night. To protect the identity of his sources, Jamieson was forced to take every precaution. He used out-of-the-way telephones, arranged for hurried meetings in hotel rooms, and engineered "casual" encounters in places where conversations could not be overheard.

4

In spite of the most intensive man hunt in police history, days passed without recovery of the baby or the apprehension of the kidnaper. There was a flurry of activity when the $50,000 ransom was paid at St. Raymond's Cemetery in the Bronx the night of April 2, 1932, and when Colonel Lindbergh searched in vain off the Massachusetts coast by air for the boat on which the baby was said to be held. The failure to recover the child turned Lindbergh to John Hughes Curtis, the Virginia boatbuilder who claimed to have been in contact with a band of kidnapers. Confidential information from police sources had led the staff at Trenton to doubt the veracity of his stories, but events in the kidnaping had been so unpredictable that anything might happen. The boatbuilder's movements were watched as closely as possible.

Another month passed with its series of perfunctory police communiqués and occasional alarms. The story had become almost routine when the air suddenly became tense again with a new epidemic of reports that an important "break" might soon occur. Colonel Lindbergh, with Curtis, was on a yacht off the New Jersey coast, combing the sea for the vessel on which the Virginian said the baby would be found.

At the State House in Trenton, May 12 droned along uneventfully until late in the afternoon. Then without warning Lieutenant Walter Coughlin, the press liaison officer of the investigation, announced that Colonel H. Norman Schwarzkopf, superintendent of the State Police, wanted all newspapermen covering the story to be at the Lindbergh estate in an hour. No reason was given for the abrupt summons but everyone felt it meant an announcement of exceptional importance.

It was after five o'clock and Jamieson decided on a course of action.

"Sam," he instructed Blackman, "you go on down to Hopewell. I'm going to try to get Governor Moore. If anything big is doing, Moore will know about it. I'll get down to Hopewell then as quickly as I can."

Blackman remembered that the nearest telephone to the Lindbergh estate was in the house of the baker he had routed out of bed the night the baby was stolen. The man worked in Trenton, so Blackman called him at the bakeshop and arranged to hire his telephone at Hopewell for as long as necessary. That done, he started over the familiar road to Sourland Mountains. At the baker's house he stopped and telephoned New York, explaining the desirability of keeping an open line in readiness for whatever Schwarzkopf's press conference might produce. New York put a member of the local staff on the wire to chat with the baker's wife and read her news items so that the line would be kept busy until needed. With the nearest line of communication assured, Blackman continued up the lane to the Lindbergh estate. The State

Police headquarters had been set up in the garage and correspondents were already gathering there.

Back in Trenton, Jamieson had no immediate success in his efforts to reach Moore. The governor was motoring to his home in Jersey City, some fifty miles away. The governor's own office seemed to guarantee the greatest privacy, so Jamieson sat down there and started telephoning. He tried to get the governor in Jersey City but without success. Instructing the operator to keep trying until she reached the governor, he called several private sources that might conceivably have an inkling of what was behind the summoning of reporters to the Lindbergh estate. No one knew.

The minutes ticked by in the quiet office. Jamieson sat and waited. The governor was his only hope. If Moore did not reach Jersey City soon, Jamieson would never be able to get to Hopewell for Schwarzkopf's conference. The telephone rang.

"On your call to Jersey City," the operator said, "we are ready."

"Hello, governor," Jamieson began in his cheery way, "this is Frank Jamieson."

"Yes, Frank, what's on your mind?"

"Governor, has there been any big development in the Lindbergh case? Colonel Schwarzkopf has called all the boys to the Lindbergh estate for a press conference within the next hour and it makes us think he has something important to say."

"I haven't heard of anything, Frank," Moore answered. "Up until the time I left the State House there was no indication anything exceptional had happened or would happen."

Jamieson knew the governor had followed the case with intense interest. He suggested:

"Couldn't you get in touch with Colonel Schwarzkopf and find out?"

"I'll do that immediately," Moore said.

"And, governor," Jamieson asked, "will you call me right back if it's anything? I'm phoning from your office."

"I'll call you right back," Moore promised.

As soon as Moore hung up, Jamieson picked up a second telephone and put in a call for New York.

Hastily sketching the situation, he said:

"I don't know what's coming, but it might be big. We'll keep this line open, so when the governor calls back on the other phone, I can shoot you the stuff without delay."

More minutes of waiting. Then the other telephone jangled. It was 6:10 P.M.

"Hello! Hello!"

"Hello, Frank? This is Governor Moore. It's horrible news. The Lindbergh baby has been found dead—"

Jamieson shouted:

"Hold it, governor, hold it!"

Snatching up the other telephone, he fired the words over the open line to New York.

F-L-A-S-H

LINDBERGH BABY FOUND DEAD.

Back on the governor's telephone, he heard Moore, obviously affected, relate all he had learned of the finding of the body that afternoon in a thicket just off the Hopewell-Princeton highway, only five miles from the Lindbergh home. The correspondent halted him occasionally in order to relay the details to New York over the other line.

Once the conversation had ended and the last facts were repeated to New York, Jamieson tumbled into a taxi for a mad ride to get to Hopewell in time for the press conference.

In the garage on the Lindbergh estate the temporary press headquarters buzzed with speculation on the nature of the information Schwarzkopf had to reveal, and a half a mile away near the estate entrance the baker's wife sat listening to news items still being read to her over the telephone line Blackman had opened to New York.

Jamieson arrived just in time to get into the garage before the doors were closed. He greeted acquaintances with a disarming smile as if nothing had happened.

After the garage doors had been locked, Colonel Schwarzkopf explained that he had ordered the action because he wanted no newspapermen to leave the building until he had concluded his announcement. Then at 6:45 P.M. he began a lengthy statement. The State Police superintendent read slowly, pausing to make sure reporters had time to copy the words verbatim.

And all the while from New York to California, the presses of member papers were already rolling, and the flood of extras was hitting the streets.

When the garage doors were flung open, there was a pell-mell scramble for the nearest telephone. But the nearest telephone was at the baker's house, and Blackman had tied it up an hour earlier. Not only that, it was on a party line and as long as it was busy other telephones in the vicinity could not be used. Jamieson and Blackman alternated, dictating Schwarzkopf's official statement.

A few rivals later reproached Governor Moore for giving Jamieson the news. Moore reminded them that the AP correspondent was the only one to get in touch with him in quest of the information, and that there had been nothing to prevent others from making a similar effort. "He caught the train," the governor said. "The others stood waiting on the platform and let it go by."

Jamieson's work throughout the eleven-week search for the stolen child won him the Pulitzer prize for the outstanding example of domestic reporting in 1932.

After the finding of the murdered child, John Hughes Curtis was indicted for obstructing justice by his tale of negotiations with an imaginary gang of kidnapers. Lawrence and Kinney reported his trial and conviction at Flemington the last week in June, and the first full chapter of the bewildering Lindbergh kidnaping mystery reach its conclusion. The crime was the first of a series of spectacular kidnapings which scourged the country through the early thirties. But no one forgot Hopewell. There was always the chance that sometime, somewhere the Lindbergh case might break open again with the capture of the kidnaper.

VII. ANOTHER ROOSEVELT

I

AT ALMOST any other time the news of the smashing Japanese advance into the Jehol province of Manchuria would have been the dominant story in the report. For days Jim Mills followed the Mikado's legions on the unsheltered top of an ammunition truck—the best transportation he could wheedle from the army. He lived on hardtack and melted snow except when bitter tea was obtainable at dirty Chinese inns. An occasional rear-bound truck or airplane was his only means of communication, and many of his stories were lost entirely, probably thrown away by negligent couriers. Nevertheless, Mills plowed on through to Jehol City to write of the final phases of the campaign.

The conquest of Jehol, however, was all but eclipsed by the succession of grave domestic events which filled the report through February, 1933.

From the Detroit Bureau: Michigan declares an eight-day bank holiday.

From Baltimore: Maryland banks closed for three days.

From St. Paul: Minnesota places two-month ban on mortgage foreclosures.

From Pennsylvania, Ohio, and Delaware: Banks authorized to restrict withdrawals.

Staff men all over the country saw long queues standing outside banks, waiting to withdraw savings. State by state, the story almost defied writing. The causes of the hysteria were obscure. Its spread had been stealthy. Its manifestations were unpredictable and deceptive. Statistics on the amount of money in circulation provided the only clue to the extent of hoarding, but any attempt to compute exact figures was conjecture. No one could report authoritatively on the psychology of fear, the fatalism, and the air of gloom. Bread lines, idle factories, and empty shops were so commonplace that they had long since ceased to be news in themselves, yet each contributed to the strange thing happening in the country. It was a struggle to keep the report factual without being alarmist, on the one hand, or without attempting to minimize conditions, on the other. Stripped of atmosphere and emotion, the confirmable facts were eloquent and ominous.

Against such a gray national background Chief of Bureau Price at Washington marshaled his staff to cover the inauguration of Franklin Delano Roosevelt as President of the United States. In spite of anxiety and faltering confidence, the capital tried to be gay. After a dozen lean years of absence from power, the occasion was a great one for Democrats and each state sent its delegation of high officials and party stalwarts to participate in the ceremonies. Over the web of wires went story after story telling of the arrival of inaugural parties—from Texas, from Pennsylvania, from California, from New York . . .

Chaplin, city editor in New York, picked up another batch of copy, including a secondary Washington dispatch. It concerned the New York delegation to the inaugural, and one line noted that the newly elected governor, Herbert H. Lehman, was not among those present although it was the afternoon preceding inauguration day. Earlier announcements that Lehman would attend made his absence conspicuous. It might be that illness had interfered with the governor's plans. In that case there should be an item for the report. Then again it might be something else.

"Here, take a look at this," said Chaplin, handing the flimsy copy to a member of his city staff. "Better check the Lehman residence and see what's the matter."

The telephone at the governor's New York home was answered promptly. The reporter thought it was the butler.

"May I speak to Governor Lehman's secretary?"

"He isn't here just now," the voice answered. "Who is calling, please?"

"This is The Associated Press. We wanted to ask the governor's secretary . . ."

"Well," said the voice, "this is the governor. Perhaps I could help you."

Momentarily surprised to find that Lehman himself had answered the telephone, the reporter began inquiries. Why had the governor changed his plans for attending the inauguration?

"Oh, so that's what you want to know?" was the light reply. "There's really nothing to it. Some personal matters arose unexpectedly and I had no choice but to stay and attend to them."

"Then there is no chance that you will be able to get away in time for the inauguration?"

"No, I'm afraid not."

"And purely personal matters are detaining you? Nothing concerning state business?"

"Oh, no!"

"Or the banking situation? We understand that withdrawals have been particularly heavy today in some parts of the city."

"Oh, everything seems quite all right. Nothing to worry about. There have been withdrawals in some cases, but the banks seem to be meeting demands very nicely."

The conversation ended there, but it was enough to send the staff into action. New York and Washington proceeded on the theory that a banking crisis in New York was keeping Lehman away from the inaugural. A reporter was sent to the governor's residence. Wall Street was enlisted to uncover whatever information might be available at the Federal Reserve Bank or the offices of leading financial figures. A message went to Albany suggesting that the bureau there start working on the superintendent of banks' department. In Washington other staff men buttonholed Treasury officials.

Through the afternoon, into the evening, and on into the night Governor Lehman held conferences at his Park Avenue home. Bank officials came and went. Finally at 4:15 A.M. on Saturday, March 4— Inauguration Day—Governor Lehman issued a proclamation. A reporter darted for a telephone.

```
F-L-A-S-H
      NEW YORK - GOVERNOR DECLARES TWO-DAY
BANK HOLIDAY.
```

On the heels of the New York announcement, Harrisburg came through with news of a similar proclamation in Pennsylvania. Then Illinois, Massachusetts, and New Jersey.

Over 200,000 miles of leased wires shuttled dispatches telling of a national crisis which found all banks closed or operating under sharp restrictions. From every important foreign date line, the cables brought the reaction to the financial paralysis which had gripped the United States.

2

Perhaps not since Gobright reported the beginning of Abraham Lincoln's second term in the dark days of the Civil War had an inauguration assignment been so important. The staff gathered the story of the capital on March 4, 1933—the end of the last "lame duck" session of Congress at noon, the swearing-in of president and vice-president, the 17-minute inaugural address pledging swift and decisive action, the color of the traditional parade, the new First Lady, the somber crowds, and the quiet departure of Herbert Clark Hoover.

That night, Francis M. Stephenson, assigned to the White House, got little news although he waited hours at the entrance of the presidential offices in the west wing of the executive mansion. There was a short story from Stephen Early, who had become Roosevelt's press liaison secretary, but nothing from the White House itself where there was much coming and going as lights burned late into the night.

The next day—Sunday. Guests argued with hotel managers to cash checks. Others counted the money in their pockets, grinned and accepted their predicament in a spirit of adventure. Tension began to appear. At the White House Stephenson resumed his vigil with a hundred other newspapermen. It was not until a few minutes before Sunday midnight that the news came and Stephenson shouted over a telephone:

```
F-L-A-S-H

    WASHINGTON - PRESIDENT ORDERS NATIONAL
4-DAY BANK HOLIDAY.
```

The holiday, subsequently extended beyond its original time limit, created a story of vast proportions, demanding accurate, complete, and prompt coverage. Not only in Washington but in each of the forty-eight states banking and government officials worked with their tremendous problem. The news was of vital concern to everyone, from the banker, wondering when his institution could reopen, to the storekeeper, harassed by the lack of small coins for making change, to the jobless depositor, dependent upon his savings for food and shelter.

In the beginning the major part of the news burden fell upon Washington as the administration worked out plans for a reorganization of the country's banking system. This news had right of way, and, with rare exceptions, member papers received the information long before state banking departments were officially advised by telegrams from Secretary of the Treasury W. H. Woodin.

New York took over the task of co-ordinating the story of the banking situation as it changed throughout the nation. Each state produced detailed stories on its own condition and the reconstructive steps being taken. In addition, the controlling bureaus regularly sent a synopsis of the latest developments in their territories. From this material

New York prepared frequent undated leads which presented the national picture in broad outline so that readers might get a general picture before reading the dated stories which gave particularized news on the crisis.

As the progressive resumption of banking operations began, these leads supplied an accurate guide to the day-to-day conditions. With bureaus reporting frequently, the leads announced how many of the country's 17,600 banks had reopened, how many were state and how many were national institutions, the number operating on restricted or unrestricted basis, and the number remaining closed.

With few exceptions, official statements issued throughout the emergency, especially the national and state regulations governing bank reopenings, were transmitted in full on the wires. To clarify the numerous steps being taken to end the crisis, Washington turned out interpretive stories which explained the facts in language the man in the street could understand.

3

The banking crisis and the Roosevelt inauguration marked the beginning of a rush of events which imposed an unparalleled load on the Washington staff. Governmental activities moved at a speed unprecedented even in wartime.

The New Deal had arrived and story followed story.

Special Session of Congress . . . Emergency Financial Powers Given President . . . 3.2 Beer Legalized . . . Civilian Conservation Corps Authorized . . . Farm Relief . . . Home Mortgage Refinancing . . . Securities Control . . . Nation Abandons Gold Standard . . . Industrial Recovery . . . NRA . . .

News gathering in Washington entered a new chapter. A vast program involving far-reaching economic, industrial, and social changes was being launched and what happened in Washington affected the lives of citizens more directly than ever before. The reading public wanted to know more about the how and why of what was happening in the capital. It wanted to be told not only a law's national significance, but also what it would mean in their communities.

This need influenced the co-operative to set up a full-fledged Washington Regional Service. The purpose was to give the general report a counterpart which would follow governmental news from the viewpoints of the various states. It was the principle of vicinage news applied to the whirl of events on the banks of the Potomac.

The idea was not born of the moment. In a limited way Paul Weir of the Washington staff had explored the field informally over two decades by developing stories of special interest to individual members on census returns and crop reports. Then in 1929 the pioneering work was put on a definite basis when the management, as an experiment, sent a correspondent to Washington to concentrate exclusively on government news affecting New Jersey. William Wight, of the Newark Bureau, got the assignment and became the co-operative's first regional reporter of capital news. The success of the experiment led to similar arrangements for several other states but it was not until 1933 that the Washington Regional Service assumed major proportions.

The enlargement of the regional staff enabled Washington to consider major stories from the two approaches which papers desired. A public works program might be a national story in the sense that it represented a detail of governmental economics. At the same time it was an important local story in every community which was to receive or hoped to receive an allotment. Under the new order the Washington Bureau could make a bifocal examination of the facts and gauge its coverage accordingly.

4

Besides the great volume of front-page news from Washington, another major story developed with unlooked-for speed. At the outset, 1933 had promised to be an off year for the Election Service, but the rapid progress of the movement for the repeal of the Prohibition Amendment to the United States Constitution altered the situation. From early in April, when Michigan started the parade of states voting for repeal, until the end of the year, the Election Department was especially active. In all, forty-three special election services were set up.

The 1933 annual meeting saw the membership adopt tentative regulations to govern the use of the association's news in radio broadcasting. The subject had been recurring in official and unofficial discussions for ten years. From the time radio appeared there had been a cleavage of opinion respecting its relation to newspapers and the co-operative. Some regarded the new medium as a partner in their publishing enterprises and became active in the operation of broadcasting stations. They favored considerable latitude in the use of the news report on the air. Others—and at first they were in the majority—were inclined to regard radio as a competitor in the field of both circulation and advertising and did not want to make any of the report available for broadcasting purposes.

Before the 1925 annual meeting the Board of Directors had forbidden any broadcasting of AP news, whether general or local. The board penalized two members who transgressed, one of them being Victor Lawson. The enormous interest in broadcasts of the 1924 presidential election returns caused members to question the wisdom of the ruling and to consider the advisability of permitting a restricted use of the report in broadcasting news of special, outstanding events. At the 1925 meeting the board was permitted to allow the broadcasting of news whenever it was of transcendent importance. The management supplied radio stations with AP returns in the 1928 and 1932 presidential elections, as well as numerous E.O.S. bulletins on extraordinary news.

At the 1933 meeting the subject was thoroughly examined again and a resolution was adopted setting forth the co-operative's current policy. The resolution stipulated that no news, regardless of its source, be made available for chain broadcasting. At a small extra assessment member papers might broadcast news of major importance with credit to The AP and the member paper. With minor changes, those regulations governed the association's relations with radio for the next several years, but eventually the great majority of members saw the advantage of a more liberalized policy and AP news began to take its place on the air.

5

By 1933 daily operations had become so complex, the members had become so numerous, that too frequently the co-operative was taken for granted even by those it served and the management was left without much positive help from the membership at large.

Occasionally, nevertheless, the times produced some man or group of men of high editorial integrity who became fired with the necessity of active support of the practical ideal on which the modern association had been built, and sought to kindle the same active interest among the hundreds of others who daily looked to the co-operative for the news which constituted the "life blood" of the daily newspaper.

Such a man was produced in 1933 and out of his efforts grew one of the healthiest journalistic influences of the times. He was Oliver Owen Kuhn, managing editor of the Washington *Star*, and he came forward with a suggestion that the managing editors of all AP papers meet annually to discuss newspaper trends and to study at close range the activities of the unsung organization which supplied the bulk of their news. The gatherings were to be entirely divorced from the customary annual meetings of the publishers in whose name membership was held, and were to discuss practical newspaper problems rather than policy or theory of operation.

General Manager Cooper saw so much potential value in the first such meeting—held at French Lick in the autumn of 1933—that he sent the heads of all departments to listen to the discussions and to answer questions. One after another these key men explained how domestic and foreign news was collected, how the market and finance reports were compiled, how news was obtained in Washington, the trend in sports, and other kindred subjects. The discussions included the development of the News Photo and Feature services, the mechanics of news dissemination, wire facilities, and the scientific advances which might be expected.

Kuhn himself was named general chairman, a position to which he was unanimously re-elected until his death in 1937, and the members of the first executive committee were M. V. Atwood, of the Gannett newspapers; C. H. Heintzelman, of the Coatesville (Pa.) *Record;* M. H. Williams, of the Worcester (Mass.) *Telegram-Gazette,* and J. E. Murphy, of the Baltimore *Evening Sun.*

In spite of the heavy emphasis on affairs of national government, the report had its share of dramatics and unexpected stories. The Reichstag burned in Berlin. One-eyed Wiley Post flew alone around the world in less than eight days. Cuba plunged into revolt and Seymour Ress, a staff cameraman, narrowly escaped a Havana firing squad because he photographed the fight. The same months produced a fresh series of front-page kidnapings, and there was a matter-of-fact reminder of 1932's celebrated case in a short piece from Washington stating that the Lindbergh mystery had been turned over to the Department of Justice for renewed investigation.

But the New Deal and its efforts to bring about a return of prosperity continued the standout news of the domestic report. As the daily file of the Financial Service indicated, conditions had improved considerably since the bleak days of February and March, but the depression was not over. Harassed by problems seemingly more complicated than ever, many member newspapers struggled to regain some of the ground lost during four years of economic reverses. Few publishers were willing to risk heavy financial commitments even though in one field of news particularly there was a crying need. The great public interest in pictorial journalism had made spot-news pictures just as important as the written word in rounding out coverage on almost any news event. Yet there was no practical way of rapid transmission of pictures to newspaper offices over the country once the pictures had been taken at the scene of one event or another.

Cooper understood the situation existing in the newspaper field, but he was also convinced that the co-operative could not survive as a static organization. Unless it kept abreast of the times, unless it anticipated them whenever possible, it was certain to deteriorate. Even the forced postponement of improvements under the "deep depression" economy program had not met with Cooper's entire approval, for in the long view the postponements meant lost time to an organization for which split seconds were vital. His responsibility was to plan not only for the present but for the future.

The moment, he realized, could not be worse for advancing a program that would be as revolutionary as had been the introduction of the Morse telegraph almost a hundred years before. The tendency was to worry about the present and let the future—even the immediate future—take care of itself. There had been an earlier failure by others who attempted to solve the picture problem, but he was convinced that The AP could and should go ahead. To wait until business conditions became prosperous might mean waiting too long.

He wanted to send pictures into member newspaper offices by wire just as the news was sent.

VIII. THE FIGHT OVER PICTURES

WHEN American newspapers first began to print news pictures from halftone engravings, Kent Cooper was an unknown cub reporter. Popular photography was a novelty. The black box camera recorded scenes for the family album, and tintype snapshot men still did a thriving business at fairs and amusement parks.

As a youngster Cooper had sat for hours studying cardboard views through the stereoscope which was as essential then in any well-furnished parlor as the horsehair sofa and antimacassars. His entry into journalism coincided with the beginnings of modern newspaper photography. The more he thought of pictures the more convinced he became that they would play an increasingly important part in the newspaper of the future.

All through his developing newspaper career he had felt that a way must be found to deliver pictures to newspapers as quickly as the written word. At first that seemed almost impossible. Ever since the early fifties inventors and scientists had labored to perfect some reliable method for telegraphing pictures. A few experimental systems were devised, but they were either impractical or fell far short of solving the problem.

The laboratories of communications companies persevered and finally were able to announce the development of equipment which would transmit pictures by wire. A commercial system was set up by The American Telephone & Telegraph Company in the early twenties, and opened irregular operations with combination sending-and-receiving stations located in eight of the metropolitan centers.

The first news of the engineers' success excited Cooper, but critical examination of the invention disappointed him. Almost an hour was required to prepare a picture for sending, the speed of transmission was slow, and the delivered picture invariably came out blurred, fuzzy, and indistinct. Detail disappeared and the total effect was a vague shadow of what the original had been.

The experience of the News Photo Service, after its formation in 1927, brought home more forcefully the handicaps which beset the prompt handling of pictures on a national scale. If photos were sent by fast train mail, they took eighty-five hours to cross the continent. Even using air express, it was twenty-four hours and airplane schedules were at the mercy of weather, particularly in winter. Telephoto transmission might expedite fuzzy reproductions of an important picture to the few cities which happened to have receiving stations, but then the problem of delivery to subscribers elsewhere began all over again.

Nevertheless, telephoto remained the only wire transmission method and the News Photo Service had no alternative but to use it whenever a picture had such news value that the few editors benefited were willing to sacrifice quality in favor of speedier delivery. The association set up divisional distribution centers at Chicago, Atlanta, and San Francisco, but there was little acceleration of picture delivery as a whole.

Telephoto's continued unsatisfactory operation could have but one result even in a picture-conscious era. In June, 1933, the A. T. & T. abandoned the system after spending $2,800,000 in an attempt to make it work and the delivery of all pictures once more became a matter of railroad timetables and airplane schedules. The problem was right back where it had been before the introduction of telephoto.

2

Cooper refused to abandon hope that engineering research would win out. This time he did not have long to wait. Toward the end of 1933 Bell Laboratories reported that, after ten years of experiments along entirely different scientific lines, it had developed a completely new picture-sending apparatus. The company claimed that the new machine could send pictures by wire at two and a half times the speed of the telephoto and that the transmitted picture was so nearly perfect it was hard to detect the difference between it and the original.

In common with all other news-picture organizations, the AP Photo Service was informed. Costly experience in the business of commercial picture transmission had convinced the sponsors that the handling of pictures as news was essentially a newspaper enterprise, and so it offered to let anyone interested take over the mechanism for its own use.

The new equipment fired Cooper's imagination. Here seemed to be the scientific miracle he had been awaiting. He had President Noyes watch a demonstration between San Diego and New York and Noyes was amazed at the fidelity of the transmitted picture.

The other picture agencies also inspected the apparatus. Hearst's International News Photos, Times Wide-World, and Acme, the commercial picture agency controlled by the owners of the United Press Associations, were not interested in the telephone company's proposal. In the depths of a depression there was no eagerness to sponsor such a project.

But Cooper was working. He conferred with Norris Huse, his picture chief, and with AP laboratory experts who had examined the equipment from a scientific standpoint. He already had told the Board of Directors what he had in mind.

A nation-wide network of leased wires flashing AP pictures to AP newspapers twenty-four hours a day!

Pictures moving into newspaper offices simultaneously with the news, appearing in print side by side with stories of the same events!

It would cost money, he acknowledged, probably more than a million dollars a year. The wire tolls alone would be $560,000 annually, but it was an opportunity for The AP to blaze the trail into a new era of journalism.

Some members of the Board of Directors were inclined to consider it an impossible undertaking, particularly during the continuing depression, but they saw nothing to be lost by authorizing Cooper to sound out likely subscribers.

Cooper selected Photo Editor Norris Huse for the "impossible" task. A list of potential subscribers in twenty-five key cities was prepared and Huse set out to interest the members in those places in the possibility of high fidelity pictures on an exclusive AP network. The cost to each prospective subscriber was based on the same pro-rata principle the co-operative had used so successfully in computing other assessments over a period of years.

The first member to pledge participation in the outlined service was the Baltimore *Sun*.

Huse next called on the Washington *Star*, the paper owned by the co-operative's president. In view of Noyes's warm personal approval of the idea, Huse expected that interesting the *Star* would be a mere formality. Instead, he found that Noyes had told his managers nothing about it. He wished them to form their own judgment without being influenced by his opinion. After the *Star's* managers had heard the details, however, they became enthusiastic.

One by one the key papers pledged support until the roster was imposing.

3

The success of all preparatory moves was more than anyone dared hope for. Huse had demonstrated ably. He brought back to New York pledges of participation from more than thirty papers, a sufficient number to underwrite a minimum of five years of operations at a total cost of between five and seven million dollars.

The news of what The AP intended to do began to leak out and a number of the members became agitated at the reports they heard. Controversy developed as to the desirability of the association's committing itself to such an undertaking. The division of opinion became sharper as the weeks passed.

Led by the Hearst and Scripps-Howard members within the ranks of the co-operative, a sizable bloc of vigorous opposition took form. It was more militant, better organized, and more capably led than any previous uprising. The insurgent forces went out industriously to recruit adherents. All sorts of charges flew—that the management proposed to squander funds on an impracticable, visionary scheme; that A. T. & T. was trying to foist its obsolete telephoto equipment on the association; that, even if the apparatus worked, only a few wealthy papers could afford the advantage; that the vast majority of the membership never would receive any benefit.

More than six hundred representatives of AP papers poured into the new Waldorf-Astoria for the annual meeting in April, 1934, and most of those who could not attend were represented by proxy. The conflict brewing was the big attraction.

No sooner had President Noyes called the meeting to order than the battle began. John Francis Neylan, California lawyer and general counsel for the Hearst newspapers, fifteen of which held memberships in the co-operative, took the floor. Standing beside his seat in the front row, he demanded a showdown on the whole proposition of AP's projected establishment of a wire picture-transmission network and charged that the telephone company which had perfected the equipment was attempting to salvage the money it had invested in experiments over a period of years by persuading The AP to take over the equipment.

Neylan professed to have only the best interests of the association at heart, but there were doubts about his altruism. The Hearst papers and their Scripps-Howard allies had their own picture services to consider and protect. If The AP Photo Service could make a success of telegraphing pictures, rival agencies would find themselves hopelessly outdistanced in delivery and would be forced to enter the business of picture wire transmission in order to keep pace. It was to the advantage of these agencies to see that AP did nothing to disturb the existing equality of competition.

Neylan made a brilliant field marshal for the opposition. He called upon the board to furnish the membership with all details of the enterprise. It affected the association's financial credit, he asserted, and it never should have been sanctioned without the approval of an annual meeting.

"Up to the present time," he shouted, "only a handful of AP members have even had unofficial knowledge of the undertaking, and none had official word."

President Noyes informed him that an illustrated booklet, *Announcing AP News Pictures by Wire*, was ready for distribution to the members at the meeting. Then he called on the general manager to report on what had happened.

Cooper outlined the growing popularity of pictures as a news medium and explained the impossibility of printing them along with the news they illustrated so long as no speedy delivery system was available.

"There are no exclusive rights to the proposed wire picture service as against any member of The Associated Press," he said. "It is available to any member, any time. Personally, I hope to see the entire membership benefit by the thing. To my mind, it is the newest and biggest departure in newspaper work since words were first telegraphed."

Replying to Neylan's demand that all financial details with the telephone company be disclosed, he said:

"I am sure our competitors would like to know all about it."

He pointed out that there had been no departure from precedent in making preparations for the new service. In every instance, dating as far back as 1908, the management had submitted its plans for supplemental services to the Board of Directors. Then when approval had been obtained, member participation on a sufficient scale had been sought to finance the cost of the projected service.

"I think the News Photo Service of The Associated Press, alone, from one angle, the Feature Service from another, and the Financial

Service from another, have made membership ten to one hundred times more valuable," he concluded. "If we had let our competitors do all these things, I don't think there would be any Associated Press today. This idea of pictures by wire can go. It will go in some form. If not by us, then by our competitors, or by anybody else who wants to take it up and do it."

Neylan returned to the attack with all his oratorical skill. Twitting the management as inexperienced in the field of photo distribution, the Hearst lawyer reminded his audience again that every other picture agency had been offered the same opportunity to take over the equipment which was the storm center of the present fight.

"Is it not strange," he inquired, "that all these institutions, which had had so much more experience in the matter of photo service than The Associated Press had, went into this matter thoroughly and refused to take up the white man's burden of the A. T. & T.?"

Neylan's attack occupied all but a few minutes of the morning session. By the time the members filed out for the annual luncheon, it was obvious that the future of the co-operative's administration was at stake. If Neylan could rally a majority, it would mean in effect a repudiation of the Board of Directors for having given the general manager authority to proceed with the new supplemental service. It was a crucial situation.

Clark Howell, publisher of the Atlanta *Constitution* and one of the elder statesmen of the board, took the floor in the afternoon session. He told the membership that, although for the present he did not intend to take the service for his own newspaper, he was convinced of the association's wisdom in entering the new field.

"Let me say," he declared, "that if Mr. Hearst's organization, or any other organization, had got to this first and had made the proposition to establish a service of this kind, then you would have been right to have criticized your general manager for his laxity."

The chair recognized Fred Schilplin, of the St. Cloud (Minn.) *Times and Journal Press*, a representative smaller paper. He went to the heart of the matter.

"Summing this thing all up," he said, "about all I can get out of it is that a group of member newspapers, which is probably able to do it even in these reconstruction times, has undertaken to underwrite this experiment. We wish them all success. I don't see anything else to it. I don't see that any of this means that they are going to get a larger assessment out of us. Eventually we are going to get some of the benefits out of it."

President Noyes took this opportunity to remind the members that the spearhead of the opposition was the Scripps-Howard and Hearst group of papers, interested in their own picture agencies and reluctant to support any service which would be in competition.

"I'm sure," he commented, "that Mr. Neylan wouldn't expect The Associated Press or the general manager to base his activities on what was especially pleasing to Mr. Hearst's picture service or the Scripps-Howard picture interests."

Turning to a point of vital interest to the smaller papers which had to have their pictures delivered to them in matted form because they could not afford to operate their own engraving plants, Noyes continued:

"I also want to say that, because of this service, the users of the picture mat service will be immensely advantaged. There is an element of time against them now, in that a mat can't be made and delivered by mail as quickly as a photograph can, but because of this new service every one of them will benefit by faster service."

4

Roy Howard, chairman of the board of Scripps-Howard papers which controls the United Press Associations, then took the floor. He made no fevered emotional appeal in urging his objections to the new service. He said its inauguration would increase the costs of newspaper production and urged its rejection for that reason.

Mechanically the new process might be all that was claimed for it, he conceded, but operation of the system would be tremendously expensive and, moreover, there were not enough important pictures to justify it.

The bitter crossfire of arguments had lasted all day, and as the debate neared its close the scraping of chairs and the hum of conversation in the crowded audience showed that the membership was impatient to have the question put to a vote. It was almost evening, however, before the last man had been heard and Frank S. Hoy, of the Lewiston (Maine) *Sun-Journal*, moved to establish the attitude of the meeting on the controversial issue. His resolution was that the act of the Board of Directors in arranging for the new service be ratified and confirmed. The motion evoked applause, but the opposition, fighting to the last ditch, proposed that the entire membership be polled by mail instead. The suggestion was lost by a decisive 5-to-1 margin and then President Noyes put the question of ratifying the board's action.

There was a chorus of "Ayes."

The immediate threat to the projected wire picture service was routed by the overwhelming vote of confidence, but its foes left the meeting as determined as ever in their opposition. Some predicted the service would "die within a year." Others were frankly skeptical that it would perform better than the discarded telephoto. The evidence of laboratory experiments and tests between two points might be compelling, but conditions would be vastly different operating a system with twenty-five stations and a transcontinental network of wires. Then, too, there was the formidable task of getting equipment manufactured and installed, and of training personnel.

5

The responsibility for perfecting the complicated arrangements necessary to start the unproved wire picture system rested jointly on the Photo Service staff and the Traffic Department's force of engineers, and they had a huge job cut out for them. They hoped to have the system in operation by a tentative fall starting date, but the months passed and it did not seem that their goal would be reached. As they redoubled their efforts news continued to follow its age-old pattern. Much of it was ephemeral, and much was surrounded by the drama which marks the making of history.

For five busy weeks that summer hour-by-hour dispatches from Europe wrote the running story of history-in-the-making on a spectacular scale. When Chancellor Hitler made the great "blood purge" of disloyal elements in his National Socialist party, Chief of Bureau Lochner circumvented official government attempts to prevent dispatches from leaving Germany with the first news for ninety minutes after its release. He had arranged beforehand to have London telephone Berlin every half hour in the event the bureau failed to hear from him. The precaution enabled him to get off his news on an incoming call at the very time the Nazis were refusing transmission of all outgoing press communications.

After the blood purge there was the drama in Vienna where the assassination of Chancellor Dollfuss in an abortive Nazi Putsch on Austria gave Chief of Bureau Wade Werner and Robert F. Schildbach a succession of tense days. Then the date lines shifted abruptly back to Germany and a telephone whisper that "a very old gentleman is extremely low" gave Lochner his first hint that President von Hindenburg was dying.

In spite of the close surveillance of secret police, G. O. Beukert of the Berlin staff got prompt news of the old field marshal's death at Neudeck a few days later and rushed it through to Lochner a minute before the sole Neudeck-Berlin telephone line was cut off for an hour by government order. Hindenburg's passing cleared the way for Hitler's final assumption of supreme power in the Reich, and the correspondence from the Berlin Bureau began a fresh and amazing chapter.

There were no doldrums that year in the domestic report. Staff men at San Francisco donned trench helmets and gas masks to cover the longshoremen's strike which paralyzed West Coast shipping. Chicago bulletined the death of John Dillinger, Public Enemy No. 1, at the hands of federal agents. The Jersey staff produced another front-page story when the luxury liner *Morro Castle* burned at sea with a loss of 134 lives.

Then, without warning, came the news break for which editors had waited two and a half years—the arrest of a Bronx carpenter named Bruno Richard Hauptman in possession of ransom money paid in the Lindbergh kidnaping case.

While the news moved, preparations went ahead for the introduction of the telegraphed picture service. Major stories such as the violent West Coast strike, Dillinger's death, the *Morro Castle* disaster, and, above all, the arrest of a suspect in the Lindbergh mystery, accentuated the acute need for faster picture delivery. Member editors wanted all the pictures they could obtain on these top-ranking stories, and trains, planes, or special messengers could not deliver them swiftly enough to meet the rapidly changing newspaper needs.

The intention to start operations of the new picture system in that fall of 1934 turned out to be optimistic. Manufacture of equipment had been slow. The installation and outfitting of the twenty-five sending and receiving stations over the country required from two to three weeks each. Training personnel to handle the mechanism proved more difficult than anticipated and a hundred and one other problems had to be met.

The fall months passed without inauguration of the service, and the vigorous opponents recalled their earlier predictions. The suspicion grew that, under the demands of actual working conditions, the new equipment was not performing with the precision it had shown in the ideal surroundings of the laboratory.

The untried service, however, had acquired an official name—Wirephoto. After weeks of search for some distinctive word or combination of words which would tersely describe pictures by telegraph, Norris Huse hit upon the designation. The name for the revolutionary new service was all very well, but the big question was yet to be answered.

Would Wirephoto really work?

6

It was almost 3 A.M. on New Year's Day, 1935, and AP Wirephoto—storm center of debate—was ready for its crucial test.

Engineers in the wire control room at New York headquarters made last-minute adjustments on the eight-foot panel containing bulbs, wires, indicators, and wavering needles. Around them stood intent members of the staff, smudgy copy boys, radio announcers, busy newsreel camera crews, and a cluster of smartly turned out New Year revelers.

Attention was focused on an odd machine which seemed out of place in the newsroom atmosphere. The contraption rested on a heavy metal base in the center of the floor and supported a horizontal cylinder. Nearby was the large panel with its glowing bulbs, a bank of dials, a telephone, and a loud-speaker. Next to the panel stood a power unit enclosed in a latticed cage of thin steel.

The technicians bent over the machine. The onlookers talked in whispers. Along a special 10,000-mile network of leased wires, other engineers and technicians stood over machines in twenty-five cities from coast to coast, all waiting to see if Wirephoto could send high fidelity pictures over a nation-wide circuit just as news was sent.

The picture selected for the first sending reported headline news. A transport air liner had crashed deep in the snow-covered Adirondack Mountains. Searchers had combed the wild country on foot and by air for days trying to find the wrecked plane. Finally one party, after floundering through heavy snows in subzero weather, reached the spot where the ship had crashed. A staff cameraman snapped the scene as the half-frozen survivors greeted their rescuers.

Rushed to New York and the darkrooms, the wet picture came out of the developing tank and passed the photo desk for an identifying caption. Then it went to the experts at the new black machine. They

WIREPHOTO WAS READY FOR ITS CRUCIAL TEST.

took the picture—an ordinary print—wrapped it, face up, around the horizontal cylinder and snapped the cylinder back into place.

Out across the continent—in Chicago, San Francisco, Atlanta, Kansas City, Boston, Syracuse, and Philadelphia, in twenty-five cities —attendants also made their receiving machines ready.

At New York, engineer Harold Carlson gave the photo-encased cylinder a final glance and stepped to the control board. He nodded to an assistant at the network telephone and out of the loud-speakers in all twenty-five cities came the announcement:

"This is New York calling all points. The first picture will be a shot of the plane survivors just rescued in the Adirondacks. Are you ready?"

Carlson clicked a button. The picture was on its way over the wires to papers in cities from 100 to 3,000 miles away.

The cylinder revolved under the small hoodlike housing which contained a photoelectric cell—the "eye" which was transmitting the photograph. From the machine came a high-pitched, harmonic whistle— the sound generated when the network was in use for transmission. For eight minutes the penetrating whistle continued, then faded and ceased.

The moment the cylinder stopped rotating in New York, the receiving cylinders halted simultaneously in the twenty-five cities of the network. Attendants carried the cylinders into darkrooms, negatives were developed and within another few minutes picture editors had on their desks the finished photographic print of the air disaster scene which New York had transmitted.

In quality and fidelity the received pictures were so remarkable that only an expert could detect the difference between them and the original on the sending cylinder. There was no trace of the blurs, fuzz, and streaks which had made the old commercial telephoto so unsatisfactory.

The first transmission was followed by an air shot of the wrecked transport and then by a series of photographs which gave a pictorial account of the New Year celebration. New York sent the boisterous scene at Times Square. San Francisco took the circuit to contribute a picture of the stars in Hollywood welcoming 1935. Miami added a picture of the holiday gaiety on the beach front. Photos of half a hundred news events were transmitted. They went racing across the country even as the news circuits were carrying the dispatches they illustrated.

7

Skeptics who had contended there were not enough important news pictures to justify a Wirephoto network found no consolation in the log for the ensuing months. The day after the new service began operation, the trial of Bruno Hauptman for the Lindbergh kidnap-murder opened at Flemington, New Jersey. Wirephoto subscribers all over the country were able to publish the pictures of what was happening at Flemington the same day the events took place, and to publish them side by side with the news stories on developments in the most publicized court case in the history of American jurisprudence. It was a compelling demonstration of the new service's ability to deliver pictures day after day on a story which monopolized front pages.

In the succeeding weeks and months there was no lack of material —a new session of Congress convened at Washington; Amelia Earhart flew nonstop from Honolulu to California; G-men killed Fred and "Ma" Barker, long-sought criminals, in a furious gun battle in Florida; a new ship disaster took forty-five lives off the Jersey coast; the navy's dirigible *Macon* broke up and sank at sea near Point Sur, California; the Pacific Northwest had its Weyerhaeuser kidnaping, and in New York James J. Braddock staged the sports upset of the year by coming back from the has-been ranks to win the World Heavyweight Boxing Championship. The trunk circuits brought the written stories and the Wirephoto network simultaneously flashed the pictures.

The forty-six papers subscribing to Wirephoto represented only a small fraction of the association's 1,340 members, but General Manager Cooper had promised from the very first to make the new service benefit the hundreds of papers which could not afford its initial expense. The vast majority of members had no engraving plants of their own, and they depended on matted pictures for the photographs they printed. The AP already was supplying these members with such a service, matted at strategic centers in the country and distributed by mail, bus, train, or airplane, as the subscriber desired. Until the advent of Wirephoto, the pictures from which these mats were made were collected by the old slow methods. With Wirephoto, pictures of outstanding news from all over the country could be assembled with unprecedented speed at the widely separated matting points. At Cooper's direction, the Photo Department made preparations for a high-speed mat service, called Telemats, to be produced from pictures transmitted by Wirephoto.

8

There was now no question about the merits of Wirephoto. It justified the great claims made for it, and it introduced a new stimulus into the field of newspaper enterprise. Nevertheless, its opponents made one last attempt to halt its progress at the 1935 annual meeting—even after the service got under way. Again they called for the membership to discredit the Board of Directors and the management, but again they were voted down.

Out of their oblique onslaught, however, came one salutary development. Seeking to gain the favor of the smaller members, they introduced a resolution calling for more representation of the smaller members on the Board of Directors. Until that time, the board had been composed of fifteen members, selected from among the various categories of membership. The opponents to Wirephoto proposed that the number be increased to eighteen, giving the small members three additional representatives on the board. It was a plan the board already had under consideration and eventually it was put into effect.

As for the Wirephoto controversy itself, it slipped into the association's historic files with one parting thrust by a representative of one of the smaller papers whom the opponents had thought to win over to their program of opposition to pictures by wire. Carl L. Estes of the Longview (Tex.) *News*, listened to the 1935 debate, seconded a motion to table one of the opposition's proposals, and declared:

"I've had enough of this self-appointed, self-anointed shepherd of the little fellow. The issue at stake is one of progress. Somebody has got to pioneer pictures by wire. If The Associated Press paid every dollar in its treasury to sponsor this thing, I, as one of the smallest newspaper publishers in the country, think it would be money well spent."

Pictures by wire had come to stay. Day in and day out the system was delivering pictures simultaneously to the receiving stations over the country in only eight minutes each, but the news log of 1935 still had to produce the transcendent story which would dramatize Wirephoto unforgettably in the minds of the public as a whole. Then it came.

Harold Turnblad, chief of bureau in Seattle, was about to leave the office late the afternoon of August 16 when a report arrived from a correspondent at Fairbanks, Alaska. Wiley Post, the round-the-world flier, and Will Rogers, the humorist philosopher, had taken off by plane for Point Barrow, five hundred miles away near the rim of the Arctic Ocean. That night the editor on duty kept in frequent touch with the United States Army Signal Corps office in Seattle on the chance that some word might come through from one of the Signal Corps outposts in the remote reaches of Alaska. There was no news. When the editor left at the end of his tour of duty, he instructed the night attendant to keep calling the Signal Corps hourly until the first day editor reported at 6 A.M.

Turnblad was fast asleep when the telephone beside his bed rang at daybreak. Drowsily he reached for the phone and heard an apologetic voice which he recognized as that of Captain Frank E. Stoner of the United States Army Signal Corps.

"I hate to wake you up," the officer began quickly, "but we've just received word that Post and Rogers were killed last night near Point Barrow."

The words jolted Turnblad wide awake.

"Say that again!"

As soon as Stoner hung up, Turnblad called the bureau.

"Put on a flash!" he shouted.

    F-L-A-S-H

    SEATTLE - SIGNAL CORPS REPORTS ROGERS
AND POST KILLED NEAR BARROW IN A PLANE CRASH.

As Turnblad and his staff went into action to develop further details of the disaster—the string correspondents in Alaska reported to Seattle—things were happening at the lonely spot where Rogers and Post met sudden death. At Point Barrow the co-operative had two stringers—a medical missionary, Dr. Greist, and a grizzled trading post storekeeper named Brower. As soon as the first reports of the crash reached Point Barrow, Dr. Greist and Brower set out for the scene with an ordinary folding camera, the kind so frequently used to record family outings or picnics.

The news that Will Rogers and Wiley Post had been killed hit the nation hard. No one had to tell Photo Editor Wilson Hicks in New York that here was the greatest picture story of the year—if only pictures had been taken at the scene of the crash in Alaska.

Then came a message. The two stringers at Point Barrow had taken pictures and they were on their way to Fairbanks in the same plane that was carrying the bodies of the humorist and his flier companion from Point Barrow.

9

A relay of planes was arranged to speed the negatives from Fairbanks to San Francisco, then the nearest station on the Wirephoto network. While the leased wires were carrying stories based on information supplied by the medical missionary, the trading post storekeeper, and other correspondents, the precious negatives were on their way.

In New York Hicks remained at the Wirephoto control board. At last the loud-speaker of the network came to life. It was Sears, photo editor at San Francisco—FX by the call designation given to bureaus. He told Hicks that the Post-Rogers negatives had arrived, were in the darkroom being developed, and that the first would be ready for transmitting within a few minutes.

The loud-speaker died for a time and then Sears was on the picture network's telephone circuit informing all points that the first picture was ready for sending.

News that the Post-Rogers pictures were about to be transmitted flew about the newspaper offices and editorial workers left their desks to crowd about the receiving equipment.

In San Francisco, Sears pushed a button and started the sending drum rotating. In eight minutes the receiving machines halted in unison, negative cartridges were rushed into darkrooms for developing, and soon the first picture was in print in subscribing newspapers throughout the country.

Through the night other pictures of the tragedy moved over the network—shots of the wrecked plane, of the bodies being loaded into a whaleboat, of the Eskimo tent where Post had come down to ask directions a few minutes before the fatal crash. Subscribing member papers printed them side by side with the front-page stories which gave columns to the tragic death of two of America's beloved figures.

Wirephoto had scored a smashing coup on a story of surpassing reader interest. The pictures found their way into thousands of private scrapbooks, readers wrote letters to editors commenting on the speed with which the pictures had been obtained and printed, and the name of Wirephoto took on a new magic whenever people saw it on pictures of other news events.

Nor were the two Alaskan stringers forgotten. The two men who had helped make the Post-Rogers coverage so spectacular were sent checks for $500 each and—appropriately enough—they also were given a dozen rolls of film for their all-important little box camera.

IX. DATE LINE: FLEMINGTON

I

SMALL towns often produce well-remembered date lines. There was Dayton, Tennessee, in 1925 with its Scopes "monkey trial." In 1932 came Hopewell and the Lindbergh kidnaping. Two years later it was Callander, Ontario, and the birth of the Dionne quintuplets. And in 1935 it was Flemington and Bruno Hauptmann.

From the time of Hauptmann's arrest until his trial opened on January 2, the report had carried a tremendous volume of copy on the Bronx carpenter accused of kidnapping and murdering Charles A. Lindbergh, Jr. Hauptmann was front-page and every scrap of news about him was snapped up. Long before the first juror was chosen it was evident that coverage of the trial would have to be both superior and comprehensive.

The mention of Flemington subsequently came to have many connotations. For some it meant one of the most widely publicized and controversial criminal cases in court history. To AP men, however, Flemington was synonymous with the most mysterious blunder in the association's records. For a long time staffers winced when they heard the name spoken.

Preparations and planning for covering the trial began weeks in advance. The staff—news, photo, and traffic—was selected. Flemington was to operate as a full-sized, specially constituted bureau.

As chief of bureau at Newark, the strategic center for New Jersey, Henry E. Mooberry headed the trial staff of seven reporters. O. K. Price was in charge of the special Traffic force assigned to handle the transmission of copy. Working space in the cramped courthouse was at a premium, but The AP obtained the use of half the sheriff's private office, which was located immediately outside the courtroom door.

The trial opened January 2, 1935, and while court was in session the Morkrum in the sheriff's office raced along at sixty-five words a minute, pouring the running story directly onto the news network.

As the end of the trial approached, Mooberry became extremely anxious to have the seven weeks of outstanding work on the story climaxed by the speediest possible flash on the jury's verdict. He anticipated difficulty in getting the verdict promptly. In all likelihood, the courtroom doors would be locked from the moment the jury returned until after it was discharged. Anyone who devised a way to circumvent the locked doors would be assured a beat on Hauptmann's fate.

The problem of reporting the verdict became a major concern in the bureau chief's mind. There was the established method—written copy coming out from the men assigned in court, just as throughout the trial. That guaranteed the cardinal consideration—accuracy—but it might mean sacrificing speed if the anticipated difficulties arose. Mooberry knew that others were exerting every resource to circumvent the barriers of closed courtroom doors and he disliked the possibility that someone else might stage a last-minute coup which would detract from the acknowledged superiority of the report he had directed throughout the trial.

The intense importance attached to the announcement of the Hauptmann verdict in the public mind strengthened Mooberry's purpose. He determined upon an alternate method of getting the verdict out of the courtroom.

Without writing to New York for authorization and approval, he worked out plans for the use of a short-range radio set. The arrangement called for Ralph Smith, a Traffic mechanic and amateur radio operator, to be in the courtroom with a portable set concealed under his overcoat, while Price, the Traffic chief, was to station himself at a receiving set in a locked storeroom in the attic of the building. Price had borrowed a teletype and installed it there and it could be connected to the same trunk wire as the Morkrum in the sheriff's office. As soon as Price received the short-wave signals from Smith, he was to cut in on the wire and flash the verdict. Control of the wire would then revert to the Morkrum downstairs without outsiders in the sheriff's office being any the wiser as to what had been sent.

2

February 13 was the last day of the trial and the long siege of work. Pressure and nerve strain were almost finished. In spite of the general atmosphere of public hysteria pervading the courthouse, it promised to be the easiest day of the trial—nothing like the hectic sessions when Lindbergh was on the witness stand, or Hauptmann, or Dr. "Jafsie" Condon.

The jury retired at 11:15 A.M. and the long wait began. State troopers cleared the courtroom of all spectators except newspapermen. Outside in the streets crowds gathered around the courthouse and the adjoining county jail where Hauptmann paced his cell. The day dragged on into the afternoon, and the afternoon into the night.

In mid-evening Mooberry summoned Price and Smith to his desk and gave them each a small card bearing the code signals for the various verdict possibilities. It had been agreed in advance that, for safety, the signal must be repeated five times and carry a prearranged signature. Any message not fulfilling all those requirements was to be ignored.

The bailiffs detailed to guard the jury sent for the sheriff. Tension rose in the courtroom. There was a commotion at the doorway leading to the jury room. At 10:20 the sheriff came out. He announced the jury had agreed upon a verdict.

The two staff men assigned to do the running story wrote identical flashes that the jury was ready to report and sent the copy flying out of the courtroom by messenger boys. Each had been instructed to do independent running stories. This was a routine precaution against any loss of copy in the confusion outside the courtroom. With duplicate flashes, bulletins, and running being sent out, there was a good chance that at least one complete set could be counted upon to reach the news desk—unless all copy was stopped completely.

Immediately after the sheriff's announcement, state troopers took command in the courtroom. The doors were locked and the window shades drawn. At every door and window a trooper mounted guard. "No one will be permitted to leave this room until dismissed by the court," newspapermen were told.

At 10:28 P.M. the bell in the courthouse cupola began to toll its traditional signal, that a murder case jury was returning to the box with a verdict.

In the locked courtroom, every member of the staff was at his post. Two men waited at the locked doors ready to write the flashes they hoped to be able to slip out across the sill. The two men assigned to the running bent over their duplicate stories. A relay of messengers lined the aisles to pass each sheet back as soon as it was torn from the thick yellow pads. Overcoated and perspiring, Smith with his concealed wireless set stood near the rear benches. Beside him stood a newsman, pencil and paper ready to scribble off the verdict which the operator was to tap out in code on the hidden sending key in his pocket.

Only a wall separated Mooberry in the sheriff's office from the courtroom, but he might have been in another world. The regular running story began to come out, describing preparations for the arrival of the jury, Hauptmann, and Justice Trenchard. Mindful of what had happened during the judge's charge that morning when copy was held up almost a half hour, Mooberry looked for a time lag of at least several minutes between events in court and the appearance of copy. Unknown to Mooberry and everyone else outside, however, the troopers behind the locked doors were making no attempt to halt news copy as they had done in the morning. The running story was being slipped over the doorsill with only negligible delay.

3

Hunched at his desk, Mooberry worked fast, editing the copy shuttled in to him by the messengers posted outside the courtroom door. Although he watched closely, he found no indication yet as to the size of the presupposed time lag. The copy was preliminary descriptive and recorded nothing requiring a time element, something the two men had been instructed to incorporate on all major developments. As rapidly as the bureau chief finished with one piece of copy, he passed the "take" over to the Morkrum in the corner where Sam Patroff, the operator, kept feeding the story onto the trunk wire.

Everything was going smoothly—like clockwork.

Patroff's fingers suddenly jerked off the keys as if they were hot.

"He's breaking, Henry," he whispered. "He's breaking!"

Mooberry jumped across to Patroff's side. Price was cutting in from the attic.

Here it came!

```
F-L-A-S-H

     FLEMINGTON - VERDICT REACHED GUILTY AND
LIFE
```

The Morkrum pulsed, idle for a second, then the typebars flipped up against the printer paper in a quick flurry. Price timed his flash—10:31 P.M.

For one jubilant moment Mooberry hung over the machine. From coast to coast, in bureaus and member offices, that flash had just hammered out on hundreds of Morkrums as fast as the letters fed onto the circuit from the secret machine in the attic at Flemington.

The verdict was out! All over the country! And the courtroom doors were still locked!

The bureau chief turned back to his desk. His immediate job was cut out for him. By the time Patroff took back control of the wire, Mooberry had a bulletin ready amplifying the flash into terse, readable newspaper copy for waiting telegraph editors and composing rooms. Then the extras could roll. Crowding on the heels of the bulletin came bulletin matter explaining that, under New Jersey law, a recommendation of mercy made life imprisonment mandatory.

Borne along by a great emotional lift, Mooberry pieced together the story, combining the explanatory, or "stock," material he wrote himself with the available running copy which had been flowing under the locked courtroom door. The courtroom copy was still entirely descriptive of the scenes preceding delivery of the verdict. A few minutes ticked by without bringing any confirmation of the verdict through the regular channels. To Mooberry, that was understandable enough. The duplicate running had mentioned the State Police guards at all doors. Apparently the troopers were holding up copy as they had done earlier.

The bureau chief looked up from his work to see Price hurry into the office.

"You're sure you're right, aren't you?" he asked in a whisper when the Traffic chief reached his side. "The verdict came awfully quick." He paused and voiced the faint suspicion which had begun to worry him. "Almost too quick."

"Sure, Henry, sure." Price was tense but positive. "I got the signals. The number was 4, and 4 means life."

With Price watching over his shoulder, Mooberry returned to the scrawled running account which had been coming out under the courtroom door. In the light of Price's positive assurance, this copy lagged at least eight minutes behind actual proceedings. That wasn't bad. Price read a few pages, and left to return to the attic.

The office boy darted in with another batch of courtroom copy. Mooberry had his thick black pencil poised to continue editing. Then he froze. Time elements had begun to appear in the "takes"—time elements impossible to reconcile with the secret wireless verdict which had been flashed at 10:31. Frantically Mooberry scanned the next pages. Perhaps one of the men had made a mistake in noting the time. A glance dashed that desperate hope. Both sets of running copy carried the times of events in court, and the times tallied. At 10:31, the time of the attic flash, the jury's verdict had not been delivered.

In that numbing moment Mooberry reacted instinctively. His pencil jabbed down on a clean sheet.

> F-L-A-S-H
>
> KILL HAUPTMANN VERDICT - ERRONEOUS

Functioning like an automaton, the bureau chief got off the bulletin obligatory after all kills—a bulletin calling editors' attention to the transmission of a mandatory kill and directing that the erroneous copy be destroyed promptly. Regardless of everything else, the error must be caught and killed without delay.

The seconds seemed ages, but it was barely a few minutes before the office boy was thrusting a sheet of paper into Mooberry's hand.

> F-L-A-S-H
>
> HAUPTMANN GUILTY DEATH SENTENCE

That was from McGrady. Identical written flashes from Ferris, Lawrence, and Kinney arrived almost simultaneously.

No doubt now. The correct verdict was: Guilty—Death.

The accurate verdict went out at 10:46—exactly one minute after the nervous jury foreman announced it from the box.

The established method had done the job accurately and with all the speed one could ask.

4

The erroneous flash had stood eleven minutes. In New York, editorial and traffic men alike had been clustered over the Morkrums when the typebars printed the four false words. All the main wire circuits had been hooked up directly to Flemington so the news would have instantaneous distribution.

Then—the Kill. Members of the New York staff went about their duties with set faces. No one felt like talking. Eleven minutes was an infinitesimal speck of time for an organization that went back eighty-seven years, but this error seemed almost a personal tragedy.

The circumstances prevailing that night gave New York little opportunity to obtain the details behind the false flash. After the wrong verdict had been killed, the first consideration was to get the correct story cleared quickly and smoothly.

Not until the next day did amazed executive editors begin to learn of the disastrous secret scheme which had caused the false flash. Assistant General Manager Elliott instituted an investigation as soon as he received intimations that irregularities were involved. The co-operative had rigorous rules against the use of special transmission systems in reporting news, unless specifically authorized by New York, and what had been done at Flemington was, bluntly, a flagrant violation of regulations.

On his own initiative and without authorization, the bureau chief had gone ahead with a scheme which placed heavy reliance on a make-shift signal system. The indictment did not stop there. The scheme required a special installation of radio and telegraph equipment, something strictly forbidden except with the approval of a Traffic Department executive. Other regulations had been ignored in the unauthorized use of the borrowed teletype, the extension of the news wire to the attic location, and even the unauthorized employment of a second operator to check the verdict signals. New York learned that Traffic Chief Price had hired a second operator to help him detect the wireless signals in the attic room and this act assumed further gravity when it was learned that the man employed was a former Traffic man who had been dismissed from the service some time before.

Mooberry offered no defense for proceeding without approval on a plan which flouted so many regulations. All his thoughts had been concentrated on getting the verdict the instant it was announced. The consequences left him dismayed.

"It is almost impossible," he wrote General Manager Cooper, "for me to express my feelings on the situation into which I have thrown you and The Associated Press."

The general manager waited until all the facts had been examined and then took action. There was no alternative but to discipline the three men involved in the unauthorized undertaking. Price was dismissed, Mooberry was suspended, and Smith was transferred to work in another part of the country.

5

What had happened in the attic storeroom during those fifteen eventful minutes immediately preceding the announcement of the Hauptmann verdict?

Even after the investigation, no one knew for certain. When Smith, the mechanic, left the courtroom on the verdict night, he encountered Price coming down the stairs from the top floor. "I got a couple of 4's and went ahead," Price explained. In the next breath he was telling the mechanic that he wasn't positive the signals he received had been 4's. They might have been letter V's, a somewhat similar combination of dots and dashes. He said, however, that the second operator with him in the attic had identified them as 4's. The code signal—whether 4 or V—recurred only twice and bore no signature, he acknowledged, but he sent the fatal flash on the strength of that reception. The prearranged code was: 1 for the death verdict; 4 for guilty, life imprisonment; 7 for acquittal; 9 for disagreement.

Having cleared the number 4 flash, Price made his trip downstairs to see Mooberry, became uneasy after seeing some copy and returned to the attic. Resetting the dial to the wave length Smith was to use, he received the correct verdict signal and then heard it repeated. By that time, however, a correct flash in writing had reached Mooberry from the courtroom.

The origin of the mysterious signal 4 could not be traced. At first some of the staff suspected that it might have come from other portable equipment which had been smuggled into the court by the representative of one of the metropolitan papers. The man who operated it was detected after Hauptmann's sentencing, was arrested and later released. His set, however, proved to be for voice transmission and not Morse code.

The erroneous flash was a sensation not only in the pressrooms at Flemington but in newspaper offices over the country. The same editions which blazoned the Hauptmann death verdict also gave prominence to accounts of the flash which caused so much confusion.

The Associated Press had made a mistake—and that was news.

That some member papers would be highly exercised was to be expected. What was totally unlooked for, however, was the spontaneous outpouring from those who took the occasion to reiterate their confidence. While regretting the mischance, they praised the over-all coverage of the trial and the efficiency with which the association gathered the news of the world day after day, year after year. A letter from George B. Armstead, managing editor of the Hartford *Courant*, the country's oldest daily newspaper, was typical of many. Addressing Cooper, he wrote:

It must be grand to preside over an organization so far famed for accuracy and speed that when it makes a slip, it becomes a national sensation.

We all regret for your sake and that of the men on the story that luck went against you, but it does serve to point out the great record of The Associated Press and the tremendous impression its accuracy has made throughout the years.

Nevertheless, the memory of the false flash remained with the staff. Realization that the slip was due to the zealousness of an individual rather than to any weakness in the established system only served as a poignant reminder that, in such an era of rapid transmission facilities, the human element became an increasingly significant factor in the quick marshaling and distribution of eagerly awaited fact. As long as that human equation was involved there would remain the possibility that some error of individual judgment, some well-intentioned act, might produce an unwanted result. But no amount of effort to minimize such possibilities could be overemphasized in an organization so conscious of its unique position in a nation's daily life.

X. "URGENT"—FROM ETHIOPIA

I

WAR clouds had been gathering over East Africa for months. There had been a frontier "incident" in December, 1934, when Italian and Ethiopian patrols clashed at Ualual in disputed territory between the boundaries of Italian Somaliland and the primitive kingdom of Haile Selassie, the Conquering Lion of Judah. By midsummer of 1935 Premier Benito Mussolini had more than 240,000 troops and labor battalions concentrated in Italy's East African colonies adjoining Ethiopia. The League of Nations threatened to invoke sanctions against Italy if Il Duce's legions invaded Ethiopia. Great Britain massed naval might in the Mediterranean area at Suez and Gibraltar.

Once it became apparent that Mussolini was not likely to abandon his Ethiopian plan, The AP ordered Jim Mills to Addis Ababa to report developments there and to be on the spot if war should come. For Mills it was another out-of-the-frying-pan-into-the-fire assignment. He had just finished covering the revolt in Crete and Greece which resulted in the flight of Venizelos and the restoration of King George.

Mills arrived at Addis Ababa early in August. He found it the same sprawling collection of dirty huts and haphazard buildings he had seen five years earlier when he reported the spectacular coronation of Haile Selassie. The news in the African capital was neither abundant nor weighty. Ethiopia was anxious to bring about a peaceful settlement. Mills renewed his acquaintance with the Emperor and secured several exclusive interviews with him and with Everett A. Colson, Selassie's American financial adviser. He also watched the bands of fierce native warriors troop into the city in their dirty white shammas, savagely eager for the conflict their monarch wished to avoid.

Little happened in the barbaric city that escaped Mills's attention and he was on hand when a plane flew in from Egypt with Francis W. Rickett, a British promoter with an extraordinary career. Mills knew him of old. Rickett had become known as the "Lawrence of Finance" because of his operations in Asia and Africa. His arrival touched off a flurry of rumors among foreign newspapermen in Addis Ababa: He had come to arrange a gigantic munitions deal. He was entrusted with

407

a secret political mission bearing on the Italo-Ethiopian crisis. He had been called for a mysterious conference with the Emperor. The reports were endless.

Suave and debonair, Rickett dismissed all such talk with a tolerant smile. There was nothing spectacular behind his visit. He said he had come as a representative of the Coptic Church of Egypt for a "benevolent" purpose. The Egyptian Patriarch of that church had instructed him to learn how the Copts of Egypt could best help their Ethiopian brethren in the event of war. As proof of his mission he exhibited a letter from the Patriarch to the Abuna—or "Pope"—of the Coptic Church in Abyssinia.

Rickett managed to disarm suspicion in the press corps. He was taken at his word and attracted no special attention thereafter.

Mills, however, was not satisfied. He could not believe that a man of Rickett's caliber would be in Addis Ababa to find out whether the Egyptian Copts should send money, ambulances, airplanes, doctors, or what not. The more he speculated the more he became convinced that something else was afoot. He discovered that he was not the only skeptic. There was one other—Sir Percival Phillips of the London *Daily Telegraph*.

Over the rare luxury of a bottle of cold beer, the two correspondents compared notes in the humid privacy of their hotel rooms. They were agreed that Rickett was in Ethiopia for no trivial, "benevolent" reason. Mills and Phillips made their plans. The only way to find out just what Rickett was doing was to keep an eye on him all the time, wherever he went.

During his first week in Addis Ababa, Rickett saw the head of the Coptic Church, the Emperor and the imperial advisers. Every place he went he found himself encountering either Mills or Phillips. At first he pretended not to notice their interest in his movements, hoping to throw them off the trail or at least discourage them into abandoning their sleuthing. But the effort was futile.

Rickett stood up under the surveillance for a few days, then made overtures for a truce. Slipping into Mills's hotel room one night the British promoter laid his cards on the table.

"You two have been following me for over a week now. In another day or two the rest of the reporters are going to wake up to the fact. That is apt to spoil everything—for you as well as for me. What I have to do here makes it imperative that I act quietly and unobserved."

"Well, that's your worry," said Mills noncommittally. "Why come to us about it?"

"I have a proposal to make. If you'll stop shadowing me, within a few days I'll give you one of the biggest stories that ever happened "

Mills and Sir Percival exchanged glances. The idea of any Ethiopian story being of the "biggest-that-ever-happened" variety was a bit too much for them. They said so. However, they wanted the story behind Rickett's mission and now they knew how to get it.

"I'll go along," said Mills.

Sir Percival nodded agreement.

2

A few nights later Addis Ababa slept under a clear sky. The full moon shone down on deserted streets and dark houses. In the Emperor's palace four intent figures moved to and fro. They were Francis M. Rickett, Haile Selassie, Everett A. Colson, and George Herouy, son of the Ethiopian foreign minister who acted as interpreter for the Emperor.

Haile Selassie yawned. He looked strained, worried and tired. For the past two weeks he had been up every night until long after midnight, negotiating with Rickett. Because of the need for secrecy about the bold coup by which he hoped to forestall an Italian invasion, the Emperor and those negotiating with him had worked only after the city was asleep.

Rickett handed the Emperor a folio of typewritten sheets.

"There is the revised contract, your Majesty," he said.

The document represented the seventh revision. The Emperor examined it page by page, announced his approval, and affixed the imperial seal.

Mills and Phillips waited in their hotel room. They knew this was the night. Rickett had told them to be ready for the story that was to be the "biggest that ever happened," but they still did not know what it was.

Then the dapper Englishman appeared. He burst into the room, smiling and elated. Mills and Phillips were on their feet.

"Here it is, signed, sealed, and delivered," he said triumphantly, throwing the document on the table. "It will make history. It may even make war. It may indeed make peace. In any case, it will be a triumph for American and British capital and industry."

Mills and his colleague pounced on the papers and began to study them in the lamplight. The two correspondents were astounded by what they read.

Haile Selassie had signed over to the Standard Oil Company and some British interests the exclusive rights for the exploitation of all Ethiopia's oil and mineral wealth in an area three times the size of New England, and for the amazing period of seventy-five years. The agreement assured the Emperor of an annual return far greater than the whole yearly national income of his kingdom. It granted the American-British interests the right to build railroads, pipe lines, bridges, refineries, new highways, ports, whole cities, and a hundred other great developments. It involved the ultimate investment of several hundred million dollars.

Sir Percival smothered a gasp. He turned to Mills.

"This thing is so gigantic," he said, "I'm afraid to send it to my paper. They won't believe it."

Mills, too, was awed by the contents of the contract.

"But it's signed and sealed by the Emperor, the minister of mines, and Rickett," he pointed out. "There can be no question of its authenticity."

"You can accept it as Scriptural truth," Rickett declared.

The significance of the document was all too clear to the two correspondents. In signing away the richest part of his domains, the Emperor had a shrewd motive. With this great area in the hands of powerful American and British interests, he believed Mussolini would never attempt to challenge their claims under the concession, nor even dare to invade that section of Ethiopia, for fear of antagonizing the two great powers.

Rickett said he was dog-tired after the negotiations of the past two weeks. He was going to bed, but he'd entrust the main points of the concession to them until daybreak so that they could prepare their dispatches. He asked them to frame a brief communiqué, based on the contract, so that the government could release it as an official announcement when the proper time came.

"I'm leaving by airplane for Cairo the first thing in the morning," he explained. "Be sure to have everything ready before I go."

Mills and Sir Percival went to work. First they prepared the "official communiqué"—a hundred-word statement reciting the broad general facts of the historic contract. Then they devoted the next few

RICKETT HANDED THE EMPEROR A FOLIO OF TYPEWRITTEN SHEETS.

hours to their own dispatches and to plans for keeping the explosive story a secret from competitors.

The government wireless station—sole link between Addis Ababa and the outside world—opened at dawn and Mills filed a 1,600-word story. Sir Percival sent off a story of similar length to his paper in London. After Rickett departed, Mills secured the complete text of the concession, a 2,000-word document, and dispatched it by wireless, giving a copy to Sir Percival. Getting out the story was comparatively costly—25 cents a word. Under normal circumstances Mills would have sent his dispatch at the even more expensive "urgent" rate, but he and his British colleague had agreed to mark their stories for release the next day, August 30, so that The AP and the London *Daily Telegraph* would be able to break the news simultaneously.

By nine o'clock that morning, Addis Ababa time, Mills had his complete story cleared. With Sir Percival he spent the next few hours in nervous anxiety lest any hint of it leak out. Their fear was justified. Word did leak out, and the rest of the press corps went rushing about the city seeking confirmation of the report and details. Some fifty correspondents descended in turn upon the Emperor, the minister of mines, the foreign minister, Mr. Colson, the American legation, the British legation, the Abuna of the Ethiopian Church. All sources, however, disclaimed knowledge and refused to comment. Some, like the American and British legations, professed complete ignorance of the concession, which was literally true. Other legations termed the reported story pure invention.

3

Halfway across the world the first "takes" of Mills's dispatch began arriving in New York. The time difference between New York and Addis Ababa made it eight hours earlier in the American metropolis, and the result was that the story reached the cable desk well over a dozen hours before the stipulated time set for its release in the night report of August 30. Working against the clock as he did, Mills had written his dispatch hurriedly, but there could be no mistaking the significance of the facts he had set down.

The story was promptly brought to the attention of Smith Reavis, then in charge of the Cable Department, and Milo Thompson, executive assistant to the general manager.

Both Reavis and Thompson were accustomed to the shocks and surprises in the daily news of the world, but they were astounded by this "break" in Ethiopia. They saw the importance of the transaction Mills described. They studied the story and its accompanying text. Then a series of editorial conferences started. One of the first subjects raised was the question of trying the two logical domestic sources for "follows"—the State Department at Washington, for comment on the international aspects of the Rickett concession, and the Standard Oil offices in New York, for a statement of the corporation's plans in the matter. The idea was weighed and tabled. Any attempt to develop follows might result in the story's leaking out before time came to release it in the night report. Mills had said it was exclusive, so both Reavis and Thompson felt the wisest course was to keep it a secret and not try any follows until the story actually began to move out on the wires.

As for the story itself, the more it was studied the more formidable it became. Even though it came from Jim Mills, a staff man of twenty-five years' service, some of the men found the news almost too overwhelming for belief. Reavis and Thompson had confidence in Mills, but the dispatch was something that must be confirmed and double checked thoroughly before a single word was transmitted. They consulted the general manager and he sent an urgent message.

The government-owned wireless station in Addis Ababa closed down for the night at seven o'clock. At five minutes before seven Mills was handed the general manager's query. The message said it was imperative that the authenticity of the story be confirmed beyond conceivable doubt and that headquarters have complete proof for every statement in the dispatch as well as the specific source of all the information.

Mills finished the cable, upset and bewildered. All day long he had been looking forward to the nightly closing of the wireless station, because then, if the Rickett story should come out into the open, competition would have no means of communication for a dozen hours. Now—five minutes before the station's closing time—came this bombshell from headquarters.

Mills made quick calculations. Unless he got a reply off to New York before 7 P.M., he would have to wait until 7 A.M.—and that would be 11 P.M., New York time. It meant losing almost a whole day. Hatless and coatless, he sprinted for the telegraph office. The operators were getting ready to go home when he burst into the station. In two minutes he scribbled off an "urgent" to "Kenper, New York." He told the general manager that all the details in the dispatch had come "straight from the horse's mouth"—from Rickett himself; that the actual text of the concession had been given him personally by Colson; and that he had personally seen the original of the contract, bearing the seals and signatures of those involved.

Front pages the next morning splurged a world copyright story—Mills's detailed disclosure of the now historic Rickett Oil Concession.

4

Haile Selassie's desperate attempt to halt an Italian invasion with the fantastic concession proved a failure. At 5 A.M. on October 3 the gray-green columns of Fascist Italy crossed the Ethiopian border from Eritrea and the undeclared Italo-Ethiopian War was on.

Andrue Berding, chief of the Rome Bureau, was in the field to report the first stages of the main Italian advance. The assignment was afterward taken over by a new recruit in the Foreign Service, Edward J. Neil, a breezy young man with prematurely gray hair, an infectious smile, and an engaging personality. Another seasoned newspaperman from New York, Mark Barron, covered the secondary Fascist thrust northward from Italian Somaliland. Joe Caneva, one of the top-ranking cameramen on the staff, was the first American photographer on the scene. He followed Il Duce's legions on a moth-eaten donkey. In Addis Ababa, Mills was joined by Al Wilson, of the London Bureau, who had been ordered to Egypt when the massing of the British naval force at the Suez Canal aroused danger of an open clash with Italy.

After Wilson's arrival, the AP establishment in the Ethiopian capital went on a semi-permanent basis. Mills and his London colleague leased a little cottage which formerly had housed the Austrian legation. The cottage was only two blocks from the wireless station, and it boasted a small truck garden and a barnyard of ducks, chickens, pigeons, and rabbits—insurance against any food shortage. Wilson lined up string correspondents in the major Ethiopian towns and helped Mills arrange with foreign free-lance photographers for pictures. The cottage headquarters accumulated a staff of eight—Ethiopians and Arabs who acted as messenger boys, runners, and men of all work. Airplanes were hired to ferry out pictures, and the two-man Addis Ababa Bureau soon found itself acquiring a truck, an automobile, and a motorcycle.

Once hostilities started, the topic in Addis Ababa was the Emperor's projected departure for the front to take personal command of his warriors. Until the Emperor left no correspondent was permitted to leave the capital for the war zone because authorities feared the ignorant tribesmen would mistake them for enemies and kill them. Mills had arranged to accompany the monarch. When the day finally came, Wilson, who remained behind, found himself in trouble with the government—very much as he expected.

Weeks before the King of Kings started for the front, the Govment Press Bureau notified all correspondents that the censors would pass no copy dealing with his Majesty's departure, the route he would travel, or his subsequent whereabouts. Officials feared the Emperor's safety would be jeopardized by Italian bombing planes. Wilson could appreciate the Ethiopian attitude, but his responsibility was to report the news. When the Emperor left for the front, it unquestionably would be news. The job was to get it out. After much thought he and his superiors in London, by a mailed exchange, devised a plan to circumvent the censor by disguising the information in a routine interoffice message regarding bureau supplies. The plan worked. No sooner had the imperial party departed in mid-November than London had Wilson's message and cabled New York that Haile Selassie had left for the front, traveling overland via Dessye.

The news got back to Addis Ababa within a short time, and a storm of Ethiopian wrath descended on Wilson's head. The correspondent offered no defense. It was news. His job was to get it out. Unfortunately that necessitated outwitting the censor. The logic was unassailable, but Ethiopian officials could not be expected to agree. Wilson was notified that all AP dispatches henceforth would be refused at the wireless station—and the wireless station was the only channel to the outside world. The ban remained in force several days and was rescinded without explanation. Perhaps the fact that the wireless was a government monopoly had something to do with it—for The AP spent as much as $1,000 a day in wireless tolls.

5

Ethiopian precautions to conceal the Emperor's whereabouts were unavailing. On December 6 a fleet of nineteen Capronis roared over the imperial field headquarters at Dessye, bombing and machine-gunning the panic-stricken natives. Three Italian bombs fell within a few feet of Mills, exploding with ear-shattering roars and setting fire to a Red Cross tent immediately adjoining the one the AP correspondent had been occupying.

The bombing of Dessye was the first air raid witnessed by any correspondent attached to the Ethiopian armies. It inflicted casualties of 84 killed and 363 wounded, but Mills came through it unscathed, started pictures back to Addis Ababa on one of the AP trucks, and cleared his story by field wireless to Wilson at the capital. Later Mills was the first correspondent to make flights over the northern and southern Ethiopian fronts—a dangerous business with the Italians supreme in the air.

For the staff men on both sides there were plenty of hardships. The temperatures ranged from blistering heat in the day to below freezing at night, and the high altitude imposed a severe physical strain. Eddie Neil had a bout with tropical fever and later suffered a chest hemorrhage from overexertion. He also suffered a leg injury in the crash of a bomber which was flying him over enemy lines. The altitude felled Wilson for a few days, inducing an acute attack of appendicitis resulting from disturbed metabolism. Before hostilities ended Barron contracted a virulent tropical disease which made it necessary to bring him out on a stretcher. Only Mills and the durable Caneva seemed immune to sickness and altitude.

Even without illness, the assignment was trying enough. Life was made up of storms, swarms of insects, omnipresent vermin, uncertain drinking water, and bad food. The men with the Italians lived on a monotonous diet of spaghetti—with a few Ethiopian flies mixed in each dish—and uncontaminated drinking water cost forty cents a bottle. Once in a while on trips back to the Italian base in Eritrea they pooled resources for a "banquet"—a huge American-style omelet and a jug of wine—and these rare gastronomic orgies cost each the equivalent of a week's salary.

Caneva had his own little group of additional troubles. Working almost entirely in the field with the army, he had to handle his photographic plates under impossible conditions. Pictures could not be developed during the day because the heat was so scorching that negatives would melt, and even at night developing was a major problem. There were no darkrooms or any other photographic facilities.

As the campaign wore on, the main source of news became more and more the staff men with the Italian troops. Not long after the bombing of Dessye, the Emperor ordered all newspaper men back to Addis Ababa and they were kept cooped up there until the government collapsed.

Flying with Italian pilots, slogging along on foot with sweating columns, or bouncing around in a careening army truck, Neil had opportunities for gathering the news, but getting it out was a different proposition. Only the briefest stories were accepted over the military communications facilities. The bulk of the material had to be sent back in any manner that offered itself—sometimes by courier, sometimes by an ambulance driver or returning supply truck, and sometimes by an obliging aviator. Neil marveled that so much of his copy got through to New York. Speaking of the uncertainty of sending dispatches, he remarked: "Once you finished a story, it was like putting it in a bottle and throwing it overboard in the middle of the ocean. All you could do was to hope somebody would find it and send it along to New York."

It was all over in a comparatively few months, and Neil went whirling into a conquered Addis Ababa with the mechanized column that formed the spearhead of the final Italian advance.

Prior to 1914 the conclusion of a war had always meant an interlude of reasonable normality for the Cable Department. But now there was nothing but turbulence. In Asia the scope of another undeclared war grew wider as Japanese troops extended operations in China. Spain seethed with unrest, in England King George V had died and Germany's Adolf Hitler, Der Führer of the Third Reich, had begun his systematic scrapping of the Versailles Treaty.

XI. MATTERS OF MOMENT

I

THROUGH three historic decades and well into a fourth, Frank B. Noyes had presided as president of The Associated Press. In all that time there had been no variation in the procedure each year when the newly constituted Board of Directors convened the day after the co-operative's annual meeting. The first business was always the election of officers. On April 21, 1936, the well-established order was followed. The name of Noyes was placed in renomination. No other candidate was offered.

As he had done so often before, Noyes told his fellow directors that he appreciated the honor more deeply than he could hope to express.

"Nevertheless," he said gravely, "the time is coming—if indeed it is not already at hand—when I shall have to lay down the cares and obligations of this high office."

The board was reluctant to accept any suggestion of immediate retirement and one after another the directors pressed him to reconsider.

In the face of their pleas, Noyes finally consented to accept re-election. He imposed one condition—that some younger member of the board be elected first vice-president and in that capacity assume any part of the president's duties and responsibilities which might be passed on to him. In effect, Noyes was asking that the man who would succeed him be designated in advance so that he might work with him for whatever time remained before he relinquished the presidency.

For first vice-president—and ultimately the next president of The Associated Press—the board unanimously selected Robert McLean, publisher of the Philadelphia *Bulletin*. His father, W. L. McLean, had been a member of the board from 1900 until his resignation in 1924, and thereafter he continued an active interest in the co-operative's affairs until his death in 1931. The new vice-president had been elected to the board to succeed his father and had served ever since. He began his newspaper career in 1913 when he was twenty-one, soon after his graduation from Princeton University, and during the World War served as a major of artillery. In his dozen or more years on the board he had been close to Noyes, particularly in the fight to prevent the defeat of Wirephoto.

Noyes's contemplated retirement was only one of the noteworthy administrative developments in the twelve-month period since the previous Board of Directors had met to organize. There had been several executive changes in the management owing to the retirement of men whose names had long been bywords in the co-operative.

The first major change involved the retirement of a character who had become an AP legend—Treasurer John R. Youatt. Back in April, 1894, Stone had offered him the position of auditor. For forty-two years he was the vigilant guardian of the association's finances. He watched pennies as closely as dollars and the stories about his thriftiness multiplied with the years. Once a staffer covering General Pershing's pursuit of Pancho Villa wired him that a fine second-hand automobile could be purchased for $800 if approval were given, and that it might facilitate coverage in Mexico. In those days second-hand automobiles were not the acme of mechanical reliability. Moreover, desert country did not present ideal operating conditions. Youatt's reply was a model of economy and wisdom. "Buy a mule," he telegraphed.

To succeed Youatt the board elected L. F. Curtis. The new treasurer had been a member of the staff for twenty-five years. During that time he handled local, national, cable, political, and financial news assignments, and one of them sent him with President Wilson to the Paris Peace Conference in 1919. Subsequently he was news editor of the Eastern Division, and in 1921, when Wilmer Stuart died, he became superintendent of markets and elections.

A few weeks after Youatt's resignation, Jackson S. Elliott, another notable figure, relinquished his duties as assistant general manager preparatory to retiring after more than thirty years of service.

2

Demands on the management as a whole had assumed such proportions that some administrative expansion was necessary. For this reason two assistant general managers—Lloyd C. Stratton and William J. McCambridge—were appointed by General Manager Cooper to help him. Stratton, the first editor of the Feature Service, was assigned to administrative duties in the field of news. McCambridge was placed in immediate charge of all matters pertaining to transmission and engineering operations.

Several months after these changes were made effective, the general manager began consideration of a step looking toward a more complete unification of all news-gathering efforts. As matters then stood, the active direction of the news report was divided among three supervising general editors—one for the day, one for the night, and one for the Sunday or weekend report. Assignments to day, night, or weekend duty made for corresponding divisions of the staff. Under this system there was sustained staff endeavor around the clock, seven days a week, and at the same time a healthy rivalry was fostered, for each division strove to produce a better report than the other. The three supervising editors—W. F. Brooks, C. E. Honce, and J. M. Kendrick—worked under the personal direction of the general manager.

The time Cooper could devote exclusively to the news report day after day was limited and he finally reached the conclusion that it was desirable to appoint an executive news editor who would be able to give exclusive attention to the news. For the position he needed a man of wide experience and proved executive ability. He wanted someone who would not disturb the rivalry existing among the day, night, and Sunday staffs.

Byron Price, chief of bureau at Washington, had the talent and training to fill the requirements Cooper had in mind. He had joined the staff in 1912, a young man with a Phi Beta Kappa key recently out of Wabash College. He got his start in the Atlanta Bureau, served as acting correspondent at New Orleans, and then was transferred to Washington. He joined the army during the World War. As a first lieutenant and later a captain of infantry, he served overseas with a regiment that was cited for conspicuous service during the Meuse-Argonne offensive immediately preceding the signing of the Armistice. Mustered out in 1919, he rejoined the Washington Bureau. His subsequent assignments covered all fields of governmental, political, and diplomatic activities.

3

The program of administrative changes, contemplated or already in effect, constituted only a part of 1936's story. Much more dramatic was the unscheduled and unheralded debut of the newest servant of modern news gathering—portable Wirephoto.

For more than a year engineers in the research laboratory had been working to perfect a convenient-sized picture-sending machine which could be hurried to the scene of big news along with staff reporters and cameramen. Size was not the only problem. They wanted a set that could utilize either the regular Wirephoto network or ordinary commercial circuits, and thus be adapted for immediate use in any place, no matter how isolated, which had a telephone.

Progress was slow. Telephone company experts had not minimized the difficulties when they expressed doubt that any practical portable apparatus could be devised. Nevertheless, the laboratory kept at it. One by one the technical difficulties were overcome, new mechanical parts designed, and knotty assembly problems worked out. At length Assistant General Manager McCambridge, Chief Engineer Biele, and their research staff believed they had developed the equipment they sought.

The miscellany of parts, vacuum tubes, and wires scattered along a laboratory workbench looked like a hopeless hodgepodge, but to the men who had spent months of experimenting they represented a splendid achievement. They could visualize the equipment mounted ingeniously in two small traveling cases weighing about forty pounds each—a power unit in one case and the sending unit in the other—ready to be rushed to the scene of any news emergency so that pictures could be transmitted onto the Wirephoto system with a minimum of delay.

The first experiments had produced satisfactory results. The picture transmissions were on a par with the performance of the stationary apparatus in the regular Wirephoto stations. The experiments, however, were performed under ideal laboratory conditions; the network had not been utilized, and the transmissions were over relatively short distances. The engineers wanted to satisfy themselves that the portable would perform with equal fidelity over long distances after being subjected to the hard knocks and rough usage incident to actual field operations. The test schedule was mapped along those lines.

But news has never respected engineering programs. The initial experiments had scarcely started when a succession of violent spring floods swept the eastern United States. In New England, New York, Maryland, Ohio, and particularly in Pennsylvania and West Virginia, bureau staffs went on emergency footing to report another national catastrophe. Hour by hour the news report brought accounts of the devastation and The AP News Photo Service obtained eloquent pictures of the ruin and havoc.

The worst-hit of the flood areas was western Pennsylvania and West Virginia. Pittsburgh was virtually isolated. The airport there was inundated and water more than six feet deep flowed through the business district—"The Golden Triangle." Johnstown, scene of the terrible flood of 1889, watched the rising water and feared an even worse disaster. In Wheeling half of the downtown section was under water, and the swollen Ohio rolled over Wheeling Island, submerging the homes of hundreds of families.

As the strategic bureau in the stricken area, Pittsburgh became the clearinghouse for the news and pictures. Once again a staff battled the problem of getting out the information after communications had been disrupted. Most telephone and telegraph lines were down, railroad and motor vehicle traffic was virtually suspended, bridges were out, power plants had failed, and planes could not take off from the airport.

In spite of the failure of regular news facilities, Pittsburgh managed to keep the news moving out by one means or another. Sometimes it was a roundabout series of shaky telephone relays, sometimes a temporary Morse circuit, sometimes amateur wireless stations. With pictures, however, the difficulties were acute. Although four staff cameramen were on the job, most of their pictures accumulated unserviced at Pittsburgh. The city was not then on the Wirephoto network and there was no means of getting out the pictures rapidly.

For photo editors in New York the situation was maddening. They had the pictures, any number of pictures, but the pictures were in Pittsburgh, isolated by the flood. Until the waters receded, there was little chance of getting them out by the usual methods. To wait until transportation facilities were restored might mean days, and member newspapers did not want to wait days.

Photo editors at headquarters held conference after conference but were unable to devise any workable solution. Finally Assistant General Manager McCambridge proposed that the unassembled portable equipment on the laboratory workbench be flown to Pittsburgh on the chance that it could meet the emergency. There was considerable doubt that a plane could negotiate a landing on the flooded Pittsburgh field. Even assuming a safe arrival, the portable would have to be able to operate under the most adverse conditions, utilizing an uncertain wire circuit for transmission and drawing on storage batteries for power. The odds were against the success of a machine which was little more than an experimental model.

The assortment of parts were hurriedly stowed away in two packing boxes and Harold Carlson and Jim Barnes, who had worked on the portable ever since research began, were chosen for the trip. Their plane was forced down at Harrisburg, two hundred miles short of its goal, and they chartered another and took to the air again. The second plane made a splashy landing on the soggy, treacherous flying field at Pittsburgh that afternoon.

The men headed for the telephone company building only a few hundred feet from the flood crest. They found conditions as bad as they had feared. There was no regular electric power, no heat, and no assurance that a wire circuit would be available. Carlson and Barnes moved in their packing boxes, tool kits, and storage batteries. The room placed at their disposal was dark and the only illumination came from candles and storage battery lights.

For hours they tested, changed, adjusted and readjusted, checking the equipment piece by piece. Then the telephone company notified them that a line had been set up and could be cut into the regular transcontinental Wirephoto network.

A few minutes later the last adjustment had been made, the last connection checked. The portable was as ready as the engineers could make it. The latest pictures had arrived by messenger from the Pittsburgh Bureau. Earphones clamped to his head, Carlson could hear the conversations and instructions going back and forth over the Wirephoto circuit. The control editor in New York gave them a "Go Ahead," and Barnes flipped a switch.

The portable's sending cylinder began to rotate.

In New York, Boston, Miami, Chicago, Kansas City, San Francisco, and all the other cities on the picture network the receiving Wirephoto cylinders revolved turn for turn with the Pittsburgh portable. Eight minutes later the transmission was finished and the first negative developed. Across the country photo editors had the wet print of the Pittsburgh picture before them. It was a photograph of a flooded newspaper pressroom in the heart of the Golden Triangle. With perfect clarity it showed the dark waters running deep across the floor, the details of the half-submerged presses and the rubber-booted press crews perched high on the machinery.

Portable Wirephoto worked.

During 1935-1936 the series of administrative changes made one major theme in the co-operative's story. The development of portable Wirephoto, together with other inventive accomplishments of Traffic Department engineers, supplied a second. To these was added a third. It was the subject of labor, although The AP had never been disposed to regard the question of its own personnel in the controversial terms of a "labor problem."

XII. BEFORE THE SUPREME COURT

I

THROUGHOUT the troubled thirties the story of American labor, its plans and its problems, its gains and its losses, its champions and its critics, took a more prominent place in the news report than ever before. The period had begun with the story of labor's struggle against unemployment and then it turned to the uncharted field of economic and social construction and experimentation. As the worst rigors of the depression began to pass, labor entered a complex period of transition. It was a period of labor legislation and great resurgence of union activities. Often it was a period of contradictions and puzzles, and it saw organized labor for the second time split into two hostile camps over the issue of craft and industrial unionism.

The controversial nature of events made the strictest accuracy and impartiality so imperative that particularized instructions were issued to the staff, admonishing everyone to exert the most scrupulous care in reporting, writing, and editing labor news. Both sides in any issue must be presented correctly, fully, without bias. Given the facts of any case, newspaper readers should be able to form their own opinions.

Recounting the story of labor was no fresh assignment. In the eighty-odd years since the association began its career the staff had been called on to report most of the history of the labor movement in the United States, but only once did that movement impinge even briefly on the operations of the organization itself. At the founding of The Associated Press in 1848, a national "labor problem," in the modern understanding of the term, did not exist. The country was largely agricultural in character, and only along the eastern seaboard were there any industrial centers.

During those early years the subject of staff personnel was one of the few problems which caused little worry, except that experienced newspapermen were difficult to find. The staff was small and salaries compared favorably with the standards of the day. Like colleagues on daily publications, the men considered their occupation professional or semi-professional in nature and looked upon it with a professional pride. People spoke of them as "journalists" and in the popular mind they constituted a class apart—an impression which most "journalists" consciously or unconsciously encouraged.

Excepting messenger boys, a few clerical workers, and kindred employes, the staff was entirely editorial in character. With leased news circuits unheard of, transmission of dispatches was the province of commercial telegraph companies and the association had no need to maintain its own corps of Morse operators although many of the men considered a knowledge of the telegraph as essential to their work as the modern reporter considers the ability to use the typewriter.

Labor news was negligible, but the years after the Civil War brought a revival of union activity and for the first time organization efforts and disputes manifested a tendency toward a national scope. By and large this movement was political rather than industrial in concept, representing an evolution from the earlier organizations which had preached a doctrine of class harmony and humanitarianism with such slogans as "Union for power, power to bless humanity." The quasi-political unions were the forerunners of the more definitely trade-union groups which developed in the years that followed.

In 1875—two years before The Associated Press covered the first large-scale industrial dispute in the country—there came a change in its personnel structure. The association leased its first news-wire circuits and manned them with its own telegraphers. This introduced a new class of employe. It was the beginning of a mechanical, or traffic, department, although that formal designation was not applied until much later.

First staff telegraphers were engaged at salaries identical with those being paid by the commercial telegraph companies—$17 a week for day work and $19 a week for night work. Then, as the operating force increased, James W. Simonton, the general agent, became convinced that the work of a staff telegrapher was more exacting than that of an operator with a commercial company. Accordingly salaries were increased to maintain a proper differential.

2

The great railway strike of 1877 introduced a new type of news. Before the strike ended seven persons were killed and millions of dollars in property destroyed. From then on, labor became increasingly productive of major stories. In 1885 there was the dispute affecting Jay Gould's Missouri Pacific and Iron Mountain Railroad, which ended with a victory for the Knights of Labor. This strike was memorable in AP history both because Charles S. Diehl's exclusive interview with Gould in Florida was credited with expediting a settlement and because Diehl's story was the first ever carried in the report with an official by-line. The eighties saw an epidemic of strikes waged on the eight-hour-day and lockout issues. From a news standpoint, the most notable story was the one which culminated in the bloody Haymarket Square riot in Chicago in 1886—one of the first assignments covered by John P. Boughan, later one of the association's best known writers.

The emergence of AP as a non-profit co-operative coincided with a period in labor history both important and turbulent. The movement was divided on the question of craft versus industrial unions. The industrial Knights of Labor had begun to decline, and a new craft union organization—the American Federation of Labor—was gaining strength, advocating the eight-hour-day. The panic of 1893 was responsible for large-scale disputes and disorders and the strikes produced the use of injunctions and federal troops.

In the nature of things, strikes and other labor disturbances made more news than the peaceful progress of the union movement or industrial amity, just as an international crisis made more news than a harmonious world. There was, inevitably, a certain amount of criticism from time to time by opposing factions, particularly in the heat of strikes when employers and employes could see only their own side of the conflict. Proportionately, however, the complaints were neither greater nor less than the number arising from political questions or other controversial matters.

The co-operative was zealous to maintain its disinterested approach to all news, whether it concerned labor or some other topic, and anything that might raise the slightest doubt about the impartiality of the staff was a matter to be rectified at once. The Board of Directors even went so far as to discourage social relationships of General Manager Stone with some of the prominent people of his day, lest they create any suspicions, however unjust, affecting the integrity and independence of the news.

The return of prosperity after the Spanish-American War gave organized labor fresh stimulus. Membership in unions increased and there was a revival of interest in unionism and its aims. As in the past, however, these activities failed to arouse any perceptible personal interest among the co-operative's staff. There was an operators' union in the country—the Commercial Telegraphers Union—but it had enlisted only a few of the association's Morse men. The salaries of staff telegraphers were higher than those paid by the commercial companies and the idea of unionization for editorial personnel had never been broached either by labor leaders or by editorial employes. As far as the editorial men were concerned, they considered themselves specialists engaged in work of a mental and creative character not amenable to the same hard and fast rules which might apply in purely commercial and industrial pursuits.

3

The first few years of the twentieth century were marked by the high cost of living, and many staff telegraphers felt its pinch. Stone met the situation by increasing the salaries of operators in the larger cities, where the rise in living costs had been sharpest.

When living conditions failed to improve by 1903, however, he received a petition signed by 254 of the 374 telegraphers in the service asking a blanket increase. The request came at a bad time, for the co-operative was operating at a deficit. Stone ascertained that the association by that time was maintaining a differential of at least 25 per cent over the salaries paid by commercial companies and railroads. Nevertheless, he recommended that the telegraphers be given two weeks annual vacation with pay—something no commercial company gave its operators—and that the men be relieved of the obligation of supplying and maintaining their own typewriters, a practice then in force universally.

The results of the 1903 petition seemed to satisfy the majority of the telegraphers and a number told Stone they thought he had obtained an equitable adjustment for them.

The C.T.U. continued its campaign to extend its strength and in 1905 sought a written contract, although it represented only a minority of the men. It presented a series of demands which included salary increases as high as 50 per cent, and a provision whereby the assignment of operators, and in some cases their employment or dismissal, would be entirely in the hands of the union. The Board of Directors rejected the contract and the C.T.U. retaliated by announcing that its members thereafter would not accept employment in the co-operative. The union's action had no effect and the attempt to impair the strength of the operating force ended in admitted failure.

In July, 1907, a series of strikes against the two commercial wire companies—Western Union and Postal Telegraph—began throughout the country. Except in so far as it delayed some news matter being handled over commercial facilities, the dispute at first did not involve The AP. The association employed only about one per cent of the 40,000 telegraphers in the United States and there had been no requests, official or otherwise, for adjustments.

Since the co-operative's New York headquarters were then housed in the Western Union building, the telegraph staff was well aware of the tension and the disturbed atmosphere. The news report, however, continued to move out over the leased wires with accustomed regularity. Then, without warning, a group of telegraphers on the night staff took possession of the circuits on August 11 and canvassed night operators at all bureau points, asking authority to sign their names to a petition.

Some agreed and the unexpected petition was placed before Stone the next morning with an ultimatum that its demands be met within twelve hours. It called for increases aggregating $200,000 a year— roughly 10 per cent of the whole annual budget at the time—and for a higher overtime rate. Stone had no authority to grant such a demand and the deadline gave him no opportunity to arrange for a meeting of the board to consider it. He offered to confer with a representative of the men pending a meeting of the board.

The offer went unheeded and a strike was ordered at 7:30 P.M. that same day—August 12. In the Eastern Division, the largest unit of the service, 59 of 180 telegraphers quit their keys. Some divisions were not affected at all, but in others enough quit to interrupt temporarily the local transmission of the report. A majority remained at their posts and volunteered to work additional hours to keep the news moving. Reporter-telegraphers on the editorial staff manned empty Morse positions and in Albany an office boy who had been studying telegraphy handled one wire like a veteran.

From the outset the strike failed of its objective—a nation-wide stoppage of the news report. The morning after the strike was called every member of the New York day telegraph staff reported for work. They condemned the strike as merely sympathetic to the dissatisfied commercial workers, termed it an unjust action by a minority element of their fellow telegraphers, and drafted a message urging the strikers to return to their posts. Stone's permission was sought for the transmission of the message on the leased wires, but he declined.

The back of the strike was broken after the first week, but it dragged on in desultory fashion for a month. Then most of the men applied for their old positions and were taken back without prejudice. The Board of Directors met in mid-September and Stone expressed himself in favor of an even higher wage level, irrespective of what the commercial companies were paying. Although an annual deficit of $100,000 already was in prospect, the directors authorized him to proceed.

4

In terms of the ensuing years, the telegraphers' strike had no lasting effect. It did not signalize the beginning of an era in which the relations between management and personnel were to assume "labor problem" proportions.

The policy of The AP had been to maintain the relations between employes and the general manager (himself an employe) on a personal basis. The size of the staff at the time made such a system practicable and the general manager had no difficulty keeping in close touch with the men and their work. Both Stone and Assistant General Manager Diehl traveled extensively and the staff knew them familiarly as "M.E.S." and "Charley Diehl."

As the staff grew, however, it became more and more difficult to maintain these personal contacts. Little by little, personnel relations became decentralized and the responsibility was divided among the superintendents in charge of the four main geographical divisions which comprised the domestic service. Dealing with these smaller units, the superintendents were able to handle their division staffs on an individual basis, but the co-operative as a whole lost something in the suspension of direct relations between the employe and the management.

By 1910, when Cooper entered the service, the handling of personnel had become, with certain limitations, entirely the province of the division superintendents. Cooper's duties called for incessant traveling and the assignment unintentionally served a twofold purpose. It restored to the staff at large a personal link with headquarters, and it gave the management a firsthand contact with the staff without the medium of division superintendents.

Several things impressed Cooper. The first was the widening difference between the editorial and telegraph departments in outlook, problems, and the type of employe attracted. Once ambitious telegraphers had made editorial positions their goal but now the younger members of this staff were thinking in terms of scientific and engineering opportunities. It was clear that the interests of the service would best be served by divorcing the news-gathering and news-disseminating staffs, and the formal organization of a Traffic Department followed.

Another matter Cooper reported was a tendency toward stagnation of the news personnel under the administration of division superintendents. The superintendents, concerned only with the most efficient operation of their respective divisions, were inclined to keep their editorial men in the same position indefinitely if they filled it well. With few exceptions, advancement depended on the death or resignation of the man who was the immediate superior. Such a system minimized merit, tended to discourage initiative, and removed the stimulus of opportunity. Furthermore, by placing divisional considerations above everything else, the General Service was being deprived of able men who might be more valuable in other positions. To remedy this situation, Cooper recommended more frequent transfer of talented men from one geographical division to another.

5

The outbreak of the World War had a tendency to "freeze" the system in its existing state. Attention was monopolized by the problems of war coverage and there was little time to study ways and means of restoring any semblance of the old direct methods in personnel relations. However, a higher salary scale was made effective to meet the increased cost of wartime living and, more important, the Board of Directors inaugurated the general pension, insurance, and sick benefit plan which Cooper had drawn up.

After the Armistice and the break in war prosperity, labor news came back with a wave of strikes and disputes largely precipitated by the reduction of wages from boom peaks. Living costs and mounting unemployment contributed to the unsettled conditions, but this industrial unrest left the co-operative unaffected because its affairs were running counter to the general trend. The postwar years saw unprecedented expansion in news gathering, wages were maintained at wartime levels, and the staff was enlarged rather than curtailed.

The sole personnel problem was the loss of experienced editorial men who were being sought by publicity-conscious organizations of one sort or another. The salary inducements often were irresistible and Stone on occasion found himself reluctantly advising valued editors to accept positions which offered greater compensation than he could match. Nevertheless, these raids led to further adjustment of salaries for editorial employes generally. The management could not always bid dollar for dollar, but it was anxious to make positions as attractive as possible because the general manager thought the association could be best served by "career" men who regarded their employment as more than just another job.

Throughout the twenties unions were aggressive in campaigns for wage increases, shorter hours, and improved working conditions. Key bureaus developed specialists on their staffs to handle the news so that coverage would be in the hands of men thoroughly familiar with the background of union activities.

Although the internal affairs of The Associated Press had progressed smoothly, no enduring changes had been made in the status of personnel administration. Division superintendents continued to discharge most of these responsibilities, and the undesirable features of such a system persisted. It was not until Cooper became general manager in 1925 that a concerted effort was made to restore as much of the old "personal" element as the size of the staff would permit.

He proceeded on a twofold principle. He wanted to centralize personnel administration at headquarters so that he could keep constantly informed on the staff and use that information to the best advantage of the service. He also wanted to put relations between headquarters and staff members back on an individual basis, in so far as possible. To accomplish these ends, he assumed complete charge of all personnel matters and instituted a new system of personnel administration.

The first step was to inaugurate a special "personal" file at New York for every member of the staff. Into these individual files went the complete record of a man's service, his successes and setbacks, salary increases and promotions, the report of superiors on his work, and a confidential letter from the employee himself setting forth his ambitions in the organization.

Cooper called for regular reports from bureau chiefs on each member of their staffs and when a man showed ability for greater opportunity he tried to see to it that he got a transfer to some bureau where opportunity existed. When a man did not seem to be advancing in proportion to his capabilities, the general manager wanted to know why. All recommendations for salary increases came to him for approval and at times he acted without recommendation.

New men were engaged and employes dismissed only after the general manager had given his approval. In cases where a discharge was recommended, the employe was informed by his superior and given opportunity to present his side of the case. Whether an employe protested or not, the general manager carefully reviewed his file before making a decision. Sometimes he rejected a recommended dismissal, either because of the case set forth in an employe's appeal or because of the record disclosed by the personal file. On such occasions the superior making the recommendation was called to task for failure to understand and handle his men properly.

6

These were the conditions existing at the advent of the depression in 1929. In many other fields the accompanying epidemic of unemployment served to make the labor problem acute, but without any noticeable immediate effect on The AP. There was no dismissals, wholesale or otherwise, to reduce the staff in line with economic conditions. Salaries finally were cut 10 per cent in 1932, but as soon as the business outlook showed promise of improvement, Cooper resumed his practice of giving increases on merit.

While the labor problem, as such, failed to involve either the co-operative's personnel or its management during the worst depression years, the nation's efforts to cope with general labor distress did have definite effects. Roosevelt called on American enterprises in July, 1933, to comply with the President's Re-employment Agreement until National Recovery Act codes were ready. The AP levels were above those the NRA suggested for minimum hours and wages, but the organization complied with the spirit of the agreement and 223 members were added at a monthly payroll increase of $15,960.61.

When the newspaper code of the NRA was approved, the association made certain that all its operations conformed. The code would have permitted a 30 per cent reduction in the salaries of one group of employes, but the general manager declined to take advantage of any provision which sanctioned wage scales below AP standards. A five-day workweek was introduced for bureaus in the larger cities as President Roosevelt requested and the general manager further directed that, in any other city where member papers adopted the five-day week, bureaus should be guided accordingly. He was not pleased to make such a distinction which benefited the staffs in some cities and not in others, but until complicated financial arrangements could be worked out it was not possible to put the entire domestic service on five-day week. Then the Supreme Court declared the NRA and its codes unconstitutional and the association not only maintained its wage and hour schedules, but continued to increase the number of employes and the payroll. In four years the staff increased 43 per cent and the payroll 47 per cent.

7

Coincident with the national efforts to get jobless men back to work, there was a phenomenal resurgence of activity in the field of organized labor. New unions appeared and for the first time the trade-union principle was extended to the editorial departments of newspapers and news gathering. The American Newspaper Guild, an organization of newspaper editorial workers, was formed and affiliated with the American Federation of Labor, a craft union group. Some time later the Guild transferred its allegiance to John L. Lewis's Congress of Industrial Organizations and expanded to include non-editorial workers in the commercial and other departments of newspapers. The new union attracted some AP employes, mainly in the larger centers, but its following in the service failed to assume large proportions.

In November, 1933, a Guild unit was organized in the New York office with Morris Watson, a reporter-editor as chairman. There was no secret about Watson's efforts to enroll members of the staff. The general manager was aware of the circumstances and as early as 1934 personally assured Watson and a Guild committee that he would countenance no discrimination against any employe because of union affiliations. As to the merits of an editorial union, Cooper pointed out that, because of his responsibility for the impartiality of the news report, he could not express opinions which might be used either pro or con by those who favored or opposed any feature of union programs.

Watson, an experienced newsman, had been active in Guild affairs for more than a year when his editorial supervisors first expressed dissatisfaction with his work on the grounds that it was not up to its former standard. Subsequently his duties were twice changed and then one day in October, 1935, he was informed that the general manager had been handed a memorandum recommending his dismissal with a month's salary.

Although Watson himself asked for no review of his dismissal by the general manager, it produced repercussions. The American Newspaper Guild charged that he had been dismissed for no reason other than his union activities—a violation of the recently enacted National Labor Relations Act—and announced it would contest the action. It filed complaint with the Regional Division of the National Labor Relations Board and before the year ended the co-operative was served notice of hearings on the Watson case.

The threat of litigation automatically brought the matter to the attention of the Board of Directors and the subject was referred to counsel. After a study of the facts involved, counsel decided the case should be contested, not on the specific point of Watson's discharge, but on the ground that the Labor Relations Act was unconstitutional and hence could not apply.

The hearings began in New York on April 7, 1936. Charles E. Clark, dean of the Yale Law School, served as examiner for the NLRB. At the request of that body, Assistant General Manager Stratton testified as to the corporate structure of the co-operative, its non-profit character, and the various operations involved in the collection and distribution of news. As stipulated by AP counsel at the outset, no testimony was produced by the co-operative as to the reasons for Watson's dismissal.

Watson himself testified at length concerning his career with the organization, followed by Mrs. Elinore M. Herrick, regional director for the Labor Board, and it was from their testimony that the co-operative's asserted reasons for the dismissal quite incidentally became known.

The reporter-editor said that, in the course of his seven years of employment, his superiors had come to know him as a capable newsman, but that more recently the general manager had told him that "every time my by-line was used in the report it brought protests from Associated Press members because I was Guild." He said the general manager also had told him there would be no discrimination against employes because of their union activities, but that a desirable Foreign Service assignment was out of the question as long as he was active in the Guild "because people would think he [the general manager] was running away from me and that I was running away from him."

He also testified concerning a number of talks that he had with his superiors about his Guild activities and their relation to and effect on his work. He told of an occasion on which he had arranged for a substitute to do his work so that he could attend a meeting held in connection with his labor activities, and expressed the opinion that his union work had led to the changes in his assignment and his eventual dismissal.

Questioned on the circumstances surrounding his discontinuance, he said he asked his immediate superior to tell him the reason for the action and that he was told:

"Because we are dissatisfied with your work, you are dissatisfied with us, and I am convinced that you will be happier elsewhere."

He said he thereupon "walked out of the office" and that he made no efforts to secure reinstatement except through the Labor Board.

The regional director of the NLRB told of the examination she had made of Watson's "personal" file, the record similar to that kept on all employes. She said it had been made available to her by the association at her request and that, with the knowledge of the management, she had taken notes on what she found.

Her testimony constituted a lengthy recital of complimentary and critical comments by Watson's superiors during the time of his employment and was climaxed by her reference to having had access to the memorandum of October 18, 1935, by Watson's superior outlining five reasons for recommending the discharge. She said she had copied the second of the reasons exactly as it appeared, and quoted it as having read:

He is an agitator and disturbs the morale of the staff at a time when we need especially their loyalty and best performance.

She said that, across the top of the five-point memorandum in penciled handwriting and initialed "KC"—initials of General Manager Cooper—was a further notation which said:

But *solely* on grounds of his work not being on a basis for which he has shown capability.

"I made a note for myself," she said, "that the 'but' was heavily written in pencil and that the 'solely' was underlined."

The hearing lasted two days and the Labor Board decision was made public on April 22. Examiner Clark ruled that the "sole" reason for Watson's discharge was his Guild activities. He held that the association had engaged in "unfair labor practice," directed it to "desist from interfering with, restraining, or coercing its employes in the right of self-organization," and ordered that Watson be reinstated.

8

The legal contest proceeded and the news report covered all developments factually and impartially, just as though the co-operative had no interest in what was happening. Then The AP carried the

NLRB ruling to the United States Circuit Court of Appeals on June 16. The court rendered an adverse decision a month later, upholding the constitutionality of the Wagner Act and ruling that it "does not hamper the legitimate right of the employer who may discharge his employes for inefficiency or any other cause agreeable to him," provided such a dismissal is not for union activity.

The decision cleared the way for an appeal to the United States Supreme Court. Briefs were filed by The Associated Press and on February 9-10, 1937, the court heard final arguments. John W. Davis, one-time Democratic candidate for President of the United States, appeared for the co-operative, Charles Fahy, general counsel for the NLRB, and Charles E. Wyzanski, special assistant to the United States attorney general, represented the government.

Davis based his attack on the Wagner Labor Relations Act on three major points: that it was invalid under the First Amendment to the Constitution because it was "a direct and palpable" invasion of the freedom of the press; that it was invalid under the Fifth Amendment because it deprived The AP of rights and liberties without due process of law; that it was invalid under the Tenth Amendment because the legislation undertook to deal with employer-employe relationships, a subject matter not committed to Congress under the commerce provisions of the Constitution.

Wyzanski and Fahy divided the government's argument. Wyzanski concentrated on the technical legal considerations involved, the propriety of the Wagner Act's application to The AP, and the court decisions which bore on the law's constitutionality. In the course of his argument he shrewdly pointed out a now-apparent salient weakness in the co-operative's case—no defense had been offered in the proceedings in the lower courts to controvert the Labor Board charge that Watson had been dismissed for reasons other than unsatisfactory work. Thus the findings of the lower courts—that the dismissal constituted unfair labor practice—stood unchallenged as far as legal considerations were concerned.

It was left to Fahy to answer Davis's arguments respecting the freedom of the press. He also pointed out that the association had offered no testimony in the lower courts to disprove the contention that Watson had been discharged only because of his union activities. This being the case, he said the argument that the Wagner Act invaded the First Amendment to the Constitution was not a valid one.

9

The Supreme Court announced its decision on April 12, 1937, in one of the celebrated 5-to-4 opinions which made the court's general attitude on New Deal legislation a subject of heated political controversy. The decision upheld the constitutionality of the Wagner Labor Relations Act and made Watson's reinstatement mandatory.

Mr. Justice Owen J. Roberts delivered the majority opinion. He noted that the co-operative "did not challenge the [Labor] Board's findings of fact" respecting the reason for Watson's dismissal and continued:

We, therefore, accept as established that The Associated Press did not, as claimed in its answer before the Board, discharge Watson because of unsatisfactory service, but, on the contrary, as found by the Board, discharged him for his activities in connection with the Newspaper Guild.

The question of the freedom of the press received extended treatment in the majority opinion. In part, it read:

The conclusion which the petitioner draws is that whatever may be the case with respect to employes in its mechanical departments, it must have absolute and unrestricted freedom to employ and to discharge those who, like Watson, edit the news; that there must not be the slightest opportunity for any bias or prejudice personally entertained by an editorial employe to color or to distort what he writes, and that The Associated Press cannot be free to furnish unbiased and impartial news reports unless it is equally free to determine for itself the partiality or bias of editorial employes.

So it is said that any regulation protective of union activities, or the right collectively to bargain on the part of such employes is necessarily an invalid invasion of the freedom of the press.

We think the contention not only has no relevance to the circumstances of the instant case but is an unsound generalization. The ostensible reason for Watson's discharge, as embodied in the records of the petitioner, is "solely on the grounds of his work not being on a basis for which he has shown capability." The petitioner did not assert and does not now claim that he has shown bias in the past. It does not claim that by reason of his connection with the union he will be likely, as the petitioner honestly believes, to show bias in the future. The actual reason for his discharge, as shown by the unattacked finding of the Board, was his Guild activity and his agitation for collective bargaining.

The statute does not preclude a discharge on the ostensible grounds for the petitioner's section; it forbids discharge for what has been found to be the real motive of the petitioner. These considerations answer the suggestion that if the petitioner believed its policy of impartiality was likely to be subverted by Watson's continued service. Congress was without power to interdict his discharge. No such question is here for decision. Neither before the Board, nor in the court below, nor here has the petitioner professed such belief. It seeks to bar all regulation by contending that regulation in a situation not presented would be invalid. Courts deal with cases upon the basis of the facts disclosed, never with non-existent and assumed circumstances.

The act does not compel the petitioner to employ anyone; it does not require that the petitioner retain in its employ an incompetent editor or one who fails faithfully to edit the news to reflect facts without bias or prejudice. The act permits a discharge for any reason other than union activity or agitation for collective bargaining with employes. The restoration of Watson to his former position in no sense guarantees his continuance in petitioner's employ. The petitioner is at liberty, whenever occasion may arise, to exercise its undoubted right to sever his relationship for any cause that seems to it proper, save only as a punishment for, or discouragement of, such activities as the act declares permissible. . . .

The dissenting opinion was delivered by Mr. Justice George Sutherland. The minority held that the Wagner Act as applied to The AP violated the First Amendment to the Constitution in that it restricted the freedom of the press. Justice Sutherland, rendering the opinion, said:

Freedom is not a mere intellectual abstraction, and is not merely a word to adorn an oration upon occasions of patriotic rejoicing. It is an intensely practical reality, capable of concrete enjoyment in a multitude of ways day by day. When applied to the press, the term freedom is not to be narrowly confined, and it obviously means more than publication and circulation. If freedom of the press does not include the right to adopt and pursue a policy without governmental restriction, it is a misnomer to call it freedom. And we might as well deny at once the right of the press freely to adopt a policy and pursue it, as to concede that right and deny the liberty to exercise an uncensored judgment in respect to the employment and discharge of the agents through whom the policy is to be effectuated. . . .

For many years there has been contention between labor and capital. Labor has become highly organized in a wide effort to secure and preserve its rights. The daily news with respect to labor disputes is now of vast proportions: and clearly a considerable part of petitioner's editorial service must be devoted to that subject. Such news is not only of great public interest, but an unbiased version of it is of the utmost public concern.

To give a group of employers on the one hand, or a labor organization on the other, power of control over such a service is obviously to endanger the fairness and accuracy of the service. Strong sympathy for or strong prejudice against a given cause or the efforts made to advance it has too often led to suppression or coloration of unwelcome facts. It would seem to be an exercise of only reasonable prudence for an association engaged in part in supplying the public with fair and accurate factual information with respect to the contests between labor and capital, to see that those whose activities include that service are free from either extreme sympathy or extreme prejudice one way or the other. . . .

. . . If petitioner concluded, as it well could, that its policy to preserve its news service free from color, bias or distortion was likely to be subverted by Watson's retention, what power has Congress in the face of the First Amendment?

At the time the Supreme Court's decision was handed down, Watson was director of the *Living Newspaper*, a Federal Theatre Project on which he had been employed since his dismissal from the staff. He expressed his gratification and returned to duty April 19, 1937.

Then the co-operative announced its readiness to enter into collective bargaining negotiations with such unions—mechanical or editorial—as the NLRB might certify to be the official representatives of a majority of employes.

After working two weeks, Watson applied for and was granted the customary vacation with pay to which all regular employes were entitled. On returning he resigned, explaining that he wished to resume his WPA activities. In his resignation, dated May 17, he wrote:

I would be remiss if I did not express here my sincere appreciation of the good grace with which The Associated Press accepted my return. I am convinced now that there never will be any discrimination against Associated Press employes for organizing or being active in a union formed for their economic betterment through collective bargaining.

10

The possibility of a misunderstanding of the co-operative's motives in challenging the Wagner Act was something which caused concern to the management. Yet as the situation developed it offered little opportunity for clarification as long as the question remained one for purely legal decision. Although the National Labor Relations Board's decision was not unexpected, since the strategy of the co-operative's counsel was to offer no testimony, nevertheless it created a practical problem which could not but be regretted by the management. There was the chance that silence as to the reasons for the co-operative's action might lead to the belief that its efforts were directed against unionism, an improved social economy, the New Deal which created the Wagner Act, and the Democratic Party which created the New Deal.

The decision of the Court of Appeals cleared the way for the Supreme Court appeal and the question of a public statement by the co-operative setting forth its case was considered. Counsel withdrew an earlier objection to such a course and Vice-President McLean and General Manager Cooper set about preparation of the document. It reviewed the whole case and stated that the co-operative's purpose in challenging the Wagner Act was to make sure that the new law did not destroy its right to supervise the work of its employes and to discipline them for cause lest it lose control over the most important element of its existence—the creation of the unprejudiced and unbiased daily news record on which millions of readers of all complexions and beliefs had come to depend.

Circumstances, however, began to militate against the release of the statement. The 1936 presidential campaign was under way and there was the likelihood that anything The AP said might be seized upon for political significance. The statement was reluctantly discarded and the co-operative continued to hold its silence.

During the time the Wagner case was pending two other matters were before the co-operative for action or decision. The first was a request by the American Newspaper Guild for collective bargaining. The Board of Directors, on advice of counsel, ruled that no action should be taken until the legal proceedings in the Wagner Act case had been concluded.

The question of a universal five-day week, however, was something on which action logically could be taken. Contrasting current standards with those at the time the association introduced its first revolutionary pension and disability plan for employes back in 1918, Cooper told the Board of Directors he was convinced that the trend toward a five-day workweek was a salutary thing and that he hoped the association could inaugurate it for all bureaus, irrespective of what others might do. The financial details represented a considerable item—a universal five-day week meant an increase of more than $300,000 annually in operating expenses—but eventually they were worked out with board approval. In 1936 the shift of the entire Traffic personnel to a five-day week started, and on January 1, 1937, the process began with the editorial staff.

That the Wagner Act case and all that it came to involve might have some effect on personnel relations in the co-operative seemed a foregone conclusion, but the general manager of The AP could not feel that it should disrupt the revived personalized basis of relations between the management and its staff. If anything, he felt more than ever that the strength of the organization, in which there was such a definite element of public service, lay in the strength of a keenly intelligent editorial staff. The Supreme Court decision, while upholding the constitutionality of the Wagner Act, nevertheless had defined the rights of both employer and employe, and those rights formed a basis for future relations.

Regardless of union affiliations, the court's decision made continuance of those relations dependent upon the competence of the employe and his ability to demonstrate to the satisfaction of the association that no act of his constituted any threat to the integrity of the report through bias or prejudice in the handling of news. For the text of this phase of the opinion clearly read:

The Act does not compel the petitioner to employ anyone; it does not require that the petitioner retain in its employ an incompetent editor or one who fails faithfully to edit the news to reflect facts without bias or prejudice.

XIII. "THE PUBLIC MUST BE
FULLY INFORMED"

I

ACROSS the Manzanares River behind the Nationalist lines Richard Massock listened to the slam of artillery as Franco's batteries hurled the first shells of 1937 into beleaguered Madrid. The guns opened up on the stroke of midnight and fired a dozen times in grim greeting to the New Year. Inside Madrid, Chief of Bureau Alexander Uhl stood in the Puerta del Sol and heard the crash as the shells struck the center of the city. About him, disdainful of the explosions, militiamen were chewing the twelve lucky grapes which Madrileños tradionally eat as a dying year is tolled out and a new year in.

Thus the Spanish Civil War entered its second year, prolonging the chronic crisis which kept Old World chancelleries in a state of nervous apprehension and the co-operative's European staff constantly on the alert. The conflict followed five years of dissension after King Alfonso XIII fled into exile in April, 1931. The Madrid Republican government was a "left" government, speaking for workers and peasants. The insurgents, under General Francisco Franco, grouped the military, the big landowners, and the aristocracy under the "right," or Fascist, banner. The Pope recognized the Franco government.

In an attempt to isolate the war, the British sponsored a "Non-Intervention Committee," but in spite of these efforts it soon became apparent that Italy and Germany were helping Franco and the Soviets were giving aid to the Madrid government. The Rome and Berlin bureaus watched Mussolini and Hitler for their next moves and the Moscow Bureau sought a better line on the Soviets' future course. Cables from London and Paris described the concern of the western powers.

The pieces in the puzzling jigsaw that was the map of Europe were slowly being matched and put together. The pattern still was not clear, but there were many who said that Spain was a mere testing ground on which some of the Old World nations were trying out their modern armaments and strategies.

The staff men in Spain had the riskiest part of the over-all

441

European assignment, but months of bitter warfare had inured them
to the perils and discomforts incidental to the task of getting the news.
The scream of shells, the rattle of machine guns, the horror of air
bombardment, all these were old things now. Massock and Elmer
Peterson had been with the insurgents since Franco raised his banner
of revolt. They accompanied the column which captured Toledo and
relieved the Alcazar after the 72-day siege, and their eyewitness stories
were frequently written under fire.

On the other side, Chief of Bureau Uhl, James Oldfield, and H.
E. Knoblaugh covered the government, or "Loyalist," forces. In the
north, where the Franco forces thrust toward the Basque cities on
the Bay of Biscay, Robert B. Parker, Jr., watched the fall of Irún and
San Sebastian.

When Franco's advance was stubbornly halted on the outskirts
of Madrid, the AP bureau at No. 4 Calle Mejia Lequerica was in a
section of the city often bombarded by the terrifying insurgent fire.
Shell splinters pockmarked its walls and bomb blasts shattered its
windows. The dozen shots from the insurgent batteries as January 1
came in were nothing new, for the staff men with the Loyalists had had
plenty to report during the weeks in which the government forces had
made their heroic defense.

Early in the war it had become obvious that one of the major
objectives of the insurgent Franco forces was to capture Madrid in
an effort to demoralize the seat of the government, and in various
circles it was freely predicted that such a development would mean
dissolution of the "Non-Intervention Committee" which had its headquarters in London.

The staff men with the government had been in the thick of things
when the Madrid forces began one of their most spectacular defenses
of the city on November 8 and 9, 1936. The assault on Madrid had
come only a few weeks after the insurgents relieved the Alcazar, forty
miles away, and the Franco strategy now was coming into the open.
His forces were fighting down from the north through the Guadarrama
Mountains and up from the south and west in an effort to throw a
semicircle of steel around the embattled capital. At the insurgent head-
quaters in Burgos, General Franco had been proclaimed "Chief of the
Spanish State" and had organized his own "government."

But the terror of modern aerial warfare on November 8 and 9
did not signal the end of Madrid. Uhl and members of his staff scurried
through the streets dodging bombs and explosions as the missiles of

death rained down from attacking insurgent planes which were being engaged by the determined government forces both on land and in the air.

During earlier attacks on surrounding towns, Uhl saw pamphlets as well as bombs rain down and in Madrid he witnessed hand-to-hand fighting. From balconies and windows he saw women, armed with guns, proudly picking off the first Franco troopers as they battled in the streets below, and from others he saw the first of the undercover, or Fifth Column, Franco sympathizers firing on government militiamen.

While the fierce fighting continued, the government forces quickly converted homes and public buildings into miniature forts from which to defend the city. Women who could not procure guns poured hot oil from the housetops on the heads of attackers.

On the insurgent side Elmer Peterson had to throw himself flat on his stomach on the roof of a suburban house to escape the gun fire, and with the government Uhl and his staff watched crowds in the center of Madrid run panic-stricken to cover, saw ambulances and fire trucks go clanging into the thick of the fray, and listened to the screams of wounded and dying women and children.

Throughout November 8 and early again the next day the insurgents continued to hurl their deadly missiles from guns and planes. No one could estimate how many dead and wounded they left in the streets and in the wreckage of homes and public buildings—but still Madrid stood.

It was still standing on January 1, 1937, and Uhl and the others with the government forces listened to the explosions, heard the scream of shells, and wondered how much longer Madrid could last.

2

The Spanish War lost the news spotlight temporarily during the spring to two memorable stories—the coronation of George VI as King-Emperor of the British Empire, and the wedding of Edward, Duke of Windsor, to the twice-divorced American woman, Mrs. Wallis Warfield. They provided the final chapters to one of the great news narratives of contemporary times, and recalled the stirring march of events not so many months earlier when Edward, in December, 1936, renounced his throne rather than abandon his determination to marry Mrs. Warfield, "the woman I love."

Accounts of the majestic ceremonies at Westminster Abbey were eagerly read, but no crowning of a king-emperor could have the reader appeal and human interest inherent in the romance of the Duke of Windsor and Wallis Warfield. People called it the "greatest love story of our time" and followed with rapt attention the news of the preparations for the marriage on June 3 in France.

For the occasion, the association set up a special five-man staff, headed by John Lloyd, chief of the Paris Bureau. With him were Louis Matzhold, Melvin K. Whiteleather, Robert Parker, who had just been relieved from duty in Spain, and Alice Maxwell, the Paris Bureau's style specialist.

Matzhold, of the Vienna Bureau, had been with Windsor during the duke's exile in Austria for the several months since the abdication. He had talked with him daily, followed him on his frequent outing trips and traveled with him to Monts, France, when the duke hurried there to join Mrs. Warfield on May 3, the day her second divorce became final. Lloyd was one of the five correspondents chosen from the world press to attend the civil and religious ceremonies when the marriage took place in the Château de Cande at Monts.

3

While the one-time king was getting married, Edward Neil, back on war duty after his experiences in Ethiopia, was plodding along in the hot June sun with the insurgent legions that pushed relentlessly on to the Basque stronghold of Bilbao in northern Spain. Neil had lived all his life literally against an AP background. Indeed, he and his father claimed they never had had an employer other than The AP. The senior Neil, when fourteen, got his first job in the Boston office as a copy boy before the turn of the century, and later became a telegraph operator. The younger Neil likewise entered the service in Boston and joined the sports staff in New York in 1926. A vivid style and a wide knowledge of athletics soon made him one of the association's best known writers, and sports editors on member papers swore by his signed stories.

Through the so-called "golden age" of sports, Neil helped cover most of the major events and in 1932 he won honorable mention for the Pulitzer prize with a thrilling account of a mile-a-minute ride he took down the bobsled run at Lake Placid during the winter Olympics. After a while sports began to pall and he applied for a Foreign Service assignment. He went to Ethiopia to cover the Italian conquest and after that came an assignment in the Holy Land, where Arab bombs and rifles waged war on returning Jewish colonists.

Now he was moving along toward Bilbao with Charles Foltz, Jr., a fellow staffer who had relieved Parker on the northern front. On June 19 Bilbao fell, and Neil, Foltz, and a Latvian newspaperman named George Timuska, in their haste not to miss anything, found themselves entering the city ahead of the troops.

With escorts of Basque militiamen, the three newspapermen set out to tour the shell-smashed city which had been besieged for eighty days. Bilbao's communications connection with Algorta, the cablehead fifteen miles to the northwest, had been severed when the Basques blew up the bridges surrounding the city and the correspondents had no way of getting their news out.

By late afternoon Foltz had rounded up five cable company employes and their equipment. He had a plan for sending the news to London and the arrival of a lone insurgent press officer, who had followed the correspondents into the city, facilitated matters. The first Franco troops had just started to move into Bilbao.

The plan was simple. The cable company employes said they could set up their equipment at the cablehead at Algorta and reach London within an hour. That would mean much to the correspondents. It was Saturday afternoon and other correspondents, who had not yet entered Bilbao, would send their stories from Vittoria or take them across the French frontier. Vittoria was a good four hours away and a telegram from there to Vigo, a cablehead, would take at least eight hours. From Bilbao a trip to the frontier would require five hours and there was no guarantee that the frontier would be open.

The insurgent captain, who acted as censor, agreed to co-operate and dragooned all the able-bodied men in the vicinity to help load the cable equipment on boats for a trip across the estuary to Algorta. On the other side automobiles were commandeered and the party roared away up the coastal road to the deserted cablehead. It was a small, forlorn building at the tip end of a low and barren peninsula. Except for a bluff a few hundred yards away, the terrain was flat and unprotected. Potentially it was not a healthy spot, for anti-Franco sharpshooters still held the opposite shore and did not hesitate to open fire on any suspected insurgent followers.

Once the party got inside the building, the blinds were drawn, the lights lighted, and the three correspondents started to pound out their stories. Assisted by two chauffeurs, the five cablemen set up their sending equipment.

The insurgent captain made a pretense of censoring the correspondents' copy, but that night he was too weary to argue and the dispatches passed his black pencil unedited. Then the newspapermen waited nervously while the cablemen tried to contact London. The London cable office had not heard from Algorta for days, but some English operator had left the Bilbao wire open.

"Hello Bilbao Hello Bilbao Do you have have something for us?" were the first words from London.

Timuska had written only a brief story, and Neil and Foltz offered to let him clear it first.

"No," declined the Latvian in his broken English. "My story, she go third. If I say to my editor in Riga: 'Timuska sent first story from Bilbao,' my editor say: 'Timuska he is a liar.' But if I say Timuska send third story from Bilbao, my editor say: 'H-m-m. Third story from Bilbao. Timuska is a good correspondent, fine correspondent.'"

Neil's story went first, then Foltz's, and then Timuska's, all speeding into London at an eighty-word-a-minute clip. It was a great moment for three war correspondents who had been accustomed to count eight to fifty-two hours good transmission time.

4

They were congratulating themselves on their good fortune when there was a loud noise in the rear of the cable building, and a crash of shattering window glass. Foltz and Timuska went back to investigate. There were round holes in the curtains and bullets buried in the wood of the opposite walls. They darted back and pulled the power switch, cutting off the lights and the cable.

A dark shape moved on the waters, heading toward the shore near the cable building. It was a boatload of government militiamen and they had opened fire on the cable office, believing it was occupied by Franco's Nationalist forces. More bullets slapped into the walls and more glass showered to the floor.

The insurgent captain, who had accompanied the reporters to the deserted cablehead, took a submachine gun and gave the two chauffeurs automatic rifles. The cable employes asked for arms as well, but the captain refused them. They were Basques who had been on the Loyalist side only the day before. "You were fighting us just yesterday," the captain said, "so you'll get no chance to try it again today."

Neil, Foltz, and Timuska watched from a window. The nearest Franco troops were a dozen miles away and the three armed men in the two-room frame building were the only defenders of a spit of land on which a trawler loaded with the attacking government militiamen intended to come ashore. There was no chance of dashing out and escaping. The flat, barren country would not give a rabbit cover from the sharpshooters in the boat.

The rifle fire from the water grew heavier, punctuated by vicious machine gun bursts. The bullets thudded into the outer walls of the building, just under the window frames. The captain and the chauffeurs opened up in return. The three correspondents exchanged glances. There was no question what would happen if the attackers succeeded in landing. To them everyone in the cable station was an enemy, and the correspondents knew what army officers said: "No one takes prisoners in night attacks. They're too much trouble."

The trawler came on deliberately until it was only seventy yards from the shore.

For another ten minutes it raked the station with rifle and machine gun bullets, as it maneuvered for a landing spot not in a direct line of fire from the building. Then, without warning, a new sound was heard amid the firing—a noise like Roman candles going off on an American Fourth of July. A battery on the Franco-controlled shore had opened fire on the approaching boat. The captain yelled excitedly.

"Tracer bullets! Tracer bullets from our shore!"

The correspondents dashed to the door. The trawler with its cargo of militiamen was moving at full speed back toward the opposite shore. It was an easy target for the white balls of fire which streaked after it —a blinding stream of bullets from a machine gun mounted on the bluff a few hundred yards inland from the cable station. The bullets cut a dazzling swath across the water.

Leaving the captain and chauffeurs blazing away at the fleeing ship, Neil, Foltz, and Timuska ran to the bluff, where they found eight Nationalist gunners busy with two machine guns. They had been stationed on the bluff to prevent enemy movements in the area. They grinned a greeting.

"We would have started firing sooner," explained one of them, "but we all went back to the village for some food and they came while we were gone."

"My friend," said Neil, "if you'd had an extra cup of coffee after that dinner, we'd have haunted you for the rest of your life!"

5

Foltz was recalled to Paris not long after that and Neil carried on alone on the northern front.

At the start of the Santander offensive, the next major operation in the north, he found his movements sharply circumscribed by official Franco restrictions. The participation of Italian "Volunteers" in the war on the insurgent side had become an open international issue, particularly since the rout of an Italian column at Guadalajara on the Madrid front, and Franco's generals had become wary about permitting correspondents to learn the exact composition of front-line forces.

When the Santander offensive got under way, rumors had it that a large number of Italian legionnaires were fighting at the front. It was virtually impossible to confirm these reports. Ubiquitous press officers on the insurgent side kept the correspondents out of harm's way at headquarters and saw to it that they got only such information as Franco headquarters thought fit to release.

For days Neil chafed at the inactivity and the strict supervision. He bided his time until one of the press custodians got careless. Then he slipped away in an old automobile in the direction of the front. It was not long before he encountered two Italian divisions moving up. He discovered that he had traveled with both units in Ethiopia and soon renewed acquaintances with the officers he remembered. They obligingly gave him the proper directions and he set out again for the firing line.

A few miles along the road he drove up to a railroad track lined by a long stone wall behind which crouched Italian combat troops in full field kit. There was no sign of action, so the correspondent halted and shouted a request for further directions. Two of the soldiers started toward him with a warning, and the others gestured frantically to him to seek shelter.

Just then Neil heard the shrill scream of shells. He froze momentarily at the steering wheel, waiting for the explosions. The first struck with a deafening roar near the left front side of the car, flinging out a storm of jagged splinters and dirt.

Automatically Neil dived out of the battered machine and made for shelter.

Another salvo shrieked toward the railroad line and a second later a direct hit landed on Neil's abandoned car. One of the soldiers who had run out to warn him was killed and the other lost an eye.

Neil had found the front. His excursion to the battle zone produced the stories which positively established large-scale Italian participation on the northern front and brought the question into the open. To circumvent censorship, the dispatches were sent by courier to the French frontier.

6

The assignments in Spain meant constant hard work and a great deal of drudgery. As in Ethiopia, the perennial nightmare was how to get dispatches to the communications point once they had been written. Often after a battle Neil had to climb into his car and drive back as many as two hundred miles to the nearest telegraph office. Then, before a story could be accepted, he had to hunt up a translator to put his story into Spanish. After that there was always the exasperating fight against the Franco censors and the long wait for a turn on wires already choked with official and private communications.

Just as with the Franco forces, the men on the Loyalist side also had their troubles.

On one occasion an American flag displayed on a balcony and the quick-wittedness of a Spanish employee saved the Madrid Bureau from attack although it was in the area occupied by government forces, and its staff had been reporting the war from the "Loyalist" side from the beginning. There had been sniping from one of the buildings in the vicinity and a detachment of militiamen moved into the district to crush it. Members of the Fifth Column—undercover Franco adherents —had been waging a guerrilla warfare against the government, and there was no mercy for them when they were caught.

The militiamen decided that the sniping must have come from the building occupied by the AP bureau. One group deployed to storm the door, while the other raised rifles and took aim at the windows. Staff men working at their desks were oblivious of the danger, but Arturo Cardona, a clerk, happened to pass a window and saw the situation. There was no time to consult anyone. Risking a volley of bullets he stepped boldly to the balcony.

"Do you see that flag?" he shouted, draping a flag over the ledge. "This is the office of the naval attaché of the United States of America. You will lose your heads if you molest this place!"

The untutored milicianos fell back. They did not know that the United States had no naval attaché in Madrid.

The relentless hunt for members of the Fifth Column, suspected spies, and other designated enemies of the government, made a correspondent's life hazardous, nevertheless. Once in Barcelona a man walking a few paces ahead of Knoblaugh was shot dead in his tracks when he failed to hear a sentry's command to halt. Another time, Knoblaugh and a government official were fired on while on an automobile tour of Madrid at night. At one time or another Uhl, Oldfield, John Lloyd, Edward Kennedy, Charles Nutter, Ramon Blardony, Henry Cassidy, and Robert Okin had comparable experiences.

Most of the news was routed out by telephone whenever possible, and that meant daily danger after the government placed an artillery observation post in the tower of the International Telephone Building, the tallest structure in Madrid. The building was hit repeatedly by shells. One day while Uhl and Knoblaugh were waiting for a telephone connection, a six-inch shell smashed through the wall and exploded over their heads.

Living in constant danger of aerial and artillery bombardment, some of the men suffered severe nervous strain—"bomb jitters," as they called it—which made them jump at a slammed door or duck when they heard the drone of an airplane motor. Because of this terrific tension, the replacements in Spain were frequent.

Censorship was an endless source of trouble and, because of efforts to circumvent it, Knoblaugh eventually found it necessary to leave the country. His difficulties arose from several reasons. He ignored taboos and wrote about interparty friction and the part foreign intervention was playing on the "Loyalist" side—two subjects authorities did not wish discussed. When the censors began striking out from controversial dispatches such qualifying phrases as "the government claimed," or "according to the government," he protested. He pointed out to press officers that such deletions had the effect of making him the authority for statements of disputed fact. It was against AP regulations to send any controversial material without stating the authority. The protests were unproductive, so Knoblaugh sent out a letter by secret courier informing New York of the situation. Once advised, the cable desk could reinsert the qualifying phrases where they belonged.

Kennedy, sent to Valencia to replace Knoblaugh, also had a hard time. He reported that the activities of the secret police became worse as the war continued. His experience was that officials were more interested in getting correspondents to write dispatches that would be good propaganda than they were in preventing military information from reaching the enemy. His hotel room was searched, some of his personal effects "disappeared," coat linings were torn in a search for "documents," and he was threatened with arrest.

On at least one occasion, however, a reporter got his story through without official hindrance.

The incident occurred one evening in 1937 when Franco batteries rammed six shells into the century-old Foreign Office in Madrid. By this time the war around the capital had settled into a virtual siege with Franco lines running three-quarters of the way around the city, cutting off all railroads and six of the seven arterial highways. The city was slowly starving on the meager supplies that could be brought in by truck and mule cart, yet few inhabitants left—they had no better place to go.

The censorship office in Madrid had been shelled out of the telephone building by the Franco artillery perched on hills across the narrow Manzanares valley scarcely a mile away. Both censors and correspondents sought refuge in the abandoned Foreign Office, below which was a labyrinth of dungeons reputedly used during the Inquisition. The walls were thick, but the building had an open court that was a constant menace because of the danger of shells dropping into the patio.

Charles Nutter, covering the government side, was sitting in the pressroom of the cold, exposed building late in the afternoon of October 13. He had just prepared his dispatch, had had it approved by the censor, and had placed a telephone call for London to transmit the story to the bureau there for relay to the United States. The established practice was for the correspondent to telephone his approved dispatch from one room while the censor listened in on another line. Then, if the correspondent deviated from his copy, the connection could be quickly cut.

The call from London came through simultaneously with a loud report just outside a window of the Foreign Office. The Franco artillery had put a six-inch shell into a near-by church and a fragment came bounding through the window past Nutter's desk. Another shell hit the Foreign Office itself, seeming to rock its very foundation. A third landed in the patio and others scooped holes in the heavy walls. It was obvious that the Foreign Office was the target.

While the shells burst Nutter sat at his desk going through the necessary motions preliminary to beginning conversation with his London office. The censor crouched at his own desk for a moment as the bombardment began, but just as the telephone connection was established he dropped his end of the telephone line and dashed for the basement where all others in the building were fleeing for safety. It was an unceremonious departure, but he paused at the door just long enough to yell to Nutter, still busy with his line:

"Tell them anything you like about this attack!"

Nutter hurriedly dictated to the London office the story as it developed, pausing occasionally when the bombardment drowned out his voice so that the man on the receiving end in London could hear the noise of the attack.

The shelling lasted for an hour, but the death toll was officially reported at only six. The only casualty at the Foreign Office was the AP automobile, which got a piece of shrapnel through its rear seat. Although no more shells penetrated the office, Nutter had to abandon his call after several minutes because of the acrid fumes of the explosives.

He explained his predicament to London, let the operator on the other end of the wire listen again to the noise of the shelling and then broke the connection. His story of another of Franco's attempts to capture Madrid had gone through without official interference.

"Cheerio," said the man on the London end as Nutter hung up his telephone.

7

Outside of Spain the world was going on. Pugilism acquired a new heavyweight champion, one Joe Louis, whom writers dubbed the "Brown Bomber." Clipper ships explored the sky lanes for aerial service across the Atlantic. In the Far East the undeclared Sino-Japanese War commanded attention after a temporary lull, this time with both sides serving notice that it was a fight to the end. Italy joined Germany and Japan in the Anti-Comintern Pact after Mussolini ostentatiously reaffirmed the strength of the Rome-Berlin Axis with a triumphal visit to Adolf Hitler at Munich and Berlin. America's recovery from the long setback of the depression encountered a sharp "recession" which sent business indices tumbling. And the Soviets celebrated the twentieth anniversary of nationhood—a celebration preceded and followed by new "purges" of "traitors," self-confessed and otherwise.

The Spanish Civil War, like so many stories of long duration, temporarily had become a matter of routine interest by mid-December of 1937. Major developments were few, for winter had retarded mili-

"TELL THEM ANYTHING YOU LIKE ABOUT THIS ATTACK."

tary operations and Franco was making preparations for a spring offensive. Moreover, front pages were given over to amazing news from the Far East—the bombing and sinking of the United States gunboat *Panay* by Japanese war planes in China. But, quiet or not, there was no relaxation of coverage efforts in Spain.

The interlude was short-lived. On December 19 the government army launched a terrific offensive, capturing the city of Teruel and threatening to sever Franco's Aragon salient at its base. The fight for Teruel developed into one of the severest battles of the war, both sides throwing their full weight into the fray.

To cover the seesawing conflict, Neil was with Franco and Bob Okin and Ramon Blardony were across the lines in the government camp, as close to the front as the milicianos would allow. The first impact of the government drive hurled the Nationalists back several miles, and for days all correspondents with Franco were refused permission to go near the fighting zone.

When the insurgent counter thrust began to gather headway, Neil again slipped away from the shepherding press officials and made his way to the front. He cabled an eyewitness account of the fighting on December 29, describing the assaults of Franco's troops on the government front and a synchronized mass attack by two hundred insurgent airplanes.

Two days later the Franco headquarters lifted the ban on correspondents at the front and Neil and his colleagues started out by automobile from the base at Zaragoza. In a little while it began to snow and got bitterly cold. The road was pitted with shell holes and choked with military traffic. Troops moving up shuffled along numbly in the freezing winds, and the press car passed knots of peasants huddled together to keep warm. As they approached the front, the press party stopped in each village to forage for scraps of news from ahead.

At noon the press cars turned off the shell-pocked main road and jolted toward the next little hamlet, Caude. Gunfire became louder and louder. Snow sifted gloomily down. The cold grew so intense that hands, feet, and ears ached.

In Caude the cars stopped near a barn and the correspondents piled out to get the latest news. There were Franco reserves everywhere waiting for the command to move into action. A heavy battery thundered on a field a hundred yards away, hurling projectiles toward Teruel. Conversation had to be in snatches, between the blasts of the guns. Four mules stood woodenly by a small pond near the barn where the press cars had halted.

The news in Caude was quickening. The Franco troops had fought their way to the outskirts of Teruel. The beleaguered garrison in the seminary would be relieved and the city recaptured by nightfall at the latest. Neil and his colleagues were disappointed when an unyielding press officer refused to permit them to go on. It was still too dangerous, he said. As a matter of fact, they were too near the fighting zone now. Someone had blundered in allowing them to come so far.

The men scattered to wait. Some went off to watch the battery and others to explore the village. Neil, Richard Sheepshanks, of Reuters Agency, and H. A. R. Philby, of the London *Times*, returned to their car, parked some distance from the others. Neil and Sheepshanks had covered the Ethiopian War together and since their reunion in Spain had been almost inseparable.

Sheepshanks slipped into the front seat as Neil and Philby climbed into the back. They sat talking, smoking, and munching chocolate. The windows were closed against the subzero cold, the snow, and the bellow of the heavy artillery near by.

Soon they were joined by Brandish Johnson, a young American who was gathering material for magazine articles. He had just come back from photographing the heavy artillery in the field.

Poring over a map alone in a parked automobile across the way, Karl Robson of the London *Daily Telegraph* heard the terrifying scream of another shell. There was a stupefying crash and a terrific concussion. Another shell exploded, and another, and another. Soldiers shouted and fled to cover. Robson dived out of his car and raced for the barn. The road rocked under a new burst of gunfire.

As abruptly as it began, the shelling ceased. The newsmen and the soldiers who had taken refuge in the barn looked out. Three of the mules near the barn lay dead. The fourth stamped the frozen ground in terror. There was no other sign of life. Then a man appeared, reeling toward the barn. Blood streaked his face and covered his clothes. It was Philby.

"They're in there! They're in there!" he yelled, pointing to the shell-wrecked automobile down the road.

The press officer got there first, with Robson at his heels. They saw three motionless figures with powder-blackened faces slumped in their seats. A shell had exploded within inches of the left front wheel of the car.

When the door was opened, Johnson's body tumbled out from be-hind the steering wheel. Sheepshanks, who had been seated next to him, lay back unconscious, his temple torn open. In the back seat sprawled Neil. He was conscious, but speech was an effort and he could not move. He had been hit many times. His left leg was torn and broken by dozens of shell fragments.

Stretcher-bearers carried off Sheepshanks to a dressing station up the street. Johnson's body lay where it had fallen. Someone threw a rug over it. The rescue workers had difficulty getting Neil out of the car. He was heavy and the two-door sedan gave little room for man-euvering behind the front seat. The Loyalist artillery resumed bom-barding the village and the rescuers were interrupted several times by the thud of shells.

"Good work, boys," Neil said when they finally got him out. "Sorry I'm so heavy. Keep an eye on my typewriter, will you?"

He saw the covered body on the ground.

"Who's that? Robson?" he asked.

They told him and hurried him off to the first-aid hut, thence into an ambulance with Sheepshanks for the journey back over rutted roads to a casualty clearing station at Santa Eulalia.

Philby, who had been sitting with Neil in the back of the car, had had a narrow escape. His head wounds proved not to be serious. Doctors could do nothing for Sheepshanks. He died that night without speaking a word. It was New Year's Eve.

Neil was not told of Sheepshanks' death. He was in good spirits and his colleagues hoped that he was not critically hurt. He joked with them.

"Well," he said, "I guess the war is over for me."

But Neil was badly wounded. He had been hit by thirty-four shell fragments and his condition was so grave that doctors at the casualty clearing station felt he could be attended properly only at the base hos-pital in Zaragoza. The ambulance made the slow trip in a blizzard and it was not until one o'clock on New Year's morning—more than twelve hours after he had been wounded—that Neil reached the hospital. Hal Philby wrote Neil's story that night and filed it for him to New York.

Philby and William P. Carney, the New York *Times* correspondent with Franco, visited Neil on New Year's Day. They found him semi-delirious. Every effort had been made to prevent his learning of Sheepshanks' death, but somehow he had heard of it in the hospital.

"They're burying poor Dick tomorrow," he said, "and I'm afraid

I can't go to the funeral. They keep me here on my back, and I am getting so sick I soon won't be able to write a story or do anything. But old Philby has told everything there is to tell by now, haven't you? Tell my office I'm going to Paris as soon as I can and I'll soon be all right again."

Then, when his visitors were leaving, he managed one of his flashing smiles.

"So long until tomorrow," he whispered. "I wish I could go to the nearest café with you guys and have a big, cold beer."

Blood transfusions seemed to help Neil, but by the next morning gangrene developed. He died late that night.

8

When the word reached The AP in New York, it was a hard shock. From copy boy to general manager, everyone had known Neil and liked him. As the story moved out over the wires into bureau after bureau, the staff's feeling of bereavement increased.

The news touched not only the staff. It affected men on member papers who remembered working with Neil at one time or another on the numerous news and sports events he had covered before entering the Foreign Service. And it meant something personal to many newspaper readers, particularly the sports enthusiasts to whom Neil's by-line had long been familiar in the days before he gave up sports writing.

The co-operative's wires were silenced for two minutes on January 3, 1938, the day Neil's body left Spain for home. Zaragoza gave Neil and his two companions in death a solemn farewell. General José Moscardo, hero of the defense of the Alcazar, was present. With members of his staff, representatives of the provincial government, a delegation of native newspapermen, and a large group of foreign correspondents, the general followed the flower-banked hearses afoot. Crowds lined the city's ancient streets and saluted as the cortege passed. In the famous Cathedral of La Seo, where the Kings of Aragon were once crowned, a funeral mass was said for Neil. Then the three coffins were placed on the train that would carry them to France. An officer called for "Vivas," and the train moved away to the echoes of "Viva America!" . . . "Viva Inglaterra!" . . . "Arriba España!"

The first matter for consideration when the Board of Directors met nine days after Neil's death was the question of extraordinary death benefits for the correspondent's widow, Mrs. Helen Nolan Neil, and his five-year-old son, Edward J. Neil, III. The general manager was directed to make special financial arrangements for Mrs. Neil, and to set up an annuity fund for the support of the boy and his education through college. Then the directors adopted this resolution:

The Board of Directors of The Associated Press, as representatives of the entire membership, by this means enter into the permanent records of the institution this memorial to Edward J. Neil, Jr., gallant reporter, who died in The Associated Press service at Zaragoza, Spain, as the result of wounds he suffered while reporting the encounter on the Teruel front.

If democratic institutions are to prevail, as we all believe they will, the public must be fully informed as to what is happening in the world. We recognize that the good reporter is the keystone of our journalistic edifice. Believing this, we also believe that Edward J. Neil's death was not in vain. He undertook a perilous assignment at our behest and he carried it out gloriously.

As chroniclers of the day's events, we are proud to pay tribute to his memory. In him we find a justification of our faith. He accepted and fulfilled that ultimate measure of devotion which is so rarely found, but which, when we find it, helps us all go on.

They buried Neil in his native Massachusetts on January 21, with flowers from all over the world heaped high over his grave. And in the snow and zero cold of the Teruel front another staff man, Dwight L. Pitkin, took up the assignment Neil had begun.

XIV. "PEACE FOR OUR TIME"

I

THE Spanish Civil War staggered on toward its close and the spotlight of news, more than ever, remained on the Old World. Those who had felt that Spain was a mere testing ground were saying they had been right. More than one government talked of peace and prepared for war. The European jigsaw had become a desperate, many-sided contest in which opposing forces were hammering on toward an inevitable end.

Adolf Hitler, in whose eyes burned the fire of an ambition to restore to Germany the power and prestige of pre-World War days, had become one of the biggest news personalities since 1914. While in prison for his attempt to overthrow the German government in 1923 the one-time Austrian corporal had written *Mein Kampf*, and by 1938 it was becoming increasingly apparent that, as Der Führer of the Third Reich, he was determined to pursue his course.

Hitler sensations had kept the foreign staff on the jump ever since his appointment as chancellor of Germany in 1933. Each move he made seemed bolder than the last, touching off a long train of international repercussions.

The first important news in 1938 came on February 12, when Chancellor Kurt Schuschnigg of Austria journeyed suddenly and secretly to Hitler's Bavarian mountain retreat at Berchtesgaden to confer with the Führer. For months the relations between the two countries had been marked by nervous apprehension and suspicion on the part of Austria—in spite of Hitler's "guarantee" of Austrian independence —and the unexpected meeting whipped up puzzled speculation. The official communiqués were vague. The Austrian version spoke of a "distinct triumph" for Schuschnigg, while in Germany there were indefinite explanations that "improved" Austro-German relations were likely in the future.

In Berlin and in Vienna the two bureaus went to work to learn the truth of what actually had happened at Berchtesgaden. What with a controlled press, propaganda ministries, and self-serving government departments, real news had a habit of going underground in Central

Europe. It was likely to come in many ways. Sometimes a hurried telephone call from a government employee who could not speak officially. Sometimes a penciled message on the back of a crumpled handbill tossed negligently into a correspondent's parked automobile. Sometimes a few words in a "chance" meeting in some out-of-the-way café.

Once the staffs in Austria and Germany began their investigations, the unexpected meeting at Berchtesgaden assumed a character far different than the innocuous communiqués had indicated. Vienna was able to report that, far from being a "triumph" for Schuschnigg, the conference had ominous implications. Hitler had served the equivalent of an ultimatum on the Austrian chancellor, demanding among other things that he include Austrian Nazis in his Cabinet under the threat of invasion.

From Berlin came an even more penetrating series of stories. Chief of Bureau Louis Lochner, who had been building up his contacts in Germany for fourteen years, pointed out that Hitler had shaken up the German army only the week before, ousting some of its old leaders and assuming supreme command himself. He mentioned the general "we-will-show-them" resentment in Nazi circles against the foreign tendency to regard the drastic shake-up as symptomatic of general unrest in the Reich, and recorded the belief in official quarters "that der Führer might decide on a dramatic step to bolster confidence in Germany's armed forces." Then he called attention to the fact that the last time Germany had threatened Austria—in 1936 when Dollfuss was assassinated—Mussolini had massed the Italian army at the Brenner Pass, but this time Mussolini was a partner in the Rome-Berlin Axis and had sanctioned the Berchtesgaden meeting. The dispatch was factual throughout, and the facts gave evidence that an important coup was in the offing.

The stories of the next several days from Vienna and Berlin began to clarify the picture. Schuschnigg admitted five Austrian Nazis to his Cabinet after German troops massed along the frontier. Hitler, in a Reichstag speech on February 20, not only failed to reaffirm his guarantee of Austrian independence, something he had promised to do in return for Schuschnigg's concessions, but he spoke pointedly of the "continuous suffering" and the "unnecessary torture" of Germans outside the Reich. Simultaneously in London the British foreign secretary, Anthony Eden, resigned because of his opposition to Prime Minister Neville Chamberlain's "appeasement" policy toward the dictator nations. There followed a deceptive lull.

The climax came with a sudden rush of cables. On March 9 Schuschnigg, finally convinced that Hitler intended to seize Austria, made a last desperate effort to forestall such a move by announcing a plebiscite to determine whether the nation wished to join the Third Reich or remain independent. The plebiscite was set for March 13. Almost immediately pressure was brought on Schuschnigg to rescind the plebiscite order, but he held firm. Disorders and violence broke out in Austrian border towns which had large pro-Nazi elements. In Berlin, officials told Lochner that the plebiscite call was an "unfriendly act" toward Germany and a "betrayal" of the Berchtesgaden "agreement." Austria began to mobilize.

The staff in Vienna—Chief of Bureau Alvin J. Steinkopf, Melvin Whiteleather, Louis Matzhold and A. D. Steffreud—wrote the story of Austria's last hours on March 11. The first break came in mid-afternoon after a day of mounting tension and sporadic disorders. Schuschnigg announced postponement of the plebiscite under threat of Nazi invasion. A few hours later Steinkopf was flashing far bigger news. Schuschnigg had resigned as chancellor, again under the renewed threat of invasion. Then the swift final impacts: the formation of a new pro-Nazi government under Seyss-Inquart as chancellor; Seyss-Inquart's request to Hitler to send troops into Austria "to preserve order"; and the march of the German army into Austria.

The next seventy-two hours brought a whirlwind of news. Storm Troopers took over control of the Austrian capital. Nazi partisans filled the streets in wild, cheering demonstrations. The beating and plundering of Jews spread. Wholesale arrests began, and a purge of "unfriendly anti-Nazi forces" together with "traitorous elements." Lochner and his Berlin staff reported the Anschluss as Germany saw it, and Wade Werner accompanied Hitler when he crossed the Salzach River into his native Austria at Braunau, where he was born, and started his triumphal progress toward Vienna.

2

The Nazi seizure of power in Austria multiplied coverage problems. A tight censorship was imposed. Local telephone conversations had to be in German and every outgoing call was tapped. There were long delays in getting calls through to London and other European points, but dispatches routed via Berlin were transmitted with reasonable promptness. Nazi surveillance extended to the mails. The handicaps under which the staff worked were not lessened by the fact that Storm Troopers generally regarded foreign correspondents with hostility and several times threatened arrests.

An incident occurred on March 15, the day of Hitler's tumultuous entry into Vienna. Steinkopf and Matzhold, together with other members of the foreign newspaper corps, were summoned to the Chancellery to obtain the permits necessary to hear Hitler speak on the Heldenplatz and to witness the ensuing parade of the Third Reich's military might.

Steinkopf and Matzhold got their permits and, with other correspondents, were hurrying downstairs to the courtyard. At the foot of the stairs their way was blocked by black-uniformed SS guards, the elite of Nazi organizations. A steel-helmeted officer waved a revolver at the correspondents.

"Get back at once, every one of you," he shouted. "Get back! Unless you clear these steps this very moment, I give the order to fire!"

There was no arguing with gun muzzles and an officer of uncertain temper. Steinkopf and the other correspondents retreated up the stairs to the press section of the Foreign Ministry where they had just obtained their permits. It became apparent that the press chief there was as much a prisoner as the correspondents themselves. He telephoned agitatedly in futile efforts to secure his own release and that of the newspapermen. He refused explanations and the best idea he had in the emergency was the suggestion that, by leaning well out the window, the men could see the Heldenplatz in the distance.

Steinkopf telephoned the American legation and explained the predicament of the men in the Chancellery building, and his colleagues made similar appeals to the diplomatic representatives of their governments. Considerable time elapsed and Hitler's speech was well under way before the correspondents finally were permitted to leave. The explanation of the Gestapo—the German Secret Police—was that "there was reason to suspect sudden danger, and immediate and ruthless measures had to be taken to counteract it. Someone perhaps went too far in detaining foreign correspondents so long in the building."

The temporary "imprisonment" of Steinkopf and Matzhold, however, did not affect coverage of Hitler's speech. Wade Werner, who was accompanying the Führer's party, was on hand to report the address from the beginning. His credentials had been issued in Berlin and were not subject to the special regulations imposed on the Vienna press corps.

3

The efforts of the Vienna Bureau to tell the swiftly moving story of Austria's annexation in pictures as well as in words met the same difficulties. As rapidly as photographs could be obtained, they were rushed to London either by plane or by wire for radio transmission to the United States. A surprisingly complete pictorial report went out in spite of the fact that authorities interposed obstacle after obstacle, many without explanation. In one instance they refused to permit the wire transmission of an AP picture showing Hitler's troops entering the town of Graz, and the messenger was threatened with a prison camp. On another occasion an employee of the Vienna Bureau was arrested.

Whiteleather was at work in the office when it happened. Busy typing out a dispatch, he was interrupted by the sound of heavy foot-falls in the corridor. He looked up as a jack-booted Storm Trooper planted himself on the threshold, blocking the doorway.

"Is Willi Jacobson here?" the trooper demanded.

Whiteleather nodded.

Jacobson was a staff photographer of German-Jewish parentage. Originally he had been attached to the Berlin Bureau, but when the Nürnberg anti-Semitic laws were enforced he was refused the permit necessary for all subjects of the Third Reich who were engaged in newspaper work. Had he stayed in Berlin, he would have been deprived of his regular livelihood, so Lochner transferred him to Vienna. The systematic German police, however, kept a careful record.

At the time of the Storm Trooper's arrival, Jacobson was developing pictures in the darkroom. Whiteleather called him out. He took one look at the Nazi and understood. The Storm Trooper ordered him to come along, and he gathered up his coat. Whiteleather's attempt to intervene was of no avail. He could get no explanation as to why the photographer was being taken into custody.

Jacobson, like so many non-Aryan Germans in Vienna, was clapped into prison and kept there for months although no formal charge was made against him. The combined efforts of the Berlin and Vienna bureaus to bring about his release accomplished nothing, and the photographer remained under arrest until the authorities decided to release him. He returned to Berlin but, being a German and subject to the country's laws, he was unable to continue newspaper work.

The tempest whipped up by Austria's Anschluss with the Reich kept

A JACK-BOOTED STORM TROOPER PLANTED HIMSELF ON THE THRESHOLD.

the foreign staff on an emergency footing not only in Vienna and Berlin, but in London, Paris, Rome, Praha, and lesser points. Hitler's coup shook Europe and there were tense days during which no one knew what might come next. In New York the cable and wireless teletypes turned out the dispatches:

Britain and France Protest in "Strongest Terms" . . . Berlin Retorts They Have No Right to be Concerned . . . Mussolini Approves Hitler's Action . . . Reinforcements Rushed to Maginot Line . . . Czechoslovakia Closes Frontiers . . . Danzig Nazis Ask Union With the Reich . . . Britain to Speed Up Rearmament, Cautions Hitler Against Designs on Czechoslovakia . . . Russia Proposes Immediate Conference to Deal With Italo-German "Menace" . . . Hitler in Reichstag Speech Cites Austria's Fate as Warning to Czechoslovakia . . . Franco Continues Advance in Spain . . .

The most succinct summary of the foreign situation appeared not in the cable report but in a story by one of the New York staff's ship news reporters who interviewed Herbert Hoover on March 28 on the return of the former President of the United States from an extended trip abroad. Hoover told him: "The only problem not acute in Europe is that of parking space."

4

The echoes aroused by the annexation of Austria were still sounding when the members of The AP met on April 25 for their 1938 meeting, but for that one day the echoes were temporarily forgotten. The gathering had one thought—to do honor to Frank B. Noyes, who was retiring as president after thirty-eight years. Since he first intimated his intention to step down, he had been prevailed upon to accept re-election. But now the inevitable time had come and he was officially surrendering to Robert McLean the gavel he had wielded since 1900. His retirement, however, did not mean a leave-taking from the association's affairs. The members were anxious that the 75-year-old Washington publisher continue to be heard in the councils of the co-operative, and Noyes consented to accept renomination as a director.

The annual luncheon was made the occasion for a remarkable tribute. A precedent was broken when the assemblage rose and drank a toast to the publisher and his wife in addition to the traditional single toast to the President of the United States and the First Lady. In the principal address, Paul Bellamy, editor of the Cleveland *Plain Dealer*, told Noyes:

"There is one gift we can give you today which will gladden your heart more than any other. We can and do rededicate ourselves to the cause of truth in the news. This cause was never in direr need of defenders than today. But we shall tell the truth—and more resolutely than ever."

The retiring president expressed his gratitude for the "exaggerations" of the speakers who had described the worth of his long service, and said:

First, I want to say that no one knows better than I that whatever the contribution I have been able to give to the modern Associated Press, its success has not been due to me, but as all of you know, has been through the staff who have daily gathered the news. Under the direction of two great men, who have served as general managers, that news was gathered under the principles that we laid down. And it is also true that if I had attempted to interfere with that unbiased report I would have been banished. If it were the general manager or his predecessor who had attempted to color the news or serve a biased report to you, he would have been banished, because that is the whole basis of the organization. Fourteen hundred members of The Associated Press, as well as the Board of Directors, are on watch hour by hour and day by day to see that that report is not contaminated, is not biased, does not represent the beliefs or the opinions or the desires of any one individual. That, after all, is the real basis of what The Associated Press is, and that is the reason why in these days at times some of us seem unreasonably opposed to private control by a private organization of a dominant news service serving the newspapers of the United States.

I certainly think that Mr. William R. Hearst would not be satisfied to have a news service controlled by Mr. Roy Howard, nor would I; and Mr. Roy Howard would not be satisfied to have a news service that was controlled by Mr. William R. Hearst, nor would I; and I would not be satisfied to have a news service controlled by Frank B. Noyes, and neither of them would either.

The truth is that no one man in the world is good enough to be trusted to color or influence the report that comes to you as the life blood of your newspapers, and I pray to God that the time may never come when any individual can dictate to the newspapers of the United States the nature of the reports that they give.

Mr. Bellamy has said truly that nothing could make me happier today than to know that this generation were not skeptics as to the things that were fought for in 1893 and from then on. It would be tragic to me if I did not feel that the same belief in the vital necessity for a free, unhampered press was with you today as it was with me in 1893. I would feel that forty-five years had been wasted so far as I am concerned and that the press of the country was in a dire situation. But I have no such thought and I am, as Mr. Bellamy said, happy in the belief that this generation goes on carrying the banner of an independent press, and the banner of The Associated Press

"THIS GENERATION GOES ON CARRYING THE BANNER OF AN INDEPENDENT PRESS."

as the representative of that independent press. I don't mean that there should be a dead hand, that times do not change, that there shouldn't be changes in the organization, that you don't have to give way for the common good, that we shouldn't modify our hours of publication, or whatever it may be. Those things are the price of living together. But when it comes to the maintenance of the principle that nobody else, save the newspapers of this country, must control the fountains of their news, I hope that you will dedicate yourselves, just as we dedicated ourselves nearly fifty years ago, to the defense of that principle.

I thank you with all my heart.

5

There was no doubt but that there were formidable forces arrayed against honest, impartial news gathering in 1938—shrewdly manipulated propaganda machines, the tremendous weight of pressure groups, and the great resources of those whose interest it was to suppress facts. "In no previous year," the general manager said, "has a graver responsibility rested on the shoulders of a profession vested with the character of a public service."

One unmistakable index of that responsibility was supplied by newspaper readers themselves. In other times most dispatches were regarded as satisfactorily complete if they simply recorded the outward or official aspects of a situation and left the rest to conjecture. But that had changed drastically. Now readers wanted something more. They wanted their information more informative than the immediate current facts could be. The news report reflected that trend. On virtually every significant story the dispatches incorporated explanatory background material clarifying the latest events, or they went beneath the surface indications to disclose information which the facts obscured. This explanatory and interpretive treatment of the news was not an innovation —The AP had been doing it for some time, particularly since 1933—but only now had it become an essential element in the composition of the report.

On the world's news fronts the uneasy spring was followed by an uneasy summer. In Central Europe the Sudeten German Czechoslovak crisis simmered. Fierce fighting in Spain marked the second anniversary of the Civil War. London and Paris reported Franco-British efforts to rearm. On the other side of the world bombers droned across China, and to the north Russian troops battled Japanese along the ill-defined Manchukuo-Siberian border. Even other stories which appeared in the report seemed to have faint overtones of remembered conflict. The Blue and Gray survivors of 1861-1865 held their reunion at Gettysburg, seventy-five years to the day after the famous battle. At a rededication service in France, the bells of ancient Reims Cathedral, silenced by artillery fire in the World War, pealed out for the first time since 1914.

6

As the first day of September drew near, the wordage of the cable report began to climb significantly. The pieces of the news pattern one by one started to slip into place.

From Berlin: Germany Masses Reservists for Maneuvers with Regular Army.

From London: Britain Warns Hitler She Might Fight if Czecho-Slovakia Is Attacked.

From Praha: Czech Government Offers "Final" Terms for Settlement of Sudeten Grievances.

From Berlin: Nazis May "Sponsor" Sudeten Demands to Speed Settlement.

From Paris: French Anxiety Deepens, Discuss National Defense.

September came and at the outset the main burden fell on the staff at the two trouble spots—Berlin and Praha. After these came the other European centers which inexorably were being drawn deeper into the developing story with each passing hour—London, Paris, Rome, Moscow, Budapest, Warsaw, Geneva.

For the first several days of the month the news moved slowly. Efforts to bring about an amicable settlement of the differences of the Sudeten German minority in Czechoslovakia got nowhere. The Sudeten Nazi demand stiffened after Hitler pledged support to Konrad Henlein, their leader.

Germany moved troops. France moved troops. Czechoslovakia moved troops.

Lochner heard Hitler call the turn at Nürnberg on September 12. The German Führer denounced the "shameless ill-treatment" of 3,500,000 Sudetens, demanded they be given self-determination, and warned "if these harassed people feel they are without rights and aid, they will get both from us." Two days before Hitler's Nürnberg address, Lochner had written a story, based on the information obtained from confidential sources, that Hitler had made up his mind to demand the annexation of Sudetenland. The Nürnberg speech marked the beginning of the story's confirmation.

The stream of dispatches in the next forty-eight hours told of a continent plunged into the most fearful tension since 1914. From one capital after another came accounts of military preparations. Disorders and fighting broke out in the Sudeten areas. At Praha, Steinkopf and Larry Allen added gas masks to their workaday equipment as anti-aircraft batteries were moved into the city and laborers dug shelters in the public parks.

Then came the break. On Wednesday, September 14, the teletypes in New York began:

```
BULLETIN
LEAD DAY BRITISH

    LONDON, SEPT. 14 - (AP) - IT WAS OFFI-
CIALLY ANNOUNCED TONIGHT THAT PRIME MINISTER
CHAMBERLAIN WOULD FLY TO GERMANY TOMORROW TO
SEE REICHSFUHRER HITLER IN AN EFFORT TO ASSURE
PEACE.
                    PL GB 410P


    BULLETIN MATTER

    LONDON - FIRST ADD LEAD DAY BRITISH X X X
ASSURE PEACE.
    THE PRIME MINISTER HIMSELF DRAMATICALLY
ANNOUNCED HE INTENDED TO SEE HITLER AND "TRY
TO FIND A PEACEFUL SOLUTION TO THE CRISIS
WHICH IS MENACING WORLD PEACE."
                    APL GB 413P


    BULLETIN MATTER

    LONDON - SECOND ADD LEAD DAY BRITISH X X X
WORLD PEACE.
    THE GERMAN CHANCELLOR NOTIFIED CHAMBERLAIN
HE WOULD "GLADLY RECEIVE" HIM ON SEPT. 15 AT
BERCHTESGADEN, HIS RETREAT IN THE BAVARIAN
MOUNTAINS.  (MORE)
                    APL GB 416P
```

When Chamberlain, carrying the umbrella which became a symbol, took off from Heston Airport the next day, DeWitt Mackenzie, one of the association's Foreign Service specialists, flew after him in a chartered press plane. For Mackenzie the assignment had an ironic significance. Twenty years before he had witnessed and reported the birth of the new Czechoslovak nation in Paris of the Versailles Treaty days. Several years later he had been a guest of Thomas G. Masaryk, Czechoslovakia's first president, at historic Hradschin Castle in Praha, and had heard his host speak of the little republic's future.

It was foul flying weather. The Berchtesgaden-bound planes were pitched about in the turbulent air. Chamberlain, making his first trip by air, got airsick, so much so that his plane landed outside Munich to permit him to continue his journey by train. He was not the only victim of the rough weather. Mackenzie, for whom air travel had ceased to be a novelty, got just as sick as the prime minister, but he could not indulge in the luxury of getting back on land at Munich. His job was to be on the scene at Berchtesgaden ahead of Chamberlain.

The British prime minister's change of plans did not catch Lochner in Berlin by surprise. He had J. A. Bouman at the Oberwiesenfeld airdrome when Chamberlain, palely clutching his umbrella and wearing a weak smile, climbed out of the plane to be greeted by Foreign Minister Joachim von Ribbentrop and other Nazi dignitaries. Bouman accompanied the party by train to Berchtesgaden where he joined Mackenzie and Edward Shanke, who had been sent from Berlin.

But even before Bouman's dispatch reached New York there was another:

```
BULLETIN
FIRST LEAD CZECH

PRAHA, SEPT. 15 - (AP) - SUDETEN LEADER
KONRAD HENLEIN ISSUED A PROCLAMATION TODAY
DEMANDING ANNEXATION OF THE SUDETEN GERMAN
REGIONS OF CZECHOSLOVAKIA TO GERMANY.
                    OMH 918 A
```

The Praha bulletin—which further confirmed Lochner's story of September 10 on Hitler's Czechoslovakian plans—served advance notice on the subject matter to be discussed at Berchtesgaden when the Führer and Britain's prime minister met.

For Mackenzie, who handled the main story there, and for the two Berlin staffers who assisted him, the assignment meant a struggle against twin handicaps of inadequate communications and official secrecy. The little village had only two telephone lines, one of which was monopolized most of the time by official Nazi business. But in spite of the fierce competition for the single remaining line, the AP men fared exceptionally well in getting their copy through to Berlin for relay to America. Many times, however, good secondary material went into the wastebasket because there was no hope of getting it on the wire.

As far as the details of the Hitler-Chamberlain discussions were concerned, each correspondent was left to his own resources to find out what he could. The official communiqué was a model of vagueness. It took fifty-four words to state that there had been an "extended, frank exchange of views on the present situation," and that "a new conversation takes place within a few days."

Canvassing private resources, Mackenzie, Shanke, and Bouman were able to establish some positive facts. No great enthusiasm was evident or expressed in quarters close to Hitler or Chamberlain. It was certain that the prime minister had obtained no guarantee of peace from Germany. Furthermore, all indications were that Hitler was adamant in supporting the Nazi Sudeten demand that Czechoslovakia's German minority be united with the Reich, and for him the only question was how this might be accomplished. The one hopeful sign was that the conversations were scheduled to continue after Chamberlain had opportunity to confer with the French. All this went into the stories from Berchtesgaden. Mackenzie's impression was that Chamberlain left Germany a far sicker man than when he arrived.

7

Chief of Bureau Lochner had remained in Berlin. His long experience with the rigid government control of news had taught him that often the real story could be obtained, not on the scene, but in apparently unlikely places miles away. Once Chamberlain took off for home, Lochner's story was the one that the New York cable desk wanted. If anyone could pierce the veil of secrecy surrounding the Berchtesgaden discussions, New York felt Lochner could. The story came through from Berlin via London:

```
    FIRST LEAD GERMAN
    BY LOUIS P. LOCHNER

        BERLIN, SEPT. 16 - (AP) - ADOLF HITLER
    WAS SAID TODAY TO HAVE DEMANDED BOTH CESSION
    TO GERMANY OF CZECHOSLOVAKIA'S SUDETEN AREA
    AND BINDING ASSURANCES THAT CZECHOSLOVAKIA'S
    FOREIGN POLICY SHOULD BE IN HARMONY WITH
    GERMANY'S.
        THIS INFORMATION WAS VOLUNTEERED BY A MAN
    WHO TALKED TO HIGH CHANCELLERY OFFICIALS AT
    BERCHTESGADEN, WHERE HITLER RECEIVED PRIME
    MINISTER CHAMBERLAIN OF GREAT BRITAIN YESTERDAY.
        ANOTHER GERMAN DEMAND, THIS SOURCE SAID,
    WAS THAT AFTER GERMAN ABSORPTION OF THE CZECHO-
    SLOVAK SUDETEN AREA, WHAT IS LEFT OF THAT RE-
    PUBLIC SHOULD FIT ITSELF INTO GERMANY'S ECONOMIC
    SYSTEM, AT LEAST TO THE EXTENT THAT CZECHO-
```

```
SLOVAKIA DID NOT HINDER REALIZATION OF GERMAN
ECONOMIC AIMS.
     THE QUESTION OF UNION OF THE SUDETEN AREA
WITH GERMANY, THIS INFORMANT SAID, IS NOT EVEN
REGARDED AS AN ISSUE BY HITLER.
     IT WAS SAID TO HAVE BEEN HITLER'S STARTING
POINT IN DISCUSSIONS WITH ALL OTHER QUESTIONS,
SUCH AS PROCEDURE UNDER WHICH THE CHANGE COULD
BE EFFECTED WITHOUT WAR GROWING OUT OF IT.
(MORE)

                  ES-1135AED
```

While the teletypes reeled off Lochner's story that Hitler, in effect, wanted a virtual protectorate over Czechoslovakia, events in Europe had resumed the furious pace which prevailed before the brief respite of Berchtesgaden. London found it increasingly difficult to communicate with Steinkopf and Allen at Praha. Telephone calls were limited to six minutes. The delays in getting a connection mounted from several minutes to six hours. On top of that, a new scene of action had developed in the Sudeten areas, where fighting was going on between members of the Nazi Free Corps and Czech gendarmes or troops.

Whiteleather of the Berlin Bureau was the first to reach the fresh trouble zone. Armed with credentials from both German and Czech authorities, he was given a roving assignment to work on both sides of the disputed frontier in the Asch-Eger district, reporting the disorders and the stormy Nazi demonstrations for a return of the Sudetenland to the Reich. Whiteleather was followed by Roy Porter, of the Paris Bureau, who took over the task of patrolling another turbulent section of Sudetenland by auto. Later a third man, Edward Kennedy of Rome, was moved into the area. Across the German frontier R. F. Schildbach took up the job of covering troop concentrations, the arrival of Sudeten "refugees," the activities of the fugitive Sudeten Nazi leader, Konrad Henlein, and the mobilization of the "Free Corps" which made its headquarters on German soil.

The border districts swarmed with secret police and the populace was infected with a spy scare. The possession of pencil and paper, and especially a map, was a good ticket to the nearest police station. Twice in one day Whiteleather found himself in the hands of the police. Because he was seen asking questions in Selb, a small Bavarian town, he was taken into custody and questioned exhaustively before the officer finally agreed to release him. The Czechs were just as suspicious. A post-office official in Eger, Nazi Sudeten stronghold, who examined the correspondent's credentials, jumped to the conclusion that the safe-conduct letter from the Czech Foreign Office was a forgery. He summoned the criminal police and Whiteleather was taken to the local headquarters.

An effort to obtain an interview with the elusive Henlein led to the worst experience. Tipped off that Henlein would address an unscheduled Sudeten rally one night in Dresden, Germany, Whiteleather set out by automobile with Kenneth Anderson, a Reuters correspondent. They did not find Henlein, but there was plenty of news in the fiery mass meeting, with one of Henlein's aides proclaiming: "With gun in hand we are going to fight for our freedom."

The meeting hall was jammed and the two correspondents joined the overflow throngs gathered outside to listen to the harangue over loud-speakers. They were busily taking notes when a Sudeten loudly began denouncing them as spies. The crowd set upon them and before the police arrived the reporters were roughly handled. The local police turned the pair over to the Gestapo and from that point on they were unable to help themselves.

Whiteleather and Anderson were stripped of everything they carried. Requests for permission to communicate with an American or British consul were a waste of breath. They were thrust into a room. A moment later an officer stalked in, planked his heavy automatic on a table, and then began to ask questions.

The questioning lasted for an hour and a half and all the while, Whiteleather realized, the exclusive Sudeten rally story was getting colder and colder. Then abruptly the officer left the room, the two newspapermen were taken back to another part of the station where their belongings and credentials were returned without comment. They were free to go.

The news was what mattered, and the tom-tom of events grew faster in a crisis which had become a war of nerves. The cable teletypes in New York were never quiet:

Czechoslovakia Dissolves Nazi Sudeten Party . . . Germany Accuses Czechs of "Provocation" . . . Ten Million Men Under Arms in Europe . . . French and British Statesmen Meet in London to Draft Answer to Hitler . . . Czechs Decree State of Emergency . . .

The outcome of the fateful Franco-British conference at London was a decision to support Hitler in his demands concerning the German minorities in Czechoslovakia. The two powers jointly "proposed" that the Czechs agree to cede the Sudeten areas to the Reich. While Czecho-

slovakia's answer was awaited, the teletypes spelled out another foot-
note to the future:

```
BULLETIN

GENEVA, SEPT. 21 - (AP) - MAXIM LITVINOFF,
SOVIET RUSSIA'S FOREIGN COMMISSAR, TODAY
BITTERLY ACCUSED BRITAIN AND FRANCE OF AVOIDING
"A PROBLEMATICAL WAR TODAY IN RETURN FOR A
CERTAIN AND LARGE-SCALE WAR TOMORROW."
                 GB 755A


BULLETIN
FOURTH LEAD CZECH

PRAHA, SEPT. 21 - (AP) - THE PROPAGANDA
MINISTRY DISCLOSED INFORMALLY TONIGHT THAT
CZECHOSLOVAKIA HAD ACCEPTED THE BRITISH
FRENCH PLAN FOR MEETING REICHSFUHRER ADOLF
HITLER'S PEACE TERMS.
                 OL145P


BULLETIN MATTER

PRAHA - FIRST ADD FOURTH LEAD CZECH X X X
TERMS.
AN OFFICIAL OF THE MINISTRY SAID AT 6:15
P.M. THAT THE GOVERNMENT HAD YIELDED TO THE
PRESSURE OF LONDON AND PARIS.
THE BRITISH AND FRENCH LEGATIONS WERE
NOTIFIED OF THIS DECISION IN NOTES DELIVERED
LATE THIS AFTERNOON.
                 GB 146P
```

8

Mackenzie, Shanke, and Fred Vanderschmidt of the London staff,
were at Godesberg on September 22 for the second of Chamberlain's
three meetings with the German Chancellor. As far as coverage problems went, it was another Berchtesgaden with inadequate communications and a stone wall of official reticence. The hotel where Hitler
stayed was surrounded by army units, Hitler elite guards and Gestapo
men. Correspondents were denied all access. Nazi officials were the soul
of politeness, but where news was concerned their co-operation ended.
A few secretly contributed some information, but the bulk of the facts
were obtained sub rosa from Britishers on the staff accompanying
Chamberlain.

The conference dragged through two nerve-racking days. Most of
the co-operative's news was routed through Berlin, and the facilities

left much to be desired. The German capital could be reached only by so-called "lightning calls" which cost ten times the ordinary tolls, and the connections were arbitrarily broken after a certain number of minutes, the time allotment varying unpredictably from hour to hour.

The story that Mackenzie, Vanderschmidt, and Shanke sent from Godesberg was the story of a deadlocked conference with Hitler increasing his Czechoslovakian demands and insisting they be met by October 1 under threat of war. From Praha, Steinkopf flashed the order for a general mobilization of Czechoslovakia's armed forces, and on the heels of that news came John Lloyd's bulletin from Paris that Premier Edouard Daladier had decided to decree general mobilization the moment Germany marched against Czechoslovakia.

Europe began to black-out.

Then with the terrific tension close to the breaking point, another respite—another momentous scrap of copy:

```
THIRD NIGHT LEAD CHAMBERLAIN
BY FRED VANDERSCHMIDT

GODESBERG, GERMANY, SEPT. 24 - (AP) - (SAT-
URDAY) - PRIME MINISTER CHAMBERLAIN SALVAGED
THE EPOCHAL "PEACE OR WAR" CONFERENCE WITH
ADOLF HITLER TODAY WITH A MIDNIGHT PROMISE TO
PUT NEW PRESSURE ON CZECHOSLOVAKIA, MENACED AND
MOBILIZED.
                    349AMA
```

If communications with Praha had been erratic before, they became virtually impossible once the Czechoslovakia mobilization was decreed. More calls were put in to Praha 236:1—Steinkopf's telephone number —than to any other single staff phone in Europe, but only rarely did one get through. Nearby Budapest refused even urgent calls to Czech points, and except for wireless, the little republic was virtually isolated. Marylla Chrzanowska, correspondent at Warsaw, managed to get through a call from Poland, but it was quickly interrupted. Without success, London enlisted the help of amateur wireless stations in an effort to contact Steinkopf or Allen. One story did come through to New York by short wave, addressed jointly to The AP and one of its local members, the *Herald Tribune*.

Other facilities developed alarming symptoms of disintegration on September 25. Telephone calls from London to Paris were subject to a forty-minute delay and were limited to six minutes. The London-Budapest delay was at least an hour. The London-Moscow lines were so uncertain under normal conditions that a change for the worse there could not make much difference. At London, peacetime hub of the organization in Europe, there was evidence that delays might soon extend to the cables, and Chief of Bureau J. C. Stark warned New York to stand ready to handle quick transatlantic telephone calls. To make communications trouble complete, atmospheric conditions badly hampered the radio transmission of pictures.

In the no man's land of the Sudeten regions, Whiteleather, Porter, and Kennedy were finding their assignments more perilous than ever, what with land mines, snipers, and barbed-wire entanglements. Although instructed to take no unnecessary risks, the men frequently faced machine gun and rifle fire to get their stories. Regulations became more severe. The Nazi Free Corps barred all correspondents from approaching within gunshot of their rear guard unless they had special passes, and these were valid for only a few hours. Because of the paralysis of Czech communications, Whiteleather had to drive sixty miles to get his stories out, while his two colleagues, lacking German credentials, could not cross the border and were forced to rely either on couriers to neighboring countries or on the uncertain telegraph.

Whiteleather's experience with spy scares and police of one sort or another convinced him it might be wise to show his nationality plainly. He got a small American flag and pinned it to his coat lapel. His confidence was deflated when an innkeeper at Asch inquired curiously: "What's that you have, a German war flag?" On another occasion he got a lift across the border from Anderson of Reuters, who had a British flag on his car. When they stopped at Selb in Germany to file their stories, a peasant girl touched the AP man's arm and pointed to the Union Jack. "Is that the new Sudeten German party flag?" she asked. After that Whiteleather gave up the flag idea.

9

The anxiety and tension before the Chamberlain-Hitler meeting at Godesberg was as nothing to what succeeded it. Dispatch after dispatch told of a continent sweeping toward a precipice which all those concerned professed every desire to avoid. Even the small, traditionally neutral nations were girding for an emergency. Occasional items such as the report of a prize fight in London or a soccer game in Dublin seemed incongruous news indeed, sandwiched as they were between stories of air raid scares in Paris and black-outs in Praha.

Editors in New York swiftly relayed the incoming flood of copy, inserting the deleted first names, articles and prepositions, then rushing the dispatches to the Morkrums:

```
BULLETIN
SECOND LEAD FRENCH

     PARIS, SEPT. 24 - (AP) - FRANCE MOBILIZED
270,000 RESERVISTS TODAY IN THE LAST STEP
BEFORE GENERAL MOBILIZATION AS EVACUATION OF
TOWNS ALONG THE GERMAN FRONTIER BEGAN.
               RFH 523 AED


BULLETIN MATTER

     PARIS - FIRST ADD SECOND LEAD FRENCH XXX
FRONTIER BEGAN.
     TWO FULL CLASSES WERE ORDERED TO THE COLORS
THIS MORNING, PUSHING FRANCE'S MEN UNDER ARMS
TO CONSIDERABLY OVER THE 2,000,000 MARK.
     AT THE SAME TIME IT WAS REPORTED THAT
PREMIER DALADIER WOULD FLY TO LONDON THIS
MORNING BECAUSE OF THE INTERNATIONAL SITUATION
GROWING FROM GERMAN EFFORTS TO TAKE OVER
CZECHOSLOVAKIA'S SUDETENLAND HAD BECOME MUCH
WORSE.
               TFH 525AED
```

More copy:

```
BULLETIN

     VICENZA, ITALY, SEPT. 25 - (AP) - PREMIER
MUSSOLINI THREATENED TODAY TO TAKE MILITARY
MEASURES IF OTHER NATIONS DO NOT CEASE MOBILIZ-
ING MEN AND WARSHIPS.
     MUSSOLINI DID NOT MENTION BY NAME EITHER
FRANCE OR GREAT BRITAIN, BOTH OF WHICH HAVE
TAKEN EMERGENCY PRECAUTIONS, BUT IT WAS BELIEVED
HIS DECLARATION WAS DIRECTED AT THEM.
               BB 1242A
```

By this time the situation had become so ominous that the question of evacuating the families of correspondents arose. Stark of London advised the general manager that he was sending the wives and children of his staff men to the country, pending provisions for their return to the United States. Boat accommodations were at a premium, he cabled, but Joseph P. Kennedy, United States ambassador to England, was canvassing all possibilities before asking for American ships. Chief of Bureau Lloyd in Paris had a similar problem, with the wives of seven staff men and their nine children to consider. He sent them off to remote French villages until a decision was reached on returning them to America. From Geneva Charles Foltz cabled his family to cancel their plans to sail from New York to join him. Wives of the men on the Berlin staff began to pack up and make ready to leave Germany.

Simultaneously preparations were made for the protection of the bureaus in event of war. Those responsible had to think in terms of sandbags, black-out paper for windows, and strips of criss-cross tape to keep the panes from shattering should bombers strike. Final arrangements were completed in cable exchanges with New York for the staff abroad to revert to a full wartime basis at a minute's notice, filing direct to New York instead of to London. London still was clearing the bulk of European copy, but an increasing proportion of dispatches were being sent direct. Stark also reported that everything was in readiness to shift the London Bureau to a previously selected secret location if war came and air raids made the British capital untenable.

All this, of course, was incidental to the main task of reporting under the most driving pressure. Yet Lloyd in Paris found time to worry about his staff and the fact that he couldn't procure gas masks for them. Foltz at Geneva proved the hero of the emergency. He found a Swiss shop where a limited supply was available at fifty francs each. He sent thirty to Paris by plane.

And the teletypes hammered on:

```
BULLETIN
FIRST LEAD FRENCH
    PARIS, SEPT. 25 - (AP) - THE FRENCH CAB-
INET AGREED UNANIMOUSLY THAT REICHSFUHRER
HITLER'S MEMORANDUM TO CZECHOSLOVAKIA DE-
MANDING QUICK OCCUPATION OF SUDETENLAND BY
GERMANY WITHOUT GUARANTEES FOR NEW CZECHO-
SLOVAK FRONTIERS WAS "UNACCEPTABLE."
                    BB1232P
    BULLETIN
FIRST LEAD BRITISH
    LONDON, SEPT. 25 - (AP) - THE CZECHO-
SLOVAK GOVERNMENT'S REPLY TO REICHSFUHRER ADOLF
HITLER'S "FINAL OFFER" FOR PEACE WAS REPORTED
RELIABLY TONIGHT TO CONSTITUTE VIRTUAL IF NOT
COMPLETE REJECTION.
                    OL 120P
    BULLETIN MATTER
    LONDON - FIRST ADD FIRST LEAD BRITISH
X X X REJECTION.
    IT WAS STATED THE REPLY WAS HANDED TO THE
BRITISH FOREIGN OFFICE BY THE CZECHOSLOVAK
```

MINISTER, JAN MASARYK, SHORTLY BEFORE FRENCH
PREMIER EDOUARD DALADIER AND FOREIGN MINISTER
GEORGES BONNET ARRIVED TO CONSULT WITH BRITISH
LEADERS.

OL 127P

Czechoslovakia's isolation had become more complete than ever.
Traffic was virtually suspended for all except the military. Most border
points were closed and censorship imposed on all telephone calls. Each
time London heard from the men in the Sudeten region it was a relief.
The dispatches Allen sent through by courier to Budapest offered
assurance that he was safe, but anxiety was felt for Steinkopf. Louis
Matzhold prevailed upon the American legation at Budapest to put
through a diplomatic call to the legation at Praha, and this established
that Steinkopf was well and working hard. Later the Czech legation at
Budapest informed The AP that the Foreign Office in Praha was
making special arrangements to permit Steinkopf to send his dispatches
via wireless.

While the world waited on September 26, the crisis which seemed
to have no end pushed to more terrible peaks. Mussolini again warned
France and Britain to leave the Czechs to their fate. Chamberlain sent
a new appeal to Hitler. And in the huge, swastika-draped Sportspalast
at Berlin the German Chancellor took the rostrum before his wildly
heiling followers for his final pronouncement on the Sudeten issue.
Lochner, Rudolf Josten, and Bouman were there to handle the spot
news, leaving the color to Shanke and Mackenzie, who had attached
himself to the Berlin staff after Berchtesgaden.

Copy—from Paris, not Berlin:

BULLETIN

PARIS, SEPT. 26 - (AP) - AN OFFICIAL
STATEMENT ISSUED BY THE FOREIGN OFFICE TODAY
SAID THAT IF, IN SPITE OF ALL EFFORTS MADE BY
PRIME MINISTER CHAMBERLAIN, GERMANY WERE TO
ATTACK CZECHOSLOVAKIA, FRANCE WOULD GO TO THE
AID OF THE LITTLE REPUBLIC AND THAT BRITAIN
AND RUSSIA WOULD STAND BY FRANCE.

EDB 336 PED

From the Sportspalast:

NIGHT LEAD HITLER
BY LOUIS P. LOCHNER

BERLIN, SEPT. 26 - (AP) - REICHSFUHRER
ADOLF HITLER TONIGHT TOLD THE WORLD THAT IF

```
CZECHOSLOVAKIA DOES NOT GIVE GERMANY THE
TERRITORY HE HAS MARKED AS SUDETENLAND BY
OCTOBER 1, HE WILL ACT.
     "THE TIME HAS COME TO TALK BUSINESS," HE
SAID.  "THE SUDETENLAND IS THE LAST TERRITORIAL
DEMAND I HAVE TO MAKE IN EUROPE, BUT IT IS A
DEMAND FROM WHICH I NEVER WILL RECEDE."
              2145 HTM 530P
```

Take after take of the story flowed across the cable desk in New York and thence to the domestic wires. Hitler Text . . . Add Hitler Descriptive . . . First Add Lochner . . . Second Add Lochner . . . And the bank of cable teletypes kept spelling out more.

The next day Ambassador Kennedy confidentially advised Stark to get the families of the London staff out of England and offered to arrange for accommodations on a Swedish liner sailing September 29. The British government started the final preliminary moves for the imposition of censorship. Because two out of three news pictures dealt with war preparations or subjects of a military nature, they had to be submitted to the War Office for approval before transmission. Paris already was feeling the censor's hand. One dispatch was held up two hours and thirty-seven minutes. Lloyd switched his entire urgent file direct to New York, reporting that delays on all channels to London had become several hours long.

At Praha the staff got ready for the terrific impact of the German Blitzkrieg which everyone expected. Steinkopf informed New York that he, Allen, and Porter, who was just back from Sudetenland, planned to divide if the government left the Czech capital. One of them, however, would remain at Praha as long as communications held out. The news would go out by radio to the Paris Bureau for relay to the United States. Steinkopf had no direct word from the border regions where Kennedy and Whiteleather were still on assignment.

Resentment in Praha ran high against France and Britain, for the Czechs felt that they had been "sold out" by the earlier concessions to Hitler. Allen was spat upon by one group of Czechs who thought he was English, but they apologized when they learned he was an American.

Not only in Czechoslovakia, but in Hungary and other Central European countries, the money problems of staff and resident correspondents became acute. Government-controlled communications facilities were insisting on prepaid tolls in all cases. Banks refused to cash checks, and in some instances no withdrawals were permitted. Treasurer

Curtis got a steady stream of urgent requests to cable dollars. No foreign exchange. Dollars.

And all the while the news:

```
          SECOND LEAD BRITISH
          BY RADER WINGET

          LONDON, SEPT. 27 - (AP) - JAN MASARYK,
     CZECHOSLOVAK MINISTER TO LONDON, TODAY MADE
     PUBLIC HIS GOVERNMENT'S NOTE FLATLY REFUSING TO
     ACCEPT ADOLF HITLER'S "FINAL" TERMS FOR CUTTING
     UP CZECHOSLOVAKIA AS THE PRICE OF EUROPEAN
     PEACE.
                        ADS 737A


          THIRD LEAD DEFENSE

          LONDON, SEPT. 27 - (AP) - THE OFFICIAL
     GAZETTE TODAY PUBLISHED A ROYAL ORDER FROM
     KING GEORGE DECLARING "A CASE OF EMERGENCY
     EXISTS" AND AUTHORIZING THE CALLING UP OF
     AUXILIARY AIR FORCES FOR DEFENSE.
                        OMH 154P


          BULLETIN
          FIRST LEAD CHAMBERLAIN

          LONDON, SEPT. 27 - (AP) - PRIME MINISTER
     CHAMBERLAIN DECLARED TONIGHT HE WOULD NOT HESI-
     TATE TO TAKE A THIRD TRIP TO GERMANY IF HE
     THOUGHT IT WOULD DO ANY GOOD, BUT AT THE
     MOMENT "I CAN SEE NOTHING FURTHER THAT I CAN
     USEFULLY DO IN THE WAY OF MEDIATION."
                        GB 211P


          LONDON - FIRST ADD FIRST LEAD CHAMBERLAIN
     X X X MEDIATION.
          "IF I WERE CONVINCED THAT ANY NATION HAD
     MADE UP ITS MIND TO DOMINATE THE WORLD BY FORCE
     I SHOULD NOT HESITATE TO RESIST IT," THE PRIME
     MINISTER DECLARED IN A BROADCAST FROM FAMED
     TEN DOWNING STREET.
          "I FIND HERR HITLER'S ATTITUDE UNREASONABLE
     IN HIS FINAL DEMANDS," HE CONTINUED.
          "BUT I SHALL NOT GIVE UP MY HOPE FOR A
     PEACEFUL SOLUTION."
                        GB 218P

          BULLETIN

          LONDON, SEPT. 27 - (AP) - THE ADMIRALTY
     TONIGHT ANNOUNCED THE IMMEDIATE MOBILIZATION OF
     THE ENTIRE NAVY.
                        CCC 614P
```

10

The night of September 27-28, taut and weary correspondents knew the explosive situation could not last much longer. For the past two weeks they had been battling a maelstrom of propaganda, inspired untruths, and false reports, endeavoring to sift out truth and actual facts and to report them honestly, without emotionalism or synthetic hysteria. A miscue, a lapse in levelheaded thinking under those circumstances might conceivably have disastrous results.

Stark sent a message the morning of September 28, saying that Witt Hancock would handle the running story and Vanderschmidt the leads when Prime Minister Chamberlain appeared in the House of Commons that day to report on the crisis and announce Britain's readiness to go to war, if need be. Everyone expected that to mark the beginning of the end.

Before the Parliament session started the news indicated how near that end might be. Germany recalled all her shipping from the seas. The British Air Ministry sent up fighting planes to guard against any lightning thrust of enemy bombers. France ordered a new partial mobilization of army reserves. The Czechs were ready to resist invasion to the last ditch.

The impersonal teletypes in New York mechanically carried on with the story which for days had been pouring from 20,000 to 30,000 words across the sea to The AP each twenty-four hours.

```
        BULLETIN
        CHAMBERLAIN RUNNING
        LONDON, SEPT. 28 - (AP) - PRIME MINISTER
   CHAMBERLAIN, OPENING HIS HISTORIC DECLARATION
   TO PARLIAMENT TODAY, SAID, "WE ARE FACED WITH
   A SITUATION WHICH HAS NO PARALLEL SINCE 1914."
                    APL GB
```

And a little later:

```
        BULLETIN
        LEAD CHAMBERLAIN
        LONDON, SEPT. 28 - (AP) - PRIME MINISTER
   CHAMBERLAIN TOLD PARLIAMENT TODAY THAT ADOLF
   HITLER HAD INFORMED HIM AT BERCHTESGADEN THAT
   "RATHER THAN WAIT" TO HELP THE SUDETEN GERMANS
   ACHIEVE SELF-DETERMINATION "HE WOULD BE PRE-
   PARED TO RISK A WORLD WAR."
                  GB 946A
```

At the cable desk and in the offices of member papers, editors gravely watched the story line after line as it came from the typebars. This looked like the end.

Then in the House of Commons, as Chamberlain was reaching the close of his speech, a cabinet minister hastily passed him a message on a folded piece of paper.

The news printers jangled with the bells that signaled only the most urgent news.

```
        BULLETIN
        SECOND LEAD CHAMBERLAIN

        LONDON, SEPT. 28 - (AP) - PRIME MINISTER
CHAMBERLAIN DRAMATICALLY ANNOUNCED TODAY THAT
HE, PREMIER DALADIER OF FRANCE, AND PREMIER
MUSSOLINI OF ITALY WOULD GO TO MUNICH TOMORROW
TO MEET CHANCELLOR HITLER.
                APL GB1024A


        BULLETIN MATTER

        LONDON - FIRST ADD SECOND LEAD CHAMBERLAIN
X X X HITLER
        THE PRIME MINISTER SAID HITLER HAD AGREED
TO POSTPONE MOBILIZATION OF THE GERMAN ARMY FOR
24 HOURS TO PERMIT THE HOLDING OF THIS CONFER-
ENCE IN SEARCH OF A WAY TO AVERT A EUROPEAN WAR.
                APL GB 1028A
```

The bureau chiefs abroad drafted plans for covering the Munich conference. Lochner, who proceeded at once to the Bavarian city, headed the staff chosen for the assignment. Mackenzie accompanied him. Vanderschmidt flew from London. His particular responsibility was the British delegation. Foltz was selected for similar work with the French. The fifth member of the staff was Whiteleather, who knew the Italian end of the axis because of his previous experience in Rome. He got word of his assignment while under fire during one of the numerous Czech-German frontier clashes that had been taking place.

The staff took over a hotel suite for its Munich headquarters. A regular news desk was set up and arrangements perfected for routing the bulk of the story to London by telephone, and the overflow to Berlin by telegraph. The story Lochner wrote on the eve of the conference stated on authoritative information that Hitler would insist on getting the Sudetenland, as he had determined all along.

Lochner and Mackenzie watched Hitler and Mussolini arrive by train the next morning, Thursday, September 29. Hitler was smiling and self-assured. His axis partner, Mussolini, was heavy-eyed and drawn. The German officials to whom Mackenzie spoke were not optimistic, but they all manifested a hopeful air. Lochner got a more positive reaction from his sources. Bavaria's governor, General Earl Ritter von Epp, a doughty old warrior, had no misgivings. "Herr Lochner," he explained, "Munich today is the center of the world. It's right here that its axis is going to be greased!"

At the airport Foltz flashed the arrival of the two Allied spokesmen, Daladier and Chamberlain. Daladier was the first to land. He came armed with plenary powers under which he could place France on a war footing by a single telephone call if the conference failed. Chamberlain's plane landed a half hour later. The prime minister was affable as he received the greeting of Foreign Minister von Ribbentrop, but his smile vanished when he was escorted across the field to review an honor guard of black-uniformed SS troops.

The conferees held three carefully guarded sessions before the final agreement was signed, sealing the fate of Czechoslovakia. The first began at 12:45 P.M. and continued until 2:45 P.M. After a two-hour interval the statesmen convened again and sat until 8:20 P.M. The final conference started at 10 P.M. and lasted until after midnight. Except for the strictly cautious and limited announcements of government spokesmen, the progress of the discussions was shrouded with secrecy and uncertainty. The air was full of all sorts of rumors, surmises, and speculation.

The interval between the first and second sessions gave Lochner the opportunity he needed and he went behind the scenes, as he had done repeatedly during the year, to determine what was actually happening. An hour after the second session began, he had a story on the cables setting forth in detail an authentic summary of what was to be the outcome of the conference. Hitler, his information ran, would get virtually everything he demanded. The only difference was that the annexation of the Sudetenland would be effected by degrees over a period of ten days, instead of in toto on October 1. The Polish and Hungarian claims to portions of the Czech state were to be settled, and then a guarantee by the four powers to protect what was left of the little nation against unprovoked aggression.

The succeeding hours produced unofficial confirmation bit by bit, not only at Munich but in European capitals involved, and finally sixteen minutes before the formal communiqué was issued:

```
BULLETIN
LEAD
      MUNICH, SEPT. 30 -- (FRIDAY) - (AP) -
WESTERN EUROPE'S FOUR MAJOR POWERS EARLY THIS
MORNING ANNOUNCED AGREEMENT "IN PRINCIPLE" ON
PLANS FOR CEDING TO GERMANY THE SUDETEN REGIONS
OF CZECHOSLOVAKIA AND THUS KEEP EUROPE AT
PEACE.
                    WW 753P
```

There followed the terms for "peace for our time"—terms which Lochner had described more than eight hours earlier—and a comprehensive roundup not only of what had happened at Munich, but also an explanation of the events and their effect on the nations of Europe. Simultaneously from Berlin, Rome, London, and Paris came stories of relief at the settlement of the crisis. Only the dispatches from Moscow and Praha struck a contrary note. In the Soviet capital the Munich powers were branded "beasts of prey," and in Praha there was the bitter grief of a nation which had sacrificed itself to "superior force" in order "to save the peace of Europe."

II

Munich produced one more major story September 30—the signing of a special statement by Hitler and Chamberlain as earnest "of the desires of our two peoples never to go to war with one another again."

Whiteleather and Mackenzie started for the German-Czech border to join Schildbach and cover the advance of the German army of occupation when it started to move into the Sudeten areas on October 1. They found strict regulations had been promulgated to govern all correspondents. Any foreigner not officially attached to headquarters or not accompanied by an army officer was subject to arrest. Reporters were promised an opportunity to see everything, but warned against independent investigations. Photographers were denied permission to accompany the troops. The only pictures available would be made by army cameramen. Across the border with the Czech troops who were waiting to fall back as the Germans advanced The AP had Kennedy, Porter, and Allen. They were not subject to the same restrictions, and photographers had the opportunity of recording the story from the Czech side without interference.

The hour when the occupation would begin on October 1 was left indefinite, but Lochner had his resident correspondents alert at all points in case the move was made at some place not immediately accessible to the staff men with the army. Konstantin Kreuzer at Salzburg stayed up all night and flashed the first word when a reconnaissance vanguard of infantry battalion strength crossed the border at 2 A.M. near Aigen, Upper Austria. Kreuzer's news of the start of the occupation—news sharply challenged at the time in a number of quarters—was confirmed many hours later by both the Propaganda Ministry in Berlin and by the headquarters of the army.

After that the story settled down to a schedule basis with the installment occupation of the ceded zones, the Führer's triumphal progress through the Sudetenland, the Polish and Hungarian annexations of the areas they claimed, and the readjustment of Czechoslovakia's national life to meet her straitened circumstances.

In the judgment of the general manager, the Czech-German crisis with its weeks of suspense, upheaval, and uncertainty was one of the greatest tests the co-operative's foreign staff had faced. He wrote an appraisal in a special message to all employes:

It has been a time when calm, sound, and accurate reporting in the midst of rumors and alarms was a requisite of highest consequence. Millions of Americans have made the reports of The Associated Press their first reliance in their eager quest for the truth. The staff has met that responsibility fully. It has recorded only the truth. It has reported no wars that did not materialize, and no peace settlements until they were arrived at.

It is gratifying to know that developments were covered with uniform promptness—in many instances with surprising and unparalleled speed.

But far beyond that, it is more satisfying than words can express that nothing you have written need be erased, but can stand as an authentic day to day history of one of the great international episodes of our times.

The Pulitzer Prize Committee voted Lochner the award for outstanding work by a foreign correspondent during 1938.

12

As the reverberating echoes of Munich began to subside, Mackenzie, free to assume his roving assignment as a Foreign Service specialist, set out to visit Eastern and Central Europe to study at first hand the long-range results of the four-power agreement. The question was: What next in Europe? As a trained observer, he sought the signs and the evidence. What Munich had meant to the nations most vitally concerned, and what officials of those nations thought it might mean in time to come—that was news.

The first country Mackenzie visited was Poland. He found the Poles, although jubilant over their share in the Czech spoils, suspicious of what Hitler might do next. They did not discount their fears of aggression, and they seemed to have little confidence in the power of Britain and France, under "appeasement" governments, to deter the German Chancellor from any subsequent move.

In Warsaw the correspondent had a long talk with an authority who had been close to the late Marshal Pilsudski, Poland's "strong man."

"Ah, Mr. Mackenzie," said the informant, "Hitler should have been stopped long ago. In 1933, the year he became the power in Germany, Marshal Pilsudski urged strongly upon our ally, France, the great need for waging a preventive war against the Reich. It would have been easy then. 'Now is the best time,' Pilsudski told the French. 'You'll have to do it sooner or later.' But France could not be persuaded."

As to Poland's future, the Pole intimated that their course depended largely on Hitler's attitude. "He's the master of Central Europe. Poland doesn't have much choice. It is prepared, as you say, to play his game economically and in other ways as long as he makes no efforts to intrude on our sovereignty. It can't do anything else, situated as it is. But if it ever becomes necessary to defend Polish sovereignty, be assured that the Poles will fight to defend themselves."

Throughout the Balkans, government officials and others of standing in the little nations were inclined to take an even gloomier view, Mackenzie found. He talked with Cabinet ministers, diplomats, army officers, businessmen, educators, and the peasants he encountered along the roadsides. Everywhere he found the same feeling that Hitler was the dominant figure on the Continent, that all Franco-British influence in Central Europe had been ended by the "defeat" at Munich. Governments feared that their nations might be the next victims. A great deal of what Mackenzie learned was in confidence or for his personal information as background in writing interpretive articles. By far the largest portion of the material, however, appeared in the series of first-person stories he wrote on conditions during the course of his travels.

Christmastide, 1938, was approaching when Mackenzie got back to London. Almost at once he felt that something fundamental had changed since he left England three months earlier to fly to Berchtesgaden for the first of the conferences which were climaxed at Munich. There had been shouts of "Stand by Czecho!" then, but the vast majority of the people were adverse to stiff measures. The attitude toward Hitler had been a mixture of tolerance, indulgence, and exasperation.

This old attitude had disappeared. Exactly when or why, Mackenzie could not ascertain. The new feeling was still extremely vague, as if it had only started to crystallize.

In search of reliable information, he arranged an appointment with one of the most important single figures in the British government—a man who delayed his appearance in Parliament half an hour for the talk which occurred.

"I have not come to you for an interview," Mackenzie explained, "because I know you cannot grant one. But I seem to have sensed the beginnings of a change in British sentiment and policy toward Germany. I will be grateful if you can tell me if I am right or wrong, and what it all means."

The statesman did not resent the direct approach.

"You're right," he replied. "The British government reluctantly has come to the conclusion that the policy of appeasement is a failure, and there is no longer any use to pursue this policy. We reluctantly have come to the conclusion that Hitler is not susceptible to any moral influence. He is a man with a dangerous obsession. We have decided that we must smash him. We hope to do it by economic or political means—but if these fail—we shall use force!"

Because of the statesman's high position, the publication of the blunt, unequivocal statement was not possible, but Mackenzie was given permission to use the information guardedly as "background" without positively indicating its source. Accordingly in one of his last first-person interpretive stories from abroad in 1938 he wrote:

I am in a position to state with assurance that many officials of the democracies have now adopted the view that Führer Hitler's mind is so inflexibly fixed on his program of empire building that nothing will stop him short of defeat in war or the collapse of his regime.

Advocates of a policy of appeasement toward the dictators clung to the last to the idea that they could bargain with Hitler.

I understand, however, this hope has been abandoned very generally and it is now agreed that the only value of such an approach to Berlin is to postpone an ultimate reckoning.

That pretty well sums up the sentiment with which England entered the Christmas holidays. There is a fairly grim determination to get down to cases and have an end to war scares, even if it takes a major war to establish peace.

Here was the answer to: What next in Europe?

13

Even before Mackenzie's illuminating confidential talk with the member of the British Cabinet, General Manager Cooper had been assaying post-Munich Europe from the standpoint of the news demands it might be likely to produce. None of the "peace for our time" developments had caused him to alter his opinion that, whether it be peace or war, Europe was a continuing emergency, certain to produce news of extraordinary calibre.

One of his first steps was the leasing of a special cable between New York headquarters and the London Bureau—something for which the association had been negotiating without success over a period of years. This represented a great advance in transatlantic communications. It gave The AP control over its cable line, and it meant that an operator could sit at his keyboard in the London Bureau and send directly into member paper offices all over the United States, for the cable and the domestic leased wire system could be hooked together when outstanding foreign news warranted.

Two other features in the post-Munich program were the additional assignments of picked staff men to the bureaus abroad, and an enlargement of the cable desk force at home. The general manager's final decision was the appointment of Milo M. Thompson, bureau chief at Washington, as resident European executive. Thompson's duties in the post were to act as co-ordinator for all the association's efforts in Europe and to take over the general administrative work abroad so that bureau chiefs there could concentrate on the news exclusively.

News considerations in Europe and plans for the year ahead were important during the Christmastide of 1938, but the season also chanced to witness one of those rare occasions when the co-operative had another job which, in the last analysis, was quite incidental to the task of gathering and distributing news. The organization was moving New York headquarters into its own building.

The dream of a special building to house the organization's general offices and related agencies was not a new one. Years earlier, both Stone and Adolph S. Ochs, as a member of the Board of Directors, had broached the idea, but the discussions had been indefinite. Cooper, as general manager, had the same idea and worked toward its realization.

The new home of The AP was a fifteen-story building in the Rockefeller Center group off midtown Fifth Avenue, six blocks from the old Madison Avenue offices. Four floors were made ready, one of them an immense newsroom of some 34,000 square feet in area. There the world's most complicated news control board and an intricate labyrinth of wires were installed to make transmission of the news virtually instantaneous to member newspapers across the nation. For the first time in any New York building the power lines of all five city power stations were cut into the switchboard. Engineers pointed out that, with this precaution, although the metropolis might be bombed or ravaged by fire, flood, or hurricane, the chances were almost negligible that all five power stations would fail simultaneously.

The move meant something more than a mere shift in geographical location. Cooper expressed it in a note to the staff:

The new Associated Press Building is a monument to the association's newspaper members and its employes. Through 90 years they have mutually striven that an accurate, unbiased chronicle of events, interestingly recorded, be available to newspaper readers. . . .

What you have aided in accomplishing in the past must continue into the future so that "By The Associated Press" shall prevail as long as the rights of a free press continue to make possible an uncensored, unfettered collection and dissemination of truthful news.

The future of which he spoke even then had started.

XV. "BY THE ASSOCIATED PRESS"

ALMOST a century of news gathering. . . .

They had been crowded, busy years. The news was always the thing, but in retrospect the unpretentious beginnings of 1848 seemed hopelessly inadequate for the task undertaken. Then the entire regular news staff consisted of the versatile and overburdened Alexander Jones and an inexperienced assistant. Only six papers received the service. Except on rare occasions, the report never exceeded a few hundred words a day and the total of all expenses was less than $20,000 annually. The organization at first boasted no regular foreign correspondents and the coverage of domestic news depended almost entirely on the enterprise of free-lance "telegraphic reporters" who peddled their dispatches at so much a word.

By the end of the first forty-five years, when The Associated Press became a non-profit co-operative, news gathering as a public service had come far indeed. But the years after 1893 wrought a much greater transformation.

The contemporary association was spending more than $11,000,000 annually to collect the world's news and news pictures for 1,400 member newspapers in the United States and for scores of others over the world. Yet it had no capital stock, made no profits, declared no dividends. For its tremendous task it could muster a staff of 7,200, supplemented by the auxiliary army of editorial workers on member newspapers and with affiliated news agencies in other countries. To produce the report of a single day approximately 100,000 men and women contributed their ability and effort, directly or indirectly. The volume of news had reached staggering proportions—1,000,000 words in every twenty-four hours, more than any one member newspaper received, more than any one member newspaper could print.

Day after day, on general, regional, and state circuits, the vast flood of copy poured over 285,000 miles of domestic wires—a news network more than twice the size of any other—and it kept a battery of 3,300 teletype machines busy around the clock, swiftly spelling out item after item. It was a flood that came from all points of the compass

—from the association's own world-wide staff, from member newspapers, from string correspondents, from bureaus in every major city in the United States, from American-manned bureaus in foreign countries, and from representatives in virtually every other city, town, and hamlet of the globe.

At first news had but one medium—the written word. Now a second had developed—the visual medium. The same forces that were on the alert around the world to report the news in textual form were equally vigilant for pictures with which to complete the story told by the written word. Wirephoto, the only regular picture network in existence, whisked photographs across the United States to record pictorially the same history which was simultaneously being written on the news wires.

2

The contrasts between the first year and the current year seemed endless, but those who looked had no difficulty in finding one surpassingly important element common to both.

The big story was the same—the fate of Europe.

In 1848 the Old World was shaken and torn. In France, Louis-Philippe lost his throne. Another Louis abdicated in Bavaria. Ferdinand of Austria surrendered his scepter to Franz Josef, who lived to see the World War. There were uprisings in Ireland, Hungary, Italy, and the German states. There was unrest in England, where the Chartist movement constituted an assault on the existing order.

Now Europe was plunged into another conflict of enormous gravity and consequence for the entire world. The key figure was Adolf Hitler and, despite Munich, Hitler was not through.

The vast world-wide resources of news gathering, all of the modern facilities afforded by the expansion of The AP into its own new building, combined to keep abreast of events which marched relentlessly toward one climax. Staff men, struggling in a whirl of contradictions and unbelievable realities, strove harder than ever for the truth.

The mechanized Nazi legions moved into Poland on September 1, 1939, and the cables rushed news of the crushing invasion to the new headquarters in New York, whence it sped along the wires and through the air to newspapers in virtually every country in the world.

As recorded by the news, that move by Hitler marked the end

of one era and the beginning of another. All that was awaited was the official Allied declaration.

Then it came—swiftly, dramatically, yet almost quietly at dawn in the newsroom of the new headquarters of The AP in New York.

It was early Sunday, three days after the German forces moved on Poland. Outside the streets were gray and empty, except for a few worshipers en route to St. Patrick's Cathedral, a block away. In the brilliantly lighted AP headquarters it might have been just another Sunday morning except that the men, alert for the momentous words from other staff men abroad, were waiting beside the pulsing cable machines for news they knew would come.

Everything was in readiness to relay on the news and picture wires the black-and-white record of history in the making.

A bell jangled on the cable machine and the men hovered to watch the words as they spelled out:

```
F-L-A-S-H
    CHAMBERLAIN PROCLAIMED BRITAIN AT WAR WITH
GERMANY.
```

The great story of the generation had begun. Immediately it was called another World War. Yet, from the outset, it appeared different, taxing as never before the resources of those whose daily duty it was to go beyond mere externals in search of all the newsworthy facts. The conflict involved the same clash of countries, the same struggle for territory, the same brands of death and destruction. But those concerned with objective reporting had to realize that it also brought into battle both physical and intellectual forces beyond anything yet recorded.

Whatever the issues, propaganda and pronouncements from both sides already had made it clear that there no longer was a question merely of who should be defeated. The story loomed larger, concerning most of the people of the world because it involved the kind of governments they might have in the future. Freedom of the press and of speech, intellectual and religious problems, and the problems of world trade, in the minds of most people seemed to depend upon the outcome of the conflict pitting Hitler, a world power after a comparatively few years in public life, against the British with their vast empire "on which the sun never sets."

Against such a background of world interest, the forces of news gathering were called upon to report the complex struggle between Hitler's conception of Germany's rights in the world and Britain's conception of what might follow a Nazi rule of Europe or the world.

Later that same September 3, France joined the conflict. Canada issued its declaration a week later.

And those events were only the beginning.

3

The association's foreign correspondents were in action. In Warsaw, Elmer Peterson and Lloyd Lehrbas dodged dive bombers and the lightning-swift destruction of a modern Nazi Blitzkrieg to witness the terror of a military attack such as history never before had known. With the Germans, Louis Lochner was the first correspondent to follow the Nazis into action. Russian troops entered Eastern Poland and with them went Melvin K. Whiteleather.

From all directions, from all vantage points, staff men moved to obtain the news, hampered by censorship, privation, physical dangers, and all the conscienceless dictates of those to whom human life seemed suddenly unimportant. The second World War was barely under way, yet the number of men already engaged in reporting it outnumbered many times over those on duty during 1914-1918.

The big story developed, consuming nation after nation in its relentless flame:

. . . Germany and Russia Agree on Partition of Poland . . . Germany Announces Capitulation of Warsaw . . . Hitler Narrowly Escapes Bomb in Munich Cellar . . . Russia Invades Finland . . . Germany Blows Up Own Pocket Battleship Admiral Graf Spee in Montevideo Harbor . . . Moscow Announces Treaty Ending Russian-Finnish War . . . German Blitzkrieg Overruns Denmark, Occupies Points in Norway . . . British Land Troops in Norway . . . Allies Begin Withdrawal from Central Norway . . . Germans Invade Netherlands, Belgium and Luxembourg . . . Winston Churchill Succeeds Neville Chamberlain as Britain's Prime Minister . . . Dutch Army Surrenders after Queen's Flight to London . . . King Leopold III Orders Surrender Belgian Army . . . Trapped Allied Troops Begin Withdrawal from Dunkerque . . . Italy Declares War on Britain and France . . . Germans Bomb Paris, 254 Dead, 652 Wounded . . . Norway Surrenders . . . Germany Occupies Paris . . . French Sign Armistice With Germany, Then With Italy . . .

Britain Fights On . . .

So the second World War continued, past the time when these

words were written, past the time they were sent to press. As a climax to almost a century of reporting daily history, Munich's "Peace for our time" had seemed a beautiful note on which to end any story of news.

But over the world AP men were busy—and the news went on.

New York, N. Y.
June 25, 1940

INDEX

Abell, Arunah S., 13
Accuracy, 198
Adams, George Matthew, 328
Advertising matter, disguised as news, 295
Airplane, 205-213
Alaska, purchase, 70, 395-397
Alexander, M. B., 326
Allen, Larry, 466, 470, 473, 477, 478, 483
America, dirigible, 208-213
America, Frank, 265-267
American Expeditionary Force, 264, 267, 271-276, 284, 288
American Federation of Labor, 425, 432
American Indians, 62, 84-87, 100
American Mining Congress, 200
American Newspaper Guild, 432, 433, 436, 439
American Telephone & Telegraph Company, 383, 384
Amis, Reese T., 325, 326
Anderson, Kenneth, 471, 474
Anglo-Irish Treaty, 300
Angly, Edward, 341
Anti-Comintern Pact, 452
Anti-Semitism, 88
Antislavery movement, 19
"Appeasement," 459, 485, 486
Appomattox, 52, 53
Archbold, John D., 220
Argonne Forest, 276
Armistice, 281-283; false, 277-281
Arms Limitation Conference, 342
Armstead, George B., 405
Arthur, Chester A., 89
Associated Press, The, administrative expansion, 418, 419; annual meetings, 381; building, new, 487, 488; change in operating methods, 317; election service, 249-255; employees' benefits, 288, 289, 429, 430, 439; "Extraordinary Occasion Service," (EOS), 229, 230; Feature Service, 329, 330, 348, 381; Financial Service, 230, 346, 347; Foreign Service, 355, 360, 484; General Mail Service, 328, 329; General Service, 318; laboratory, 361; leased wires (*see* Wires); logotype, 286; moves (1924), 307; New York meeting (Stone anniversary), 273; news credited, 263, 286; News Department, 230, 271; News Photo Service, 334, 335, 348, 381, 383, 387, 390, 394; 1900 incorporation, 155-157, 175, 310, 314; personnel administration, 428-431; postwar expansion, 303, 317, 318; radio and, 379, 380; "reports human spectacle," 315-317;

retrenchment program, 359-363; science editor, 318; South America, 274, 275; Special Survey Committee, 201, 204, 230, 231, report, 201, 202; State Services, 317, 318; Traffic Department, 230, 233, 263, 264, 390, 424; war coverage expenses, 287; Washington Regional Service, 378, 379
Associated Press of Germany, The, 362
Associated Press of Great Britain, The, 362
Associated Press of Illinois, 117-124; conflict with *Inter-Ocean*, 148-155; co-operative non-profit, 119, 122, 123, 132, 136, 151-156; dissolution, 156, 157; Eastern papers join, 130-134; meetings, Chicago (1893), 125-129, (1900), 154; struggle with UP, 124-135; "unifying contract" with UP, 119, 120; victory celebration, 136, 137
Associated Press, New York (*see* New York Associated Press)
Atlanta *Constitution*, 388
Atlantic cable, 32-35, 50, 63, 67, 69, 78
Atlantic City *Press*, 364
Atter, Robert, 235, 236
Atwood, M. V., 381
Austria, *Anschluss*, 458-463; first World War, 235-237, 269, 276
Aviation, 336-342

Bailey, R. O., 185
Baker, Newton D., 263
Baldwin, Stanley, 321
Balfour, Sir Arthur, 298
Balkans, 235, 241, 276, 290, 485
Baltimore *American*, 132
Baltimore Press, 29
Baltimore *Sun*, 13, 14, 22, 132, 354, 385
Bank failures (1893), 116; (1933), 374-376
Barnes, Jim, 421, 422
Barrère, M. 167
Barron, Mark, 413, 415
Bartley, E. R., 303, 304
Barton, Bruce, 325
Barton, Clara, 107
Baseball, 78, 231, 245, 246, 292, 320, 342
Bassett, Fred N., 83
Beach, Harrison L., 140, 142-144
Beach, Joseph P., 64, 66, 76
Beach, Moses, 13, 19
Beasley, Lawrence, 229
Beebe, Katherine, 368
Belgium, 235-238, 241, 276, 492
Bell, Alexander Graham, 83
Bell, Brian, 319, 336-339
Belo, Alfred H., 155
Benedict XV, Pope, 169

495